'War on terror'

'War on terror'

The Oxford Amnesty Lectures 2006

edited by

Chris Miller

Manchester University Press

Manchester and New York

distributed in the United States exclusively by Palgrave Macmillan

While copyright in the volume as a whole is vested in Manchester University Press, copyright in individual chapters belongs to their respective authors, and no chapter may be reproduced wholly or in part without the express permission in writing of both author and publisher. The opinions expressed in this volume by the contributors and editor are their own. They do not reflect the positions of Amnesty International, Oxford Amnesty Lectures or Manchester University Press.

Published by Manchester University Press
Oxford Road, Manchester M13 9NR, UK
and Room 400, 175 Fifth Avenue, New York, NY 10010, USA
www.manchesteruniversitypress.co.uk

Distributed in the United States exclusively by
Palgrave Macmillan, 175 Fifth Avenue, New York,
NY 10010, USA

Distributed in Canada exclusively by
UBC Press, University of British Columbia, 2029 West Mall,
Vancouver, BC, Canada V6T 1Z2

British Library Cataloguing-in-Publication Data
A catalogue record for this book is available from the British Library

Library of Congress Cataloging-in-Publication Data applied for

ISBN 978 07190 7974 0 *hardback*
ISBN 978 07190 7975 7 *paperback*

First published 2009

18 17 16 15 14 13 12 11 0 09   10 9 8 7 6 5 4 3 2 1

Typeset 10.5/12.5pt GraphArnoPro by Graphicraft Limited, Hong Kong
Printed in Great Britain by the MPG Books Group, Bodmin

Contents

Preface

The Oxford Amnesty Lectures is a registered charity. Its purpose is to raise funds for Amnesty International and to raise awareness of human rights in the academic and wider communities. It is otherwise independent of Amnesty International. It began as a fund-raising project for the Oxford Amnesty group and is now one of the world's leading lecture series. To date, Oxford Amnesty Lectures has raised over £105,000 for Amnesty International.

Acknowledgements

The lectures on which this book is based were given in Oxford in 2006. I should like to thank the lecturers – Khaled Abou El Fadl, Joanna Bourke, Conor Gearty, Jeff McMahan, Bat-Ami Bar On, Thomas Pogge and Ahdaf Soueif – for coming to Oxford to speak and for giving us permission to publish their lectures in aid of Amnesty International. I am also very grateful to Michael Byers for writing a contribution without lecturing and to Afifi al-Akiti for permitting the inclusion of his *fatwa* and Gibril F. Haddad for his introduction and *taqriz* and glossary to the *fatwa* and to both for their assistance in stylistic revision. I should also like to express my gratitude to the respondents – Afifi al-Akiti, Elleke Boehmer, Thomas Dublin, Sandra Fredman, H.A. Hellyer, Dino Kritsiotis, David Miller, Avner Offer and David Rodin – for their contributions to this volume. All of the contributors have been most generous in dealing with my queries, comments and editing; my contact with them has been a pleasure and a privilege. My thanks also to Wes Williams, Kate Tunstall and Nick Owen for reading and criticizing the introduction and to Khaled Abou El Fadl and Cathryn Costello for expert advice. Remaining errors are my own.

The organizing of the lectures was, as always, a collective venture. The members of the organizing committee for OAL 2006 were Tim Chesters, Melissa McCarthy, Chris Miller, Nick Owen, Fabienne Pagnier, Deana Rankin, Richard Scholar, Stephen Shute, Kate Tunstall, Katrin Wehling and Wes Williams.

Notes on contributors

KHALED ABOU EL FADL is Professor of Law and the Alfi Distinguished Chair in Islamic Law at the University of California, Los Angeles (UCLA) School of Law. One of the world's leading authorities on Islamic law, he won the 2007 University of Oslo Human Rights Award. Among his best known books are: *The Search for Beauty in Islam: A Conference of the Books* (2006); *The Great Theft: Wrestling Islam from the Extremists* (2005); and *Speaking in God's Name: Islamic Law, Authority and Women* (2001).

MUHAMMAD AFIFI AL-AKITI is a Fellow at the Oxford Centre for Islamic Studies. Trained in Muslim seminaries of the Far East with a long tradition in Shafi'i jurisprudence, he has recently completed his doctorate on a newly discovered theological text of al-Ghazali.

ELLEKE BOEHMER is Professor of World Writing in English at Oxford University. She is the author of *Stories of Women: Gender and Narrative in the Postcolonial Nation* (2005), *Nelson Mandela: Postcolonial Thinker* (2008), and of four novels including *Nile Baby* (2008).

JOANNA BOURKE is Professor of History at Birkbeck College, University of London. A distinguished social historian, she won the Fraenkel (1998) and Wolfson (2000) Prizes for *An Intimate History of Killing* (1998). Her most recent book is *Rape: A History from 1860 to the Present* (2007).

MICHAEL BYERS holds the Canadian Research Chair in International Politics and Law at the University of British Columbia. He is the author of the widely translated *War Law: Understanding International Law and Armed Conflict* (2005) and most recently of *Intent for a Nation: What is Canada For?* (2007).

THOMAS DUBLIN is Co-Director of the Center for Historical Study of Women and Gender and the Center for the Teaching of American History at the State University of New York, Binghamton. He is co-author with Walter Licht of *The Face of Decline* (2005).

SANDRA FREDMAN is a Professor of Law at Oxford University. She is the author of *Human Rights Transformed: Positive Rights and Positive Duties* (2008), *Women and the Law* (1997) and *Discrimination Law* (2002). She has acted as expert adviser to the E.U., Northern Ireland, the U.K. and Canada, and is a barrister practising at Old Square Chambers.

CONOR GEARTY is Director of the Centre for Human Rights and Professor of Human Rights Law at the London School of Economics. He is the author of *Can Human Rights Survive?* (2006) and *Civil Liberties* (2007). He has appeared in human rights cases in the House of Lords, the Court of Appeal and the High Court.

Born in Beirut, DR. GIBRIL FOUAD HADDAD embraced Islam as a graduate student at Columbia University. He studied in Damascus 1997–2006 and now lives in Brunei. His latest book is *The Four Imams and Their Schools: Abu Hanifa, Malik, al-Shafi'i, Ahmad ibn Hanbal.*

DR. H.A. HELLYER is Senior Research Fellow of the Centre for Research in Ethnic Relations at Warwick University, a Member of the Oxford Centre for Islamic Studies, and founding director of the Visionary Consultants Group. He is the author of *The European 'Other': Muslims and Multiculturalism* (2009).

DINO KRITSIOTIS is Reader in Public International Law at the University of Nottingham and Visiting Professor at the University of Michigan Law School. He serves on the Board of Editors of the *Journal of Conflict & Security Law* and the *Human Rights Law Review.*

JEFF MCMAHAN is Professor of Philosophy at Rutgers University. He is the author of *The Ethics of Killing: Problems at the Margin of Life* (2002) and *Killing in War* (2009).

DAVID MILLER is Professor of Political Theory at the University of Oxford. He is the author of many books, including *Principles of Social Justice* (1999) and most recently *National Responsibility and Global Justice* (2007).

AVNER OFFER is Chichele Professor of Economic History, Oxford University, and a Fellow of All Souls College. He is the author of many books, including the prize-winning *The First World War: An Agrarian Interpretation* (1989) and most recently *The Challenge of Affluence* (2006).

BAT-AMI BAR ON is Professor of Philosophy and Women's Studies at Binghamton University – SUNY. She is the author of *The Subject of Violence* (2002), a study of the relation of violence to politics, and has edited several collections, notably the *Hypatia* symposium on the 'just war tradition'.

THOMAS POGGE is Professor of Philosophy at Yale and Professorial Fellow at ANU's Centre for Applied Philosophy and Public Ethics. He is the author of *World Poverty and Human Rights* (2002/8) and editor of *Freedom from Poverty as a Human Right* (2007), *Global Justice: Seminal Essays* and *Global Ethics: Seminal Essays* (both 2008).

DAVID RODIN is a Research Fellow in Philosophy at Oxford University and Co-Director of the Oxford Institute for the Norms and Ethics of War. He is the author of *War and Self-Defense* (2002) and editor of *War, Torture and Terrorism* (2007).

AHDAF SOUEIF was born in Cairo and educated in Egypt and England. She divides her life between Cairo and London and fiction and journalism. She is the author of two celebrated novels, *In the Eye of the Sun* (1992) and *The Map of Love* (1999, shortlisted for the Booker Prize). Her essays are published in *Mezzaterra* (2004).

CHRIS MILLER, translator and critic, is co-founder of the Oxford Amnesty Lectures.

Chris Miller

Introduction: some notes on 'terror'

Terrorism is a form of human sacrifice. It treats humans not as ends in themselves but as means to a political goal. It asks no permissions of those whose lives it takes or mars; they are sacrificed to a cause that they may never have heard of. Ritual human sacrifice is found in societies that have an erroneous notion of the instrumentality of this procedure and suppose that the gods or other influential entities are appeased or sated by slaughter. For a society afflicted by terrorism, the easy choice is to suppose that the deaths and traumas inflicted by terrorism are like those inflicted by ritual sacrifice; that terrorism too is mistaken in its methods and as futile as it is murderous.

I do not think we can say this, though I believe that terrorism is never justified. On this point, we must shift the grounds of our analogy. Terrorism (in the common understanding of the term, which I shall call 'non-state terrorism') does not seek to placate 'influential entities', to sate or appease by slaughter. On the contrary, it seeks to provoke the powerful.[1] In this, of course, it is often very successful. And the 'gods' whom this terrorism provokes, like those to whom it sacrifices, are invariably political. To dismiss it as the product of religious fanaticism is self-deluding. From the point of view of the victims and their loved ones, of course, terrorism is nothing other than human sacrifice. They have been chosen at random as representatives of a targeted society. But there is some evidence to show that, however repugnant the practice, when terrorism sacrifices other human beings to a cause, it not only ensures that the cause for which they are sacrificed is not forgotten but that ultimately, if the non-state terrorism persists, realistic questions will eventually be asked as to the terrorists' motives. And there is therefore every reason to suppose that terrorism will continue.

For, when inquiry is made into the motives of non-state terrorism, it frequently emerges that an injustice has occurred; that 'Others' in a specified place and time have previously been sacrificed to 'higher interests' and that the survivors of this injustice are not prepared simply to concede defeat, abandon their own dignity and accept the new status quo. And insofar as human societies have a concern with justice, nor should they. History cannot be reversed but sometimes injustices can be remedied or at least not perpetuated. In principle, none of us wishes to perpetuate a recognized injustice, however difficult we may find it to perceive the injustice of our actions.

For the analogy with ritual human sacrifice to be complete, then, we should have to be able to say that the victims of terrorism die for no reason at all. And this, I think, we cannot say. We can say, perhaps, that they are sacrificed for no reasons of their own and that this is what makes death by terrorism so hideous. But even this formulation must be attenuated. For when we say that the victims of terrorism are innocent, we are making a technical point.

The standard definitions of terrorism involve variants on the following: terrorism means inflicting violence on the innocent for political purposes. Michael Walzer defines it as 'the random murder of innocent people'.[2] Jeff McMahan in this volume defines 'acts of terrorism' as 'intentional efforts to kill or seriously harm innocent people as a means of affecting other members of a group with which the immediate victims are identified'. Here Walzer and McMahan might seem at variance over 'random'. But the experience of terrorist outrages has told us all too clearly what is meant. Terrorism is not the same as assassination – a deliberate attempt to kill specified individuals – but nor is it wholly random.[3] Osama bin Laden writes: 'And know that targeting Americans and Jews the length and breadth of the world is one of the greatest duties'.[4]

The body of doctrine and law under which terrorism is generally thought to fall is the law of war, which is twofold. It is customarily divided into '*jus ad bellum*, the justice of war' and '*jus in bello*, justice in war'.[5] Detailed discussion of the principles of international law can be found here in the essay of Michael Byers and the very significant response by Dino Kritsiotis. I wish to make just two points about it here. First, international law is not an immutable code that stands forever remote from public opinion. There are grounds for saying that the Bush government has sought and even obtained a change in international law in favour of pre-emptive aggression. It is possible that overwhelmingly large anti-war demonstrations in the United States and Western Europe could have blocked this (though this is contested here by Thomas Dublin and the demonstrations were very large). Second, the function of the codes of war is or should be that of ensuring that, if war breaks out, as little harm as possible is done by the belligerents to innocents on either side.

Within this body of law, there is nothing to legitimate terrorism and its deliberate targeting of innocents. Who, then, *are* the terrorists? The terrorists from whom everyone has most to fear are states. 'Inflicting violence on the innocent for political ends' is something that can be done most effectively with the arsenal of the state. This point is at variance with the common public understanding of terrorists as ideologically driven individuals who infiltrate a country in order to blow up innocents in its public places. (This is an understanding promoted, as Conor Gearty argues here, in order to let state terrorism off the hook.) But it is easy to conceive that a terrorist campaign conducted by a hostile nation's air force will have even more terrifying results; that an army put to terrorizing a population can achieve this more easily than a gang of individuals. If you want to frighten people, fire-bombing an entire city is more effective than blowing up a bus or a train. Londoners may have been terrified by the bombings of '7/7' but they were probably less frightened, shall we say, than the (surviving) population of Hamburg in July 1943, when 45,000 died in the four-night RAF fire-bombing, some caught up and instantly incinerated in the firestorm, some suffocated in shelters as all the oxygen was drawn into the flames, some killed by the delayed-action bombs intended to discourage the emergency services.[6]

We have come to two new points here: terrorist actions may be accomplished during wartime as they may during peace. And they make take place during a war declared for just ends. World War II is conventionally and justifiably thought of as a 'just war' par excellence, unavoidably fought against an aggressive, tyrannical and genocidal regime. But 'just war theory' also requires that a war be fought in certain ways. 'The two sorts of judgement are logically independent. It is perfectly possible for a just war to be fought unjustly and an unjust war to be fought in strict accordance with the rules'.[7] There is an obligation to discriminate between the combatant and the non-combatant and a requirement to observe the two principles of necessity and proportionality. As Jeff McMahan puts it here, an unjust war 'might be fought for a just cause but be unnecessary for the achievement of that cause, or disproportionately destructive relative to the importance of the cause'. The RAF bombing of Dresden took place late in World War II (February 1945), at a point at which it seemed clear that defeating Nazi Germany was simply a matter of time. Dresden was an important transport hub close to the eastern front but the bombing was not focused on roads and railways and the city was known to be full of refugees.[8] Its bombing was intended to strike a blow at morale, not least by destroying a city of little military but immense cultural value. It was never likely to have the effect on morale claimed for it at the time, as London's reaction to the Blitz had already shown. It was a culturecidal and a terrorist act.[9] It might be added that it was not, as such, exceptional in the British campaign of bombing cities that did not constitute military targets.[10] This policy was not observed by the United States in the European theatre of combat, but in the war against Japan it was. Tokyo was fire-bombed after Japan's defeat had become inevitable and the atomic bombs were dropped on Hiroshima and Nagasaki not only to demonstrate to the Japanese that they were facing overwhelming military might but also to demonstrate this destructive power to a likely future enemy: the Soviet Union.[11] As Ami Bar On notes, these particular acts were exceptional in their scale alone: some 50 per cent of the casualties in World War II were civilians.

Who, then, are the innocent? This is the 'technical point' referred to earlier. In just war theory, the 'innocent' are non-combatants. We say nothing about their moral character when we refer to 'innocents'. Some of the civilian victims of Allied bombing during the Second World War were Nazi voters or convinced Nazis; many of those will have adhered to the Nazis' genocidal anti-Semitism. Others may have colluded with Nazism only as the victims of a tyrannical state. These are controversial propositions, which I do not intend to argue here. But the victims' innocence in this context was and is that of non-combatants, a category whose targeting is forbidden in the laws of war developed in the aftermath of World War II.

And it takes little thought to understand that the punishment of even an active exponent of genocide should not take the form of random incineration. This is a different sense of innocent, but is the one from which the former sense derives. Those who serve in the army do so in the knowledge that, on declaration of war, they are at all times legitimate targets. The non-combatant has the right not to be killed. If he or she is suspected of taking part in atrocities, the courts must adjudicate. Incendiary bombs cannot be used to further the rule of law. In a fire-bombing like that of Dresden, the dissident is caught up in the flames alongside the concentration camp commandant. The innocence of the non-combatant is ultimately reducible to innocence before the law.

I have said that non-state terrorism normally has its origins in a specific injustice or a series of injustices. However, I do not wish to suggest that terrorism is ever justified by injustice. Nor can it be described as caused by injustice. It is, however, generally *motivated* by injustice or the perception of injustice. But we must repeat that it is a strategy of deliberately targeting the innocent and this is not generally the only strategy available to the oppressed seeking to remedy an injustice.[12] Where it is the only strategy available, their dilemma is indeed a desperate one. The commission of atrocities in the pursuit of justice leaves no one unharmed. Terrorism is a training in moral insensitivity and a deplorable preparation for civil government, as many post-independence 'liberation' regimes have shown.

The terms we use here are excessively broad. We might wish to distinguish the actions of insurrectionary groups that target strategic property or infrastructure (with only accidental loss of life) from those of terrorists who deliberately target the innocent civilian. In the 1960s, the ANC began a campaign of violence intended to overthrow the apartheid South African state. It did not initially target people. But Umkhonto we Sizwe (Spear of the Nation) went on to use car bombs and other forms of violence that killed innocent people, often, the perpetrators subsequently claimed, in response to atrocities committed by the apartheid government. Once insurrectionary violence has begun against an efficiently oppressive state, this form

of escalation is all too predictable. We should contrast Umkhonto's initial principles with those of the Real IRA and those responsible for 9/11. In one of the worst
non-state terrorist outrages in Northern Ireland, the Real IRA killed 29 people on
15 August 1998 in Omagh.[13] It did, however, issue several warnings before the bomb
went off. It is possible to think that, had these warnings been clearer, the death toll
might have been lower, and that the obscurity of the warnings (which in fact contributed to the loss of life) was not intended.[14] When planes were flown into the
Twin Towers on 11 September 2001, no warning was given and the maximum possible loss of life was clearly sought. This was not merely a terrorist act, it was a
terrorist spectacular.

What should a government faced with non-state terrorists do? The outrage of its
citizenry at seeing their innocent compatriots blown up normally results in a punitive military reaction: a 'crackdown'. That this should be the government's first reaction is entirely predictable. But we have said that terrorism often arises out of injustice and though its method might seem to disgrace its cause, the next thing that a
government should do is attempt to recognize and deal with that injustice. To suggest this is, of course, to beg the question of why violence was adopted in the first
place. If we take the example of Umkhonto, the apartheid state was dedicated to
racial injustice: that was its primary function, in the name of which it justified torture and killing. But there have been occasions in the recent past in which a political solution has been found to a conflict in which terrorist violence was the
principal expression of one side's sense of injustice. Northern Ireland is a classic case.
The difficulty for a government is then to negotiate with an entity whose methods
are abhorrent. But this is what the U.K. government (at first secretly) did. The results
are clear today.

To point this out is to point out that a 'war on terror' could never be successful. 'Terror' is a diffuse notion that takes no account of local particularities and 'war
on terror' is a contradiction in terms.[15] If the object was to reduce the incidence of
either state or non-state terrorism in the world, it has failed. If the object was to
combat the Jihadist terror associated with the figure of Bin Laden, it has failed in
this objective too, opening in Iraq an unrelated new front in which Jihadist terrorism has proliferated.[16] Those who wish to reduce the incidence of Jihadist terror
will have to go about in a different way. One such way is to listen to what the terrorists have to say and see if there is an injustice that has given rise to this outbreak
of violence. But no such thing has been attempted by either of the main particip-
ants in the 'war on terror', the U.S.A. and the U.K.

Let us therefore consider what Bin Laden has to say. His writings are in some respects
exemplary and in the Arab street he holds a symbolic position perhaps analogous
to that once held by Che Guevara for the European left. Bin Laden's primary

concern is Saudi Arabia. He finds the current Saudi regime corrupt and believes that it has deviated from the Wahhabi variant of Islam with which it has always endeavoured to associate itself. His principal objection is to its inviting 'infidel' (U.S.) troops into Saudi Arabia against Wahhabi tradition but his objections do not stop there. He believes that it has corrupted a section of the Islamic scholarly community and is thus able to rely on pliant Islamic authorities to support its policies and require obedience to it. It is, he says, a tyrannical and unjust government and he believes that Muslims should therefore take up arms against it, citing Koranic instructions to rebel against the unjust ruler. The Saudi government should 'bring back Islamic law and . . . practise real consultative government'.[17]

There is no doubt that, outside the ruling circles in Saudi Arabia, these policies would be exceedingly popular.[18] If a democratically elected government came to power in Saudi Arabia tomorrow and if its actions were not constrained by American influence, a Wahhabi version of Shari'a (Islamic law) would surely be instituted, almost certainly as repressive and cruel as that of the current regime and at least as oppressive towards women. American soldiers would be immediately expelled. A situation might prevail in Sunni Saudi Arabia not unlike that of Shi'ite Iran in the immediate aftermath of the Iranian revolution. Such a Saudi government could not be counted on to regulate the price of oil in favour of the West. The question then arises, whether democracy in Saudi Arabia would be a *bad thing*? This question is at the heart of the issues raised in this volume, notably in Abou El Fadl's essay.

Of course, the 'consultative government' that Bin Laden proposes would not be a democracy. Nor is this the place to discuss a point ably discussed by Abou El Fadl in his symposium *Islam and the Challenge of Democracy*.[19] The point I wish to make here is: does the West favour democracy? Or are we only prepared to countenance democracy where it 'gives the right answer'? If the latter, the analogy between the avowed principles of the West and the Saudi regime's tame clerics is clear enough.

The second issue with which Bin Laden is concerned is what he describes as the 'Judaeo-Christian' or 'Zionist-Crusader' alliance ('Judaeo-American' alliance is also found).[20] This term identifies Judaism (Israel) and the Christian West, particularly the United States, and suggests that they are together set on undermining and attacking Islam wherever possible. The conflicts in which he sees Muslims being killed include Palestine, Lebanon, Afghanistan, Iraq, Kashmir, Bosnia and Chechnya. This overall view is a misunderstanding. Indeed, it is a misunderstanding of a kind precisely analogous to the misunderstanding represented by the 'war on terror'. It takes no account of the historical circumstances of the conflicts that he refers to. Judaism and Christianity are not – to take one example – responsible for the repression exercised by India in Kashmir. At the partition of India, the rulers of individual states were given the authority to decide whether their states should form part of India or Pakistan. The Maharaja of Kashmir hesitated, then opted for India and Indian assistance in the face of a guerrilla campaign partly supported by Pakistan. A ceasefire between India and Pakistan was brokered by the U.N., which incorporated an obligation on the part of India to discover by means of a plebiscite the preference of the Kashmiris. This has never been fulfilled. The injustice is clear though it may no longer be soluble simply by the implementation of the U.N. resolution.[21]

It is similarly difficult to blame Zionist-Crusader tendencies for Russian atrocities in Chechnya, a country long under the domination of the atheistic and often anti-Semitic U.S.S.R. and now oppressed (the word is hardly sufficient) by secular Russia. The Russian interest in Chechnya is strictly imperialist and is not guided by Russian Orthodox religion. Similarly, when Orthodox Serbs began the ethnic cleansing of Bosnian Muslims in former Yugoslavia, the enmities involved were demarcated by religion but were primarily concerned with territory and power. Nor was Russian support for the Serbs of primarily religious motivation. There can be no denying that the West – and indeed the rest of the world – was, for a time, insufficiently exercised by ethnic cleansing in Bosnia and elsewhere to risk the lives of soldiers. The U.N. was officially in charge of Srebrenica when in July 1995 the largest act of mass murder in Europe since the end of World War II took place, the genocidal massacre of 8,000 Bosniac (Bosnian Muslim) boys and men.

In certain details, then, Bin Laden's account of Western attacks on Muslims is a misinterpretation of historical circumstance. It will be noted, however, that I have not yet entered into any detail of the Middle Eastern conflicts cited. Moreover, in its general outlines, Bin Laden's complaint might be translated into other terms. Russian oppression of Chechnya is clearly imperialist in tendency, and in this imperialist perspective retention of control of Chechnya is clearly more important than the lives of its inhabitants. The Serbian hostility towards the Bosniacs is itself a relic of the Ottoman oppression of Serbia. Imperialism is not known for excessive caution with the lives of those it regards as its subjects. If Bin Laden's objections were recast in terms of politics (imperialism) rather than religion, they would be more reasonable – though perhaps less persuasive to the sections of the *umma* (the community of all Muslims) that he is trying to conscript. Some of those close to him do speak in terms of colonialism. Thus a document from the Center for Islamic Studies and Research – said to form part of al-Qaeda – includes the word 'colonialism' ('The Muslim countries today are colonized. Colonialism is either direct or veiled') and uses the name 'Karzai' as an equivalent of 'Quisling'.[22] Since religious difference tends in any case to envenom conflict, the notion that religious affiliation has been irrelevant in the treatment of Muslims by the West should perhaps be discarded. It is inconceivable that the United Kingdom would have been allowed by the international community to combat terrorism in Ulster in the way that it has been dealt with in Afghanistan and Iraq, and the fact that greater value is attached to Western lives than to those of (non-Western) Muslims is a point on which Bin Laden rightly insists.

In his most explicit attack on the U.S., 'To the Americans' (dated 6 October, 2002), Bin Laden's sentiments echo those of many who would never accept his terrorist goals. 'The British handed over Palestine, with your help and support, to the Jews, who have occupied it for more than 50 years; years overflowing with oppression, tyranny, crimes, killing, expulsion, destruction, and devastation'.[23] (The creation of Israel in Palestine was indeed made possible by the U.K. and the U.S.A.) 'You supported the Russian atrocities against us in Chechnya, the Indian oppression against us in Kashmir and the Jewish aggression against us in Lebanon'.[24] (We have dealt with two of these heads above; the last is, of course, true if we substitute Israeli for Jewish.) 'Your forces occupy our countries'.[25] (This is a reference to the U.S. troops in Saudi Arabia and precedes the invasion of Iraq.) 'You have starved the Muslims of Iraq, where children die every day. It is a wonder that more than 1.5 million Iraqi children have died as a result of your sanctions, and that you have not shown concern. Yet when 3,000 of your people died, the entire world rises up and has not yet sat down'.[26] (In this volume, Thomas Pogge cites Dennis Halliday, former coordinator of humanitarian relief to Iraq and Assistant Secretary-General of the United Nations: 'I had been instructed to implement a policy that satisfies the definition of genocide: a deliberate policy that has effectively killed well over a million individuals, children and adults'.) Bin Laden goes on to talk about democracy: 'When the Islamic party in Algeria wanted to practice democracy and they won the election, you unleashed your collaborators in the Algerian army on them, and attacked them with tanks and guns, imprisoned them and tortured them – a new lesson from the "American book of democracy"'.[27] (The West showed no taste for democracy in Algeria when an Islamist regime was on the point of taking power. It is not an isolated case.[28] This Western refusal of the verdict of the people was repeated when Hamas won a majority in the Palestinian parliamentary elections. The party was elected having clearly stated its non-recognition of Israel but was required to reverse this policy before any other government was prepared to recognize it.[29] By contrast, no disavowal of the project of Eretz Israel ('Greater Israel') is required of Israel.) Bin Laden continues: 'You are the last ones to respect the resolutions and policies of International Law, yet you claim to want to selectively punish anyone who does the same. Israel has for more than fifty years been pushing U.N. resolutions and rules to the wall with the full support of America'.[30] (Between 1972 and 2006, the U.S.A. vetoed thirty-two U.N. Security Council Resolutions condemning Israel, thus exercising its veto more often than all the other members combined.)[31] He adds: 'You have claimed to be the vanguards of Human Rights, and your Ministry of Foreign Affairs issues annual reports containing statistics of those countries that violate any Human Rights. However, all these values vanished when the *mujahidin* hit you [on 9/11] and you then implemented the methods of the same documented governments that you used to curse'.[32] (This is true. 'Extraordinary rendition' means handing over terrorist suspects, some of them kidnapped from allied countries such as Italy, to the security services of countries in which torture is routinely used. One reason for this, apparently, was a lack of Arabic-speaking intelligence operatives in the U.S.A.[33] We know, of course, that the U.S.A. itself has used torture routinely[34] and that it attempted to alter the definition of torture in order to avoid having to admit that it had done so. The subject is eloquently dealt with in this volume by Thomas Pogge, Joanna Bourke and Khaled Abou El Fadl.) 'What happens in Guantánamo is a historical embarrassment to America and its values, and it screams into your hypocritical faces'.[35] This surely is true.

Bin Laden's indictment is an impressive one. When he adds: 'You are a nation that exploits women like consumer products or advertising tools'[36] and 'You also permit drugs, and only forbid the trade of them, even though your nation is the largest consumer of them',[37] there is also considerable truth in what he writes. But I should say again that there is nothing in his indictment that justifies, let alone demands, the killing of the innocent. Bin Laden, of course, does not regard the U.S. population as innocent. 'The American people are the ones who pay the taxes which fund the planes that bomb us in Afghanistan, the tanks that strike and destroy our homes in Palestine, the armies which occupy our lands in the Arabian Gulf, and the fleets which ensure the blockage of Iraq . . . That is why the American people cannot be considered innocent of all the crimes committed by the Americans and Jews against us'.[38] The failure of logic here is the one that we have seen before. Even in the country responsible for the Holocaust, it was members of the executive who were charged with responsibility for the atrocities committed and they were individually charged. Those who had committed smaller-scale individual atrocities were charged for their crimes. But I should emphasize again that the innocence of the non-combatant is the innocence of the individual before the law. It says nothing about moral innocence. A democracy can indeed consider itself tarred by its leaders' policies. Let us now return to the expression 'Zionist-Crusader alliance' in the context of the Middle East.

In 1995, NATO intervened in former Yugoslavia to end the ethnic cleansing conducted by the Bosnian Serb Army, which had proceeded by means of massacre, rape and demolition. American military power was essential to the NATO operation. The purpose of ethnic cleansing is not generally genocidal. Massacres are 'merely' intended to 'encourager les autres'. Demolitions are conducted so that return becomes unattractive. And the brutality of ethnic cleansing is not necessarily the product of long-standing hatreds; it is often intended to create hatred so that a return to the status quo becomes impossible. We know that the ethnic groups in historical

Yugoslavia often intermingled in ways that have come to seem exotic in the aftermath of its implosion. This was also true in pre-Zionist Palestine.

Following Ilan Pappe,[39] I wish to make a parallel between the ethnic cleansing in former Yugoslavia and the ethnic cleansing of Palestine. This requires a brief historical excursus. The story of the creation of Israel is the story of a nineteenth-century colonial project rewarded with permanent status in the twenty-first. Much of the responsibility for the injustice committed belongs to the British government, under whose mandate the Jewish desire for a homeland in Palestine was effectively authorized and the interests of the Palestinians explicitly sacrificed to this end. The infamous 1919 Balfour memorandum is an egregious expression of racial and religious prejudice: 'in Palestine, we do not propose even to go through the form of consulting the wishes of the present inhabitants of the country . . . The four great powers are committed to Zionism, and Zionism, be it right or wrong, good or bad, is rooted in age-long tradition, in present needs, in future hopes, of far profounder import than the desires and prejudices of the 700,000 Arabs who now inhabit that ancient land [Palestine]'.[40] When the Zionists began a terrorist campaign against the British mandate in the aftermath of World War II, the U.K. handed the problem over to the United Nations, which on 29 November 1947 voted for the partition of Palestine and the creation within it of a Jewish state. The vote was obtained by intense U.S. pressure on countries such as Liberia and the Philippines that had much to lose from U.S. disfavour.[41] It granted the Jewish state 5,700 square miles of the 10,000 or so constituting Palestine. Yet in 1947, only one-third of the Palestinian population was Jewish and most of them had arrived since the 1920s. They owned less than 6 per cent of Palestine; within the designated Jewish borders, they owned only eleven per cent of the land and were a minority in every district.[42] As Hirst puts it, 'Overnight, the comity of nations solemnly laid the foundations of a new moral order by which the Jews, the great majority of whom had been in Palestine less than thirty years, were deemed to have claims equal, indeed superior, to those of the Arabs who had lived there since time immemorial'.[43]

But it was not enough. The Zionists were glad to have their state recognized but had no intention of accepting its proposed dimensions. By 1947 they had developed a map of the Jewish state that 'anticipated almost to the last dot pre-1967 Israel, i.e., Palestine without the West Bank and the Gaza Strip'.[44] The plan for implementing it was Plan Dalet (Plan D). It was based on a very detailed register of Palestinian villages. The plan's prime mover was David Ben-Gurion, subsequently for many years Israel's prime minister. He was explicit about his ethnic goal: 'There are 40% non-Jews in the areas allocated to the Jewish state . . . Only a state with at least 80% Jews is a viable and stable state'.[45] Even before Plan Dalet was implemented, operations kicked off with an attack on the village of Khisas on 18 December 1947. Houses were blown up during the night with the occupants still inside.[46] In Haifa, the Jewish neighbourhoods were high above the Arab ones. So barrels of explosives were rolled down the hill, and oil and fuel sent flowing down the roads, which were then ignited. Car bombs were sent for 'repair' in Palestinian garages.[47] On 31 December 1947, the village of Balad al-Shaykh was attacked with the loss of 60 Palestinian lives. The Wadi Rushmiyya neighbourhood of Haifa was 'cleansed' on the same day and its houses demolished. The British stood by and watched.[48] The Stern Gang (led by another future Israeli Prime Minister, Menachem Begin) issued pamphlets to its activists: 'Destroy Arab neighbourhoods and punish Arab villages'.[49] The attack on Sa'sa was reported in the *New York Times*. Thirty-five houses were blown up while the families slept inside them. Some 60–80 Palestinians were killed, quite a few of them children.[50] The implementation of Plan Dalet began in April 1948. Among the first and most famous victims were the villagers of Deir Yassin, which had made a non-aggression pact with the Haganah, the Jewish army. So the Irgun and Stern Gang were sent in instead. There were 93 victims including 30 babies.[51] The Deir Yassin massacre took place before the end of the British Mandate and outside the area assigned to the Jewish state. Four nearby villages were razed in an hour each. The cleansing of Haifa was assisted by the British withdrawal; British troops were in Haifa in great numbers and could have prevented it. The commander of the Carmeli Brigade, later Israeli Chief of Staff, issued orders: 'Kill any Arab you encounter'.[52] The fleeing Palestinians gathered in Haifa market, near the port gate. There they were mortar-bombed from the surrounding heights.[53] In Acre, which held out for a while, the water supply was poisoned with typhoid germs. A similar attempt was made on the wells in Gaza. This was part of a biological warfare effort directed by Aharon and Ephraim Katzir. (Ephraim Katzir later became president of Israel.)[54] In a standard procedure, villages were attacked simultaneously from three sides. Then a hooded collaborator identified all those between 10 and 50 suspected of resistance to the Jews. These were summarily shot. The surviving men, women and children were then expelled from the 78 per cent of Palestine that the Zionists were intent on capturing.

The intervention of the Arab Liberation Army has been presented in Zionist history as a threat to the existence of Israel as severe as the Nazi threat to the existence of European Jews. In fact, in 1948, Ben-Gurion wrote: 'If we . . . receive in time the arms we have already purchased . . . we will be able not only to defend [ourselves] but also to inflict death blows on the Syrians in their own country – and take over Palestine as a whole . . . We can face all the Arab forces. This is . . . a cold and rational calculation based on practical examination'.[55]

The result we know. Around a million Palestinians were expelled from their villages at gunpoint. Hundreds of Palestinian villages were destroyed. Pine forests were often planted over their remains. Where villages were repopulated by settlers, the names were changed. Names from Biblical times replaced Palestinian ones. Mosques and churches were frequently destroyed. A culturecide was attempted. Efforts were made to efface all traces of Palestinian inhabitation.

Such operations were repeated after the Six-Day War in 1967, though now without the massacres. Beit Nuba, Imwas, Yalu, Beit Marsam, Beit Awa, Habla and Jifliq
were demolished and their inhabitants driven out. About a fifth of the population
of the West Bank, something over 200,000, crossed the Jordan.[56] Even before
this, other land-grabbing processes had been established. The 1950 Law for the
Acquisition of Absentee Property proved very useful. 'For under the new law any
person who left his usual place of residence between 29 November 1947 and 1
September 1948 for any place outside Palestine, or any place inside Palestine but
outside Jewish control, was considered to be an absentee', no matter why or for how
long absent. Absentee Property was acquired by a Custodian of Absentee Property,
who could hand it over to the Jewish authorities for settlement. In cases where the
Custodian was mistaken, the law provided that the decision would remain the same
'even if it is later proved that such property was not absentee property at that time'.[57]
The Emergency Article for the Exploitation of Uncultivated Areas was used in common with the Defence Regulations. The Ministry of Defence could declare a
Palestinian area 'closed'. Now no one could enter it without permission. No per-
mits were given to farmers. Therefore it was not cultivated. Therefore it was, in
accordance with the law, handed over to those who *would* cultivate it: the nearest
Jewish colony.[58] When the Israeli Supreme Court allowed the villagers of Kafr Bar'am
to return to their 'closed' village, the authorities were irritated. So it was bombed
by Israeli Defence Force aircraft and razed to the ground.[59]

The Israeli connections with ethnic cleansing and terrorism are made clear in
its choice of leadership. Its first Prime Ministers were David Ben-Gurion (1948–53,
1955–63) and Moshe Sharett (1954–55), the two architects of the ethnic cleansing of Palestine. Menachem Begin (1977–83) was the leader of the Stern Gang.
Yitzhak Shamir (1983–84, 1986–92) was one of the leaders of the LEHI (Fighters
for the Freedom of Israel), a terrorist organization responsible for the assassination of U.N. Peace Mediator Count Bernadotte. Ariel Sharon (2001–6) was commander of Unit 101, responsible for the cross-border reprisal attack on Qibya in
which 66 men, women and children were killed in revenge for a mother and two
children killed by a Palestinian grenade attack. The operation 'reminded even pro-
Israeli newspapers like the *New York Post* of [the Nazi atrocity at] Lidice'.[60] He was
also the commander of the Israeli forces in Lebanon that permitted and apparently
watched the Phalangist massacre of Palestinian civilians at the Chatila and Sabra
refugee camps. The Israeli forward command post was a seven-storey building with
a direct view of the camps, 'like the front row of the theatre'.[61] Israeli soldiers prevented
the refugees escaping. 'Women and small girls were raped, sometimes half a dozen
times, before, breasts severed, they were finished off with axes'.[62] In 1983, the Kahan
Commission found that Sharon bore personal responsibility for this massacre.[63] These
facts make Israeli objections to terrorism exercised against the Israeli state look rather
hollow. Israel was founded on terrorism exercised first against the British Mandate

and then against the Palestinians. It has persistently chosen ex-terrorists as its democratically elected leaders. These are matters about which no well-informed Israeli
citizen can any longer claim to be ignorant.

Enough has been said in the previous two sections to indicate that an injustice did
indeed take place in Palestine. Let us therefore return to Bin Laden's expression
'Judaeo-American alliance'. Is it justified? On this point, there can be little doubt.
Throughout the history of Israel, the United States has supported Israel to an extraordinary extent. It has been the largest recipient of U.S. foreign aid since 1976 and
receives about one-sixth of all U.S. foreign aid annually, amounting to some $3 billion
a year, though Israel's per capita income is higher than that of South Korea or Spain.
This equates to a per capita subsidy of $500 per Israeli (the number two recipient,
Egypt, receives $20 per person).[64] Why? As I noted above, the United States was
instrumental in the NATO intervention to prevent ethnic cleansing in Bosnia and
is not thought to approve of ethnic cleansing. It is also famously hostile to the proliferation of WMD in the Middle East. The possibility that a Middle Eastern
nation might be surreptitiously developing a nuclear weapon allegedly drove U.S.
policy on Iraq. However, Israel had long since developed such a weapon by means
of 'systematically lying' to the United States and its inspectors throughout the process, exactly as Iraq was alleged to have done.[65] More recently, the United States
has developed a rooted objection to terrorism.[66] Yet it conserves its alliance with
a nation founded on terrorism. Israel may have served some purpose during the
Cold War as an experimental weapon platform in which U.S. weaponry could be
pitted against the Soviet weaponry of the Syrian armed forces. What purpose is served
today by U.S. aid to Israel? When George W. Bush attempted to order Sharon to
withdraw his troops from the West Bank in the aftermath of 9/11, he was forced
to back down.[67] Apparently, U.S. aid does not even provide the U.S. with a lever
for enforcing its own policies.

We have seen, then, that a historical injustice did indeed occur in Palestine, and
that the expression Judaeo-American alliance is justified. Moreover, we remember
that this is not Bin Laden's only complaint. He also objects to the containment
policy in Iraq described by the U.N. official responsible for its implementation as
effectively genocidal. To this he can now add the estimated 10,000 innocent dead
in the Afghan War[68] and the innumerable Iraqi civilians killed in the occupation of
Iraq,[69] in a war wholly unrelated to terrorism. But what does Bin Laden mean by
'Zionist-Crusader alliance'? In stating that 'The Bush-Blair axis claims that it wants
to annihilate terrorism, but it is no longer a secret – even to the masses – that it
really wants to annihilate Islam',[70] Bin Laden is simply mistaken. As we shall see,
both the U.S. and the U.K. have supported political Islam (as they did Saddam
Hussein) when it suited them. His principal heads of accusation seem to be

associated with four points: the killing of Muslims worldwide; American and
Israeli occupation of Islamic holy sites; the establishment of non-representative pro-
American governments in Islamic countries; and the project of Eretz Israel. On the
eve of the invasion of Iraq, Bin Laden wrote 'One of the more important objectives of this new Crusader campaign, after dividing up the region, is to prepare it
for the establishment of what is called the state of Greater Israel, which would incorporate large parts of Iraq and Egypt within its borders, as well as Syria, Lebanon,
and Jordan, the whole of Palestine, and a large part of Saudi Arabia'.[71] We have dealt
with the first head above. Concerning the second head, it should be noted that the
term 'occupation' does not, in Bin Laden, refer only to invasion but, for example,
to the stationing of U.S. troops in Saudi Arabia. He regards the holy places of Saudi
Arabia as being, in this limited sense, occupied, and considers them profaned by
this occupation. Islamic holy cities in countries that are under the U.S. sphere of
influence are presumably also thus 'occupied', for example Kairouan in Tunisia. And
today the Shi'ite holy cities of Karbala and Najaf are militarily occupied by the U.S.
For the West, this notion of occupation may seem absurd. But we have already seen
that for most Saudis the notion is legitimate, at least as regards Saudi Arabia. And
it will be seen below that this notion of occupation clearly resonates with suicide
terrorists. Indeed, it seems to apply to many of the Gulf States too. On the third
head, Bin Laden asks: 'Who was it that installed the rulers of the Gulf States? It
was the Crusaders, the same people who installed the Karzai of Pakistan, who installed
the Karzai of Kuwait, the Karzai of Bahrain, Qatar and others. Who was it that installed
the Karzai of Riyadh . . . to fight on their side against the Ottoman state?'[72] Though
all these states have some form of parliamentary democracy (however limited the
suffrage), none of them choose their own heads of state with the exception of Pakistan
– where the 'Karzai' in question, General Musharaff, took power by a military coup
largely unopposed and subsequently favoured by the West. The ruling families of
the other states acquired their status by treaty with the U.K.

Finally, what should we say of the accusation concerning Eretz Israel? The con-
venant made with Abraham in the Bible at Genesis 15 specifies 'Unto thy seed have
I given this land, from the river of Egypt unto the great river, the river Euphrates'.
This would bring the northern borders of Eretz Israel close to Medina and is the
definition proposed by the 'founder' of Zionism, Theodor Herzl.[73] Is there any evidence that the invasion of Iraq was undertaken for the purposes suggested by Bin
Laden? The fact that U.S. policy in the Middle East is largely driven by its alliance
with Israel is, I would say, uncontroversial. Bin Laden, however, believes that there
is no distinction between Israeli and U.S. policy.[74] It seems at least fair to mention
the 'Clean Break' plan developed by the U.S. Institute for Advanced Strategic and
Political Studies. The study group that drafted it included influential 'neo-cons' such
as Richard Perle, Douglas Feith and David Wurmser, all of them part of the Bush

administration at the time of the invasion of Iraq. In 2000, the plan was presented not to the U.S. government but to the Israeli PM Benjamin Netanyahu. It states that 'Israel can shape its strategic environment . . . this effort can focus on removing Saddam Hussein from power in Iraq – an important Israeli strategic objective in its own right'. Wurmser was allegedly among those who suggested to the Bush administration an attack on a 'non-al Qaeda target like Iraq'.[75] We also know that this possibility was raised at the National Security Council by then Secretary of Defense, Donald Rumsfeld, another neo-con, as early as 12/11: 'Rumsfeld was raising the possibility that they could take advantage of the opportunity offered by the terrorist attacks to go after Saddam immediately' – and that he was afterwards furious that this fact was known.[76] Mearsheimer and Walt have made an impressive case for a generalized Israeli capture of the U.S. foreign policy agenda. But there are also grounds for thinking that, as Saudi Arabia came to seem less politically stable, Iraq's potential 220–300 billon barrels of undiscovered oil were increasingly tempting.[77] This is the view of Alan Greenspan, the former Chairman of the Federal Reserve: 'the Iraq war is largely about oil'.[78] A combination of motives is not ruled out. As for the relation of Christianity to Eretz Israel, many Christians in the United States believe that the completion of the Israeli project of Eretz Israel would herald the Second Coming of Christ; they therefore support Israel even though the Second Coming would also mean the destruction of all the Jews (thus putting the Nazi holocaust entirely in the shade). This is a case of Christian religious support for Israeli expansionism. From the perspective of the Palestinians and the Lebanese, however, we might frame the question differently: what has the United States ever done to oppose the establishment of Eretz Israel? That question is more difficult to answer. If we acknowledge, for example, that countries should not keep territory outside their own borders occupied in the course of war defensive or aggressive, we are bound to acknowledge that (at very least) Israeli occupation of the West Bank is indefensible. But Israel has held this territory since 1967. The United States alone has the political and economic authority to insist that Israel return this land and has not done so. Even its protests at the methods used by Israel to settle it have lacked conviction. The expression 'Zionist-Crusader alliance' is therefore misleading insofar as it suggests either that the destruction of Islam is a Western goal or that the West is much concerned to occupy the holy places of Islam. But concerning Eretz Israel we may say that the jury is still out. The United States' unyielding loyalty to Israel, regardless of its acts, suggests that it is not wholly opposed to the advance of Israeli settlements. Where would it draw the line? It seems hard to expect that the Arab street should make the distinctions necessary to perceive that the United States does not have Crusader ambitions or to distinguish between the legend of the 'World Zionist conspiracy' and the unalterable support for Israel by the one remaining superpower. But it would not be hard to make the distinctions clearer.

Who then are the non-state terrorists? In the context of the 'War on Terror', they are the Islamist suicide bombers. And with the publication of Robert Pape's *Dying to Win*, a summary of the findings of the Chicago Project on Suicide Terrorism, we now know a good deal about them. They come into two categories: the first comprises the Jihadists of Middle Eastern political Islam, the second the 'home-grown' terrorists. Neither group, as we know from the Pew Global Attitudes surveys, hates Western values, though they hate American military policy.[79] Pape has shown that suicide terrorism is a response to the occupation *by a democracy* of a country of different religious belief – occupation including cases such as the U.S. soldiers stationed in Saudi Arabia. It is not a product of religious fanaticism. It seems to be a calculated strategy of the occupied to obtain political gains, predicated on the belief that democracies will not long persist in the face of the losses suicide terrorism can inflict. As Pape observes, 'the main reason that suicide terrorism is growing is that terrorists have learned that it works'.[80] Surveying suicide attacks in Sri Lanka, Lebanon, India, Palestine, and Turkish Kurdistan, Pape indicates a 50 per cent success rate in the attainment of the attackers' objectives, a level higher than that expected of international military and economic coercion.[81] The most prolific suicide bombers, the Tamil Tigers, are neither Islamic nor indeed religious in ideology. They and other such groups are motivated by nationalism and not religious fanaticism. Thus, of the 41 Hezbollah suicide bombers in 1982–86, 30 were affiliated with groups opposed to Islamic fundamentalism.[82] There is no pan-Islamic project for suicide terrorism. Each nationalist campaign has been fought independently: al-Qaeda has never attacked Israel while Hamas has never operated outside Palestine or Hezbollah outside Lebanon.[83] Al-Qaeda is Sunni and Salafiyya[84] but few countries combining these two influences are represented among the al-Qaeda suicide terrorists: 'the overwhelming majority [of al-Qaeda suicide terrorists] emanate from a narrow range of Muslim countries, those with American combat troops stationed on or immediately adjacent to their soil and those that received substantial military backing by the United States'.[85] Suicide terrorism is the product of organizations systematically enrooted in their local communities. The criterion of success is taken seriously, as it must be, given the Islamic taboo on suicide: 'The self-martyring operation is not permitted unless it can convulse the enemy. The believer cannot blow himself up unless the results will equal or exceed the loss of the believer's soul. Self-martyring operations are not fatal accidents but legal obligations governed by rules'.[86]

The justification for suicide bombing offered by the bombing organizations thus takes the form of necessity; they cannot defend their community militarily, and undertake suicide bombings because they believe them to be effective in a context in which political protest has proved ineffectual. This point takes us to one of the recurrent topics in the discussions of 'just war' theory, the 'supreme emergency' as a justification for transgressing the code of war. It is discussed in the sixteenth chapter of Walzer's *Just and Unjust Wars* and is taken up in John Rawls's *The Law of Peoples*.[87] The question is whether a supreme danger to a community could ever justify disregarding the conventions of war – that is, indulging in terrorism. Walzer's answer in that volume is a qualified 'yes': 'Utilitarian calculation can force us to violate the rules of war only when we are face-to-face with a defeat likely to bring disaster to a human community'.[88] In a more recent volume, *Arguing About War*, Walzer qualifies the condition still further, saying that terrorism might be justified 'if the oppression to which the terrorists claimed to be responding was genocidal in nature'.[89] Walzer's first formulation seems to be substantiated in practice by Pape's researches. As Pape puts it, 'the most important goal that a community can have is the independence of its homeland (population, property, and way of life) from foreign influence or control'.[90] Moreover, 'disaster' is precisely the translation of *nakba*, the word used by the Palestinians to refer to their expulsion from most of Palestine. On his first formulation, Walzer might seem bound to approve Palestinian terrorism – unless it had no chance of success, something that is any case largely determined by the U.S. I do not myself believe that the concept of the 'supreme emergency' can cast much moral light on the actions of the desperate. Even Nazi Germany was a community and defended itself as such. Rawls, as Ami Bar On points out, argues that only certain communities are of such value that they may invoke the supreme emergency condition – but surely few communities see themselves as so lacking in merit that they never would invoke it. Though Walzer is right to argue against *realpolitik* even in cases where a country or community faces imminent defeat, I believe he is closer to the mark when he says about terrorism: 'Certainly, there are historical moments when armed struggle is necessary for the sake of human free-dom. But if dignity and self-respect are to be the outcomes of that struggle, it can-not consist of terrorist attacks upon children. One can argue that such attacks are the inevitable products of oppression, and in a sense, I suppose, that is right'.[91] Those enduring severe oppression who (rightly or wrongly) believe that they must choose between resignation and killing the innocent are in a hard place. I can see that the former choice is unacceptable. But I cannot see that the latter choice is any more acceptable.

The reaction in the United States to 9/11 seemed to suggest that the ambitions of political Islam were previously unheard of, limited as we have seen that they are in their terrorist form. It may therefore be worth explicating this error. In fact, though frequently involved in violence, political Islam has enjoyed the steady support of the major imperialist powers: the U.K. before World War II and the United States after it. (Here I follow Robert Dreyfuss's study, *Devil's Game*.) What is perhaps the founding force in political Islam, the Egyptian Muslim Brotherhood, was founded by Hassan al-Banna with the aid of a grant from the British Suez Canal Company,

which helped build his mosque in Ismalia.[92] The Brotherhood was a strange mix-
ture of Salafiyya Islam and European fascism. Between the wars, the British in Egypt
were happy to pit it against the Nationalists. But its principal influence came after
World War II when an Islamic revival was combined with the race for oil. By the
late 1940s, it was already known for its terrorism, having been involved in the assassination of an Egyptian prime minister.[93] Banned in Egypt, it began spreading its
influence through Jordan, Syria and Kuwait. After Banna's death, its principal
agent was Said Ramadan, who travelled widely, spreading the creed to Palestine
and notably Pakistan, where he helped Abdul-Ala Mawdudi create a similar organization, the Islamic Group, with its Islamic Student Society, a student grouping
modelled on Mussolini's *squadristi*.[94] Ramadan met Eisenhower in 1953.[95] The Cold
War had begun and American imperialism had begun to replace British imperialism in the Middle East. And the enemy of either imperialism was socialist nationalism. What could be a better bulwark against communism and socialism than the
Muslim Brotherhood? Christianity and Islam could make common cause against
'godless' Soviet Communism.

As Saudi Arabia grew richer on oil revenue, it was a precious source of funds
for organizations such as the Muslim Brotherhood, since its claim to rule was based
on its alliance with the Wahhabi clerisy and so it was anxious to be seen to export
the Wahhabi version of Islam, which chimed nicely with the Salafiyya tendencies
in political Islam. And it was most in danger from the form of socialist pan-
Arabism promoted by Egypt's Nasser. The wave of revolts in Arab countries in the
mid- to late 1950s seemed to suggest that an entire socialist, nationalist Arab bloc
might be built. This was against Saudi interests, against the perceived interests of
the United States and, incidentally, against Israel's interests. (In the Yemen, where
Nasser sponsored a coup against the Yemeni monarchy, there was the surreal
spectacle of Yemeni Jews from Israel disguised as Arab Yemenis serving as military
instructors to the Saudi-sponsored royalist opposition.)[96] King Faisal meanwhile
described Marxism as a 'subversive creed originated by a vile Jew'.[97] In the 1970s,
Sadat brought the Muslim Brotherhood back into mainstream politics, where its
youth wing, the *jama'at Islamiyya* returned to old Brotherhood tactics, intimidating students on the campuses.[98] By now, provision had been made within the Salaffiya
brotherhood for forms of Islamic banking: the Faisal Islamic Bank of Egypt and Al
Tawqa gave the Muslim Brotherhood the ability to move capital internationally.[99]

Rich in petro-dollars, the Islamic banking movement became a vehicle for
exporting Islam – and for sponsoring violence. In the occupied territories, Israel
helped create Hamas as the Islamic opposition to the anti-colonialist socialism of
the PLO. ' "Israel started Hamas", says Charles Freeman, the veteran U.S. diplo-
mat. "It was a project of Shin Bet [the Israeli domestic intelligence service], which
had a feeling that they could use it to hem in the PLO" '.[100] Shin Bet was assisted
by the Saudis. (This might seem to be an own goal for the Israelis, but in fact Hamas

has proved so wonderfully productive in disrupting the peace process that one begs to doubt this. While Sharon knew that he could precipitate a suicide bombing by a targeted assassination, he was sure that the peace process could not go ahead.[101] And the division of the Gaza Strip and the occupied territories into Hamas and Al Fatah territories is a clear strategic advance for the Israelis, who can claim that there is no one to negotiate with while continuing to alter 'the facts on the ground'.) This was consistent with Israeli support for the Muslim Brotherhood against the al-Assad regime in Syria.[102] The culminating action in Western incitement of militant Islam against Soviet Communism came, of course, in Afghanistan, where the CIA supported Islamist opposition to the Soviet invasion of 1979. (The CIA hoped that this procedure could be repeated throughout Central Asia.)[103] Even before the Soviet invasion, in the 1970s, the CIA and the Shah's secret service, the Savak, had cooperated in promoting the Brotherhood in Afghanistan, where it and other Islamist organizations conducted a terrorist assassination campaign against secular and educated Afghanis.[104] After the Iranian revolution, Iran favoured the *mujahidin* even more strongly. Afghanistan became the Spanish Civil War of the Jihadists. Between 1982 and 1992, Ahmed Rashid tells us, 35,000 radical Islamists fought alongside the Afghans and tens of thousands more trained in the madrasas along the Pakistan-Afghanistan border.[105] In Afghanistan, the result was the Taliban, initially encouraged by the United States, which saw in a unified Afghanistan the possibility of a pipeline from Central Asia that avoided the Ayatollah's Iran combined with the further possibility of a clampdown on Afghanistan's opium crop.[106]

Meanwhile, the Saudis continued to export the Wahhabi version of Islam throughout the world. If you wanted a mosque (or a university department), the petro-dollars came with a doctrine. And this doctrine was a very simplified, crude version of Islam that lent itself perfectly to the new Jihadists' orientation – one (as Abou El Fadl notes in *The Great Theft*[107]) with a very destructive view of the wealth of Islamic juridical, theological and artistic achievements. The spectre of large-scale Jihadism (of which al-Qaeda is only part) was therefore conjured from the frustration of the pan-Arabic socialism of the Nasser years, the failings of the autocratic Arabic states (along with the Shah's Iran) and the alliance of the CIA with Wahhabi petro-dollars. When Iraq invaded Kuwait, Bin Laden offered to lead his Jihadi legions against Iraq and thus liberate Kuwait while obviating the need for the Arabic peninsula to be defiled by foreign troops. The Saudi rejection of this offer and its repression of the clerics who favoured it was one of the main factors in Bin Laden's break with the Saudi regime.

Who are the home-grown terrorists? In a series of interviews with al-Qaeda sympathizers in mainly French jails, Farhad Khosrokhavar elicits a remarkable homogeneity of response.[108] For some, delinquents for whom the freedoms of the West had meant sex, drugs and alcohol, a reversion to a strict form of Islam imparted a moral fibre and a sense of moral superiority through which to resist the daily humiliations of discrimination. A Jihadi outlook further identified them with the *umma* and gave them a sense of destiny. For others – second-generation immigrants – their famil-ies' acceptance both of discrimination and of Western lifestyles (among which female nudity in advertising is often cited) oriented them towards a new Islamic identity, in which the nation state was not as important as the *umma*. At this point, the scenes of violence in Chechnya, Bosnia, Iraq, and above all the intifida in Palestine gave them a new sense of the West constantly attempting to repress Islam. By coming to identify with Islamic principles and the *umma*, they saw imperialist violence in terms of a Western attack on Islam. Where discrimination in the West induces Muslims to identify principally with their co-religionists, this view is entirely predictable.

We can put this point in another way by pointing out that a small proportion of the Western population now consists of persons related by kinship, religion or extraction to those who have in the past been the victims of Western imperialism. It would be proper to understand this as finally imposing on the West standards in foreign policy such as would befit its treatment of its own citizenry (this is the doctrine known as 'human rights'). In the 'Judaeo-Christian' West we are asked to love our neighbours. In the past, it was clearly not our literal neighbours whom we were exploiting and oppressing abroad.

This point is particularly important in the age of 24/7 televisual news. As Conor Gearty argues here, the standard notion of terrorism in the West has been that of individual agents and there has therefore has been a failure to perceive state terrorism in 'counter-terrorist' wars. In turn, this has led to a failure to understand what the standard military methods in anti-insurrectionary campaigns look like to those who sympathize with the victims.[109] This is not just a matter of occasional military errors. It is at least partly a function of the way in which the world's largest democracy conducts war, with a very substantial disregard for the consequences to the civilians among whom insurrectionists shelter. This in turn is a consequence of U.S. domestic policies and a kind of bottleneck in neo-con policy. The U.S., in the neo-cons' belief, is almost always strong enough to go it alone. But to attain political goals by military force will mean U.S. soldiers returning in bodybags and this tends to alienate the electorate. It follows that military goals must be obtained with minimum casualties to U.S. personnel. There is therefore a tendency for the U.S. army to prefer (for example) air strikes to house-to-house fighting, an under-standable choice but one which will always tend to look a little one-sided to the viewer not associating the householders with evil-doers or al-Qaeda but with neighbours, family, or co-religionists. Fallujah would seem to be a classic case of this. The doctrines of proportionality and necessity are carefully considered in this volume but a question arises whether proportionality is something that can any longer be expected on the part of a Western democracy in a non-conventional war. This is outstandingly true of anti-insurrectionary campaigns such as Iraq has now become. Indiscriminate air strikes answer the definition of terrorism very precisely. A hi-tech war fought against insurrectionists who are all but indistinguishable from the rest of the population does not and perhaps cannot meet the criteria of 'just war'.

It will be observed that the focus of this introduction has not been the atrocities committed by non-state terrorists in the West but the wrongs perpetrated by the West. The reason for this emphasis is that the very formulation 'War on Terror' suggests that the West is the innocent victim of some inexplicable animus now taking terrorist form. And this is simply not the case. Throughout the twentieth century, the Arab-speaking world and Iran have experienced constant interference in their affairs by the West. (The most egregious of these was of course the imposition of the Israeli state.) The fissiparous nature of a state such as Iraq is owed very largely to the arbitrary carve-up of the region agreed by the European powers in the wake of the defeat of the Ottoman Empire in World War I. Since World War II, the Western need for oil combined with its Cold War strategy have consistently trumped any other considerations, notably those of human rights and democratization. Western attitudes to the Arab-speaking world seem to have been compounded of a profound contempt mitigated only by the consideration due to petro-dollars. After World War II, it seems that a sense of collective guilt for the Holocaust in Europe reinforced this contempt and ensured that the state of Israel could act with impunity. The role of the U.K. and the U.S. in the Palestinian catastrophe or *nakba* has already been touched on. But it should be remembered that European support for Zionism long precedes the Holocaust and the abominable loss inflicted on European Jewry cannot in any sense justify Israel's treatment of the Palestinians as if they should not or, in Golda Meir's words, did not exist.[110] This treatment continues in the project of Eretz Israel, which should be compared with the policy of *Lebensraum*. The Palestinians' willingness to acknowledge the existence of Israel and sacrifice 78 per cent of Palestine constituted an extraordinary endeavour to bring a peaceful solution to one of the major historical injustices of the twentieth century. They have been rewarded with further oppression.

As Abou El Fadl notes in this volume, one of the most frequently encountered responses to the 'human rights culture' outside the West is to suggest that human rights are Eurocentric in their concerns and in fact a form of disguised imperialism, exporting in the form of individual freedoms the tenets of capitalism and indeed globalization. No doubt the promotion of rights by the West has often taken this form. But in the 'War on Terror', it is the Western commitment to human rights that has been called into question. And no historical lessons have been learnt by the West from its previous encounters with terrorism and insurrection in its colonies. Within ten years of its horrified discovery of the Nazi extermination camps, the U.K. was building its own 'gulag' in Kenya to deal with an uprising transparently caused

by the award of the best agricultural land in the country to white settlers.[111] In
the Algerian war of independence, torture was institutionalized among the French
military. Thus in 1957 a French lieutenant in the paras, drunk and requesting a drink
after hours, was so incensed by the barman's refusal that he arrested him and took
him away for torture.[112] The interest of this story is that the then-lieutenant was
subsequently elected to the second round of the 2005 French presidential elections.
Uninterested by historical precedent, the Bush administration in the aftermath of
9/11 has broken almost every rule prescribed by the post-World War II human rights
settlement. Now the methods previously associated with star chambers and dictatorships have been adopted by the Bush administration: unlimited arbitrary detention in grotesque conditions in prisons such as Guantánamo and Abu Ghraib, the
promulgation of torture from the top down, extrajudicial killings of alleged terrorists outside the borders of the United States, secret prisons in a number of countries and a wide variety of tortures. The torture chambers of countries such as Egypt,
Syria and Jordan, previously stigmatized by the State Department, have been put
to use through 'extraordinary rendition'. As I write, President Bush is preparing to
strike out a bill outlawing the use of a variant of a torture practised at least since
the Spanish Inquisition: waterboarding. For Vice-President Cheney, 'dunking' of
this kind is famously a 'no-brainer'.[113] When Amnesty International described the
United States as a violator of human rights, he nevertheless said: 'I frankly just don't
take them seriously'.[114] Meanwhile the United States continues to fight an insurrectionary urban war in Iraq with air-strikes and punitive demolitions.[115] What moral
authority remains to a government that preaches human rights and indulges in these
practices? If other countries, such as Burma, Indonesia, Syria or Saudi Arabia, now
cynically conclude that human rights are merely Western propaganda, who can con-
tradict them? And this point matters because human rights matter – to each and
every one of us who would prefer to live our lives unaffected by arbitrary detention or torture. If the theorists of human rights are correct in alleging that certain
freedoms are in fact universally desired, this ground may eventually be won back
by democratic impetus in the United States and in the many countries such as Burma
where a human rights settlement is urgently desired by the population if not by the
government. That would be a consummation devoutly to be wished. For now, political activism in support of human rights is more urgently required than ever. There
is otherwise some danger that the 'human rights culture', that fragile post-World
War II achievement, will, in the wake of the 'War on Terror', be entirely discredited as the rhetoric of Western imperialism.

Notes

1 'One of the most positive effects of our attacks on New York and Washington was to
   expose the reality of the struggle between the Crusaders and the Muslims, and to demonstrate the enormous hostility that the Crusaders feel toward us'. Bin Laden in Bruce

Lawrence, ed., *Messages to the World: The Statements of Osama Bin Laden* (London/ New York: Verso, 2005), 205.

2 'Its method is the random murder of innocent people'. Michael Walzer, *Just and Unjust Wars: A Moral Argument with Historical Illustrations*, 3rd edn. (New York: Basic Books, 2000), 197.

3 There are, of course, forms of terrorism that do not target at random but focus on particular categories, such as trade-unionists (Colombia) or intellectuals (the French pro-colonialist Organisation de l'armée secrète in Algeria, whose example was subsequently followed by the home-grown Islamist Islamic Salvation Front). We might categorize them as terrorist assassinations.

4 *Messages to the World* (note 1), 205.

5 *Just and Unjust Wars* (note 2), 21.

6 See A.C. Grayling, *Among the Dead Cities: Was the Allied Bombing of Civlians in WWII a Necessity or a Crime?* (London: Bloomsbury, 2006), 16–20.

7 *Just and Unjust Wars* (note 2), 21.

8 *Among the Dead Cities* (note 6), 259–60.

9 'If Operation Gomorrah [the fire-bombing of Hamburg] was *unnecessary* and *disproportionate* . . . then how much more so were the attacks on Dresden, Hiroshima and Nagasaki'. *Among the Dead Cities* (note 6), 272 (original emphasis).

10 'Yet the bombing of Germany gives every appearance in hindsight of a concerted smashing of as much of Germany, its people and its cultural heritage as possible'. *Among the Dead Cities* (note 6), 168.

11 Ibid., 260.

12 Walzer is eloquent on this point in his chapter on terrorism in *Arguing About War* (New Haven and London: Yale University Press, 2004).

13 See Kevin Connolly, 'How the Omagh Case Unravelled', http://news.bbc.co.uk/ 1/hi/northern_ireland/7154952.stm.

14 See 'Omagh Bomb Warnings Released' at http://news.bbc.co.uk/1/hi/events/ northern_ireland/latest_news/153818.stm.

15 See Robert Pape, *Dying to Win* (New York: Random House, 2005), 42: 'Winning the war on terrorism requires a clear conception of victory. The enemy is not "terrorism" per se. This is a tactic that has existed throughout history and that will continue to exist long after the threat to the United States and its allies comes to an end'.

16 'In Iraq, suicide terrorism has gone from nothing in all the years before the U.S. invasion to doubling every year that nearly 150,000 American combat forces have been stationed there'. *Dying to Win* (note 15), 258.

17 *Messages to the World* (note 1), 38.

18 In *Dying to Win* (note 15), 42, Pape notes 'over 95% of Saudi society reportedly agrees with Osama Bin Laden in this matter'. The evidence on which he draws is an article by Elaine Sciolino in the *New York Times*, 27 January 2002, available online at: http:// query.nytimes.com/gst/fullpage.html?res=950CE4DD153AF934A15752C0A9649C8B63.

19 Khaled Abou El Fadl, *Islam and the Challenge of Democracy* (Princeton: Princeton University Press, 2004).

20 *Messages to the World* (note 1): 'Judaeo-Christian alliance', 25–6, 27, 42, 60, 73; 'Zionist-Crusader alliance', 191, 214, 215, 218–19, 246, 251.

21 For a summary of this situation, see the Commons Library Research Paper at www.parliament.uk/**commons**/lib/**research**/rp2004/rp04-028.pdf.

22 See *Dying to Win* (note 15), 118, especially note 25. By 2003, Bin Laden himself had begun to use some language of this kind, referring to 'Quislings' in 'Among a Band of Knights' just before the invasion of Iraq. He has long since referred to 'puppet' Arabic governments (*Messages to the World* (note 1), 197, 38).

23 *Messages to the World* (note 1), 162.

24 Ibid., 163.

25 Ibid.

26 Ibid., 164.

27 Ibid., 169.

28 See Abou El Fadl's essay in this volume, in particular notes 52–3.

29 Documents have recently come to light showing that the United States attempted to foment a civil war between Fatah and Hamas in order to overthrow this democratic decision. See Seumas Milne, 'To Blame the Victims For This Killing Spree Defies Both Morality and Sense', *Guardian*, 5 March 2008.

30 *Messages to the World* (note 1), 169.

31 J. Mearsheimer and S. M. Walt, *The Israel Lobby and U.S. Foreign Policy*. (London: Allen Lane, 2007), 40.

32 *Messages to the World* (note 1), 170.

33 See S. Grey, *Ghost Plane: The Inside Story of the CIA's Secret Rendition Programme* (London: C. Hurst, 2006), 133.

34 For a particular instructive case, see www.amnesty.org/en/news-and-updates/feature-stories/former-detainee-reveals-details-secret-cia-program-20080314.

35 *Messages to the World* (note 1), 170.

36 Ibid., 167.

37 Ibid. In citing those of Bin Laden's arguments that seem to me justified, I do not mean to suggest that I accept his worldview in general, such as his condemnation of homosexuality. A state realized along the lines of Bin Laden's views would, from the Western secular perspective, be like a puritanical Fascist state. Some notion of the extremity of his views is given by the fact that he believes that Andalusia should form part of the new Islamic world order. The views that I have selected here emphasize the hypocrisy of the West and on this point alone I find it hard to disagree with him.

38 *Messages to the World* (note 1), 165.

39 I. Pappe, *The Ethnic Cleansing of Palestine* (Oxford: One World, 2006).

40 See Edward W. Said, 'Nationalism, Human Rights and Interpretation', in *Freedom and Interpretation: The Oxford Amnesty Lectures 1992*, ed. B. Johnson (New York: Basic Books, 1993), 200.

41 David Hirst, *The Gun and the Olive Branch*, new edn. (London: Faber and Faber, 2003), 256.

42 Ibid., 256.

43 Ibid., 256–7.

44 *The Ethnic Cleansing of Palestine* (note 39), 27.

45 Ibid., 48.

46 Ibid., 57.

47 Ibid., 58–9.

48 Ibid., 60.

49 Ibid., 67.

50 Ibid., 78. The record is that of Moshe Kalman, who led the attack: 'We left behind 35 demolished houses and some 60–80 dead bodies'. See Walid Khalidi, ed., *All That Remains: The Palestinian Villages Occupied and Depopulated by Israel in 1948* (Washington, DC: Washington Institute for Palestinian Studies, 1992), 181–2.

51 *The Ethnic Cleansing of Palestine* (note 39), 91. Hirst notes that the Palmach (an elite section of the Haganah) nevertheless took part. See *The Gun and the Olive Branch* (note 41), 248–53.

52 *The Ethnic Cleansing of Palestine* (note 39), 95.

53 Ibid., 96.

54 Ibid., 101.

55 Ibid., 46.

56 *The Gun and the Olive Branch* (note 41), 354.

57 Ibid., 314.

58 Ibid., 315.

59 Ibid., 317.

60 Ibid., 307.

61 Hirst's source here (*The Gun and the Olive Branch* (note 41), 558) is an Israeli officer cited in the study by the Israeli journalist Amnon Kapeliouk, *Sabra et Chatila: enquête sur un massacre* (Paris: Seuil, 1982), 30. The Kahan Report (which Hirst, partly on this account, dismisses as 'by and large a whitewash', 556) did not corroborate this.

62 *The Gun and the Olive Branch* (note 41), 558.

63 'It is our view that responsibility is to be imputed to the Minister of Defense for having disregarded the danger of acts of vengeance and bloodshed by the Phalangists against the population of the refugee camps, and having failed to take this danger into account when he decided to have the Phalangists enter the camps. In addition, responsibility is to be imputed to the Minister of Defense for not ordering appropriate measures for preventing or reducing the danger of massacre as a condition for the Phalangists' entry into the camps. These blunders constitute the non-fulfillment of a duty with which the Defense Minister was charged'. See www.mideastweb.org/Kahan_report.htm.

64 See *The Israel Lobby* (note 31), 26.

65 See *The Gun and the Olive Branch* (note 41), 109.

66 Prior to 9/11, the U.S.A. had not infrequently been involved in supporting terrorist groups, notably the Contras in Nicaragua and the *mujahidin* in Afghanistan. When it objects to Iranian 'meddling' in Iraq, it is objecting to precisely the kind of action it undertook against the Soviet invasion of Afghanistan: funding and arming local militias.

67 See *The Gun and the Olive Branch* (note 41), 37–40.

68 Michael Mann notes that the civilian deaths in Afghanistan caused by U.S. bombing 'must have been close to 10,000' (Michael Mann, *Incoherent Empire* (London: Verso, 2003), 30).

69 See the Johns Hopkins Bloomberg School of Public Health survey published at www.jhsph.edu/publichealthnews/press_releases/2006/burnham_iraq_2006.html for a revised estimate confirming the results of the famous estimate published in the *Lancet*.

70 *Messages to the World* (note 1), 188.

71 Ibid., 189.

72 Ibid., 197. According to Dreyfuss, Ibn Saud was put on a £5,000 monthly retainer by the U.K. in 1917. Robert Dreyfuss, *Devil's Game: How the United States Helped Unleash Fundamentalist Islam* (New York: Henry Holt, 2005), 42.

73 Raphael Patai, ed., *The Complete Diaries of Theodor Herzl*, tr. Harry Zohn, vol. 2 (New York/London, Yoseloff Press, 1973), 711. Herzl is considering what demands he should put to the Ottoman Sultan.

74 *Messages to the World* (note 1), 60, 143, etc.

75 Mark Hosenball and Michael Isikoff, 'Secret Proposals: Fighting Terror by Attacking . . . South America?', *Newsweek*, 9 August 2006.

76 Bob Woodward, *Bush at War* (London: Pocket Books, 2003), 49. This was also the policy of Rumsfeld's deputy, Paul D. Wolfowitz (39). For Rumsfeld's anger, see ibid., 319.

77 Jim Holt, 'It's the Oil', *London Review of Books* 29.20 (18 October 2007), www.lrb.co.uk/v29/n20/holt01_.html.

78 See Graham Petersen, 'Alan Greenspan Claims Iraq War Was Really About Oil', Times Online, 16 September 2007, www.timesonline.co.uk/tol/news/world/article2461214.ece.

79 See *Dying to Win* (note 15), 244. Bin Laden refers disparagingly to the claims by America's 'idiotic leader' that 'we despise their way of life' (*Messages to the World* (note 1), 193), though he also refers to 'the deceptive idea of democracy' (191).

80 *Dying to Win* (note 15), 61.

81 Ibid., 65.

82 Ibid., 205.

83 Ibid., 243.

84 Derived from the word *salaf* (ancestors or predecessors), the word is currently used to refer to a kind of *prisco more* Islam associated with the first generations after the Prophet and therefore translating as 'fundamentalism'. See for example Ian Richard Netton, *A Popular Dictionary of Islam* (London: Curzon Press, 1992), 221.

85 *Dying to Win* (note 15), 125.

86 Ibid., 190. These are the words of Ayatollah Fadlallah, Hezbollah's spiritual leader.

87 John Rawls, *The Law of Peoples with 'The Idea of Public Reason Revisited'*, 4th printing (Cambridge, MA/London, England: Harvard University Press, 2004), §14.3, 98–103. The first 'draft' of Rawls' ideas on the 'Law of Peoples' was of course given as an Oxford Amnesty Lecture on 12 February 1993.

88 *Just and Unjust Wars* (note 2), 268.

89 It is worth observing that, according to the U.N. official quoted by Pogge, the U.N. policies in Iraq met this condition. Walzer notes (60) of the terrorist strategists, 'we ought never to excuse such leaders', a point that obviously reflects on Israel's historical choice of leaders.

90 *Dying to Win* (note 15), 42. Note that the definition of the 'homeland' is likely to be in the hands of the terrorists/the oppressed. The Tamil Tigers occupy a part of Sri Lanka that has no official 'homeland' status. Obtaining that status is, of course, the object of their campaigns.

91 *Just and Unjust Wars* (note 2), 205.
92 Robert Dreyfuss, *Devil's Game: How the United States Helped Unleash Fundamentalist Islam* (New York: Henry Holt, 2006), 47 and 51.
93 Ibid., 63.
94 Ibid., 74–5.
95 Ibid., 72.
96 Ibid., 141.
97 Ibid., 142.
98 Ibid., 149–53.
99 Ibid., 164–6.
100 Ibid., 191.
101 See ibid., 212 and *The Gun and the Olive Branch* (note 41), 73: 'Again, in 2002, only twenty minutes before Hamas's Yassin was to announce a ceasefire, Israel bombed a Hamas headquarters in Gaza, killing seventeen people, including eleven children'.
102 *Devil's Game* (note 92), 200.
103 Ibid., 255.
104 Ibid., 261–3.
105 Ahmed Rashid, *Taliban: The Story of the Afghan Warlords*, new edn. (London: Macmillan, 2001), 130.
106 See ibid., chapters 12 and 13.
107 Khaled Abou El Fadl, *The Great Theft: Wrestling Islam from the Extremists* (San Francisco: Harper San Francisco, 2005).
108 See Farhad Khosrokhavar, *Quand Al-Qaïda parle: témoignages derrière les barreaux* (Paris: Grasset et Fasquelle, 2006), *passim*.
109 The leader of the 7/7 London bombers stated 'democratically elected governments continuously perpetrate atrocities against my people all over the world'. *Dying to Win* (note 15), 253.
110 See *The Gun and the Olive Branch* (note 41), 391–2: 'It is not as though there was a Palestinian people . . . and we came and threw them out and took their country away from them. They did not exist'. The quote is from the *Sunday Times*, 15 June 1969.
111 For an account of this, see David Anderson, *Histories of the Hanged: The Dirty War in Kenya and the End of Empire* (New York: W.W. Norton, 2005) and Caroline Elkins, *Britain's Gulag: The Brutal End of Empire in Kenya* (London: Jonathan Cape, 2005).
112 See Pierre Vidal Naquet, *La Torture dans la république* (Paris: Maspero, 1983), 72.
113 See www.guardian.co.uk, Friday 27 October 2006, 'Cheney Endorses Simulated Drowning': ' "Would you agree a dunk in water is a no-brainer if it can save lives?" "Well, it's a no-brainer for me", Mr Cheney replied'. His spokesman later denied that this was a reference to waterboarding. This is perhaps encouraging as it suggests some sense of shame.
114 See www.cnn.com, 'Cheney Offended by Amnesty Criticism', 31 May 2005.
115 See Dahr Jamail, *Beyond the Green Zone: Dispatches from an Unembeded Journalist in Occupied Iraq* (Chicago: Haymarket Books, 2007), 73 and 260ff.

1 Ahdaf Soueif

The function of narrative in the 'war on terror'

In his introduction to *The Mind of Egypt* the philosopher and Egyptologist, Jan Assmann, states that his purpose is not to examine Ancient Egyptian history, but to examine what the Ancient Egyptians *said* their history was; he would listen to and interpret the stories the Ancient Egyptians told about themselves. He distinguishes between three types of subject for historical research:

1 Traces: archaeological remains that are objectively what they are and from which we attempt to construct a picture of a particular moment; shards of pottery, tools, bones.
2 Messages: objects that were intended to convey a particular reality at a particular moment; texts, pictures, letters.
3 Myth: which, he says, 'is not to be understood as "in opposition" to history. On the contrary: all history that finds its way into normative tradition becomes myth. Myths are the basic figures of memory. Their constant repetition and actualisation is one of the ways in which a society or culture affirms its identity'.[1]

It is almost irrelevant to Assmann's study whether any particular event in the past actually occurred. He cites Burckhardt on the narratives of Ancient Greece: 'those events passed down to us in the form of narration . . . are in many ways uncertain, controversial, coloured, or else . . . fictions entirely dictated by imagination or bias'.[2] The function of these narratives is to give a meaningful structure to the world in which we live, act and feel. 'It is precisely the fabrications, constructions and projections – the fashioning of meaning – that are my concern'.[3]

Amnesty has rightly described this 'war on terror' as a war on human rights. It is also a contest of narratives: stories that the protagonists tell about themselves, about their enemies, and about what is happening now. The President of the United States and the Prime Minister of Britain tell us that what is under threat today is a set of values and a way of life – Western of course, and American specifically – that constitute civilization itself. And that the threat comes from forces of darkness, from a great evil that emanates from Muslim countries – although, they've learned to add, not from Islam itself, or at least not from what they call 'moderate' Islam.

The American narrative

What makes it possible for the President of the United States to identify his way of life with 'civilization'? Or, to put it another way: what is the story that America tells itself about itself, the founding narrative to which it refers in order to give coherence to its present and call it 'civilization'? Here are some elements of the American Myth: Dissent, the Pilgrim Fathers, the Puritans, the Pioneers, the push westward, the taming of the frontier, the Constitution: Life, Liberty and the pursuit of Happiness, President Wilson's Rights of Man; the Land of Opportunity: 'Give us your poor, your weak, your hungry'; the Melting-Pot: anyone can be American; the American Dream: anyone can build an empire, anyone can be president; the peaceable nation that seeks to trade not to conquer, the Little Man standing up to adversity or to the Big Bad Guys, the right to carry arms, the American Woman: liberated, wholesome, strong-minded and equal; absence of class, no embarrassment about money, philanthropy, democracy, the rule of law, free speech, excellence and technology, Silicon Valley and Nasa – and Goodness. To be American is to be Good.

Some of these elements are by definition of dubious moral quality. Some are true and good. Some used to be true but are fast becoming untrue. And, of course, the gaps are obvious.

What happens when the story we tell about ourselves is not consonant with reality? Well, as Assmann says, these narratives are fictions, cultural constructs; they are, if you like, spin. They are meant to show off our best self: the self that we communally aspire to. Everyone expects there to be a certain amount of divergence between the actual and the ideal. Still, if the narrative is what we use to give coherence to our lives and meaning to our actions, surely it can only diverge from reality up to a point?

If we transfer this conceit to an individual it becomes clear that, when a wide enough distance opens up between the way a person sees himself and the way others see him, he is considered delusional. And at a certain level of delusion he becomes a danger to himself and to others.

We all know that you can have a domestic face and a face for the outside world. You can have a country that is, as it were, the converse of the bloke down the pub who's a good mate, buys his rounds, is the life of the party and goes home and beats his wife. In fact you did have something like that with old-fashioned colonialism: reasonably well behaved at home but horrid abroad. Then, in the late nineteenth century, when Europe was articulating its position on Liberty and Nationhood and Rights while at the same time engaged in colonial expansion, a discourse was created to accommodate this dissonance. This discourse, to continue my simile, was like the chap going back to the pub and explaining – to those who had heard his wife's screams – that she thrived on the occasional beating. This position was elaborated by (otherwise fine) intellectuals. Ernest Renan, for example:

> The regeneration of the inferior or degenerate races by the superior races is part of the providential order of things for humanity . . . *Regere imperio populos*, that is our vocation. Pour forth this all-consuming activity onto countries which, like China, are crying aloud for conquest. Turn the adventurers who disturb European society into a *ver sacrum*, a horde like those of the Franks, the Lombards, or the Normans, and every man will be in his right role. Nature has made a race of workers, the Chinese race, who have wonderful manual dexterity and almost no sense of honour; govern them with justice, levying from them, in return for the blessing of such a government, an ample allowance for the conquering race, and they will be satisfied; a race of tillers of the soil, the Negro; treat him with kindness and humanity, and all will be as it should; a race of masters and soldiers, the European race . . . Let each do what he is made for, and all will be well.[4]

Renan was not a Fascist; the spirit of the age rendered this kind of discourse so unremarkable that it was incorporated into the European self-narrative under the heading 'The White Man's Burden' or France's 'Mission civilisatrice'. But that was colonialism old-style. The world has moved on. For Britain the watershed came – or was supposed to have come – with Anthony Eden's Suez adventure, when the British people – even though they did not know the full extent of the plotting that their Prime Minister had engaged in with France and Israel – came out on the streets to reject the war. In effect, the British had decided that colonial wars were no longer acceptable as part of their story about themselves.

Several things about the world today contribute to the Bush administration's difficulties in reconciling what they are doing on the ground with America's story about herself.

(1) The spirit of the age is not – yet – hospitable to neo-colonialism. Or, if you like, the story that the world now tells about itself rejects colonialism. For one thing, there is now a global story, not just a White Man's story. As our great friend and example, Edward Said, said when he gave a lecture in the first of the Amnesty-Oxford series in 1992: 'Constructing a "new universality" has preoccupied various international authorities since World War II. Two milestones are, of course, the Universal Declaration of Human Rights and the Geneva Conventions . . . In addition a wide range of nongovernmental, national, and international agencies, such as Amnesty, or the Organisation for Human Rights, or the Human Rights Watch committees, monitor and publicise human rights abuses'.[5]

(2) The people who find themselves in the path of the neo-colonialist enterprise have already been through the colonial experience. Liberating themselves from colonization is the central plank, the main theme, of the modern part of *their* story

about themselves. Indeed, they attribute their failings and misfortunes post-liberation to the legacy the colonial powers left behind and to the fact that these powers never stopped interfering in their affairs. To incorporate a fresh colonization into their narrative at this stage would be a defeat too far. All the tactics of the colonizer are familiar to them: the fine words, the 'we have come to make your lives better', 'we'll only be here for a while', the puppet rulers, the divide-and-stir-up-strife policies – they are all clichéd tropes. These people can be subdued, but not easily and not for long.

(3) So the war, or conflict or insurgency or resistance, lasts and lasts. Which gives a chance for information about it to come out into the world. And even though the mainstream Western media are fairly docile – not to say supine – sometimes the news is so sensational (as in the case of the Abu Ghraib photographs) that they have to run it. Then there are other channels: the 'alternative' media, for example, and the blogs coming out of Iraq and other Arab or Eastern countries. So when the White House website claims that 'Since the terrorist attacks of September 11th, the United States has waged two of the swiftest and most humane wars in history'[6] everyone who cares to know, knows that they're being lied to – on a massive scale.

(4) Finally and very importantly: the American narrative is not the property of the administration. That's the thing about these founding narratives; that even if to begin with parts of them are constructed by the authorities, they become the property of the people, and the people use them as compasses or yardsticks or at least as backdrops for their lives. Today, those Americans of alert heart who are disposed to examine the world find themselves complicit in the actions of an administration which every day moves them further from their ideal narrative of themselves. A great many Americans see themselves also as co-owners of the global move to universality and human rights that Edward Said described. It is not surprising that one of the first American anti-war groups to be formed after 9/11 called itself 'Not In Our Name'.[7] Nor is it surprising that these groups have proliferated and that their level of both dismay and commitment is very high indeed.[8]

The Israeli narrative

In a discussion of founding narratives and how they inform and are informed by the present Israel's is perhaps the most interesting; for this is a young narrative – barely a hundred years old, still under construction, but attempting to root itself in antiquity. It is also a narrative that insists on its own exceptionalism – in a world that is trying to construct a universalist story.

In a discussion of the relationship between East and West, Israel has placed itself in a central, and self-contradictory, position; presenting itself as of the West but not *in* it, and in the East but not *of* it, attempting to derive legitimacy from both belonging in the East yesterday and repudiating it today.

Finally, the relationship between Israel and the U.S.A. is of central importance to the unfolding events in the so-called 'war on terror'. Since the events of 9/11 we have seen a deliberate and powerful attempt to create a symmetry between the Israeli and the American narratives that serves to underpin the growing unification of their political and military enterprise.

We may look at the Israeli narrative in three parts.

(1) An ancient part that seeks to give the state legitimacy as a 'returning' or an 'ingathering' to a land where Jews had lived and ruled two thousand years ago. This is basically the Jewish narrative up to the beginning of the twentieth century and it is not to my purpose to attempt a full account of it. Here I give only those components of the ancient part that bear a direct political relation to Israel today: Jews are the chosen people through a Covenant with God. They were subject to tyranny in Egypt and fled to safety in Palestine where they established their kingdom. Since the fall of their kingdom they have been dispersed through the world. Their history has been one of persecution but also of survival. They maintained their identity and coherence through the diaspora. When not subject to persecution they have excelled.

(2) The modern part starts with the birth of Zionism just before the beginning of the twentieth century. In the main it is the official history of the state of Israel plus the Holocaust in Europe: Jewish people, after centuries of persecution in Europe, started to come back to their homeland at the beginning of the century. They were socialists and intellectuals who were trying to set up a kibbutz utopia. They wanted to be friendly with the Arabs and to bring them modernity. The Arabs rejected them and mounted terror attacks against them. The Jews refused to be victims any longer; they organized and armed. The British, who were in charge of Palestine, sided with the Arabs. The Jews fought a War of Independence against them. In World War II the Jews of Europe suffered the worst genocide in history. Some of them managed to flee to Israel. The new homeland was the only place where Jewish people could be safe. The U.N. acknowledged it as a state and Israel was born. Whatever Arabs were in the area fled on orders from their leaders. The Arabs refuse to recognize Israel: they hate it, fight wars and mount terror attacks against it. Israel wins the wars and occupies east Jerusalem, the West Bank, Gaza and the Golan.

(3) This part may be called the abstract part of the story, the one that articulates the qualities of the community: Israel is the only democracy in the region. By its nature, it is part of the Western system of values. It is a beacon of civilization in a sea of backwardness and barbarity. It has made the desert bloom. It is cosmopolitan and varied and technological and artistic and advanced. Arabs who live in Israel refuse to leave and go and live in the West Bank because they are happy in Israel. Israel is willing to live in peace with its neighbours, to make big sacrifices and to give them some contested land so that the Palestinians can have their own

state, one that lives peaceably side by side with Israel. But it can never find a partner for peace. Israel has been and continues to be under existential threat. The Israeli
army is a Defence Force. It is the most humane army in the world. It adheres to
'purity of arms'. It weeps as it shoots.

As with the American national narrative it is clear that some elements here are
true and some are false. More than any other story in the world today, the Israeli
narrative is under challenge. It is challenged and defended because its acceptance
or rejection crucially affects the lives of millions of people. And if the narrative, or
the founding myth, is one level of presented history, in the case of Israel, the other
two types of historical evidence – the traces (the rubble of pre-1948 Palestinian
villages for example) and the messages (memoirs, letters, reports, etc.) – are still
very much the province of research. The Israeli narrative, still in the course of
formation, is fascinating because it is in such a dynamic relationship both with the
evidence against it and with its present.

The four fronts I described earlier that are causing problems for the American
narrative are causing more acute problems for the Israeli one – which is also facing one challenge the American narrative has been spared.

(1) Israel's claim, as a state, to the ancient part of its narrative is contested by varied groupings of Jewish people who object that they have not given the state of Israel
a mandate to speak for them or to appropriate the history of all Jews. Among these
are 'Jews for Justice for Palestinians', 'Naturei Karta', 'Rabbis of Palestine', 'Rabbis
for Peace' and others. They are very vocal in trying to reclaim the Jewish story.[9]

(2) One could say that, as far as Israel is concerned, the 'spirit of the age' in the
West is or has been conflicted. It was prepared – despite its general anti-colonial
stance – to extend special privileges to Israel after World War II. Until the 1980s,
for example, you were hard pressed to find a voice in the Western liberal press that
would criticize Israel's policies even though they ran counter to the new universalist spirit of respect for international law and human rights. U.N. resolutions could
be ignored, poets could be assassinated, lands annexed, communities punished, friends
spied on: the young Israel was indulged, partly because its cultural and civilizational
placing of itself rendered it immune, and partly because it had come from such an
'abused' background. It took not just the invasion of Lebanon in 1982 but the massacres of Sabra and Chatila for the world to wake up to the activities of the Israeli
generals.

(3) The Palestinians have already been through the experience of Israeli colonization. When families that had been unable to return to Safad or Yafa or Ramle
in 1948 come under attack today in their refugee camps or in the homes they have
managed to build in Tulkarm or Jenin or Nablus, they sit on the rubble of their
homes and declare that they will not leave. Many Palestinians are holding on to
the keys of their homes in Yafa, Nazareth and countless other towns and villages
inside the 1948 border and demanding their legal right of return – which some

scholars have pointed out (in great detail) can be done without displacing any Israelis.[10] The Palestinians are not going away or keeping quiet: they are recounting *their* narrative of dispossession, imprisonment, siege and torture. And their narrative contradicts the Israeli narrative. The worse the Palestinian condition becomes the more the world is reminded that Israel is out of sync: the last existing classical colonial-settler state, the last state defined explicitly and exclusively in religious or ethnic terms.

(4) The information is out there; available for anyone who wants it, unavoidable for anyone who isn't deliberately closing their eyes. The presence of more than three million Palestinians scattered across the globe also spreads the word. And then there is the information co-ordinated and produced from within the Occupied Territories via the Web.[11]

(5) Again, as with the U.S. administration, large parts of Israel's story about itself are under attack from within what the state would like to regard as its home constituency: there is resistance to its claim to speak for every Jewish person everywhere in the world. And this resistance is very vocal. Many young Jewish people now go to Israel with the aim of finding out what is really happening[12] – and we all know what happened to Rachel Corrie.[13] A quarter of the people who work for the International Solidarity Movement in the U.S.A. are Jewish.

The state's account of Israel's modern period up to 1948 has been discredited by what have come to be known as 'revisionist' Israeli historians and now by Jewish grass-roots organizations, which aim to remind people of 1948. Its account of what it is now is contradicted by Jewish human rights activists, anti-war activists, plant-a-tree activists, journalists like Amira Hass and Gideon Levy, refusenik soldiers who even tour the world to speak against the Occupation, post-Zionists like Uri Avnery and Meron Benvenisti, writers like Yitzhaq Laor, film-makers like Yigal Alon, Eyal Sivan and Juliano Mer Khemis.

This is not to say that the Israeli community as a whole is challenging its narrative. Far from it. Nor is it to say that the dissidents want Israel dismantled or even that they all want it to become a secular democracy. But there is enough dissent to make matters uncomfortable. And Israeli (like American) dissidents are drawing both on their own narrative of Jewishness which puts a premium on bearing witness to the truth, on critical thought and noisy dissent and argumentativeness, and on their sense of belonging to a universal community which guarantees that what happened to their ancestors can never happen to them. The lessons they have drawn from the terrible events of the past, the meaning they have derived from it is 'never again shall this happen to *anyone*'. Or as Amira Hass has said 'Never will I be a bystander and watch as the event goes by'.[14]

The 'war on terror'

Without the elision of the American and Israeli narrative, which the events of 9/11 were used to cement; without the superimposition of the Israeli narrative on to the

American narrative, the U.S.A. would probably not be fighting a 'war on terror' now. It also would probably not be in Iraq, nor would it be threatening Iran and Syria.

The Israeli and American narratives already shared a quality of youthfulness, an idea of a homeland haven, a democracy, a land of opportunity and individual rights, a laboratory and launch pad for self-invention. They also share the imagery of the taming of the frontier and making the desert bloom. With this there seems to come the implicit agreement that if there happen to be natives in that desert or on that frontier the way to deal with them is by extermination, ejection or forced settling into enclosed communities. You then obliterate their history and appropriate their culture. Perhaps it is this, as much as the powerful lobby and the *realpolitik*, that led to the indispensable support that the U.S. accorded to Israel. Support that went well beyond the official $3 billion per annum. On 18 May 2000, when Al Gore was running for the presidency he addressed the powerful American Israel Public Affairs Committee (AIPAC) thus:

> The United States has an absolute, uncompromising commitment to Israel's security and an absolute conviction that Israel alone must decide the steps necessary to ensure that security. That is Israel's prerogative. We accept that. We endorse that. Whatever Israel decides cannot, will not, will never, not ever alter our fundamental commitment to her security.[15]

You might have thought support couldn't come much stronger. But the 'neo-cons' were waiting for a chance to demonstrate even higher levels of commitment. The policies they dreamed of before coming to power are well documented.[16] They were handed the opportunity to lever these policies into action on 11 September 2001. That day four major Israeli politicians, Ehud Barak, Benjamin Netanyahu, Shimon Peres and Ariel Sharon, took to the TV screens to assert that the terror just suffered by Americans was the identical terror endured by Israel since its establishment – to finally drive home the point Israel had been pushing for years: that Israel's enemies were America's enemies. We now hear talk of America's 'manifest destiny' and of a 'shared mission' as in House Republican leader Tom DeLay's speech at Boca Raton (on the occasion of the death of the astronauts – among them the Israeli Ilan Ramon) in which he talked of a destiny shared by America and Israel and asked for divine assistance in protecting both.[17]

Narrative strategies

In the wake of September 11, the U.S. administration introduced an elaboration into the current episode of the American narrative: it adopted Israel's enemy as its very own.[18] Throughout the 1990s scholars and pundits like Samuel Huntington and Bernard Lewis had been setting the stage for this development. 'Palestinian', 'Arab' and 'Muslim' dissolved into each other and swam into the focusing lens of the unfolding narrative – as 'terrorist'. The trope of the 'suicide bomber' – the enemy motivated not by economics, history or politics but only by a fanatical ideology – was born.

But although the world was prepared to agree that the attacks of 9/11 were the work of terrorists it did not agree that every Palestinian attack on every Israeli target – even suicide or martyrdom attacks – was the work of terrorists. And the world was prepared to consider, as Arundhati Roy put it, the 'long road it took the bomber to get to where he did'.[19] Not so official U.S. websites. Look up 'terror' and the U.S. administration website will direct you to a report by the RAND Corporation with examples of events that can be classed as terrorist events. It starts with: 'A member of a known terrorist organisation (e.g. the Hamas) bombs a mall, a bus-stop, a grocery store etc.' This, naturally, would be classed as a terrorist act. Second example: A member of the Hamas attaches a bomb to himself . . . third example: a member of the Hamas bombs the house of a government official . . . eighth example: Hamas attacks a livestock farm infecting the animals with a biological agent . . .'[20]

The U.S. set out to do battle while Ariel Sharon re-invaded the West Bank. Within a very short time of 9/11, and under cover of the 'war on terror', the U.S. was implicated in Israeli trade-mark activities such as:

- manipulating or sidelining international institutions;
- ignoring accepted principles of international law (e.g. setting up Guantánamo Bay, sanctioning assassinations worldwide);[21]
- ignoring accepted principles of human rights (e.g. carrying out illegal detentions including the detention of children, condoning the use of torture);[22]
- adopting military policies to achieve its political ends, embracing a policy of 'pre-emptive' war;
- moving to curtail the civil rights of its own citizens (e.g. The Patriot Act);
- encouraging the media to adopt government views and attempting to gag foreign media.[23]

The identification between the U.S. and Israel was now a manifest fact. But Israel had been losing credibility since its invasion of Lebanon in 1982, then with the Palestinian intifada in 1987 and again with the Second Intifada in 2000. And now the unwillingness of Iraqis to fall in with the American scenario, not to mention the folly and ill-preparedness of the project to 'tame' Iraq, is such that the episode has come to erode the U.S. administration's own credibility. The war on Iraq is proving more and more difficult to incorporate into the narrative of the 'war on terror' and into a narrative about themselves that the American people will accept.

Today the sound of dissent is growing louder. People's tribunals are being convened. Huge advertisements are taken out. The official narrative of the war is being challenged – and it is helping to strengthen the challenge to the Israeli official narrative as well as the American one.

We see, in response, the articulation of a number of strategies for control of the narrative:

- *Controlling access to information* through control of the media, 'embedding' journalists in the war(s), attempts to control libraries and attempts to control the net.
- *Minimizing the importance of the information* that does get out: taking women hostage in Iraq to pressure their menfolk to surrender is 'ungentlemanly conduct',[24] pornographic torture is carried out by 'a few bad apples'.
- *Controlling the interpretation of information* through surveillance of the academy: representing this mindset is Hoover Institute anthropologist, Stanley Kurtz, testifying before the House Subcommittee on Select Education in 2003 that Edward Said's post-colonial critique had left American Middle East Studies scholars impotent to contribute to the 'war on terror'.[25] Infamous examples are Daniel Pipes's Campus Watch campaign, his David Project and the activities of UCLAProfs.com.
- *Inventing alternative narratives* such as the story of Private Jessica Lynch and creating platforms for them such as the American-financed Iraqi TV station, al-Hurra, and radio station, Radio Sawa.
- *Inventing false narratives for the enemy* through the activities of agencies like MEMRI,[26] and the use of what Hamid Dabashi has called 'The Comprador Intellectual', the Arab or Muslim intellectual who doubles as a 'native informant' and utilizes discussion of a negative practice from 'home' to discredit the entire culture.
- *Discrediting anyone who points to unwelcome facts* by using labels such as 'un-American' or 'anti-Semitic' or even 'self-hating Jew'. Examples are Hugo Chavez, Norman Finkelstein, Ilan Pappe, Baruch Kimmerling – and there are many others.

Strategies also include attempts to change the interpretation of the law (so that the word 'torture', for example, no longer means what everyone knows it means), to introduce new laws (against protests, against 'glorifying terror') and generally to adopt practices that have such far-reaching effects that they in essence alter the nature of the state. What price democracy without consent? And what price consent without information?

And yet all these activities at least acknowledge the 'ideal' narrative; they chop off the toes of the administration's activities so that it may jam its foot into the dainty glass slipper of the myth. But there is another current which seeks to address the divergence between narrative and fact by stretching, or if need be smashing, the narrative to accommodate the reality. Perhaps the most stark manifestation of this current is the neo-conservative manifesto, *The Project for the New American Century*.[27] Here the neo-conservatives express a preference for power politics over diplomacy, a disdain for international law and its institutions, and a belief in the desirability of military spread – even into space.[28] This attitude is finding an echo among writers and scholars who now celebrate Empire. It is filtering down to the soldiers in the army. Robert D. Kaplan, accepting that 'Despite our anti-imperial traditions, and despite the fact that imperialism is delegitimised in public discourse, an imperial reality already dominates our foreign policy', continues ' "Welcome to Injun Country" was the refrain I heard from troops from Colombia to the Philippines, including Afghanistan and Iraq . . . The war on terrorism was really about taming the frontier'. Here we have an admission and embrace of a component of the American myth in its brutal rather than sanitized version. And we have an updating of it into a contemporary, desirable, consumerist image; an American soldier in Afghanistan celebrates: 'You get to see places tourists never do. We're like tourists with guns'.[29]

Israel too is moving to a more publicly brutal discourse. Opinion polls show that large numbers of Israelis regard Arabs as 'dirty', 'primitive' and violent. The *Guardian* report of 7 February 2002 bears reading in its entirety for its tracking of the development of openly racist and violent discourse in Israel. The revisionist historian Benny Morris epitomized the new mood when, having been one of the first scholars to expose the extent of Israel's ethnic cleansing of Palestinians in 1948, he then suggested that – in the interests of lasting peace – they should have cleansed them out some more.[30]

What now?

Jan Assmann, describing some critical moments in Egyptian history, could be analysing the period the U.S. and Israel are living through now:

> Periods of crisis, junctures where civilisation breaks with its own traditions, regularly engender discourses that illuminate the terms of reference within which that civilisation has been operating. Sometimes this illumination may result in profound changes to the prevailing semantic paradigms; sometimes those paradigms advance from more or less unconscious collective 'mentalities' to the status of conscious ideologies.[31]

Assmann is describing a specific crisis that Egyptians went through some four thousand years ago when, after fifteen centuries of living a reasonably well-ordered life within a defined and congenial system, it seemed as if their world was coming apart. Several consecutive years of low floods brought famine, central government collapsed, foreigners made incursions into the country from East and West, law and order broke down, customs and traditions were violated and people's image of themselves, of their lives and what they stood for was shattered. This was the time historians call the First Intermediate. The Egyptians called it the 'Time of the Nations' because the country was divided. But out of this time of fragmentation there emerged the Egypt of the Middle Kingdom; an era of economic prosperity, of scientific achievement, artistic flowering and a media revolution. And what seems to have been the engine at the heart of all this was that some Egyptians took a good look at their traditions, at their image of themselves and what they valued in that image, at what they were in imminent danger of losing, and then they refor-mulated it all into what became the nation's story about itself.

In essence, the Egyptian national myth can be summarized as: all humans are equal. Ra, the solar deity declares: 'I made the four winds that every man might breathe thereof like his fellow in his time. I made the great inundation that the poor man might have rights like the nobles. I made every man like his fellow, I did not command that they do evil: it was their hearts which violated what I said' (*Coffin Text no. 269*).[32] If people are unequal that is because of an imbalance in the world. It is the duty of the rich and powerful to correct this imbalance by practising ver-tical solidarity and by adhering to the law. The law exists to guarantee equality and to protect the poor and the weak from the rich and the strong. The law, not force, is the arbiter (the story of the battles of Horus and Seth). With patience, love shall prevail over hatred and life over death (the story of Isis and Osiris).[33]

The values that were given prominence in this scheme were to do with com-munality and collectivity, with every person being part of ever larger units from the family to the cosmos, with responsibility, patience, receptivity (hearkening), pro-activeness, good manners, compromise, *joie de vivre* and what we might today call a 'light footprint': not wasting water, not spoiling crops, not killing animals except for food. 'The ethic of self-effacement, integration and altruism [was] certainly funda-mental to civilisation in Egypt'.[34] In time these values became articulated as the Rules of Maat – the rules of courteous and responsible conduct towards the com-munity, the earth and the cosmos. All of which is not to say that every Egyptian from then on behaved impeccably. It is not even to say that Egyptian society of the time offers a model for today. But it is a noteworthy example of a people appeal-ing at a time of crisis to the highest ideals of their narrative – ideals still worthy of our attention today.

In an Oxford Amnesty Lecture in 1993, the philosopher Richard Rorty, discussing the old problematic of the 'nature' of man, suggested that man is a 'flexible, pro-tean, self-shaping animal' and that the most useful aspect of human nature to focus on is 'our extraordinary malleability'.[35]

Four thousand years ago, with their world in ruins, some Egyptians decided they would not allow that moment to be the end of their society and its aspirations. What has come down to us from their endeavours is 'social tractates, the earliest known discussions of society, written by their ancient authors as campaign propaganda in the earliest crusade [*sic*] for social justice'.[36] In effect, those early thinkers gambled on the 'malleability' of man; on people's ability to be whatever they decide to be. They searched their history and their traditions and they extracted the values most useful to them and elaborated them into a system which gained consensus as the approved way of behaviour that everyone should strive towards. It gave their nation two thousand further years of success. And it may even be responsible for its survival to this day.

Today, the question is: forced to re-assess their relationships to their founding narratives, will the U.S. and Israel decide to abandon current policies and try to draw closer to the ideals those narratives express? Or will they jettison the narratives and the ideals in favour of making gains on the ground (and in the air, and in space) and accept that their story from now on will be brutal, bloody – and short?

This is the time when the real owners of these narratives, the people, need to speak. And there is, now, a global voice that is making itself heard. The story it is telling speaks of the history of man on earth as one narrative. It tells of how man started to fashion tools and weapons a million years ago, but started to fashion an ethical vision of life only five thousand years ago. This vision, based on concern for man and concern for the planet, on principles of justice and solidarity, became global in the second half of the twentieth century. Now, in the twenty-first century, it remains to be seen whether it can lead to a unified narrative for all mankind. For it is in that larger narrative that our hope lies, a narrative made of reconciling, of braiding together, the stories of the different nations of the world.

Notes

1 Jan Assmann, *The Mind of Egypt* (Cambridge, MA: Harvard University Press, 2003), 10.

2 Ibid., 7, quoting Jakob Burckhardt, *Die Kunst der Betrachtung: Aufsätze und Vorträge zur Bildenden Kunst*, ed. Henning Ritter (Cologne: Dumout, 1984), 175.

3 *The Mind of Egypt* (note 1), 8.

4 Ernest Renan, *La Réforme intellectuelle et morale* (1871), quoted in Aimé Césaire, *Discourses on Colonialism*, tr. Joan Pinkham (New York: Monthly Review Press, 1972), 16. See Edward W. Said, 'Nationalism, Human Rights and Interpretation', in *Freedom and Interpretation: The Oxford Amnesty Lectures 1992*, ed. B. Johnson (New York: Basic Books, 1993), 184–5.

5 *Freedom and Interpretation* (note 4), 196–7.

6 www.whitehouse.gov/infocus/achievement/chap1-nrn.html.

7 See www.notinourname.net/index.html.

8 The websites of World Can't Wait, CodePink and Another Day in the Empire are well worth a visit and lead to a multitude of other sites.

9 See www.jfjfp.org/.

10 See Salman H. Abu-Sitta, *Atlas of Palestine 1948* (London: Palestine Land Society, 2004).

11 See particularly http://electronicintifada.net/new.shtml.

12 Matt Bradley, 'Flap Over Young Jews' Visit to Holy Land', *Christian Science Monitor*, 12 January 2006.

13 For Rachel Corrie, see www.guardian.co.uk/world/2003/mar/18/usa.israel (Editor's note).

14 Amira Hass quoting her mother Hannah in conversation with Ahdaf Soueif on 13 April 2005 at the Lannan Foundation, Santa Fe, New Mexico. See www.Lannan.org/lf/cf/detail/amira-hass-with-ahdaf-soueif/.

15 See Ahdaf Soueif, 'The Israelisation of America', *Al-Ahram Weekly*, 11–17 September 2003 and www.middleeast.org/archives/7-00-6.htm.

16 See Ahdaf Soueif, *Mezzaterra: Fragments from the Common Ground* (London: Bloomsbury, 2004), 127 and footnote 4.

17 *Newsweek*, 2 June 2003.

18 See the 'Letter to President Bush on Israel', *The Project for the New American Century*, 3 April 2002.

19 Arundhati Roy in conversation with Howard Zinn, in *Come September*, Lannan Foundation, Santa Fe, 18 September 2002.

20 www.tkb.org/RandSummary.jsp.

21 *Mezzaterra* (note 16), 130.

22 Ibid.

23 Examples are the killing of Reuters photographer (the Palestinian) Mazen Da'na on assignment in Baghdad, the bombing of the Al Jazeera offices in Kabul and Baghdad, the arrest and killing of Al Jazeera staff.

24 *ABC News*, 28 January 2006.

25 David Price, 'How the FBI Spied on Edward Said', *Counterpunch*, 13 January 2006.

26 See Brian Whitaker, 'Selective Memri', *Guardian*, 12 August 2002, www.guardian.co.uk/elsewhere/journalist/story/0,7792,773258,00.html, reply by Yigal Carmon, www.guardian.co.uk/israel/comment/0,,778373,00.html and Juan Cole, 'Repressive Memri', Antiwar.com, 24 November 2004 at www.antiwar.com/cole/?articleid=4047.

27 www.newamericancentury.org.

28 'The Project for the New American Century, Rebuilding America's Defenses: Strategy, Forces and Resources for a New Century'. See www.newamericancentury.org/RebuildingAmericasDefenses.pdf.

29 Robert D. Kaplan, *Imperial Grunts: The American Military on the Ground* (New York: Random House, 2006) quoted in *New York Review of Books*, 12 January 2006 in a review by John Gray.

30 For a discussion of Morris's ideas see Baruch Kimmerling in *History News Network*, 26 January 2004.

31 *The Mind of Egypt* (note 1), 6.

32 James Henry Breasted, *The Dawn of Conscience* (London and New York: Charles Scribner's Sons, 1939), 221.

33 The two mythical stories are best dealt with together. Osiris was the divine ruler of Egypt who brought civilization to its people. He was envied by his brother Set, who arranged a banquet in honour of Osiris, where he presented a beautiful ivory chest; this was to belong to the person it fitted. When Osiris tried it, he was immediately sealed into the chest and cast into the Nile. Set became the ruler of Egypt. Osiris's wife Isis long sought the chest. But when she found it, Set discovered its hiding place and tore the body of Osiris into pieces, scattering them throughout Egypt. Isis having recovered all the pieces and bound them together, Osiris was restored to life as the ruler of the underworld. Set now attempted to destroy Horus, the son of Isis and Osiris. But Horus was protected by Ra, the god of the sun, and in due course reclaimed his kingdom. A jury of gods gave judgement in his favour but Set nevertheless fought Horus for eighty

years. In some versions of the story, Set is finally vanquished. In others, he remains as the god of the desert and of evil.

34 *The Mind of Egypt* (note 1), 125.

35 Richard Rorty, 'Human Rights, Rationality and Sentimentality', in *On Human Rights: The Oxford Amnesty Lectures 1993*, ed. Stephen Shute and Susan Hurley (New York: Basic Books, 1993), 115.

36 *The Dawn of Conscience* (note 32), xiii.

Elleke Boehmer

Response to Ahdaf Soueif

As a fluent speaker of Arabic and English and a self-described resident of the *mezzaterra* or middle ground that exists between linguistic and cultural worlds, Ahdaf Soueif in her writing and journalism charts the difficult territory between what we sweepingly call the Middle East and the West.[1] This is a territory that has been and still is riven by powerful divergent forces that she terms *narratives*, thus suggesting the imaginative, structural and visceral power ascribed to them. These forces or narratives belong in the main to empire, religion and nationalism and take in the paranoias, frets and fears elicited as a matter of course by these powerful forces – responses which Edward Said memorably diagnosed as Orientalism.[2]

For Ahdaf Soueif the novelist, narrative is how the dominant ideology of a society or nation translates into individual or community lives. It is how ideology is acted on; how it comes to be part of our day-to-day reality and give meaning to what we do. As this suggests, the founding narratives of nations – America as the land of opportunity, Israel as the promised land, Australia as the lucky country – work on us most powerfully when we are least aware of them. Hence the volatile situation that can ensue when divergent stories of genesis and belonging are told about the same piece of land or about different peoples inhabiting the same land. People live by and are willing to die for the stories they tell about themselves: this is Soueif's central message.

Stereotypes and suspicions are the quotidian forms taken by such narratives and Soueif has examined them memorably in her writing. In *The Map of Love*, she evokes Egypt's love affair with Western modernity and its simultaneous insistence on sticking to its own cultural path and values; its fierce resistance to being represented as underling or victim or as lacking in humanity.[3] In her journalism, too, she has been tireless in showing how Western media tend to represent Arabs, particularly Muslim Arabs, as 'deranged by lust, grief, hatred or greed'.[4]

We must never stop scrutinizing the narratives that generate our central hates and resentments. This anxious exhortation subtends Soueif's Amnesty Lecture. And we should focus above all on narratives whose operation within our society is overt and apparently transparent. But how can such vigilance be achieved, given that these stories comfort us and underpin the way we think about ourselves? Pointing to the gaps that can open between the actual and the ideal, between the world we live in and the world as we imagine it, Soueif points out a pathway to such vigilance. It can be enacted by the seemingly simple yet demanding task of scrutinizing the foundational values of our national myths and converting their truisms into questions – questions that may at first seem preposterous. For example, we take the truism that America is the land of the free, or that the West is the world's honest broker and we produce these potentially troubling questions: Is America repressive abroad? Are the stories that the West tells about others always true?

Ahdaf Soueif's relentless piling-up of examples shows how, in the conflicted situation of Israel-and-Palestine where different stories striate the same communities, we are bound to interrogate the major narratives and turn the rooted truisms on their heads. One reason why that situation has become so complicated is that the narratives of the powerful have here been made to coincide in the word 'terror'. Israel claims that it has, since 1948, been fighting a war on terror, a war against the combined forces of Muslim fanaticism and fundamentalism. So convincing has this narrative been that, with the 9/11/2001 'Attack on America', the U.S. was all too ready to adopt Israel's story, and Israel to share it open-handedly with the U.S. The result was the fusion of two geographically and historically distinct stories. In Soueif's opinion, the U.S. would not be fighting a war on terror today had this fusion not taken place. On 11 September 2001, America adopted Israel's enemy – the 'fundamentalist' Arab world – as its own.

Ahdaf Soueif's call is clear: let us not so much overturn (this may be impossible) as relentlessly investigate the worst in the narratives that produce the conflict. If narratives at loggerheads produce countervailing teleologies pointing to mutually exclusive endings (as in fierce claims to the same piece of earth), then we are compelled by history to modify and disturb these teleologies. We are forced to see that these governing symbols no longer help us to address the dilemmas of our time. Other teleologies and symbols more accommodating of others – symbols and values perhaps buried in those selfsame narratives – may offer wider counsel.

In this respect, David Scott's *Conscripts of Modernity*, an analysis of the 'colonial enlightenment' played out in the Caribbean, is useful. He considers how we set about finding new teleologies to address changing socio-political conditions.[5] This does not mean generating alternatives in a hit-and-miss way, one of which may eventually work better than the current one. No, we have 'to reconceive the object of discontent'. This too, Scott says, is a problem of narrative: of thinking outside the mythic frame–romance, comedy, epic or tragedy – in which we are effectively caught. Thus if America is currently beginning to think of itself as an empire not unlike ancient Rome – heading for the same decline, as several commentators report

– then perhaps a new story, differing from the romance of liberation, is entering the frame.[6]

But here a question arises. How does one go about thinking outside the myths and stories that shape our consciousness? How, to modify Derek Walcott's words in his early poem 'A Far Cry from Africa', do we stand apart from these bloodline stories and still live; how do we move beyond the ideas and images that structure how we think and are? The sign of this difficulty in Soueif's lecture is that she grasps at (to her) familiar stories from ancient history in order, however uncertainly and tentatively, to seek alternatives to the hell-bent stories overlaid on the Middle East and the West today. Yet, as she herself acknowledges, the most compelling narratives are generally those backed by power and technology. Poetically convincing and full of regenerative tragedy as they are, the stories of Ancient Egypt – of Ra the equalizer and of Isis retrieving the dismembered Osiris's body – may not possess the political and institutional endorsement required to produce general agreement today.

We live in a crowded world – a world we all share with a myriad strangers. We are constantly bumping up against one another, physically and otherwise. In this world, the difficult territory that links and divides East and West has become more conflicted than ever before. The *mezzaterra* so valued by Soueif has come under intense pressure. It appears to be shrinking by the day. As Tabish Khair writes, on the field where the so-called clash of civilizations is being fought out, the in-between spaces are getting compressed; moderate views are being inexorably squeezed.[7]

We are so interconnected that we have no buffer zones. We need to find ways of living together. In this situation Soueif's work is important because it insists that common ground *does* remain. But the survival of that common ground depends on slow, arduous, unglamorous processes. It depends on the recognition of common purpose. And that in turn depends on listening and waiting, on careful translation, on doing comparative work between rival narratives, on finding sources of courage and honesty within our own narratives, on the willingness to shuttle back and forth across the middle ground. It depends on a kind of ethical commuting, on persistent and vigilant negotiation in order that our shared humanity be more profoundly recognized. In the words of Kwame Anthony Appiah, we need to begin with the human in humanity.[8]

In her fiction, Soueif suggests that where strangers (or representatives of estranged cultures) meet, the best they can do is to immerse themselves in the other culture – difficult as this may be. This is challenging. Soueif is not the advocate of an anodyne middle way. She speaks out emphatically where she feels an act of inhospitality has been committed. She is first and foremost a commentator of intense principle. Perhaps the most eloquent homage to her achievement is her own homage to her long-time mentor and friend, Edward Said. In a memorial address in 2003, she spoke of the importance to him of '[holding] on to our humanity, our tolerance, our inclusiveness, always. To denounce cruelty, hypocrisy and phoniness wherever we find them. [And perhaps above all] to keep our friendships in good repair'.[9]

Notes

1 Ahdaf Soueif, *Mezzaterra: Fragments from the Common Ground* (London: Bloomsbury, 2004). See also Mourid Barhouti, *I Saw Ramallah*, tr. Ahdaf Soueif (London: Bloomsbury, 2004).

2 Edward W. Said, *Orientalism* (London: Routledge, Kegan, Paul, 1978).

3 Ahdaf Soueif, *The Map of Love* (London: Bloomsbury, 1999).

4 *Mezzaterra* (note 1), 223.

5 David Scott, *Conscripts of Modernity: The Tragedy of Colonial Enlightenment* (London and Durham: Duke University Press, 2001), especially page 6.

6 See Cullen Murphy, *Are We Rome? The Fall of an Empire and the Fate of America* (New York: Houghton Mifflin, 2007).

7 Tabish Khair, Commentary, *The Guardian*, 7 February 2006.

8 See Kwame Anthony Appiah, *Cosmopolitanism: Ethics in a World of Strangers* (London: Allen Lane, 2006), 134.

9 *Mezzaterra* (note 1), 317. See also Ahdaf Soueif, 'The Heart of the Matter: Palestine in the World Today', *Wasafiri* 22.2 (July 2007), 65–73.

2 Michael Byers

Terrorism, war and international law

Introduction

Most of humanity shares two searing memories: the collapse of the World Trade
Center on 11 September 2001; and a hooded man standing on a box with wires
dangling from his outstretched hands. These images capture the painful truth that
both sides in the so-called 'war on terror' have violated fundamental rules. But while
non-state actors can violate international law, only states are able to change the law,
making their breaches of greater potential consequence. In this chapter, I consider
how the recent actions of the United States have stressed and stretched two distinct but related areas of international law: the right of self-defence, and the rules
of international humanitarian law. I conclude by arguing that even a disproportionately
powerful state is constrained, in its ability to change international law, by the actions
of other countries and public opinion – both at home and abroad.

There are two principal sources of international law. 'Customary international
law' is an informal, unwritten body of rules deriving from a combination of 'state
practice' and *opinio juris*. State practice is what governments do and say; *opinio juris*
is a belief, on the part of governments, that their conduct is obligated by international law. Rules of customary international law usually apply universally: they
bind all countries and all countries contribute to their development and change.
Whenever a new rule of customary international law is being formed, or an existing rule changed, every country has a choice: support the developing rule through
its actions or statements, or actively and publicly oppose the rule. A new rule will
not come into force until it receives widespread support, either expressly or tacitly.

Treaties are the second main source of international law. They are contractual,
written instruments entered into by two or more countries and registered with a
third party, nowadays usually the U.N. Secretary-General. Treaties may be referred
to by any number of different names – including 'charter', 'covenant', 'convention'
or 'protocol' – but legally speaking are any written instrument entered into by two
or more countries with the intent of creating binding rights and obligations.

With customary international law dependent on the practice of states, and treaty negotiations replete with political, economic and military pressures, it comes as no surprise that powerful countries can exercise disproportionate influence on the making and changing of international rules. And because they can, countries such as the United States deliberately seek to modify international law in accordance with their changing interests, for instance, by pushing for a right of self-defence against terrorism, or more flexible rules concerning the treatment of detainees. Yet the fact that powerful states carry more weight in law-making does not necessarily spell the end of widely accepted and legitimate standards. For international law is nowadays made and changed by nearly two hundred countries and indirectly influenced by an even larger number of non-state actors, including human rights NGOs and other activist groups. As the following examples demonstrate, even when the U.S. administration of George W. Bush has pushed hard for change to international rules, the potential for countervailing influences has always remained present, giving hope to those who envisage a more peaceful and humane world.

Self-defence

In 1837, the British were crushing a rebellion in Upper Canada (now Ontario). Although the U.S. government chose not to support the rebels directly, it failed to prevent a private militia from being formed in upstate New York. The 'volunteers' used a steamboat, the *Caroline*, to transport reinforcements and weapons to the Canadian side of the Niagara River. The British responded with a night raid, capturing the vessel as it was docked at Fort Schlosser, New York. They set the boat on fire and sent it over Niagara Falls.

The incident caused disquiet in Washington. The United States was still a relatively weak country, while Britain was a superpower that had torched the White House and Capitol Building just twenty-three years before. Some careful diplomacy followed, with U.S. Secretary of State Daniel Webster suggesting that the use of force in self-defence could be justified when 'the necessity of that self-defence is instant, overwhelming, leaving no choice of means, and no moment of deliberation', and provided that nothing 'unreasonable or excessive' was done.[1] The British accepted Webster's criteria, and an important legal precedent was born. Over time, as other countries expressed similar views on the law, the *Caroline* criteria – often referred to simply as 'necessity and proportionality' – were transformed into a new right of self-defence in customary international law.

By 1945, the United States had become a superpower. At San Francisco, the drafters of the U.N. Charter – heavily influenced by U.S. negotiators – included self-defence as an exception to their new, general prohibition on the use of force.[2] In addition to the existing customary criteria, three further restrictions were introduced: (1) a state could act in self-defence only if subject to an 'armed attack'; (2) acts of self-defence had to be reported immediately to the Security Council; and (3) the right to respond would terminate as soon as the Council took action. However, despite this attempt at a more precise definition, the limits of self-defence still depend greatly on customary international law, in part because the U.N. Charter also refers to the 'inherent' character of the right. And so, while the right of self-defence has been codified in an almost universally ratified treaty, its parameters have evolved gradually – or at least become more easily discernible – as a result of the behaviour of countries since 1945. One instance of this concerns the use of force against state sponsors of terrorism. Such use was, until recently, proscribed by international law.

Self-defence against terrorism

In 1986, a terrorist attack on a West Berlin nightclub killed one U.S. soldier and wounded 50 more. Two weeks later, the United States responded by bombing several targets in Libya. It claimed the strikes were legally justified acts of self-defence, on the basis that the Libyan government was behind the attack in Berlin.[3] But the legal claim was rejected by many other countries, including France and Spain – both NATO allies of the United States – which refused to allow their airspace to be used by the planes conducting the raid. The widespread negative reactions meant that the legal claim and associated military action did not succeed in changing international law.

Instead, the process of legal change began after bombs exploded outside the U.S. embassies in Kenya and Tanzania in 1998. Twelve Americans and almost 300 other people were killed. U.S. intelligence sources indicated that al-Qaeda was responsible for the attacks. Two weeks later, the United States used cruise missiles to attack terrorist training camps in Afghanistan and a pharmaceutical plant in Sudan that were allegedly being operated by al-Qaeda with the tacit support of the Afghan and Sudanese regimes. Again, the United States claimed that the strikes were legally justified acts of self-defence.[4] But on this occasion it used its political influence to bolster the claim, with President Bill Clinton phoning Tony Blair, Jacques Chirac and German Chancellor Helmut Kohl shortly before the missile strikes to ask for their support. Without having time to consult their legal experts, all three agreed – and made concurring public statements immediately after the U.S. action. As a result of these quick expressions of support by three influential states, other countries were more restrained in their responses than they might have been. This in turn helped obfuscate the limits of self-defence, rendering the rule more susceptible to change in any subsequent situation.

That situation arose when terrorists struck the World Trade Center and Pentagon on 11 September 2001. The United States quickly implicated the Taliban who, by giving refuge to al-Qaeda and refusing to hand them over, were alleged to have knowingly facilitated and endorsed their actions. In this way, the United States framed its legal claim in a manner that encompassed action against the state of Afghanistan, rather than asserting a right to use force against terrorists regardless of their location.[5] And again, the United States deployed its political influence to secure support in advance of military action. The collective self-defence provisions of the 1949 North Atlantic Treaty and the 1947 Inter-American Treaty of Reciprocal Assistance were engaged, and both NATO and the OAS formally deemed the events of 11 September an 'armed attack' – legally relevant language under the self-defence provision of the U.N. Charter. Similarly, Security Council resolutions adopted on 12 and 28 September were carefully worded to affirm the right of self-defence in the context of the terrorist attacks.[6] Just as importantly, only two countries – Iraq and Cuba – publicly opposed the U.S. claim.

As a result of this widespread support and acquiescence, the right of self-defence now includes military action against countries that willingly harbour or support terrorist groups – provided the terrorists have already struck the responding state, and done so in a manner that constitutes an 'armed attack' (essentially, by being on the level of an invasion by foreign tanks or the destruction of the World Trade Center). The long-term consequences of this development may be significant. Having seized the opportunity to establish self-defence as a basis for military action against state sponsors of terrorism, it is only a matter of time before the United States invokes it again – in circumstances which are less grave, or where the responsibility of the targeted state is less clear.

Pre-emptive self-defence

In 1981, Israel bombed a nuclear reactor under construction near Baghdad and claimed pre-emptive self-defence, on the basis that a nuclear-armed Iraq would constitute an unacceptable threat. The U.N. Security Council unanimously condemned the action as illegal.[7] Since the U.N. Charter imposes certain restraints on the 'inherent' right of self-defence, including the words 'if an armed attack occurs', both customary international law and the so-called 'law of treaties' were at issue.

Under international law, treaties are interpreted in accordance with the 'ordinary meaning of the terms'.[8] Applying this approach, any pre-existing right of pre-emption is apparently superseded by the 'if an armed attack occurs' clause. At the same time, however, the reference to the 'inherent' right of self-defence can be read as implicitly incorporating the pre-existing customary international law of self-defence into the U.N. Charter. For this reason, it has been argued that pre-emption remains justified whenever there is a 'necessity of . . . self-defence . . . instant, overwhelming, leaving no choice of means, and no moment of deliberation' – the *Caroline* criteria in their full expression.

During the latter half of the twentieth century, countries – with the exception of Israel in 1981 – avoided claiming any such right. The United States implausibly justified its 1962 blockade of Cuba as 'regional peacekeeping'. Israel justified the strikes that initiated the 1967 Six-Day War as a response to a prior act of aggression. The United States argued that the shooting down of an Iranian airliner in 1988, although mistaken, was in response to an ongoing attack. For the most part, these and other countries chose not to claim or condone a right of pre-emptive self-defence during the Cold War when nuclear missile submarines on hair-trigger alert ensured 'mutually assured destruction' if things went wrong. The Security Council's unanimous condemnation of Israel in 1981 was but the clearest indication of this thinking.

In the first few years of the twenty-first century, the situation looked quite different – at least from the perspective of the Bush administration. Relations with Russia had improved, no other potential adversary had submarine-based nuclear missiles, and the first phase of a missile defence system was being implemented. In June 2002, George W. Bush announced a new policy of pre-emption that extended towards the preventive or even precautionary use of force: 'We must take the battle to the enemy, disrupt his plans, and confront the worst threats before they emerge'.[9] The 'Bush doctrine' made no attempt to satisfy the *Caroline* criteria.

Lawyers in the U.S. State Department knew there was little chance that the policy, as presented, would achieve the widespread support necessary to change international law. Relatively few countries possess enough of a military deterrence to be able to contemplate a world without the combined protections of the U.N. Charter and the *Caroline* criteria. Accordingly, the legal claim inherent in the Bush doctrine was reformulated to make it more acceptable to others, and thereby more likely to promote legal change. The National Security Strategy released in September 2002 explicitly adopted, and sought to extend, the traditional criteria:

> For centuries, international law recognized that nations need not suffer an attack before they can lawfully take action to defend themselves against forces that present an imminent danger of attack. Legal scholars and international jurists often conditioned the legitimacy of preemption on the existence of an imminent threat – most often a visible mobilization of armies, navies, and air forces preparing to attack.
>
> We must adapt the concept of imminent threat to the capabilities and objectives of today's adversaries.[10]

The National Security Strategy took the new policy of prevention or precaution and recast it within the widely accepted, pre-existing framework of customary international law. It did so, first, by omitting any mention of the U.N. Charter, thus implicitly asserting that the pre-1945 customary rule remained the applicable law. It then asserted that imminence (one facet of the traditional criterion of 'necessity') now extends beyond threats which are 'instant, overwhelming, leaving no choice of means, and no moment of deliberation'. It did this within a context that at least suggested the need for legal change, since few would contest that terrorism and weapons of mass destruction are serious problems. And most significantly, other governments were not actually asked to agree to a change in the rule. Instead, all that was proposed was an adaptation of how the (supposed) existing rule is applied in practice.

As recast in the National Security Strategy, the claim was designed to appear patently reasonable and therefore deserving of widespread support. Yet the reformulated doctrine was hardly innocuous. By stretching imminence to encompass new perceived threats, the approach being advocated would have created further ambiguity which would, in turn, have permitted power and influence to play a greater role. Whether or not an imminent threat exists depends in large part on how the factual circumstances are assessed by states. And the ability of the powerful to influence these assessments is considerable, given the various forms of political, economic and military pressure that can be brought to bear. It is even more considerable when imminence is understood as a broad rather than narrow concept. Under the Bush doctrine, agreement on the existence of an imminent threat would have been much more likely when the United States wished to act militarily, than when others wished to do the same. The present law on self-defence would have remained generally applicable – available as a diplomatic tool to be deployed against weak states – while more powerful countries would have gained greater freedom to act as they chose.

A few regional powers, notably India, Israel and Russia, responded favourably to the claim set out in the National Security Strategy, as did Australian Prime Minister John Howard, who suggested that the U.N. Charter be amended to allow for a right of unilateral pre-emptive action. But Howard's comments sparked angry protests from other Southeast Asian states – protests that contributed to reinforcing the current law. Other countries such as Japan voiced support for a right of pre-emptive self-defence but were careful to confine their claims to the *Caroline* criteria. And several important European countries, notably France and Germany, expressed concern – albeit in moderated tones. More recently, it was revealed that the British Attorney General deemed the Bush doctrine illegal in an opinion provided to Tony Blair in March 2003.[11]

This mixed reaction would, in itself, have prevented any significant change in the law of self-defence. As the Iraq crisis escalated, it also contributed to bringing the United States to the U.N. Security Council where Resolution 1441 was then adopted unanimously in November 2002.[12] Although the resolution did not expressly authorize force, it did provide some support for an argument that a previous authorization, accorded in 1990, had been revived as a result of Iraq's 'material breaches' of the 1991 cease-fire resolution and, later, Resolution 1441. The Bush administration relied on both this argument and pre-emptive self-defence to justify the 2003 Iraq War, while Britain and Australia relied solely on the resolutions. The advancement of two distinct arguments, with the latter receiving broader support, reduced any effect that the pre-emption claim might have had on customary international law.

After the Iraq War, opposition to the Bush doctrine mounted. In December 2004, the U.N. Secretary General's High Level Panel on Threats, Challenges and Change, a group of sixteen former prime ministers, foreign ministers and ambassadors, presented its own highly authoritative response:

> The short answer is that if there are good arguments for preventive military action, with good evidence to support them, they should be put to the Security Council, which can authorize such action if it chooses to. If it does not so choose, there will be, by definition, time to pursue other strategies, including persuasion, negotiation, deterrence and containment – and to visit again the military option.
>
> For those impatient with such a response, the answer must be that, in a world full of perceived potential threats, the risk to the global order and the norm of non-intervention on which it continues to be based is simply too great for the legality of unilateral preventive action, as distinct from collectively endorsed action, to be accepted. Allowing one to so act is to allow all.[13]

So far, the Bush doctrine has failed as an attempt to change international law, though it has resulted in a small degree of legal modification, or at least clarification. Today, much more so than a decade ago, it is difficult to find any international lawyer who argues that there is *no* right of pre-emptive self-defence. The debates over the significance of 'if an armed attack occurs' have been replaced by a general acceptance that a narrow right of pre-emptive self-defence does exist, as it did before 1945, in 'cases in which the necessity of that self-defence is instant, overwhelming, leaving no choice of means, and no moment of deliberation'. Although the concept of imminence remains tightly circumscribed, the influence of the single superpower is such that, even when it fails to achieve law-making goals, it still leaves a mark on international rules.

Self-defence and Iran

As I write, it seems possible that the Bush administration will soon launch air strikes against targets in Iran, including facilities that are allegedly part of a nuclear weapons programme. If so, the United States will probably claim self-defence in both of the respects described above: self-defence against state sponsors of terrorism; and pre-emptive self-defence in the context of a somewhat imminent threat involving WMD.

The Bush administration has already asserted that Iran is supporting terrorists who are attacking U.S. forces in Iraq, notably by providing sophisticated explosive devices. On 5 March 2007, in the *New Yorker*, Seymour Hersh quoted a former senior intelligence officer as saying 'The White House goal is to build a case that the Iranians have been fomenting the insurgency and they've been doing it all along – that Iran is, in fact, supporting the killing of Americans'.[14] Here, the Bush administration is working towards the same legal argument that it used against the Taliban government of Afghanistan in 2001. Yet the fact that the argument was accepted then does not mean that it fits the situation today. Clear and unassailable evidence of direct Iranian involvement in violence directed against U.S. forces is required. And even then, the violence must rise to the level of an 'armed attack' before it can justify military action within the territory of a sovereign Iran. Finally, even if self-defence is justified, any responsive action will have to remain within the traditional bounds of necessity and proportionality – ruling out the 'right of self-defence against state sponsors of terrorism' being used to justify strikes on Iranian nuclear facilities.

For this reason, the Bush administration is also working towards an argument of pre-emptive self-defence. Already, Vice-President Dick Cheney has warned of the possibility, in a few years, 'of a nuclear-armed Iran, astride the world's supply of oil, able to affect adversely the global economy, prepared to use terrorist organizations and/or their nuclear weapons to threaten their neighbours and others around the world'.[15] The Bush doctrine, as reformulated in the 2002 National Security Strategy, is being brought back into play. But as was explained above, most countries adhere to the view that self-defence is only justified when a threat is 'instant, overwhelming, leaving no choice of means, and no moment of deliberation'. For the moment, this requirement is far from being met with regard to Iran. On 19 February 2007, Mohamed ElBaradei, the Director General of the International Atomic Energy Agency, said that the country was at least five to ten years away from developing a nuclear bomb.[16] On 5 March 2007, ElBaradei said that his agency had 'not seen any diversion of nuclear materials . . . nor the capacity to produce weapons-usable materials'.[17] The Bush administration's assertions to the contrary can hardly be taken seriously, given the misrepresentations about weapons of mass destruction made in 2002–3. The time left for diplomacy and other non-violent forms of persuasion and pressure extends well beyond the date when the current president is required to leave the White House.

Some of George W. Bush's advisers will be aware of these legal constraints, which may explain why the United States is trying to provoke Iran into a first strike. In his March 2007 *New Yorker* piece, Seymour Hersh quotes Flynt Leverett, a former Bush administration National Security Council official, speaking of 'a campaign of provocative steps to increase the pressure on Iran. The idea is that at some point the Iranians will respond and then the Administration will have an open door to strike at them'.[18] As was demonstrated by the arrest of fifteen British sailors in March 2007, it would be easy to provoke some sort of incident involving Iran and one of the very many U.S. naval vessels in the region. At this point, any recourse to force by the United States would be limited only by the traditional criteria of necessity and proportionality, which, while important, might not stop the slide into an all-out war.

International humanitarian law

International humanitarian law – the *jus in bello* – imposes restraints on how wars may be fought. It is distinct from the law governing when wars may be fought: the *jus ad bellum* of the U.N. Charter and self-defence. Also known as the 'laws of war' or the 'law of armed conflict', international humanitarian law originated in 1859 when the Swiss businessman Henri Dunant witnessed the aftermath of the Franco-Austrian Battle of Solferino – where 40,000 men died, many as the result of untreated wounds – and initiated a movement that became the International Committee of the Red Cross.

Today, the rules of international humanitarian law are found primarily in the four Geneva Conventions of 1949. The protections guaranteed under these treaties are replicated and elaborated in two Additional Protocols of 1977, a multitude of more specific treaties, and a parallel body of customary international law.

Protection of civilians

More than 300 Iraqi civilians died on 13 February 1991 when U.S. stealth bombers targeted the Al'Amiriya bunker in Baghdad. Photographs of the charred and twisted bodies of women and children shocked a world which, thanks to General Norman Schwarzkopf and CNN, had seen little of the horrors of the Gulf War. Pentagon officials, who claimed to have intelligence indicating the bunker was a command and control centre, denied knowledge of the civilian presence. Had they known, the attack would probably have been a war crime, since a key principle of international humanitarian law prohibits the direct targeting of civilians. As Article 51(2) of Additional Protocol One explains:

> The civilian population as such, as well as individual civilians, shall not be the object of attack. Acts or threats of violence the primary purpose of which is to spread terror among the civilian population are prohibited.[19]

It follows that civilians cannot be collectively punished. Indeed, attacks on civilians or civilian infrastructure may never be justified by similar violations on the other side. The actions of U.S. forces in Fallujah, Iraq in April 2004, following the killing and mutilation of four U.S. contractors, certainly looked like war crimes from afar. Hundreds of civilians were killed, many of them with apparent indiscrimination, as U.S. marines fought their way into the densely populated city – before retreating out of concern about public opinion in the United States and elsewhere. Then, immediately after the U.S. presidential election on 2 November 2004, the marines moved back into Fallujah. Howitzers and 2,000 pound bombs, neither of which are particularly precise weapons, were used to soften up the city. Fuel-air explosives were dropped on residential neighbourhoods and virtually every house was struck by U.S. tank, machine-gun or rifle fire.

Even if the assault on Fallujah was not motivated by revenge, it appears to have been an illegally indiscriminate attack – because all reasonable measures were not taken to avoid harming civilians. The 'carpet bombing' of North Vietnam in the early 1970s was a violation of international humanitarian law, as were moves to designate certain villages as 'free fire zones' – including, famously, My Lai. Iraq violated the same rule when it fired eleven Scud missiles at Tel Aviv during the 1991 Gulf War, as did Hezbollah when it launched thousands of missiles at Tiberias and Haifa in the summer of 2006. On both occasions, the missiles were aimed at the general vicinity of Israeli cities rather than at specific military targets. On the later occasion, Israel also violated the rules. Of the more than 1,000 Lebanese civilians killed during the summer of 2006, some were struck by Israeli missiles as they followed Israeli instructions to leave their homes and villages. Others were hit because blasted roads, bridges and gasoline stations had made it impossible for them to flee. More civilians died when bombs were dropped in densely populated neighbour-hoods where the military advantage could virtually never justify the civilian harm.

Given the indiscriminate character of the assault on Fallujah in 2004, the duty to protect civilians was probably also violated when U.S. forces refused to allow men between the ages of 15 and 45 to leave the city beforehand. Hundreds if not thousands of innocents may have perished as a result not just of the violence but of the discrimination on the basis of sex and age that put them in harm's way. And the United States continued to breach international humanitarian law by refusing to count and document the Iraqi dead. Article 16 of the First Geneva Convention is categorical on this point: 'Parties to the conflict shall record as soon as possible, in respect of each wounded, sick or dead person of the adverse Party falling into their hands, any particulars which may assist in his identification . . . [and] shall pre-pare . . . certificates of death or duly authenticated lists of the dead'. In this, and in too many other circumstances, the United States has committed war crimes that could easily be avoided.

International humanitarian law seeks to draw the clearest possible distinction between combatants and civilians. In order to be considered soldiers, individuals should be in a chain of command, wear identifiable insignia, carry their weapons openly and act in accordance with the laws of war. The sanction for non-compliance with these requirements is the loss, if captured, of 'prisoner of war' status and the excep-tionally high standards of treatment it requires. The rationale is that individuals who do not fight fairly – wearing uniforms, carrying their weapons openly, etc. – do not deserve the protection of all of the rules. The distinction simultaneously rewards soldiers for being readily identifiable and deters civilians from entering the fray, thereby keeping the line between combatants and civilians as discernible as possible and maximizing civilian safety.

Mercenaries – persons who fight solely for financial gain – are not entitled to be treated as prisoners of war. The increasing use of private contractors by the U.S. military, in some cases very near or even in combat zones, raises questions as to what, if any, rights – beyond international human rights – these individuals have if captured by opposing armies. At the same time, the involvement of these contractors in activities traditionally reserved to military personnel is obfuscating

the all-important distinction between combatants and civilians, with potentially serious consequences. Journalists, for instance, are considered civilians even when
'embedded' within armed units, provided they do not themselves take up arms. For
this reason, journalists may not be targeted by military forces, though they put themselves at risk of being accidentally or incidentally harmed whenever they approach
or enter a combat zone. The risk to journalists has increased in proportion to the
growth in numbers of militarily active contractors wearing civilian clothes, since
enemy forces cannot readily distinguish one group from the other.

The protection afforded civilians is not absolute, for wars are fought to be won.
Beyond prohibiting the direct targeting of civilians, international humanitarian law
simply requires that soldiers balance the protection of civilians against 'military necessity' when selecting targets or choosing weapons. This obligation includes some
general constraints: attacks must be deliberate and tend towards the military defeat
of the enemy; they must not cause harm to civilians or civilian objects that is excessive in relation to the direct military advantage anticipated; and military necessity
does not justify violating other rules of international humanitarian law. Usually, the
boundary between acceptable and unacceptable targets will depend on the facts of
the specific situation. For example, the tower of a mosque is normally inviolable,
especially since places of worship and cultural property enjoy special protection,
but may become a legitimate target if used by an enemy sniper.

Stretching (or breaking?) international humanitarian law

During the 1991 Gulf War, the United States paid close heed to international humanitarian law. Desert Storm was the first major combat operation undertaken by the
United States after the Vietnam War. Fearful of another domestic backlash if things
went wrong, the politicians left the conduct of hostilities to professional soldiers –
who are trained to fight by the book. Adherence to the rule of law was further aided
by the fact that the United States was part of a thirty-member coalition. Some allies
of the United States accord considerable importance to the requirements of international humanitarian law, and so, in order to maintain the coalition, the United
States had to fight according to the rules.

Some two hundred military lawyers were dispatched to the Gulf, where they
vetted every targeting decision. A strike on a statue of Saddam Hussein in Baghdad
was ruled out on the basis that only targets that contribute to the war effort are
permissible under international humanitarian law. Those legal controversies that
arose stemmed from differing interpretations of the law, rather than any desire to
ignore legal constraints. At least five British officers resigned their commissions after
the United States used cluster bombs and fuel-air explosives to attack Iraqi armour,
with devastating effects on enemy soldiers. A similar divergence of views arose over
the use of earthmovers and tank-mounted ploughs to bury Iraqi soldiers alive in
their trenches, thus avoiding the dangers of hand-to-hand combat. International

humanitarian law forbids methods of warfare that cause 'unnecessary suffering or superfluous injury', but where one sets the balance between military necessity and humanitarian concerns also depends, perhaps inevitably, on where one is coming from – during the 1990s, the U.S. government was particularly concerned to avoid American casualties.

Today, in Washington, it has become accepted wisdom that current and future opponents are unlikely to abide by international humanitarian law. This assumption has been fuelled by events. During the 1991 Gulf War, captured American pilots were brutalized in several ways, some having been raped. The September 2001 attacks on the Twin Towers breached international humanitarian law as 'crimes against humanity', defined as violent acts committed as part of a systematic attack on a civilian population. And during the 2003 war, Iraqi soldiers committed the war crime of 'perfidy' by using civilian clothes and white flags to trick and then kill opposing forces. If your enemy is going to cheat, why bother playing by the rules?

Former Defense Secretary Donald Rumsfeld was a key proponent of this kind of thinking, a position that put him at loggerheads with the professional lawyers in the Pentagon. In October 2002, CIA operatives used an unmanned Predator reconnaissance aircraft to track the Taliban leader Mullah Omar to a building in a residential area of Kabul. The air strike to kill Omar was called off because a lawyer at U.S. Central Command was concerned about the risk of disproportionate civilian casualties. According to a report in the New Yorker, the incident left Rumsfeld 'kicking a lot of glass and breaking doors'.[20] The Secretary subsequently took steps to reduce the number of lawyers in uniform.

Rumsfeld also encouraged a re-evaluation of the prohibition on targeting civilians, particularly with regard to actions directed at shattering support for opponent regimes. This kind of thinking was popular during World War II – as evidenced by the fire-bombing of Dresden, Hamburg and several cities in Japan – but was subsequently rejected during the negotiation of the 1949 Geneva Conventions. More recently, a theory claiming that every regime has 'five strategic rings' has attracted adherents in Washington. According to this view, each ring represents a different facet of a society: political leadership, economic system, supporting infrastructure, population and military forces. Air power is supposed to enable the United States to target opponents from the 'inside out', bypassing military forces and attacking the political leadership directly. In this context, the indirect harm caused to civilians – through the destruction of bridges, electrical grids, oil refineries and water-filtration plants – is considered justified because it promotes dissatisfaction within the regime and thus hastens the course of the conflict.

During the 1991 Gulf War, the United States targeted the Iraqi national electrical grid, shutting down hospitals as well as water and sewage stations. The health consequences for civilians were severe, but the strikes were legal because Iraqi military communications depended heavily on the grid. In 1999, when Slobodan

Milosevic's forces proved much more resilient than expected, the United States pushed for the adoption of a looser approach which led to more questionable military tactics. Electrical grids and water-filtration plants in Serbia were targeted, not to disrupt the actions of the Yugoslav Army in Kosovo, but to provoke domestic opposition to Milosevic's government in Belgrade.

Equally problematic was the targeting of the State Serbian Television and Radio station in April 1999, as well as the Iraqi State Television station in March 2003. The two stations were legitimate targets if they had been integrated into military communications networks, but not if they were simply being used for propaganda. Again, applying the rules often has as much to do with finer points of fact as it does with those of law. In 1991, a number of coalition warplanes (notably British Tornados) were lost to Iraqi anti-aircraft fire because they were bombing from low altitudes in order to reduce civilian casualties. Less accurate high-altitude strikes by B-52s were restricted to targets well clear of civilian areas. In contrast, almost all the bombing during the Kosovo War was carried out above the reach of Serbian air defences. As a result of the high altitudes, NATO pilots were sometimes unable to distinguish between military and civilian targets, with disastrous results for several refugee convoys. In 2003, the 'strategic ring' approach was given a new title: 'shock and awe'.

Again, as a result of the United States taking a somewhat different approach to these issues, there is now a different reckoning of the balance between military necessity and humanitarian concerns. Most worryingly, the new approach is now manifesting itself in the behaviour of at least some other countries: in 2006, the Israeli Chief of Staff promised to 'turn back the clock in Lebanon by 20 years'.[21] His forces bombed Beirut's international airport, striking at the heart of Lebanon's tourism-based economy. They destroyed arterial roads, bridges, power plants and gasoline stations – in a campaign that was explicitly designed to pressure the Lebanese people into rejecting Hezbollah.

Precision-guided munitions give rise to a further complication. When civilians are present, international humanitarian law requires belligerents to use weapons that can distinguish between civilians and combatants; they should therefore use the most accurate weapons available to them. There are those who argue that this requirement imposes an unfair burden on the United States, given the substantial production costs of smart missiles and bombs. But the same logic would lead to the conclusion that, because precision-guided weapons reduce the number of civilian casualties across a campaign, attacking forces using them may exercise less concern for the protection of civilians when making individual targeting decisions, since the overall collateral damage will still be less than in a low-tech war. Applying such calculations to rules designed to protect human beings is not only inappropriate, but also immoral.

The prohibition on weapons that cause superfluous injury or unnecessary suffering has led to taboos on certain weapons. Explosive or expanding ('dum-dum') bullets, booby traps and blinding laser weapons are banned on the basis that the military benefits of their use can never be proportionate to the suffering they cause. A special treaty – the 1925 Geneva Protocol – precludes the use of poisonous gas and biological weapons. These prohibitions have achieved the status of customary international law, as was confirmed by the harshly negative reaction of other countries to the use of nerve and mustard gas during the Iran-Iraq War of the 1980s. Other weapons, such as anti-personnel landmines, have been banned by most but not all countries. Today, the United States', refusal to ratify the 1997 Ottawa Landmines Convention sometimes creates awkward situations for its allies. In 2002, Canadian soldiers operating in Afghanistan were ordered by their U.S. commander to lay mines around their camp. When the Canadians refused to do so, U.S. soldiers, who were not subject to the same restrictions, laid the mines for them.

Depleted uranium, cluster bombs and fuel-air explosives are among the weapons whose use remains legally uncertain. Favoured for their armour-piercing abilities, depleted uranium shells leave radioactive residues that can pose health problems for civilians and combatants alike. Given the scientific uncertainty as to the extent of the risk, humanitarian concerns should prevail – though depleted uranium was used extensively by American and British forces during the 2003 invasion of Iraq. Cluster bombs, for their part, are the aerial equivalent of a shotgun. A single cluster bomb contains hundreds of individual bomblets which are deliberately scattered over a wide area, killing everything there. Worse yet, depending on the model and age of the particular bomb, the hardness of the ground, the presence of vegetation, and weather conditions, between 5 and 30 per cent of the bomblets fail to explode on impact. They lie in wait until disturbed by an unsuspecting passer-by, usually a civilian, often a child. Cluster bombs have been used by the United States in Vietnam, Laos and Cambodia; by the United States and Britain in Kosovo, Afghanistan and Iraq; by Russia in Chechnya; and by Israel in Lebanon. The use of cluster bombs by the Israeli Defence Forces in 2006 attracted particular attention, in part because 90 per cent of the cluster bomb strikes occurred in the last 72 hours of the conflict, when everyone knew that the hostilities were about to end.[22] At the same time, Hezbollah's use of rockets packed with ball-bearings was just as contemptible.

At an arms control conference in Geneva in November 2006, the United States and Britain defeated a proposal to begin negotiations on a treaty banning cluster bombs. Although the U.S. and British delegations argued that any discussion of cluster bombs belonged within the framework of the 1980 U.N. Convention on Conventional Weapons, this move was clearly intended to stymie any attempt at a meaningful ban. The same two countries had used the exact same tactic when opposing a ban on anti-personnel landmines a decade earlier. Fortunately, Norway refused to treat the defeat as determinative. Its foreign minister, Jonas Gahr Stoere, immediately announced: 'We must now establish concrete measures that will put an end to the untold human suffering caused by cluster munitions. Norway will

organize an international conference in Oslo to start a process toward an international ban on cluster munitions that have unacceptable humanitarian consequences'.[23]
On 23 February 2007, forty-six countries adopted a declaration calling for a treaty
banning the use of cluster bombs by 2008.[24]

Although nuclear weapons are not banned, their use is subject to the general
constraints of international humanitarian law. And while it is difficult to envision
how any use of such weapons could produce a military advantage that was proportionate to the extreme suffering caused, the legal constraints have, again, been shrugged
off by the Bush administration. In March 2002, the Pentagon issued a Nuclear Posture
Review that cited the need for new nuclear weapons specifically designed to
destroy deeply buried command centres and biological weapon facilities. Not to
be left out, the British Defence Secretary, Geoff Hoon, affirmed in February 2003
that Britain reserved the right to use nuclear weapons against Iraq in 'extreme self-
defence' – overlooking the fact that Iraq was, at the time, the only country in serious danger of being attacked.[25]

Protection of prisoners

Soldiers are legitimate targets during armed conflict. Killing members of the enemy's
armed forces is one of the goals of military action. Still, soldiers – referred to under
international humanitarian law as 'combatants' – benefit from some protections,
including the prohibitions on certain types of weapons discussed above. Important
protections are also available to wounded soldiers as well as to those who lay down
their arms.

Soldiers who have been wounded are deemed 'hors de combat' (out of combat) and accorded protections similar to those that apply to civilians. Soldiers who
clearly express 'an intention to surrender' become prisoners of war. Wounded
soldiers and prisoners of war cannot be killed, used as human shields, held hostage,
or used to clear landmines. The execution-style shooting of a wounded and unarmed
Iraqi in Fallujah in November 2004, as captured on tape by an embedded television cameraman, was almost certainly a war crime. Medical personnel benefit from
similarly strict protections, while medical facilities, ambulances and hospital ships
are off-limits as targets unless used as locations from which to launch attacks. As
with many rules of international humanitarian law, this rule is sometimes honoured
in the breach. In 1992 and early 1993, the main hospital in Sarajevo, Bosnia-
Herzegovina, was hit by no less than 172 mortar shells while full of patients.

In January 2002, the first Taliban and suspected al-Qaeda members were trans-
ported from the Afghan battlefield to Guantánamo Bay. Against the advice of the
Pentagon's professional lawyers in the State Department and Pentagon and despite
expressions of concern from a number of European leaders, Donald Rumsfeld insisted
the detainees could not be prisoners of war and refused to convene the tribunals
required under the Geneva Conventions to determine their status. Even now,

more than five years after the intervention in Afghanistan, hundreds of the detainees have neither been charged nor granted access to lawyers.

Guantánamo Bay has been the focus of public concern about the Bush administration's efforts to evade legal strictures during its 'war on terrorism'. The President and his advisers have consistently maintained that the naval base, located on leased land in Cuba, is beyond the reach of U.S. law and courts. The assertion of extra-legality prompted scathing criticism from around the world. In November 2002, the English Court of Appeal described the position of the Guantánamo Bay detainees as 'legally objectionable'; it was as if they were in a 'legal black hole'.

The U.S. Supreme Court was finally shamed into action in June 2004. On behalf of a 6–3 majority of judges, Justice John Paul Stevens wrote:

> Executive imprisonment has been considered oppressive and lawless since John, at Runnymede, pledged that no free man should be imprisoned, dispossessed, outlawed, or exiled save by judgment of his peers or by the law of the land. The judges of England developed the writ of habeas corpus largely to preserve these immunities from executive restraint.[26]

Sadly, the judicial victory was short-lived. A cross-party majority of Congressmen and women, anxious to affirm their commitment to national security in the lead-up to the November 2006 mid-term elections, adopted legislation that stripped the detainees of the right to contest their imprisonment.[27]

The Bush administration is now moving ahead with the first prosecutions of Guantánamo Bay detainees before special 'military commissions' designed to restrict the release of evidence to defence counsel and journalists. The commissions are authorized to impose the death penalty if all three of the military officers who serve like judges agree. The first prosecution took place in March 2007 against David Hicks, an Australian charged with providing 'material support for terrorism' as a result of having guarded a tank for the Taliban. In the end, Hicks, who had already spent five years at Guantánamo Bay, agreed to a plea bargain. In return for promising never to allege that he was mistreated in U.S. custody, Hicks will serve just nine months in an Australian prison.[28]

Unfortunately, the focus on Guantánamo Bay has drawn attention away from many other, arguably more serious, violations against detainees elsewhere. In November 2001, a prisoner revolt at Mazar-i-Sharif, Afghanistan, was put down with air-to-surface missiles and B-52 launched bombs. More than 175 detainees were killed; 50 died with their hands tied behind their backs. In December 2002, the *Washington Post* reported on the use of 'stress and duress' techniques at Bagram Air Base.[29] In March 2003, the *New York Times* reported that, while in custody over a three-month period, a suspected member of al-Qaeda was 'fed very little, while being subjected to sleep and light deprivation, prolonged isolation and room temperatures that varied from 100 degrees to 10 degrees'.[30] That same month, the *New*

York Times reported that a death certificate, signed by a U.S. military pathologist, stated the cause of death of a 22-year-old Afghan detainee at Bagram Air Base in December 2002 as 'blunt force injuries to lower extremities complicating coronary artery disease'.[31] The form gave the pathologist four choices for 'mode of death': 'natural, accident, suicide, homicide'. She marked the box for homicide.

In July 2003, U.N. Secretary-General Kofi Annan reported that his Special Representative for Iraq had expressed concern to the United States about its treatment of detained Iraqis. One week later, Amnesty International claimed that U.S. forces were resorting to 'prolonged sleep deprivation, prolonged restraint in painful positions – sometimes combined with exposure to loud music, prolonged hooding and exposure to bright lights'.[32] The reports attracted little attention until March 2004 when CBS television aired photographs showing prisoners at Abu Ghraib prison in Iraq who had been stripped naked, sexually and culturally ridiculed, terrorized with dogs and threatened with electrocution. The actions were blatant violations of international humanitarian law and some of them violated the 1984 Torture Convention, a treaty ratified by the United States and 143 other countries.

Additional violations were committed when the International Committee of the Red Cross was denied access to some detainees, as reportedly occurred in Iraq early in 2004. Under the Geneva Conventions, the ICRC is mandated to visit and register prisoners of war: this promotes their good treatment and ensures they do not disappear. Although the ICRC traditionally does not publicly denounce governments that fail to uphold the law – in order to preserve its neutrality, thereby ensuring future access to individuals in need – it has, on several occasions since 2001, openly expressed concern about the actions of the United States.

Torture

In December 2005, Louise Arbour, the U.N. High Commissioner for Human Rights, said:

> The absolute ban on torture, a cornerstone of the international human rights edifice, is under attack. The principle we once believed to be unassailable – the inherent right to physical integrity and dignity of the person – is becoming a casualty of the so-called war on terror.[33]

President Bush and his advisers vehemently deny that the United States engages in torture. However, these denials have failed to address either the sharp distinction between the international definition of torture and the more flexible definition favoured by the Bush administration, or their fall-back position: that any method of interrogation may still be used if authorized by the American president.

The Torture Convention defines torture as 'any act by which severe pain or suffering, whether physical or mental, is intentionally inflicted on a person'.[34] The Bush administration prefers a standard articulated by the Justice Department in an

August 2002 memorandum, namely that, to constitute torture, the pain caused 'must be equivalent in intensity to the pain accompanying serious physical injury, such as organ failure, impairment of bodily functions, or even death'.[35] Many methods of what is generally understood as 'torture' would be permitted by this definition. When that legal memorandum became public, it was retracted and replaced by an ostensibly moderated legal opinion.[36]

Still, the replacement memorandum refused to address a key aspect of the first, namely its expansive interpretation of the president's powers to ignore or override domestic legislation and even international law, and to apply whichever definition of torture he sees fit. The central figure in the advancement of this gaping loophole was John Yoo, a political appointee within the Justice Department who has since returned to his tenured position as a law professor at Berkeley. In December 2005, Yoo had the following exchange with University of Notre Dame professor Douglas Cassel during a debate in Chicago:

> *Cassel*: If the president deems that he's got to torture somebody, including by crushing the testicles of the person's child, there is no law that can stop him?
> *Yoo*: No treaty.
> *Cassel*: Also no law by Congress – that is what you wrote in the August 2002 memo.
> *Yoo*: I think it depends on why the president thinks he needs to do that.[37]

It is this extreme privileging of executive power that has enabled the CIA to maintain its list of 'enhanced interrogation techniques' for use in clandestine operations approved by the president. These techniques include 'water boarding', whereby a prisoner is made to believe that he or she will drown. In October 2006, a radio interview asked Dick Cheney: 'Would you agree a dunk in water is a no-brainer if it can save lives?' He replied, 'Well, it's a no-brainer for me'.[38]

Not all Americans agree with the Vice-President. Senator John McCain, who was tortured by the North Vietnamese, describes water boarding as 'torture, very exquisite torture'.[39] In 2005, McCain sponsored legislation confirming that 'No individual in the custody or under the physical control of the United States Government, regardless of nationality or physical location, shall be subject to cruel, inhuman, or degrading treatment or punishment'.[40] The more encompassing language of McCain's legislation clearly extends to methods such as water boarding. The legislation was fiercely opposed by Cheney, who – by invoking the threat of a presidential veto – successfully negotiated some important exemptions. The legislation, as eventually passed and signed into law, does not ban torture contracted out to other countries. It provides U.S. government employees with legal immunity for acts of torture that were 'officially authorized and determined to be lawful at the time that they were conducted'. And, as mentioned above, it denies the detainees at Guantánamo Bay the right to contest their imprisonment in federal court.[41]

Worse yet, when Bush signed McCain's bill, he issued a statement declaring the new law would, again, be interpreted within the broader context of the president's powers to protect national security – in other words, that any method of interrogation may still be used, if and when Bush deems it necessary. This outright rejection of Congressional intent is breathtaking; as Sidney Blumenthal observed, it reflects 'a basic ideology of absolute power'.[42]

'Extraordinary rendition'

In December 2005, Colin Powell said:

> There's a little bit of the movie *Casablanca* in this, where, you know, the inspector says 'I'm shocked, shocked that this kind of thing takes place'.[43]

The former Secretary of State was seeking to extinguish a scandal over the use of European airspace and airports for the 'extraordinary rendition' of terrorist suspects, either to secret CIA prisons, or into the hands of foreign intelligence services notorious for torture, such those of Jordan, Egypt and Syria. Yet Powell's words could not change the fact that secret prisons, and at least some of the renditions and methods of interrogation used by the CIA, constitute serious violations of international law. His words could not change the fact that those who facilitate these activities – for instance, by allowing the CIA aircraft to land and refuel – might themselves be engaged in international crimes.

International law has well-established rules on the involuntary transfer of persons across borders. Criminal suspects who flee overseas are usually returned on the basis of extradition treaties. These treaties provide basic protections by requiring: first, that the alleged offence would be a serious crime if committed in the country to which the suspect has fled; and second, that he or she is tried only for the offence specified in the extradition request. Most extradition treaties also require that some evidence of the crime be presented. Of greatest importance, suspects are allowed to contest their extraditions before the courts. In the late 1990s, Augusto Pinochet made full use of this right – before being released by the British government on the basis of a dementia which then, remarkably, disappeared.

Foreign nationals who have entered the country illegally or committed some minor offence are generally deported. Provided they are not being returned to face trial, the protections provided by extradition law are unnecessary. However, deportation is sometimes used to bypass the requirements and delays of extradition. Courts tend to frown upon so-called 'disguised extraditions'. In 1993, the British House of Lords ordered the release of a New Zealand citizen who, at the encouragement of the London Police, was deported from South Africa to New Zealand on a suspiciously circuitous route that took him through Heathrow Airport – where he was arrested and charged with fraud.

In other instances, there is simply no extradition treaty between the two countries. In 1994, the terrorist Carlos the Jackal was deported from Sudan to France to face trial. The transfer occurred with the full knowledge and consent of the Sudanese government and was therefore legal. However, it is illegal to deport or otherwise return someone when, in the words of the 1984 Torture Convention, 'there are substantial grounds for believing that he would be in danger of being subjected to torture'. In 2002, the Canadian Supreme Court held that this prohibition does not necessarily apply when national security is at risk and an assurance of good treatment has been obtained from the receiving state. The judgment was properly criticized by Manfred Nowak, the U.N. Special Rapporteur on Torture, on the basis that 'diplomatic assurances are unreliable and ineffective', not least because they 'are sought usually from States where the practice of torture is systematic'.[44]

Abducting a person from another country without its consent is always illegal. In 1960, Mossad agents captured Adolf Eichmann in Argentina and flew him to Israel where he was tried and executed. Argentina complained loudly about the violation of sovereignty until Israel quietly offered a generous settlement. In 1990, a Mexican doctor named Humberto Alvarez Machain was abducted to face trial for the torture and murder of a U.S. drug enforcement agent. Although the Mexican government protested the infringement of sovereignty, the U.S. Supreme Court ruled that the suspect could still be tried, on the dubious basis that the U.S.-Mexico extradition treaty did not explicitly prohibit abductions. In 1999, Turkish commandos lured Kurdish rebel leader Abdullah Öcalan out of the Greek embassy in Nairobi, where he had sought refuge, and flew him to Turkey. In the ensuing scandal, three Greek cabinet ministers resigned and the chief of intelligence was fired.

The U.S. practice of 'extraordinary rendition' involves a mix of deportations and abductions. Six days after the terrorist attacks of 11 September 2001, George W. Bush signed a presidential finding that provided the CIA with broad authorization to disrupt terrorist activity, including by killing, capturing or detaining al-Qaeda members anywhere in the world. On this basis, the CIA began secretly transferring suspects, either to the intelligence services of countries notorious for torture, or to clandestine prisons located outside the United States and therefore beyond the reach – or at least the scrutiny – of U.S. courts.[45]

In September 2002, Maher Arar – a Canadian who is also Syrian by virtue of that country's refusal to accept renunciations of citizenship – was arrested while transiting through New York's JFK Airport. After twelve days of questioning, he was taken to Syria where he was imprisoned without charge. An independent fact-finder appointed by a Canadian judicial inquiry later determined conclusively that Arar was tortured, including by being beaten with an electrical cable and by being confined for ten months to a cell measuring 6 feet long, 3 feet wide and 7 feet high.[46]

Other terrorist suspects have been captured in Pakistan and moved elsewhere with the apparent consent of the government in Islamabad. Binyam Mohamed, an

Ethiopian-born British resident, was taken to Morocco where, he claims, a scalpel was applied to his penis.[47] Khalid Shaikh Mohammed, the alleged mastermind of the 11 September 2001 attacks, disappeared into U.S. custody in March 2003; the *New York Times* later reported that he was subjected to 'graduated levels of force, including... "water boarding"'.[48] And in Macedonia, a German citizen named Khaled el-Masri was arrested, handed over to U.S. agents and transferred to a secret CIA prison in Afghanistan where he claims to have been psychologically tortured. Although the CIA soon realized it had the wrong man, el-Masri languished in prison for five months before being released.[49]

Other renditions have involved straightforward abductions. In January 2002, the Bosnian Supreme Court found six Algerians innocent of terrorist plotting and ordered their release. As the men left prison, they were seized by U.S. military personnel and flown to Guantánamo Bay.[50] In 2003, Islamic cleric Osama Nasr was abducted from Milan while under Italian surveillance and flown to Egypt where, he claims, he was tortured. The Italian authorities, incensed at this interference in their own investigation, have pressed charges against twenty-five CIA agents and a U.S. Air Force colonel.[51]

An additional form of rendition has involved the transfer of detainees out of occupied, pre-'sovereign' Iraq in violation of a provision in the Fourth Geneva Convention that unequivocally prohibits 'individual or mass forcible transfers, as well as deportations of protected persons from occupied territory... regardless of their motive'.[52] In October 2004, the *Washington Post* reported that a legal opinion prepared by the U.S. Department of Justice had reinterpreted this provision – in a completely Orwellian manner – as actually allowing such transfers.[53] A further violation occurred when the suspects, before being transferred out of Iraq, were never registered as detainees, and were moved around within and between prisons, to conceal their existence from the International Committee of the Red Cross.

The detainees from Iraq may have ended up in the secret CIA prisons, which have been located in at least eight countries including Thailand, Afghanistan, Romania and Poland.[54] The parallels to these secret prisons – the Soviet Gulag and the Latin American 'disappearances' – are obvious, as is their international illegality. Secret prisons contravene the prohibition on arbitrary arrest or detention set out in the Universal Declaration of Human Rights and numerous treaties, including the European Convention on Human Rights. It is this latter aspect that has attracted the attention of the Council of Europe and European Parliament, both of which have condemned European governments for their involvement in extraordinary rendition, as well as their ongoing reluctance to admit – or co-operate with investigations into – their roles.[55]

CIA aircraft have used British airports on at least 170 occasions since September 2001, and German, Irish and Portuguese airports almost as often.[56] In addition, British agents are alleged to have conducted interrogations under threat of torture, at

Guantánamo and elsewhere; according to Binyam Mohamed, MI6 agents visited him in Pakistan and threatened that he would be 'tortured by Arabs'.[57] It also seems the British government has used information obtained by other governments through torture. Craig Murray, a former British ambassador to Uzbekistan, posted secret documents on his website that, if authentic, showed British officials deciding that information obtained through torture by other governments could be used for British intelligence purposes.[58] When Murray questioned the practice, the government produced a legal opinion which, by focusing narrowly on the express language of the Torture Convention, carefully sidesteps two decisive points: the convention codifies a general prohibition on complicity in torture, and international law requires that any treaty's provisions must be interpreted in light of its 'object and purpose'.[59] The documents are all the more troubling because Uzbekistan is notorious for using especially horrific methods of torture, such as immersing detainees in boiling water.

There has also been Canadian complicity, above and beyond the Arar affair. According to government documents obtained by the Canadian Press, as many as twenty airplanes linked to the CIA have used Canadian airports since 11 September 2001, including for refuelling stops in Newfoundland and Nunavut.[60] Many more rendition flights presumably crossed Canadian airspace, given that the shortest flight-lines from the United States to Europe or the Middle East cross that country's vast territory.

In September 2006, after months of denials, George W. Bush finally admitted the existence of the secret prisons – and declared that they'd been closed. However, it has since emerged that the practice of extraordinary rendition has simply been shifted elsewhere, including to Ethiopia, which in April 2007 admitted to holding 41 terrorist suspects from 17 countries. According to a report in the *New York Times*, U.S. intelligence officials had questioned several of the detainees in Ethiopian prisons.[61]

All this complicity demonstrates how the law-breaking of a powerful state can tempt other, less powerful countries to engage in their own violations on the basis of the same dubious justifications. The mass of violations can then lead to the undermining and eventual change of international rules. This is all the more likely today because, prior to George W. Bush's presidency, the United States often acted as a champion of robust legal protections for both combatants and civilians. Under Bush, the United States has shifted from positive role model to very bad example, with deleterious consequences for human beings everywhere.

Conclusion

At first, many experts predicted that the terrorist attacks of 11 September 2001 would prompt the United States to adopt a mutilateralist approach. These predictions were initially reinforced when a 'coalition' was constructed to facilitate the freezing of terrorist assets and the gathering of intelligence overseas. But they were then quickly shattered, when the Bush administration rejected offers of a U.N. Security Council resolution to authorize the Afghan War, forged new alliances with illiberal regimes in Pakistan, Kyrgyzstan, Tajikistan and Uzbekistan, and began mistreating detainees. Most disturbing, however, were some of the threats uttered by George W. Bush. The assertion that 'you're either with us or against us' obviated a central aspect of state sovereignty – the right not to be involved – and recast the United States as the ultimate arbiter of right and wrong. The identification of an 'axis of evil' between Iran, Iraq and North Korea, and the concurrent claim to a greatly extended right of pre-emptive self-defence, challenged one of the twentieth century's greatest achievements: the prohibition of the threat or use of force in international affairs.

Powerful countries have always shaped the international system to their advantage. In the sixteenth century, Spain redefined basic concepts of justice and universality to justify the conquest of indigenous Americans. In the eighteenth century, France developed the modern concepts of borders and the 'balance of power' to suit its continental strengths. In the nineteenth century, Britain introduced new rules on piracy, neutrality and colonialism, again to suit its interests as the predominant power of the day. George W. Bush's United States has been no different – except that the world has fundamentally changed.

The international legal system has grown more complex, with a far broader and denser network of customary international law and treaties and an unprecedented multiplicity and diversity of actors, both state and non-state. The involvement of these new actors – former colonies, inter-governmental organizations, transnational corporations and NGOs – makes the contemporary legal system qualitatively different from before and makes the exercise of hegemonic influence more difficult.

That said, a role for non-state actors has long been recognized in the domain of international humanitarian law. Most treaties in this field contain something called the Martens Clause, which in its original form was drafted by the Russian delegate to the conferences that produced the Hague Conventions of 1907:

> Until a more complete code of the laws of war is issued, the high contracting Parties think it right to declare that in cases not included in the Regulations adopted by them, populations and belligerents remain under the protection and empire of the principles of international law, as they result from the usages established between civilised nations, from the laws of humanity, and the requirements of the public conscience.

During the last few years, the public conscience has had a discernible effect on the conduct of war. Recall the delay in the assault on Fallujah in 2004, or the Bush administration's withdrawal of its most obviously odious memorandum on torture, or the recent push for a treaty banning cluster bombs. Even governments that disrespect international rules do their best to court public opinion, and to avoid sustained and public criticism. For this reason, human rights and other activists must press continuously for transparency and accountability, especially with regard to the location, treatment and due process rights of detainees. How many people, swept up in the 'war on terrorism', remain 'disappeared'?

Public opinion also has an important role to play with regard to the recourse to military force. In 2003, public opinion kept Canada and Germany out of the Iraq War; in 2004 and 2005, it led to the withdrawal of Spanish and Italian forces from that country; in 2005–7, it caused nineteen NATO governments to hold back from deploying forces to Afghanistan's volatile south. Arguably, one of the reasons why Colin Powell spent eight weeks negotiating Security Council Resolution 1441 in the autumn of 2002 was that two-thirds of Americans thought the U.S. should co-operate fully with the U.N.[62]

However, public opinion may be of limited effect in undemocratic countries, or with respect to presidents who cannot be elected again. The November 2006 mid-term elections constituted a 'pummelling' – to quote George W. Bush himself – but rather than heeding the will of the electorate he has actually increased U.S. troop levels in Iraq. For this reason, public opinion should ideally be marshalled before military force is used and then applied not only to potential belligerents but to all governments and other actors on which the belligerents might potentially rely. To do this effectively, NGOs and other activists need to develop their capacity for geopolitical risk analysis, forward planning, and public education about foreign affairs, international organizations and international law. The same holds true for international humanitarian law, which is too often ignored until after violations have been committed. The public needs to know about the Geneva Conventions and what they require well before their soldiers march off to war.

To some degree, the Bush administration was able to disregard so much of international law because our fellow citizens understood so little about it. From now on, all of us – academics, activists and journalists – must do better, to ensure that the dogs of war remain tightly leashed by strong rules and a well-informed and engaged public conscience.

Notes

1 See: R.Y. Jennings, 'The *Caroline* and McLeod Cases', *American Journal of International Law* 32 (1938), 82.

2 Article 51, U.N. Charter, available at www.un.org/aboutun/charter/index.html.

3 See, e.g., 'Address by Secretary of State George P. Shultz, Low-Intensity Warfare Conference, National Defense University, Washington, D.C., 15 January 1986', reproduced in *International Legal Materials* 25 (1986), 204.

4 See, e.g., Secretary of State Madeleine Albright and National Security Adviser Samuel ('Sandy') Berger, 'News Briefing', FDCH Political Transcripts, 20 August 1998, Thursday.

5 See Michael Byers, 'Terrorism, the Use of Force and International Law after 11 September', *International and Comparative Law Quarterly* 51 (2002), 401; reprinted in *International Relations* 16 (2002), 155.

6 SC Res. 1368, U.N. Doc. SC/7143; SC Res. 1373, U.N. Doc. SC/7158; both available at www.un.org/Docs/scres/2001/sc2001.htm.

7 SC Res. 487 (1981), www.un.org/Docs/scres/1981/scres81.htm.

8 Article 31, 1969 *Vienna Convention on the Law of Treaties*, available at www.un.org/law/ilc/texts/treatfra.htm.

9 Remarks by President George W. Bush at 2002 Graduation Exercise of the United States Military Academy West Point, New York, www.whitehouse.gov/news/releases/2002/06/20020601-3.html.

10 National Security Strategy of the United States, 20 September 2002, p. 19, www.whitehouse.gov/nsc/nss.html.

11 Richard Norton-Taylor, 'Revealed: The Government's Secret Legal Advice on Iraq War', *Guardian*, 28 April 2005. For the original document, see http://image.guardian.co.uk/sys-files/Guardian/documents/2005/04/28/legal.pdf.

12 SC Res. 1441 (2002), available at www.un.org/Docs/scres/2002/sc2002.htm.

13 'A More Secure World: Our Shared Responsibility. Report of the Secretary General's High Level Panel on Threats, Challenges and Change' (2004), p. 63, www.un.org/secureworld/.

14 Seymour M. Hersh, 'The Redirection: Is the Administration's New Policy Benefiting Our Enemies in the War on Terrorism?' *New Yorker*, 5 March 2007.

15 Vice-President Richard Cheney, Fox News, 14 January 2007, quoted in 'The Redirection' (note 14).

16 Daniel Dombey, 'FT Interview: Mohamed ElBaradei', *Financial Times*, 19 February 2007.

17 'Director General Briefs Press On Iran/DPRK', IAEA News Center, 5 March 2007, www.iaea.org/NewsCenter/News/2007/dg_iran-dprk.html.

18 'The Redirection' (note 14).

19 Protocol Additional to the Geneva Conventions of 12 August 1949, and relating to the Protection of Victims of International Armed Conflicts (Protocol 1), 8 June 1977, available at www.icrc.org/Wes/Eng/siteeng0.nsf/htmlall/genevaconventions.

20 Seymour M. Hersh, 'The Gray Zone: How a Secret Pentagon Program Came to Abu Ghraib', *New Yorker*, 24 May 2004.

21 Donald Macintyre, 'Israel Launches Ferocious Assault on Lebanon After Capture of Troops', *Independent*, 13 July 2006, 4.

22 'Press Conference by Emergency Relief Coordinator', Department of Public Information: News and Media Division: New York, 30 August 2006, United Nations.

23 Associated Press, 'Norway Leads Move to Ban Cluster Bombs Despite Objections of U.S.', 17 November 2006, available at www.foxnews.com/story/0,2933,230278,00.html.

24 Doug Mellgren (Associated Press), '46 Nations Push for Cluster Bomb Treaty', *Washington Post*, 24 February 2007.

25 Paul Waugh, 'Defence: Britain is Ready to Use Nuclear Strike 'in right conditions', *Independent*, 3 February 2003, 9.

26 *Rasul* v. *Bush*, 321 F.3d 1134, 8 June 2004, available at http://supct.law.cornell.edu/supct/html/03-334.ZO.html.

27 Military Commissions Act of 2006, S.3930.

28 Carol J. Williams, 'Terror Detainee To Get Nine Months', *Los Angeles Times*, 31 March 2007, 12.

29 Dana Priest and Barton Gellman, 'U.S. Decries Abuse but Defends Interrogations; "Stress and Duress" Tactics Used on Terrorism Suspects Held in Secret Overseas Facilities', *Washington Post*, 26 December 2002, A1.

30 Don Van Natta, Jr., 'Questioning Terror Suspects in a Dark and Surreal World', *New York Times*, 9 March 2003, 1.

31 Carlotta Gall, 'U.S. Military Investigating Death of Afghan in Custody', *New York Times*, 4 March 2003, A14.

32 Amnesty International, 'The Threat of a Bad Example: Undermining International Standards as "War on Terror" Detentions Continue', AI Index: AMR 51/114/2003, 19 August 2003, available at http://web.amnesty.org/library/Index/ENGAMR511142003.

33 Louise Arbour, 'No Exceptions to the Ban on Torture', *International Herald Tribune*, 6 December 2005.

34 1984 Convention against Torture and Other Cruel, Inhuman or Degrading Treatment or Punishment, available at www.ohchr.org/english/law/cat.htm.

35 Dana Priest and R. Jeffrey Smith, 'Memo Offered Justification for Use of Torture; Justice Dept. Gave Advice in 2002', *Washington Post*, 8 June 2004, A1; Karen J. Greenberg and Joshua L. Dratel, *The Torture Papers: The Road to Abu Ghraib* (Cambridge: Cambridge University Press, 2005), 172.

36 'Memorandum of 30 December 2004 from Daniel Levin, Acting Assistant Attorney General, Office of Legal Counsel, for James B. Comey, Deputy Attorney General, Regarding Legal Standards Applicable Under 18 U.S.C. §§2340–2340A', available at www.justice.gov/olc/2004opinions.htm.

37 Nat Hentoff, 'Don't Ask, Don't Tell: The Bush Team Chants, "We do not torture", but Nobody Around the World Believes Them', *Village Voice*, 27 January 2006, available at www.villagevoice.com/2006-01-24/news/don-t-ask-don-t-tell/. For another expression of Yoo's views, see Jane Mayer, 'Outsourcing Torture', *New Yorker*, 14 February 2005.

38 Dan Eggen, 'Cheney's Remarks Fuel Torture Debate; Critics Say He Backed Waterboarding', *Washington Post*, 27 October 2006, A09.

39 John McCain, 'Torture's Terrible Toll', Newsweek, 21 November 2005, available at www.msnbc.msn.com/id/10019179/site/newsweek/.

40 Detainee Treatment Act of 2005, available at www.milnet.com/House/HR-6166-Military%20Commissions%20Act%20of%202006/Detainee%20Treatment%20Act%20of%202005.html.

41 Military Commissions Act of 2006, S.3930, overturning *Rasul v. Bush*, 321 F.3d 1134, 8 June 2004, available at http://supct.law.cornell.edu/supct/html/03-334.ZO.html.

42 Sidney Blumenthal, 'Bush's War On Professionals', Salon.com, 5 January 2006, www.salon.com/opinion/blumenthal/2006/01/05/spying/.

43 'Powell Raps Europe on CIA Flights', BBC News, 17 December 2005, http://news.bbc.co.uk/1/hi/world/americas/4538788.stm.

44 Manfred Nowak, Special Rapporteur on torture and other cruel, inhuman or degrading treatment or punishment, 2005 Report to the General Assembly, U.N. Doc. A/60/316, available at www.ohchr.org/english/issues/torture/rapporteur/.

45 For the most comprehensive study, see Stephen Grey, *Ghost Plane: The True Story of the CIA Torture Program* (New York: St. Martin's Press, 2006).

46 Commission of Inquiry into the Actions of Canadian Officials in Relation to Maher Arar, *Report of the Events Relating to Maher Arar: Analysis and Recommendations*, 18 September 2006, available at www.ararcommission.ca/eng/AR_English.pdf; *Ghost Plane* (note 42), 62–78.

47 Colin Brown, 'Straw Faces MPs Over Claims MI6 Delivered Suspect for Torture', *Independent*, 12 December 2005; *Ghost Plane* (note 45), 45–61.

48 James Risen, David Johnston and Neil A. Lewis, 'Harsh C.I.A. Methods Cited in Top Qaeda Interrogations', *New York Times*, 13 May 2004.

49 Dana Priest, 'Wrongful Imprisonment: Anatomy of a CIA Mistake', *Washington Post*, 4 December 2005, A1; *Ghost Plane* (note 45), 79–102.

50 Craig Whitlock, 'At Guantanamo, Caught in a Legal Trap; 6 Algerians Languish Despite Foreign Rulings, Dropped Charges', *Washington Post*, 21 August 2006, A01.

51 Sarah Delaney and Craig Whitlock, 'Milan Court Indicts 26 Americans in Abduction', *Washington Post*, 17 February 2007, A01; *Ghost Plane* (note 45), 190–213.

52 Convention (IV) relative to the Protection of Civilian Persons in Time of War. Geneva, 12 August 1949, available at www.icrc.org/Wes/Eng/siteeng0.nsf/htmlall/genevaconventions.

53 Dana Priest, 'Memo Lets CIA Take Detainees Out of Iraq', *Washington Post*, 24 October 2004, A1.

54 Dana Priest, 'CIA Holds Terror Suspects in Secret Prisons', *Washington Post*, 2 November 2005, A1.

55 See 'PACE Calls for Oversight of Foreign Intelligence Agencies Operating in Europe', 27 June 2007, http://assembly.coe.int/ASP/Press/StopPressView.asp?CPID=1781; 'European Parliament Resolution on the Alleged Use of European Countries by the CIA for the Transportation and Illegal Detention of Prisoners', adopted 23 February 2007, available at www.europarl.europa.eu.

56 'European Parliament Resolution on the Alleged Use of European Countries by the CIA' (note 55).

57 Stephen Grey and Ian Cobain, 'Suspect's Tale of Travel and Torture', *Guardian*, 2 August 2005; *Ghost Plane* (note 45), 54.

58 See Telegraph from Craig Murray, U.K. Ambassador to Uzbekistan, to Foreign and Commonwealth Office, 4 July 2004, available at http://dahrjamailiraq.com/murray/Telegram.pdf; *Ghost Plane* (note 45), 170–89.

59 See Legal Opinion from Michael Wood, Foreign Office Legal Adviser, 13 March 2003, available at http://dahrjamailiraq.com/murray/wood.php; *Ghost Plane* (note 45), 182.

60 Jim Bronskill (Canadian Press) 'More Than Six Dozen CIA-Linked Landings in Canada: Declassified Memos', 22 February 2006.

61 Jeffrey Gettleman and Mark Mazzetti, 'Ethiopia Holding 41 Suspects Who Fought With Somali Islamists, Officials Confirm', *New York Times*, 11 April 2007, A12.

62 'Public More Internationalist Than In 1990s', Poll released 12 December 2002 by the Pew Research Center for People and the Press, available at http://people-press.org/reports/display.php3?ReportID=166.

Dino Kritsiotis

Response to Michael Byers

As Michael Byers intimates in his essay on terrorism, war and international law, certain iconic images have come to define the way the Bush administration has waged its 'war on terror' since September 2001, when war was declared by President George W. Bush on al-Qaeda and 'every terrorist group of global reach'.[1] These images are potent portrayals of the administration's endeavours and exploits, though it is international law that has supplied states with the conceptual arsenal and vocabulary for their critical appraisal of the actions undertaken by the United States and its allies in the prosecution of this 'war on terror'. As Byers makes clear, international law has done so via the separate canons of the *jus ad bellum* and the *jus in bello* – though, to these, we might wish to add the *jus post bellum*, or the rights and responsibilities that accrue in the aftermath of armed conflict.[2]

Within this framework, determinations regarding the activation of the laws of the *jus ad bellum* and/or the *jus in bello* are of signal importance because they locate us within that part of the spectrum of international law appropriate for application in a given situation. They tell us which of the detailed prescriptions – which of the principles and rules – of international law are relevant to our purposes, and, by implication, they tell us which are not. As such, these determinations must occur before any of the ritual legal tasks of interpretation, argument and counter-argument can begin in earnest.

And it matters a great deal what answers are reached in this respect, for they in turn will instruct us as to what the governing legal regimen is – what legal rights and obligations are active and applicable to the facts before us. So, at this stage of our enquiries, we would need to address such questions as whether the acts of al-Qaeda on 11 September 2001 were sufficient to constitute an armed attack under the *jus ad bellum*. Did they also initiate an armed conflict and, in so doing, trigger the laws of the *jus in bello*? Or did those acts form part of an existing armed conflict that stretched as far back as Osama bin Laden's *Declaration of War Against the Americans Occupying the Two Holy Places* of August 1996, or, possibly, farther than that still?[3] Indeed, is talk of 'war' and 'armed conflict' apposite at all when we are confronted by acts of terrorism – even of this scale and order?[4] How should we then view the missile fired in November 2002 from a U.S. Predator drone against a vehicle in Yemen? According to the laws of the *jus ad bellum*? Or is that action more properly considered from the perspective of an ongoing 'armed conflict' and the targeting rules of *jus in bello*?[5] If so, who were the parties to this armed conflict and to whom did the rules apply? The United States and Yemen? Or the United States and al-Qaeda?

Such conceptual questions have surfaced before. Consider the interpretations of the June 1981 Israeli strike on the nuclear reactor at Osiraq in Iraq.[6] On that occasion, Israel argued the matter in terms of the *jus ad bellum* and the right of self-defence assured to all states under Article 51 of the 1945 United Nations Charter.[7] None of the member states of the United Nations was prepared to share Israel's understanding of an expanded scope of this right: Israel was not deemed by any state to be under any specific or imminent threat from Iraq at that point in time, the threshold that has come to define the right of (anticipatory) self-defence since the time of the *Caroline* correspondence (1838–42).[8] The Security Council approached the incident in the terms of *jus ad bellum*: it invoked the prohibition of force from Article 2(4) of the Charter against Israel in Resolution 487 of 19 June 1981, calling upon Israel 'to refrain in the future from any such acts or threats thereof'. We can see how a very different outcome on the lawfulness of Israel's action might have been reached had Israel's action been viewed as an aspect of an existing armed conflict between Israel and Iraq – as some have argued[9] – for, then, the laws of the *jus in bello* would have required us to ask whether the nuclear reactor at Osiraq met the requirements for a military objective as set out in the 1977 Additional Protocol One.[10]

Importantly, however, solving these matters of broad principle will not enlighten us as to which of the elements of the *jus ad bellum* or the *jus in bello* are actually applicable in the circumstances. We need to be sensitive to this issue because both of these branches of international law comprise a multitude of provisions and argumentative possibilities (the *jus in bello*, it must be said, much more so than the *jus ad bellum*). It is therefore possible that we have correctly concluded which branch of international law is relevant to our purposes (*jus ad bellum* or *jus in bello*) but have not tackled all aspects of its corpus, or not tackled all aspects of its corpus in finite and even-handed detail. In his essay, Byers focuses on the right of self-defence in his treatment of the *jus ad bellum*, and he is of course right to do so. This is where a good share of the argumentative action of the United States has taken place – first, for Operation Enduring Freedom against Afghanistan in October 2001 and at least in the initial phase of preparations for Operation Iraqi Freedom (March 2003). Here, we marvel at international law in action – at the dynamics of its evolution and change, at the episodes of state practice collecting

like sediments over time and willing either slight or significant shifts in the normative landscape.[11] Yet, as the Bush administration discovered in proclaiming a right
of pre-emptive self-defence,[12] there can be no guarantees that an argument will be
acceptable to other states – including one's own allies.[13] Perhaps this was what led
to a change in the argumentation adopted by the United States for Operation Iraqi
Freedom, and to its embrace of the authority of the United Nations in the form of
Security Council resolutions for that intervention.

But the laws of the *jus ad bellum* do go beyond the mere prohibition of force
and the right of self-defence, for Article 2(4) of the Charter proscribes the threat
as well as the use of force. They are not therefore limited to actual applications or
instances of force – at least not in theory – and it is important that we recognize
the actual or potential relevance of these rules well before the 'launch' of any 'air
strikes' (considered by Byers in respect of the United States and Iran). So the Security
Council seemed to say in Resolution 487 (1981) when it advised Israel against making any 'threats' of force. Yet such threats have become a recurring theme in international politics since September 2001, never more starkly so than on the eve of
Operation Iraqi Freedom in March 2003, when President Bush noted that 'All the
decades of deceit and cruelty have now reached an end' and informed Iraq that
'Saddam Hussein and his sons must leave Iraq within 48 hours. Their refusal to do
so will result in military conflict, commenced at a time of our choosing'.[14]

It is worth considering the 'idiomatic unity' of the *prohibitions* contained in Article
2(4) of the Charter.[15] As the International Court of Justice put it in its *Nuclear
Weapons Advisory Opinion* of July 1996, 'if the envisaged use of force is itself
unlawful, the stated readiness to use it would be a threat prohibited under [Article
2(4)] ... The notions of "threat" and "use" of force under ... the Charter stand
together in the sense that if the use of force itself in a given case is illegal – for whatever reason – the threat to use such force will likewise be illegal. In short, if it is to
be lawful, the declared readiness of a State to use force must be a use of force that
is in conformity with the Charter'.[16] Does this mean, then, that when the United
States made good on its threat of force and intervened in Iraq with its allies on 19
March 2003, *both* of the Charter's prohibitions of force were violated? For its part
in the charged politics of the Middle East, Iran later notified the Security Council
of the 'public and thinly veiled threats of resort to force' made against it by the United
States, actions it considered forbidden under Charter law.[17] All of this at a time when
Iran has engaged in a hostile rhetoric of its own: consider the relentless position it
has taken towards Israel, with President Mahmoud Ahmadinejad claiming in
October 2005 that Israel should be wiped off the map.[18]

The *jus in bello*, meanwhile, becomes applicable in the event of 'declared war
or of any other armed conflict which may arise between two or more of the High
Contracting Parties [to the four Geneva Conventions of August 1949], even if the
state of war is not recognized by one of them' (common Article 2) or of an 'armed

conflict not of an international character occurring in the territory of one of the High Contracting Parties' (common Article 3). These provisions need to be read with considerable care, for they mark out the modern provenance(s) of the *jus in bello* and, as is immediately clear, they remove the tremendous significance that the *jus in bello* has traditionally attached to a legal state of 'war'.[19] As we can observe from their language, the emphasis of both of these provisions is on the existence of an 'armed conflict', a concept that is broader in its reach than that of 'war' (we can tell this because common Article 2 specifies that a 'declared war' is one *example* of an armed conflict; it does not represent that concept's totality).

As far as international law is concerned, therefore, it is incumbent on us to cut through the considerable political verbiage that has accompanied the 'war on terror' – including the very term 'war on terror' itself – in order to determine *whether* the laws of the *jus in bello* are applicable, and, if so, *which* of these laws are applicable. We say this because the laws differ depending on what *form* an armed conflict assumes: hence the differentiation between armed conflicts in common Article 2 and common Article 3 of the Geneva Conventions noted above. According to these schemata, common Article 2 concerns international armed conflicts, to which the full panoply of rules in the Geneva Conventions then becomes applicable, and common Article 3 concerns non-international armed conflicts, to which the more limited coda – contained in common Article 3 – becomes applicable:

> (1) Persons taking no active part in the hostilities, including members of armed forces who have laid down their arms and those placed *hors de combat* by sickness, wounds, detention, or any other cause, shall in all circumstances be treated humanely, without any adverse distinction founded on race, colour, religion or faith, sex, birth or wealth, or any other similar criteria.
>
> To this end the following acts are and shall remain prohibited at any time and in any place whatsoever with respect to the above-mentioned persons:
> (a) violence to life and person, in particular murder of all kinds, mutilation, cruel treatment and torture;
> (b) taking of hostages;
> (c) outrages upon personal dignity, in particular, humiliating and degrading treatment;
> (d) the passing of sentences and the carrying out of executions without previous judgment pronounced by a regularly constituted court affording all the judicial guarantees which are recognized as indispensable by civilized peoples.
> (2) The wounded and sick shall be collected and cared for.[20]

This dichotomy presents us with difficulties for the 'war on terror' because of common Article 2's specification of an international armed conflict existing between High Contracting Parties to the Geneva Conventions, and because of the pervasive assumption that common Article 3 was created with a very particular understanding of the meaning of 'armed conflict not of an international character occurring in the territory of one of the High Contracting Parties'. Consider the Constitutional Court of South Africa's understanding of this schemata as it deliberated whether the struggle against apartheid constituted an international or non-international armed conflict for the purpose of the 1949 Geneva Conventions:

> It is one thing to allow the officers of a hostile power which has invaded a foreign state to remain unpunished for gross violations of human rights perpetrated against others during the course of such conflict. It is another thing to compel such punishment in circumstances where such violations have substantially occurred in consequence of conflict between different formations within the same state in respect of the permissible political direction which that state should take with regard to the structures of the state and the parameters of its political policies and where it becomes necessary after the cessation of such conflict for the society traumatised by such a conflict to reconstruct itself. The erstwhile adversaries of such a conflict inhabit the same sovereign territory. They have to live with each other and work with each other and the state concerned is best equipped to determine what measures may be most conducive for the facilitation of such reconciliation and reconstruction. That is a difficult exercise which the nation within such a state has to perform by having regard to its own peculiar history, its complexities, even its contradictions and its emotional and institutional traditions.[21]

Given these particularities of definition, the question must arise as to whether an armed conflict between the United States and al-Qaeda can exist in law at all. We say this because an armed conflict of whatever character cannot – and should not – be assumed. Does their relationship not fall into a regulatory gap of the *jus in bello*, an 'armed conflict' not envisaged by the schemata of the Geneva Conventions? Or should we analyse their relationship within the traditional framework of the international armed conflicts that the United States has entered with Afghanistan and then Iraq? Or perhaps this set of experiences has been constitutive of a new normative paradigm, ushering in a new arrangement not known to the law before 11 September 2001? Byers appears to pinpoint 11 September 2001 as a critical date in his reasoning, but he does so in problematic fashion when he refers to the 'breach[ing] [of] international humanitarian law as "crimes against humanity"'. ('Crimes against humanity' are not contingent upon the existence of war or armed conflict; they can exist independent of an armed conflict.[22] By definition, international humanitarian law, a more contemporary periphrasis for the *jus in bello*, cannot).

As urgent as these matters are, they have proved perplexing, and interminably so – even for the likes of the United States Supreme Court in *Hamdan* v. *Rumsfeld, Secretary of Defense, et al.* in June 2006.[23] There, the Supreme Court was content to follow the lead of the International Court of Justice in *Military and Paramilitary Activities In and Against Nicaragua* (*Nicaragua* v. *United States of America*) (1986), where the Court referred to the 'fundamental general principles of humanitarian law' in common Article 3 of the Conventions. These rules, the Court said, 'constitute a minimum yardstick, in addition to the more elaborate rules which are also to apply to international conflicts; and they are rules which, in the Court's opinion, reflect what the Court in 1949 called "elementary considerations of humanity"'.[24] Why the International Court of Justice adopted this approach rather than reaffirm the customary rules applicable to 'the actions of the United States in and against Nicaragua'[25] – that is, the custom applicable to international armed conflicts – is not clear. But it is an approach that has gained traction elsewhere, as with the ruling of the Appeals Chamber of the International Criminal Tribunal for the Former Yugoslavia in October 1995: 'at least with respect to the minimum rules in common Article 3, the character of the conflict is irrelevant'.[26]

Appealing though these jurisprudential pronouncements might be, it remains the case that determinations as to the form of an armed conflict are necessary in order to map out the range – the full extent – of the rights and obligations of the *jus in bello*. They are as central to claims of how the 'war on terror' is being fought – or how it *ought* to be fought – as they are to determining individual accountability under international criminal law (recall how the war crimes itemized in Article 8 of the 1998 Rome Statute of the International Criminal Court proceed on the basis of the occurrence of either an international or non-international armed conflict). And we need to be vigilant on the decisions that are and have been made on this front – whether by governments or national judiciaries (in *Hamdan*, the United States Supreme Court concluded that 'Common Article 3 [of the Geneva Conventions] is applicable here and . . . requires that Hamdan be tried by a "regularly constituted court affording all the judicial guarantees which are recognized as indispensable by civilized peoples"'.)

As we try to make sense of this detail, we should remain conscious of the efforts that have been undertaken to 'humanize' the *jus in bello*, to make its substantive components for international and non-international armed conflicts as equal or as identical as possible.[27] Yet, one consequence of these humanization efforts has meant that the once-cherished dichotomies of the *jus in bello* (such as the iconic status of prisoners of war in international armed conflicts against all else) are now no more; they have given way to a much more nuanced set of distinctions, priorities and prerogatives so that, we find, the current protections for international armed conflicts extend to 'persons who are in the power of a Party to the conflict *and who do not benefit from more favourable treatment under the [Geneva] Conventions or under this Protocol*'.[28] The law thus affords protections to *all* combatants in an international armed conflict: it is no longer a question (as Byers appears to assume in parts) of whether unlawful combatants have protections, but of what the scope and meaning of these protections might be. With so-called 'fundamental guarantees' in place, the law has thus become a much more humanitarian proposition than what went or existed before, as it is now as much a law for the suspected terrorist and the mercenary as it is (and always has been) for those who have fought as members of the regular armed forces of a state.

Notes

1 Office of the Press Secretary to the White House, 'President Declares "Freedom at War with Fear"', Address to the Joint Session of Congress and the American People, 20 September 2001, www.whitehouse.gov/news/releases/2001/09/20010920-8.html.

2 Carsten Stahn, '"Jus ad bellum", "jus in bello" . . . "jus post bellum"? Rethinking the Conception of the Law of Armed Force', *European Journal of International Law* 17 (2006), 943.

3 On the battleground of Somalia – in 1992 and 1993 – see Lawrence Wright, *The Looming Tower: Al-Qaeda and the Road to 9/11* (New York: Alfred A. Knopf, 2006), 188–9.

4 See the exchange between Kenneth Roth, 'The Law of War in the War on Terror: Washington's Abuse of "Enemy Combatants"' *Foreign Affairs* 83 (2004), 2 and Ruth Wedgwood, 'Fighting a War Under its Rules', *Foreign Affairs* 83 (2004), 126.

5 The United States has also used force against similar targets in Somalia – on more than one occasion: see David S. Cloud, 'U.S. Airstrike Aims at Qaeda Cell in Somalia', *New York Times*, 9 January 2007, A3 and Jeffrey Gettleman, 'U.S. Strikes Inside Somalia, Bombing Suspected Militant Hide-Out', *New York Times*, 9 June 2007, A10.

6 See, for instance, Yoram Dinstein, *War, Aggression and Self-Defence* 4th edn. (Cambridge: Cambridge University Press, 2005), 186.

7 U.N. Doc. S/PV. 2280 (12 June 1981), 38.

8 See R.Y. Jennings, 'The *Caroline* and McLeod Cases', *American Journal of International Law* 32 (1938), 82.

9 See *War, Aggression and Self-Defence* (note 6).

10 According to Art. 52(2) of the Protocol, 'military objectives are limited to those objects which by their nature, location, purpose or use make an effective contribution to military action and whose total or partial destruction, capture or neutralization, in the circumstances ruling at the time, offers a definite military advantage'. Though Israel is not a party to the Protocol, the Protocol's provision in this respect is widely considered to reflect customary international law: Theodor Meron, *Human Rights and Humanitarian Norms As Customary Law* (Oxford: Clarendon Press, 1989), 64–5.

11 Though in Byers' recounting of the history of this point of law on the invocation of the right of self-defence in response to acts of terrorism, there is a curious omission of the U.S. action against Iraq in June 1993: see Dino Kritsiotis, 'The Legality of the 1993 US Missile Strike on Iraq and the Right of Self-Defence in International Law', *International and Comparative Law Quarterly* 45 (1996), 173.

12 A matter on which the United States may prove redoubtable: see Christine Gray, 'The Bush Doctrine Revisited: The 2006 National Security Strategy of the USA', *Chinese Journal of International Law* 5 (2006), 555, and John Lichfield, 'France May Allow "First Strikes" on Rogue States in Policy Shift', *Independent*, 28 October 2003, 1.

13 See the remarks of British Prime Minister Tony Blair before the Liaison Committee of the House of Commons on 21 January 2003: www.parliament.the-stationery-office.co.uk/pa/cm200203/cmselect/cmliaisn/uc334-i/uc33402.htm.

14 Office of the Press Secretary, President Says Saddam Hussein Must Leave Iraq Within 48 Hours, www.whitehouse.gov/news/releases/2003/03/20030317-7.html (17 March 2003). Indeed, President Bush invoked the notion of a 'threat' as the basis of the ultimatum he was about to issue: 'The danger is clear: using chemical, biological or, one day, nuclear weapons, obtained with the help of Iraq, the terrorists could fulfil their stated ambitions and kill thousands or hundreds of thousands of innocent people in our country, or any other. The United States and other nations did nothing to deserve or invite this threat. But we will do everything to defeat it. Instead of drifting along toward tragedy, we will set a course toward safety. Before the day of horror can come, before it is too late to act, this danger will be removed'. See further Nikolas Sturkler, *The Threat of Force in International Law* (Cambridge: Cambridge University Press, 2007), 157–68.

15 *The Threat of Force* (note 14), 2.

16 *Legality of the Threat or Use of Nuclear Weapons (Advisory Opinion)* (1996) I.C.J. Rep. 225 (§47).

17 U.N. Doc. S/2006/178 (22 March 2006) and U.N. Doc. S/2006/273 (1 May 2006).

18 See Ewen MacAskill and Chris McGreal, 'Israel Should Be Wiped Off the Map, Says Iran's President' *Guardian*, 27 October 2005, 1. In June 2007, President Ahmadinejad announced that a 'countdown button' for Israel's destruction had been activated. See 'Iranian's Remark on Israel is Condemned', *New York Times*, 5 June 2007, A9.

19 Christopher Greenwood, 'The Concept of War in Modern International Law', *International and Comparative Law Quarterly* 36 (1987), 283.

20 We would need to make accommodation for the additional treaty rules developed for international armed conflicts in the 1977 Additional Protocol One and for non-international armed conflicts in the 1977 Additional Protocol Two – as well as, of course, for the customary arrangements for both forms of armed conflict as identified, for instance, in Jean-Marie Henckaerts and Louise Doswald-Beck, *Customary International Humanitarian Law* (Cambridge: Cambridge University Press, 2005), vols. I and II (although this study does not make clear where and when each of its 161 'rules' came into being).

21 Case CCT 17/96, *Azanian Peoples Organization et al. v. The President of South Africa*, Constitutional Court of South Africa: Judgment of 25 July 1996 (§31).

22 Cf. Article 7 of the 1998 Rome Statute of the International Criminal Court and Article 3 of the 1994 Statute of the International Tribunal for Rwanda with Art. 5 of the 1993 Statute of International Tribunal for Former Yugoslavia ('The International Tribunal shall have the power to prosecute persons responsible for the following crimes *when committed in armed conflict*, whether international or internal in character, and directed against any civilian population: (a) murder; (b) extermination; (c) enslavement; (d) deportation; (e) imprisonment; (f) torture; (g) rape; (h) persecutions on political, racial and religious grounds; (i) other inhumane acts'.) (Emphasis added.)

23 415 F. 3d 33 (2006). The Supreme Court contented itself with the conclusion that it 'need not decide the merits of [the] argument [on the nature of armed conflict between the United States and al-Qaeda] because there is at least one provision of the Geneva Conventions that applies here even if the relevant conflict is not between signatories' – i.e. common Article 3.

24 *Military and Paramilitary Activities In and Against Nicaragua (Nicaragua* v. *United States of America) (Merits)* (1986) I.C.J. Rep. 14 (§218). The Court's reference to its earlier jurisprudence is that of the *Corfu Channel (United Kingdom* v. *Albania) (Merits)* (1949) I.C.J. Rep. 22 (§215).

25 *Military and Paramilitary Activities In and Against Nicaragua* (note 24), at §219.

26 Case No. IT–94–1, *Prosecutor* v. *Tadic*, Decision on the Defence Motion for Interlocutory Appeal on Jurisdiction, para. 102 (International Criminal Tribunal for the Former Yugoslavia, App. Chamber, 2 October 1995). Cited – as with the *Nicaragua* Case – by the United States Supreme Court in *Hamdan* v. *Rumsfeld, Secretary of Defense, et al.*, see note 23.

27 See especially Theodor Meron, 'The Humanization of Humanitarian Law', *American Journal of International Law* 94 (2000), 239.

28 I.e. Article 75 of 1977 Additional Protocol One (emphasis added) – a provision which, one hastens to add, the United States has accepted as customary international law: William H. Taft, IV, 'The Law of Armed Conflict After 9/11: Some Salient Features', *Yale Journal of International Law* 28 (2003), 319, 321–2.

3 Conor Gearty

Human rights in an age of counter-terrorism

Terror and terrorism

For many years I worried with all the other so-called 'terrorism experts' about the fact that there was no proper, objective definition of terrorism. I even abandoned a law textbook I planned on the subject on account of the inadequacy of my introductory chapter. In the end I wrote a book on terrorism that was more about language and the power of labels than it was about killing and kidnapping.[1] This was because it had eventually dawned on me that the whole point of the subject of terrorism was that there was no definition. The importance of the subject, its utility to those who mattered, relied upon the impossibility of it ever being tied down. For the moment terrorism is given an objective meaning, one that can be commonly agreed, is a dangerous moment for the experts, a point in time when the term risks taking on a rational life of its own.[2] Take as an example a straightforward definition, one that sees as terrorist violence the intentional or reckless killing or injuring of non-combatants or the doing of severe damage to their property, in order to communicate a political message. Expressed like this, it is clear that terrorism is a method of violence, and as such can be used by any actor who has chosen to deploy violence in pursuit of this or that political goal. It can, it is true, be used by the kind of weak group that has few other military or political options in its locker: the al-Qaedas and ETAs of this world. But it can equally be deployed as a method of violence by other, stronger forces, by guerrilla organizations for example that are able to muster other kinds of military action, and by insurgent forces in a civil war situation where terror-oriented violence may be just one option among many. In failed states it is available, among other brutal techniques, to all the ambitious, power-hungry factions.

It is equally clearly a kind of political violence that can be deployed by state forces, either in isolation – the French action in sinking Greenpeace's *Rainbow Warrior* in 1985 is a good example, as might be the American decision to bomb Tripoli in

1986 – or in tandem with other kinds of violence in the context of a serious armed conflict – examples that come to mind would be the allied bombing of Dresden and other German cities towards the end of World War II and the nuclear attacks on Hiroshima and Nagasaki in 1945. Describing terrorism as a kind of political violence in this way is not necessarily to say that it is wrong, just as to call something an aerial bombardment or an invasion or a siege is not to condemn it. The question of morality is separate from the issue of classification. On this account, to call this or that action terrorist is to prepare the ground for a discussion of its legitimacy – it sets up rather than answers that important question.

Now of course this is not at all how we use the term today. First and most importantly we have come to view terrorism not as a method of violence but rather as a category of person, a kind of militant rather than a kind of tactic, the sort of thing a person is rather than the kind of thing a person does. So we have terrorist organizations, terrorist groups, terrorist leaders and so on, and these labels do not require evidence of specific actions in order to be made to stick, to secure coherence in our discourse. Second, legal definitions of terrorism are invariably much wider than the core meaning I have just given to the term,[3] incorporating violence against property, attacks on a country's infrastructure, and even on some accounts direct action and extreme forms of civil disobedience.[4] Once a group is labelled terrorist by reference to one or other of this wide set of criteria, it is then terrorist, not only (as I earlier said) *regardless* of what it does but also sometimes *in spite of* what it does. A group might be terrorist without ever having lifted a finger in anger against anybody whatsoever. It might still be terrorist even when it is involved in specifically non-violent actions. Thus, as has happened recently in Palestine, when Hamas's political wing engaged in electoral politics and, indeed, won an election, it was nevertheless regarded as terrorist and therefore as beyond the pale of proper political discourse. That 'therefore' is important. For, third, we have completely lost sight of the fact that political terror is a description of a kind of violence and not necessarily a moral condemnation of that violence. To contemporary ears, to call something terrorist is at the same time to condemn it as morally wrong: the value judgement is packed into the description, the 'is' has been elided into the 'ought' or, more accurately in this case, the 'ought not'. Fourth and finally, to complete this story of verbal degradation, we have so contrived matters that terrorism is now widely thought of as something of which state authorities – acting either directly or through authorized paramilitary forces – are incapable. Even if what the state does is both violent and designed to spread terror among its own people – a sadly not uncommon occurrence as is obvious from a perusal of the recent annual reports from Amnesty[5] and Human Rights Watch[6] – it nevertheless cannot be described as terror or terrorist action because those terms have now come to be invariably applied to sub-state actors. Even worse, this kind of terror by the state might find itself with luck and a bit of careful spin being reclassified as counter-terrorism, in other words as inherently good in the same way that terrorism is inherently bad.

The evolution of the term 'terrorism' from a description of a kind of violence to a morally loaded condemnation of the actions of subversive groups regardless of the context of their actions – or even sometimes their non-violent nature – should not surprise us. It is a movement in language that operates wholly in favour of state authorities, taking their conduct, however horrible, out of the realm of terror, while at the same time giving them the opportunity to dump this powerfully opprobrious label on their political opponents. No wonder authoritarian leaders everywhere, the Mugabes and Burmese juntas of this world, are such counter-terrorist enthusiasts. None of this explains, however, a further twist in deployment of the language of terrorism, one that has great and direct relevance today. This is the way in which the term has shed any kind of locational exactitude and become a manifestation of a universal crisis, a violent version of the plague, something that crosses boundaries at will, swooping upon unsuspecting peoples out of the blue and bringing destruction and death in its wake. In its contemporary form, terrorism is no longer a particular kind of violence that this or that gang or group in this or that country does; rather it is said to be part of a pattern of systematic international violence against which a 'global war on terror' now needs to be waged. This idea of a worldwide contagion of terror inspired by evil forces with designs on Western civilization – so commonly spoken of today as something new and unprecedented and uniquely terrifying – in fact originates well before 11 September 2001. Exploring its origins takes us back to the very beginnings of the modern distortion of our subject, the late 1960s.

We need now to turn to Israel and Palestine, the *fons et origo* of our subject in its modern form. Until 1968, descriptions of post-World War II sub-state political violence were largely informed by an anti-colonial narrative, one that saw the use of such force as designed to secure freedom for local people from domination by this or that Western power. The term that was used to describe such insurgents was usually something like 'guerrilla' or (if they looked as though they might succeed) 'freedom fighter'. The first attempts to force Israel to concede a Palestinian state were entirely conventional, involving acts of war and guerrilla action. These foundered on the ruthless implacability of the Israeli reaction: Arab and PLO fighters were being killed too easily; it simply did not pay to try to fight Israel on equal terms: it was a kind of surrender with a simultaneous death sentence attached. So the Palestinians turned to isolated acts of political violence, by both official and renegade factions, on occasion very bloody it is true, but as not much more than a kind of consolation prize that had to be accepted because it was all that was available. It is in this sense that it is right to say that Arafat was a reluctant terrorist and in this sense it is also absolutely right to describe terrorism as 'the weapon of the weak'.[7]

The 1970s and 1980s were marked by high levels of violence in the region, in particular by the armed forces of the state of Israel but also, albeit to a much lesser extent, by Palestinian factions and as time went on (and particularly after the Iranian revolution in 1979) by more religiously oriented movements such as Hezbollah and Islamic Jihad, working in southern Lebanon but also increasingly in the occupied territories themselves. During this period as well, some Palestinian factions took their fight to the streets and airports of Europe with occasional forays into extremely bloody violence. But in any head count of casualties or any impartial assessment of levels of terror during this period, it is obvious that the lavishly equipped, well-organized and dominant military force in the region – the Israeli Army – was responsible for by far the greatest numbers of killings and acts of politically motivated violence. If there were any doubt about this then all that needs to be recalled are the invasions of Lebanon that took place in 1978 and 1982, and in particular the two-month siege of Beirut that took place during the summer of the latter year.[8] This was political terror by any ordinary definition of the term. Assisted by the aforementioned internationalization of the violence by some Palestinian factions, a brilliantly successful campaign was then conducted by U.S. and Israeli strategists and their academic and intellectual allies to castigate Palestinian violence as terrorist and therefore as uniquely evil. This had two powerful effects: first it disconnected Palestinian violence from its context and turned it into a more generalized problem, one that was faced by the Western World in general, rather than something that grew out of the injustice of the Israeli occupation. What helped here was that the generally very peaceful West was indeed suffering from occasional acts of subversive violence, from leftist ideological groups in Germany and Italy (the Red Brigades and the Bader-Meinhoff gang respectively) and from irredentist nationalist groups in Corsica, Spain and Northern Ireland.[9] Even the U.S. had its own internal subversives, in the form of the Weathermen, afterwards the Weather Underground. All these groups became elided together under the general terrorist rubric, one within which, in the 1970s, the violent exponents of the Palestinian cause now also found themselves becoming helplessly enmeshed. 'Freedom fighter' was long gone; 'guerrilla' and 'urban guerrilla' were fast becoming distant dreams. All the talk was of 'terrorists' and 'terrorism'.

Second, the same neat manoeuvre saw the Israeli defence forces identified with the counter-terrorist authorities in the West and therefore cast in the same sort of benign light – and this was regardless of the extreme, terror-inducing nature of their own violence, far in excess of what the U.S., British and Spanish authorities needed to do to cope with their own subversives. One book from this period for example, *Terrorism: How the West Can Win*, contained a contribution from Israel's ambassador to the United Nations Benjamin Netanyahu which described the 'war against terror' as 'part of a much larger struggle, one between the forces of civilization and the forces of barbarism'.[10] This volume – edited by Netanyahu who was also a leading 'terrorism expert' and was to become Israeli prime minister in due course – was published seven years before Samuel Huntingdon's famous article on the 'clash of civilisations'.[11] Taking advantage of the fact that Palestinian radicals struck outside Israel, institutes and think-tanks were established to study the 'problem' of 'international terrorism': one such particularly influential organization, the Jonathan Institute, held large conferences in Jerusalem in 1979 and in Washington in 1984, calling for the 'need for a better understanding of terrorism and for mobilizing the West against it'.[12] It was named after the Israeli commando who had died in the raid on Entebbe in 1976. After Iran began to support anti-Israeli forces in Lebanon, new studies began of 'state-sponsored terrorism' and if countries in the region fell out with the U.S., they found themselves at risk of being classified as 'terrorist states' – a label that came and went as relations with Washington ebbed and flowed.[13]

The joint interest of the West and Israel in developing a common front against terrorism was consolidated in the 1980s. These were the Reagan years when pressure was being ratcheted up on the Soviet Union, or Evil Empire (as opposed to Axis of Evil) as it was then often described, without a trace of irony. A succession of books and articles and terrorist commentaries made the link between the Soviet Union and the sponsorship of international terrorism in general and of the PLO in particular. This was the first global terrorist campaign; though it is now largely forgotten, much was made of it at the time. Books with titles like *The Soviet Strategy of Terror*,[14] *The Grand Strategy of the Soviet Union*,[15] *The Soviet Union and Terrorism*,[16] *The Soviet Connection: State Sponsorship of Terrorism*[17] and the evocatively titled *Hydra of Carnage*[18] flowed from the presses and the think-tanks. Especially influential was Clare Sterling's *The Terror Network: The Secret War of International Terrorism*, published by Weidenfeld and Nicolson in 1981.[19] The point being made by all this academic scholarship was that Soviet support for the Palestinian cause essentially made it a Godfather of international terrorism the world over. So successful was this strategy of linkage between Palestinian actions and international terrorism that the attempted murder of the Israeli ambassador to the U.K. in London in 1982 (by the Abu Nidhal faction) was capable of being made into a plausible *casus belli* of the invasion of Lebanon – Operation Peace in Galilee – which was launched two days later. An eye for an eye has never been the counter-terrorist's motto in the Middle East, more like 10,000 eyes for every eye. But the invasion, and the siege of Beirut that followed, were not terrorism; they were counter-terrorism, 'acts of peace' – regardless of the terror that actually happened on the ground.

This framework for seeing the Israeli-Arab conflict, embedded so brilliantly in our public discourse in the 1970s as part of a worldwide contagion of irrational terror, remains with us to this day. Of course the Soviet dimension has declined, but it has been replaced by a new pernicious supremo, radical Islam. Where once it was the Kremlin it is now al-Qaeda. The Politbureau has been replaced by Osama bin Laden, with brief stops for Abu Nidhal and President Gaddafi along the way.

The transfer began to take place much earlier than is commonly understood, during the mid-1980s as Soviet power declined and political Islam asserted itself against Western and Israeli interests, first in Iran (against the American-sponsored Shah) and later in Lebanon (against Israeli, U.S. and French military forces buttressing the Christian regime in power in that country). In a book for the Institute for the Study of Conflict, entitled *The New Terrorism* and published as early as 1986, the terrorism expert William Gutteridge, sounded the following warning note about the future:

> The new wave of political violence in the Middle East and South Asia in the mid 1980s in which religious sectarianism is a potent factor has added other dangerous dimensions to the problem and at the same time focused attention sharply on the real danger to civilisation and international order which epidemic terrorism could pose.[20]

The point grew in substance with the increase in the 1990s both in violence within the occupied territories and in the outbreaks of political violence across the world from subversives now increasingly purporting to act in the name of Islam. This was when Hamas got properly under way. Against this kind of background, it was not surprising that the attacks on 11 September came quickly to be seen as another part of the savage terrorist 'war' being waged by political Islam against the West in general and against that honorary part of the West, Israel, in particular. The government of Ariel Sharon repeated the triumph of an earlier generation of Israeli strategists in linking its private quarrel with the Palestinians to this global epidemic of terror. Speaking to the Knesset on 16 September 2001, the then Israeli prime minister put it in the following way:

> The subject of terror is unfortunately not new to us. The state of Israel has been fighting the Arab, Palestinian and Islamic fundamentalist's terror for over 120 years. Thousands of Jews have been murdered in terrorist attacks . . . The bereavement of the American people is known well to us.
>
> The war against terror has to be an international war. A war of the free world coalition against the forces of terror . . . It is a war between the humans and the blood thirsty.
>
> We know this as we have been in this battle for many years now. . . . We weren't surprised by the evilness of the Arab, Palestinian and radical Islamic terror. Arafat chose the strategy of terror and formed a coalition of terror. The terrorist attacks against Israeli citizens aren't any different than Bin Laden's terror attack against the American citizens – terror is terror.
>
> We must remember it was Arafat who gave the legitimacy to hijacking planes, and it was the Palestinian terror groups that started sending suicide bombers. All the radical movements got their legitimacy from Arafat . . .
>
> There is no such thing as terrorists who are 'good guys' as there is no such thing as terrorists who are 'bad guys', they are all bad.

I applaud President Bush for his decision to form a coalition against terror. This coalition must fight all terror organizations, including Arafat's.[21]

As was the case in the 1980s, a large number of intellectuals, politicians and non-governmental bodies promptly echoed this theme of a new global war on Israel and the West, one which embraced all elements of the Palestinian resistance as well as the al-Qaeda 'terror network'.[22] What was true of the Palestinian Liberation Organization in the 1970s and 1980s is also true of the militant groups to be found today in the occupied territories, in Afghanistan, in Iraq and elsewhere in the region. No attention, or no serious attention, needs to be paid to the political violence – by Israeli forces, by the Russian army in Chechnya, or by U.S. forces and other armies in the latest 'Coalition of the Willing' – which creates the conditions for this subversive violence and helps to ensure its perpetuation. There are literally no words left to describe state violence of this sort – all the truly bad words have been exclusively allocated to small, weak groups that cause a fraction of the fatalities of their more powerful opponents and whose principal mistake is to kill people like us.

Human rights and terrorism

Thus the greatest violence the term 'terrorism' does to human rights is the way in which it frames public discussion. The primary effect of this is to deprive the criminal justice model of the space in which to breathe. The terrorism model blows a hole in this system, one rooted in fair procedures, settled rules and carefully calibrated international co-operation against defined criminal mischiefs. It disregards the criminal in favour of a language rooted in generalities which has little time for individual dignity or the rule of law. U.K. law has certainly drifted in this direction, with administrative powers rooted in executive judgments about involvement in terrorism (very broadly defined) being used against individuals and groups without the safeguards that would be regarded as normal if the criminal justice model were being followed. Human rights law in the United Kingdom has largely accommodated these security-oriented changes, and the effect of this has been to render them seemingly compliant with rather than inherently hostile to human rights principles. This has been achieved by a combination of, on the one hand, a code of human rights law that concedes within itself the need for occasional state action to safeguard national security and, on the other, an executive branch that has been sensitive to the need to give up some of the power it wants in order to secure a satisfactory human rights outcome.[23] So in Britain we have long periods of pre-charge detention on suspicion, albeit overseen by a judicial officer on the basis of rather general criteria sympathetic to state necessity.[24] There is an executive power to ban political associations but an independent tribunal (albeit without the security of a court) to which affected organizations can appeal.[25] The anti-terrorism control orders provided for in the terrorism law enacted in 2005 by way of a response to the Belmarsh decision accept the need for some judicial safeguards, although these do appear very weak when looked at from the perspective of criminal law. And so on. Some believe that this packaging of terrorism law in a kind of ersatz due process is merely brilliant salesmanship, a clever way of attacking human rights while seemingly complying with them, of salving the conscience of New Labour authoritarians. I have said as much myself recently, likening such safeguards to 'confetti at a funeral'.[26] It is certainly right that we would be better off with an improved code of criminal law outlining specific offences and providing mainstream procedural safeguards against abuse. At another level, however, this entanglement of terrorism law in the criminal process, and in particular the use of judges and lawyers from the historically independent legal professions to make it work, may over time transform such alien codes into something which much more closely resembles ordinary criminal law than it does at present. Given that terrorism laws are unlikely to disappear any time soon, this is certainly a goal worth working towards.

And where would you prefer to be a suspected terrorist, London or Washington? Before critics of the U.K.'s determination to make terrorism law human rights compatible become too shrill in their attacks, we should look at the United States to see what happens when no such efforts are made. In that jurisdiction, of course, there are no human rights as such to control the security instincts of the federal authorities, but there is supposed to be the Constitution; and guaranteeing its omnipotence, and thereby the supremacy of the rule of law, is supposed to be the main task of the U.S. Supreme Court. Aspects of the Bush administration's response to the attacks of 11 September 2001 have mimicked the British in that efforts have been made to secure legislative changes which have empowered the authorities to act in certain new – and undeniably draconian – ways. This is playing the game essentially by the old rules: you push something through Congress before you do what it will empower you to do, and you hope that the powers will not be struck down by the courts. The highly controversial Patriot Act is a good example. But it is now clear that this was only a small part of the administration's response, and that in fact the major commitment was to executive action without the authority of any law whatsoever. Since shortly after the 11 September attacks the National Security Agency in the U.S. has been empowered by presidential order to monitor international telephone calls and e-mails of U.S. citizens and residents without the warrant that is required by a secret foreign intelligence court. It is estimated that hundreds, perhaps thousands, of people have been under such surveillance. According to the President this is a 'limited program' aimed at those suspected of having links with terrorism and that it is 'vital and necessary' to protect the country.[27] These may be good arguments as to why there should be such a law, but these are not reasons in themselves for bypassing the law-making process altogether. The language of terrorism provides the justification for these egregious breaches of the right to privacy: they could not have arisen if we had stuck to the criminal model.

Lacking the enforcement arm of a state, international law has been even easier to ignore than domestic law. In November 2005, the Pentagon conceded that the U.S. had detained more than 80,000 people in facilities from Afghanistan to Cuba since the attacks on 11 September.[28] A large proportion of the 500 or so detainees being held at Guantánamo is believed to be on hunger strike and is being forcibly fed by the authorities.[29] Naturally enough lawyers can be found who will argue that the U.S. policy of detentions is in accord with international law, just as there are some who say that the president can do what he wants within the jurisdiction as well. Fortunately they are few and far between. Unfortunately they occupy positions of immense power.[30] And their opinions dovetail nicely with the prejudices of their bosses. For it has to be acknowledged that scepticism about the rule of law goes right to the very heart of this American administration. As President Bush said in his State of the Union Address in 2004, 'It is not enough to serve our enemies with legal papers'. Ever more brutally to the point, this is how Defense Secretary Rumsfeld put it in the 2005 *National Defense Strategy of the United States*: 'Our strength as a nation state will continue to be challenged by those who employ a strategy of the weak using international fora, judicial processes, and terrorism'.[31] If you took this quote, located it in the twentieth rather than early twenty-first century and asked an informed audience who had said it, I wonder which characters would first spring to mind? American names would not be likely to be first on the list.

And then of course there is the torture. It is an important part of the U.S. sense of itself that the country is not a place where torture has ever been officially contemplated. This is to put it mildly and – contra the idealists like Senator John McCain – ahistorical. Torture has directly and through its proxies been integral to U.S. foreign policy since the Vietnam War. Mechanisms of no-touch torture based on sensory deprivation and self-inflicted pain were developed as part of the Phoenix program during that conflict and were then exported to Latin America and Asia under the guise of police training programs.[32] The School of Americas based in Panama from 1946 until 1984 became so notorious that it was thought wiser to relocate the establishment to Fort Benning, Georgia. What was new after 11 September was the openness with which the previously covert policy was now being promulgated. Memos and legal opinions began to flow from the administration which argued that the president, in his constitutional role as commander-in-chief, had the power to order torture whatever the domestic law might say. It was also asserted that the Geneva Conventions did not apply to the unlawful combatants held by the U.S. authorities, and that the Convention against Torture did not apply to actions against non-Americans outside the United States. It was also suggested that torture was not after all quite what everybody else believed: conduct could be described as such only where it produced pain equivalent to that from serious physical injury, such as organ failure, impairment of bodily function, or even death. Anything else – no matter how awful – simply wasn't torture.[33]

The details of the various moves that the Bush White House has made away from democratic accountability, the rule of law and human dignity, all in the name of the 'Global War on Terror' that it says it has to fight, need not to detain us here. The challenge to human rights is manifest. We have already seen how the discourse of terrorism challenges universality and by positing a version of the world rooted in good and evil makes possible the kinds of subversions of our subject that I have been discussing. Our interest at this juncture lies in the reaction that these attacks on our human rights – liberty, bodily integrity, life and so on – have provoked from human rights defenders. The majority of progressives and public intellectuals have been fierce in their denunciations. But this has not been a unanimous response by any means. A substantial number of lawyers, media commentators and academics, particularly in the United States, have supported, either in whole or in part, the actions of the administration. Many of these have been supposed 'human rights experts', professors and lawyers allegedly well versed in the requirements of the field. This is not to say that they all give the Bush White House carte blanche; enough differences are maintained for critical distance to continue to appear to be preserved. And they disagree among themselves as well. Some of them do not go as far as others in what they would permit: at their conferences and in each other's edited books they argue among themselves about the morality of this or that kind of sensory deprivation and sometimes they even come down against indefinite detention without charge.[34] The details matter less than the fact of the discussions: internment, torture, coercive interrogation, covert surveillance and other manifestations of lawless state power are not any longer simple wrongs to be avoided and severely punished when they occur; rather they have become a set of proposed solutions to supposed ethical dilemmas that need now to be considered and debated, as you might consider and debate any other kind of policy proposal. The unspeakable is no longer unspoken. Even the greatest of our human rights taboos – the prohibition on torture and inhuman and degrading treatment – has become just another point of view – and to some people an eccentrically absolutist one at that.

It is not hard to see how President Bush, Vice-President Cheney and then-Defense Secretary Rumsfeld took such a position. But how have a substantial number of liberal progressives and human rights intellectuals coped with taking such a line? This is where the war on terror plays its part – it supplies the 'ethical dilemma' from which all else flows. Those who take the line I have just outlined tend also to accept the idea of a global campaign of terrorism that threatens us all. This leads them to see human rights not as a subject concerned with the powerless individual wherever he or she might be in the world but rather as an idea which finds its clearest expression in the West, indeed as something highly particular to the West, one of the reasons why the West considers its culture to be superior to that of others. In this way the 'human' is taken out of 'human rights', the particular is superseded by the general, and the subject becomes one that is more about values than about people. On this analysis respect for human rights becomes this abstract thing that we in the West have and which we must defend against those who would by destroying our culture also wreck this precious but vulnerable commitment. Michael Ignatieff's recent book *The Lesser Evil* is perhaps the best example of the genre.[35] To Ignatieff, we are faced with 'evil' people and 'either we fight evil with evil or we succumb'. 'Terrorist movements like al-Qaeda or Hamas are death cults' and it 'is redemption they are after, and they seek death sure that they have attained it'. The 'we' here is unavoidable because pervasive: intellectuals like Michael Ignatieff writing about the dangers of terrorism are speaking for the decent 'West' against a horrible other; it is a conversation with friends about what to do about the neighbour from hell. And it needs to be said that in these accounts of good and evil Israel always figures in the Western family. Just as in the 1970s global war on terror against the 'Evil Empire', Israel is our friend, the bastion of our values in a hostile zone, a beacon of good in a region of evil.

Once these assumptions about terrorism and good and evil are accepted, it becomes clear that the Western/Israeli democracies are indeed entitled to do some wrong in their struggle for survival. The human rights justification goes along the following lines. Unlike the terrorists, the defenders of democracy know that what they are doing (or what they say they have to do) is wrong (or at least a bit wrong) even when they are doing it, and they have a set of democratic values to hand to stop things getting out of control. Those values commit them to respecting the moral status of human beings and to guaranteeing 'to respect the rights of those who have shown no respect for rights at all, to show mercy to those who are merciless, [and] to treat as human those who have behaved inhumanly'.[36] But, precisely because we democratic people are special in this way, value everybody so highly and so on, 'necessity may require us to take actions in defence of democracy which will stray from democracy's own foundational commitments to dignity'.[37] So if we change our rules to allow us to respond in an evil way, or our operatives stray over the boundary into evil behaviour without our explicit authorization, it is really not so bad (fine even?) because all that is happening is that evil is being met with (lesser/theoretically accountable) evil. Indeed it is hard to be at all angry with (much less punish) 'the carnivores who disgrace the society they are charged to protect'[38] when what they are doing is protecting us not merely from our political opponents, nor even only from our enemies, but rather from evil itself. Our evil is better (because less bad) than theirs. If Abu Ghraib was wrong, then that wrongness consisted not in stepping across the line into evil behaviour but rather in allowing a 'necessary evil' (as framed by the intellectuals) to stray into 'unnecessary evil' (as practiced by the military on the ground).

Exactly this kind of human rights language has also played a part in the invasion of Iraq. A kind of militant humanitarianism had grown up during the late 1990s, which argued for a more robust strategy of intervention to secure human rights goals in faraway lands. This led many liberals to support the U.S. attacks on Afghanistan which followed the 11 September attacks.[39] While Stephen Holmes is right when he says that the 'heady support' of 'certain sparkling intellects . . . played little or no role in the decision to invade Iraq', he is also correct to note that 'it did diminish and isolate voices of dissent'.[40] Had the Iraqi occupation turned out as Washington strategists intended, there can be little doubt that the focus would now be on Syria's abysmal human rights record and its unlawful interference with Lebanon's affairs. The threat of military action would probably by now have been ratcheted up against Iran in the light particularly of its apparent effort to secure nuclear weapons – a hardly surprising policy choice, it must be said, given what has been happening in recent years in its two neighbouring countries Iraq and Afghanistan. (How would the U.S. react if Mexico and Canada were invaded and occupied by Iranian forces in possession of weapons of mass destruction of which it had none?) But we can be equally sure that, in this hypothetical future following a successful pacifying of Iraq, about Israel there would not have been a single murmur: its development of nuclear-weapon capacity would have remained unpunished, its illegal occupation of Palestinian land would have gone largely unnoticed, its invasion of neighbouring countries would still be a thing of the past, to be glossed over or forgotten. The human rights militants who would have been in the front row demanding action against Syria and Iran would have justified their silence on Israel by asserting that it is a country that subscribes to human rights values and that it is engaged in necessary evil against a global terrorist enemy, and that therefore its actions are morally better even when objectively they look a whole lot worse.

Conclusion: human rights fights back

In order to ensure its survival, the human rights idea needs to stand firmly against this kind of distortion of its essence, this move to turn it into a basis for selective aggression abroad and an alibi for brutality at home. The moment the human rights discourse moves into the realm of good and evil is the moment when it has fatally compromised its integrity. For once these grand terms are deployed in the discussion, all bets are off as far as equality of esteem is concerned. If we are good and they are bad, then of course equality of esteem between all of us is ludicrous. Why esteem the evildoer in the same way as he or she who does good? These are not now any longer human beings *simpliciter* but different kinds of humans: one good, one bad. The latter, being evil, are not only different, but worse; worse even than animals, since animals are, after all, incapable of evil. The wonder is not that we good guys abuse their human rights but that we continue to use human rights language in relation to them at all, that we recognize that they have any residual human rights worth noticing. And who is this 'they' that fills the category of lesser (because evil) humans? In theory of course the Bush administration and the liberal advocates of necessary evil agree that it is just the members of the terrorist brigades, the few truly rotten apples intent on destroying all that we civilized, good people stand for. In fact, when terrorists act in the name of a particular community, that entire community is likely to be tarred by the same brush. When this occurs, there is a danger of consistent discrimination against it; 'they' ('we' say) shelter terrorists and their human rights are likely to suffer in consequence. This process was clear enough in relation to the nationalist communities of Northern Ireland. The danger is all the greater when terrorists claim to be acting in the name of a major world religion and an entire religious community is therefore likely to be stigmatized by association. Abuses perpetrated in that context contribute to any disaffection that might already be felt within that community and the blanket suspicion can become self-fulfilling.

Again we are back with the single most disastrous legacy of the war on terror from a human rights point of view, the supersession of the criminal model based on justice and due process by a security model that is based on fear and suspicion. One of the great achievements of international law has been to remove the language of good and evil from the relationship between states. The 'just war' theory having the rather fatal flaw that 'justice' is in the eye of the beholder, it was thought far better to tie states down to specific rules and treaties into which morality (rival versions of good and evil) did not stray.[41] International humanitarian and human rights law represents the apogee of this civilizing trend in global affairs, with rules of decent conduct that took their colour from the fact of our shared humanity rather than the superiority of our particular cause being agreed and promulgated. Now, thanks primarily to the crude actions of this American administration but also to the willingness of important liberals to embrace the 'moral' language, we are back in a pre-rule phase where, in effect, despite the liberals' best hopes, anything goes. What is good for one side is good for the other as well, so we have seen a bleak escalation in the inhumanity shown towards Western captives, towards aid workers and others – journalists, support staff – working in the theatre of war. Various axes of evil bestride the world, with the exact centres of evil depending entirely on where you are standing.

The 'war on terror' has already done serious damage to the integrity of human rights, turning our subject into a kind of moral mask behind which lurk cruelty and oppression. But the signs are that the mood is turning and that resistance to this narrative is gathering momentum. The furore over extraordinary rendition that has taken up so much attention recently is in some ways good news, especially allied to the strong anti-torture assertions made by the Secretary of State Dr. Rice during a visit to Europe in December 2005. It seems that under the pressure of Abu

Ghraib and conceding a little in the face of international opinion, the Bush administration has returned to the traditional U.S. approach to torture, that of plausible deniability. In an imperfect world this realization that it is embarrassing to admit that you torture must count as a moral advance. Even better would be a move, possibly led by the European Union[42] or the Council of Europe, for far better enforcement of the Convention against Torture, and for the punishment of those states – allegedly some of them European – that have facilitated the U.S. desire to ill-treat captives in a deniable way.[43] Elements within the legislative, the judicial and even the executive branches of both the U.S. and the U.K. have become more voluble of late, subjecting assertions of terrorist threats and claims about danger to national security to more scrutiny than has been the case in the past.[44] Perhaps this is a consequence of the exposure of the faultiness of much of the intelligence with which the general public in both countries were persuaded to back the invasion and occupation of Iraq. These are advances that can be built on. But the subject of human rights will not be truly safe until the language of terrorism, and with it all dangerous talk of good and evil, is removed entirely from political rhetoric and from national and international law. In political rhetoric, it needs to be replaced with a more nuanced approach to international relations and in the legal sphere with a code of law that emphasizes the primacy of the criminal model over that of emergency or national-security driven approaches. And for either of these outcomes to be regarded even as possibilities, a just solution must first be found to the political problems in Palestine and Israel.

Notes

1 C.A. Gearty, *Terror* (London: Faber and Faber, 1991).
2 For an elaboration on what follows see C.A. Gearty, 'Terrorism and Morality', *European Human Rights Law Review* (2003), 377.
3 The Terrorism Act 2000 s. 1 is a good case in point. See also the draft U.N. Comprehensive Convention on International Terrorism as recommended by the Ad Hoc Committee on Terrorism: GA Official Records, 57th Session, Supplement No. 37 (A/57/37), 11 February 2002.
4 See B. Saul, 'Defining "Terrorism" to Protect Human Rights', Fride Working Paper, Madrid 2006.
5 Amnesty International Report 2005, *The State of the World's Human Rights* (London: Amnesty International, 2005).
6 Human Rights Watch, *World Report 2006* (New York: Human Rights Watch and Seven Stories Press, 2006).
7 The phrase is that of Walter Laqueur. See his *The Age of Terrorism* (London: Weidenfeld and Nicolson, 1987) where he makes this point about terrorism groups generally and not just the PLO.
8 R. Fisk, *Pity the Nation: Lebanon at War* (London: A. Deutsch, 1990) is a particularly harrowing account.

9   The best general study of the terrorism of the period is A. Guelke, *The Age of Terrorism and the International Political System* (London: I.B. Tauris Publishers, 1995).

10 B. Netanyahu, ed., *Terrorism: How the West Can Win* (London: Weidenfeld and Nicolson, 1986). See also B. Netanyahu, *Fighting Terrorism: How Democracies Can Defeat Domestic and International Terrorists* (London: Allison and Busby Ltd, 1996).

11 S. Huntingdon, 'The Clash of Civilisations', *Foreign Affairs* 72 (1993), 22.

12 *Terrorism: How the West Can Win* (note 10), ix.

13 To the frustration of serious academics striving to impose order in the field: see G. Wardlaw, *Political Terrorism: Theories, Tactics and Counter-Measures*, 2nd edn. (Cambridge: Cambridge University Press, 1989), 176–8.

14 S.T. Francis, *The Soviet Strategy of Terror* (Washington DC: The Heritage Foundation, 1981).

15 E. Luttwak, *The Grand Strategy of the Soviet Union* (London: Weidenfeld and Nicolson, 1983).

16 R. Goren, *The Soviet Union and Terrorism* (London: Allen and Unwin, 1984).

17 J. Becker, *The Soviet Connection: State Sponsorship of Terrorism* (London: Institute for European and Defence and Strategic Studies, Occasional Paper No. 13, 1985).

18 U. Ra'anan, R.L. Pfaltzgraff, R.H. Schultz, E. Halperin and I. Lukes, *Hydra of Carnage* (Lexington: Lexington Books, 1986).

19 C. Sterling, *The Terror Network: The Secret War of International Terrorism* (London: Weidenfeld and Nicolson, 1981).

20 W. Gutteridge, ed., *The New Terrorism* (London: Mansell Publishers, 1986), ix.

21 Prime Minister Sharon's Knesset speech, 16.9.2001, Prime Minister's Office online archives, at www.pmo.gov.il/PMO/Archive/Speeches/2001/09/Speeches5175.htm. Many thanks to Abigail Eshel (M.Sc. student, 2005–6) for finding the quotation and for the translation.

22 See J. Burnett and D. Whyte, 'Embedded Expertise and the New Terrorism', *Journal for Crime Conflict and the Media* 1 (2005), 1–18.

23 For further details, see C.A. Gearty, '11 September 2001, Counter-terrorism and the Human Rights Act', *Journal of Legal Studies* 32 (2005), 18. Cf. K.D. Ewing, 'The Futility of the Human Rights Act', *Public Law* (2004), 829.

24 Terrorism Act 2000, part V.

25 Ibid., part II.

26 C.A. Gearty, 'Human Rights in an Age of Counter-Terrorism: Injurious, Irrelevant or Indispensable?', *Current Legal Problems* 58 (2005), 31.

27 *Washington Post*, 2 January 2006, A2.

28 *Guardian*, 18 November 2005.

29 *Guardian*, 19 November 2005.

30 The definitive account is Mark Danner, ed., *Torture and Truth: America, Abu Ghraib and the War on Terror* (London: Granta Books, 2005). There is a good summary by A. Lewis in *The Nation*, 26 December 2005, 13–15.

31 See K.J. Greenberg, 'Secrets and Lies', *The Nation*, 26 December 2005, 40.

32 See N. Klein, ' "Never Before!" Our Amnesiac Torture Debate', *The Nation*, 26 December 2005, 11–12.

33 See *passim*, *Torture and Truth* (note 30).

34 Among the books recently published on the subject are: S. Levinson, ed., *Torture: A Collection* (Oxford: Oxford University Press, 2004); R.A. Wilson, *Human Rights in the 'War on Terror'* (Cambridge: Cambridge University Press, 2005); K. Roth and M. Worden, eds., *Torture: Does It Make Us Safer? Is It Ever OK?* (New York: The New Press, Human Rights Watch, 2005); A.M. Dershowitz, *Why Terrorism Works: Understanding the Threat, Responding to the Challenge* (New Haven: Yale University Press, 2002). For a comprehensive guide to those who have supported torture or some forms of what has in the past been thought to be ill-treatment see 'The Torture Tree' published in *The Nation*, 26 December 2005, 28–9.

35 *The Lesser Evil: Political Ethics in an Age of Terror* (Edinburgh: Edinburgh University Press, 2004). (See for a longer critique from which some extracts are drawn here, C.A. Gearty, 'With a Little Help From Our Friends', *Index on Censorship* 34 (2005), 46–51.)

36 *The Lesser Evil* (note 35), 34.

37 Ibid., 8.

38 Ibid., 144.

39 D. Chandler, *From Kosovo to Kabul and Beyond: Human Rights and International Intervention*, new edn. (London: Pluto Press, 2006).

40 'The War of the Liberals', *The Nation*, 14 November 2005, 29.

41 G. Oberleitner, 'A Just War Against Terror', *Peace Review* 16 (2004), 263.

42 'E.U. Threat to Countries With Secret CIA Prisons', *Guardian*, 29 November 2005.

43 See M. Bright, 'Rendition: The Cover-Up', *New Statesman*, 23 January 2006, 12–13.

44 Thus both the U.K. Parliament and the American Senate have recently taken liberal initiatives, on detention and torture respectively. Judicial authorities in both jurisdictions have handed down decisions that have overturned executive policy in sensitive anti-terrorism areas, most recently in Britain in relation to the use that can be made (or rather not made) of torture evidence: *A v. Secretary of State for the Home Department (No. 2)* [2005] UKHL 71. See www.publications.parliament.uk/pa/ld/ldjudgmt.htm. Even the U.K. executive has been slowly relenting on its steadfast refusal to allow intercept evidence to be used in court: see 'Free Foreign Suspects on Control Orders, Says Terror Watchdog', *Guardian*, 3 February 2006.

Sandra Fredman

Response to Conor Gearty

It is the tragic paradox of our times that democratic governments, facing what they see as threats to their democracy, are so quick to surrender the values of that very democracy. From Guantánamo Bay to Belmarsh, human rights are seen as increasingly disposable in the name of preserving democracy against terrorism. For me, as a human rights lawyer and a South African who grew up during apartheid, where all opposition was labelled terrorist and detention without trial was an ever-present reality for all who opposed the state, it is chilling to witness the ease with which democratic leaders seem able to give up on human rights principles. Yet as Lord Hoffmann recently put it: 'The real threat to the life of the nation . . . comes not from terrorism but from laws such as these'.[1]

Terrorism poses grave dilemmas for democratic governments. Faced with the need to protect their citizens against death or injury by groups willing to strike randomly to achieve political ends, the temptation is to respond with measures outside the rule of law and in breach of human rights standards. Yet as Chief Justice Barak stated when the Israeli Supreme Court struck down torture: 'It is the destiny of democracy that not all means are acceptable to it, and not all practices employed by its enemies are open before it. Although a democracy must often fight with one hand tied behind its back, it nonetheless has the upper hand. Preserving the Rule of Law and recognition of an individual's liberty constitutes an important component in its understanding of security. At the end of the day, they strengthen its spirit and its strength and allow it to overcome its difficulties'.[2]

Lord Hoffmann and Chief Justice Barak are, sadly, increasingly lone voices in a world in which counter-terrorism is seen as a ready excuse for giving up on human rights. It is thus particularly apposite for a leading human rights lawyer like Professor Gearty to focus his lecture on 'Human Rights in an age of counter-terrorism'. Gearty's focus is on ideology. For him, the real problem is not *acts* of terrorism, but the *language* of terrorism: the ways in which the terminology is used by powerful states to legitimate their own wrongful actions, both domestically and internationally. In his view, the language of terrorism has become inextricably bound up with moral condemnation of sub-state actors. By the same sleight of hand, terror by the state is artfully reclassified as counter-terrorism, which is 'inherently good in the same way that terrorism is inherently bad'. Thus, he concludes, 'the subject of human rights will not be truly safe until the language of terrorism, and with it all dangerous talk of good and evil, is removed entirely from political rhetoric'. Instead, it should be replaced 'with a code of law that emphasizes the primacy of the criminal model over that of emergency or national-security driven approaches'.

Gearty is right to argue against a false polarization of good and evil, where those on the side of good feel justified in taking any measures they wish in order to achieve their victory over evil. He is also right to propose that it be replaced with a more nuanced approach. It is unfortunate, however, that instead of replacing the terminology with a consistent and objective language of human rights, he succumbs to the temptation of simply inverting the ideology he currently condemns. Indeed, a central mission of the paper seems to be to unmask those posing as champions of the 'good' or 'counter-terrorism' and show them up as perpetrators of true 'terrorism'; while those currently labelled as 'evil' or 'terrorist' should be recognized as 'good' and victims of overwhelming power. This can be seen from his depiction of the origin of the language of terrorism and counter-terrorism. On his account, one country, Israel, aided and abetted by the U.S., has masterminded the rhetoric of terrorism. Thus, according to Gearty, after 1968, a 'brilliantly successful campaign' was conducted by U.S. and Israeli strategists and their academic and intellectual allies to represent Palestinian violence as 'terrorist and therefore as uniquely evil', while the same 'neat manoeuvre' saw Israel identified as counter-terrorist and therefore cast in a 'benign' light, despite the 'extreme terror-inducing nature of their own violence'. Having unmasked the real source of evil, he argues that 'terrorism' can be seen to be the 'weapon of the weak'. According to the dominant rhetoric, he maintains, Hamas is labelled 'terrorist' without 'ever having lifted a finger . . . against anybody'. Al-Qaeda is a 'kind of weak group that has few other military or political options in its locker'. For the Arab countries who attempted to eliminate Israel by conventional wars, the 'ruthless implacability of the Israeli reaction' meant that acts of political violence, 'on occasion very bloody it is true' were just a consolation prize against the 'lavishly equipped' Israeli army, 'which used extreme, terror-inducing . . . violence, far in excess of what the U.S., Britain or Spanish authorities needed'. His passing mention of Syria's 'abysmal human rights record' and its unlawful interference with Lebanon is immediately countered by his depiction of Syria as the next in a series of victims of U.S. aggression.

For a human rights regime to play its essential role in resolving conflict, it must be unflinchingly objective. Demonization of Israel and the corresponding elevation of al-Qaeda and other groups reintroduces the language of good and evil in a way which does Gearty's own argument for the primacy of human rights a great disservice. In his high velocity narrative of recent political history, complex historical events are represented as straightforward conflicts between right and wrong. It is particularly problematic to begin an account of the history of the Middle East as late as 1968, as Gearty does, when there are long and multifaceted antecedents to the conflict. Israel's illegal occupation of the West Bank and Gaza and its use of disproportionate force in its response to attacks are rightly condemned by international law as breaches of human rights. Indeed, Israel has committed many serious breaches of human rights, although it is a credit to its judicial commitment that its own Supreme Court has said so on several occasions. But to cite these abuses as justifications for the acts and rhetoric of those carrying out violence against innocent civilians is an unhelpful distortion. Similarly, it does human rights a disservice to leave out of account the context in which Israel has operated since its formation in 1948. Thus Gearty cites statements of right-wing Israeli leaders without mentioning the stream of statements by both governments and sub-state groups declaring their commitment to the destruction of Israel. As a typical example, one could cite the statements of the Egyptian President Gamal Nasser in the United Nations on 8 March 1965 when he said: 'We shall not enter Palestine with its soil covered in sand. We shall enter it with its soil saturated in blood'. A few months later, Nasser expressed the Arabs' goal to be 'the destruction of the State of Israel. The immediate aim: perfection of Arab military might. The national aim: the eradication of Israel'.[3] Nor have these in any sense waned in recent years. Thus in 2005, Iranian President Mahmoud Ahmadinejad called for Israel to be 'wiped off the map', declaring that it was a 'disgraceful stain' on the Islamic world. It is only by accounting for the full complexity of the struggles in the Middle East that a credible role for a human rights approach can be re-established.

To call for consistency in the application of human rights is not to condone Israel's actions. On the contrary, to focus on Israel alone is to negate the very real claims to human rights protection of victims of other perpetrators of terror, whether state or sub-state. Condemnation of Israel is relatively easy given that it is a relatively transparent society, with a free press, access for journalists, and an accountable government. More difficult to access but equally problematic are actions of state terror committed by governments which give little access to the international press. A particularly salient example is the state-sponsored 'terror' couched in the language of 'counter-terrorism' in Syria. Lebanese dissidents accuse Syria of consistently carrying out terrorist attacks in Syria, killing civilians and assassinating political leaders, culminating in a series of assassinations of high-profile Lebanese leaders in 2005.[4] The assassination of former Lebanese Prime Minister Rafiq Hariri has led a U.N. Commission to conclude that much of the evidence points directly towards Syrian security officials being involved with the assassination.[5] In addition, Syria regularly suppresses its own dissidents. In a strongly worded report in 2001, the Human Rights Committee of the United Nations expressed its deep concern at human rights violations in Syria, referring in particular to the number of offences punishable by the death penalty; the number of people held in pre-trial detention and

solitary confinement; the 'disappearance' following arrest of many Syrian and Lebanese nationals; the constant and 'duly substantiated' allegations of torture including
cases in Syrian prisons, and violation of the right to fair trial in trials conducted by
the State Security Court and the military courts.[6] Yet year by year, both before and
after this report, such abuses continue, not least in 2006, in what the *Guardian*
called 'Syria's silent purge', when dozens of pro-democracy dissidents in Syria have
been subjected to arrest, detention and torture.[7] Gearty's brief mention of Syria's
human rights record in the context of its vulnerability to U.S. attack belies the very
cogent claim of these people to human rights protection.

Also given only a passing mention are the Chechens, where a similar problematic
discourse of terrorism and counter-terrorism has been used to legitimate the overwhelming force of Russian military might. Particularly problematic is the fact that
Darfur gets no mention at all, rendering entirely invisible the effects of a combination of state and sub-state terrorism, leading to one of today's 'worst humanitarian crises directly caused by war crimes and crimes against humanity for which
the Sudanese government is responsible'.[8] According to Amnesty International reports,
the Sudanese government is systematically killing the black Sudanese of Darfur,
using Arab militias, its air force, and organized starvation. The result has been the
brutal killing of hundreds of thousands of black Sudanese and a further 1.8 million
displaced people left to starve. Amnesty concludes that 'there is a large amount of
information pointing at the responsibility of the Sudanese government in the human
rights violations committed in Darfur. In addition to the military and logistical support and the impunity that it provides to the Janjawid, the Sudanese government
has used a policy of repression to deal with the problems of Darfur. It has engaged
in arbitrary arrests, incommunicado detentions, "disappearances" and torture in order
to punish human rights activists, lawyers, leaders and members of communities in
Darfur. The Sudanese government has also used unfair and summary trials, using
confessions sometimes extracted under torture without the right to defence, and
applied cruel, inhuman and degrading punishments, such as amputations, flog-
gings and the death penalty'.[9]

It is particularly unfortunate that Gearty has chosen to devote this lecture largely
to a polemical account of the history of the language of terrorism and counter-
terrorism, rather than using his piercing mind and considerable legal skills to address
the very real challenges to human rights created by violent acts targeted at innocent civilians. In his conclusion he refers to the need to move away from emergency
measures and replace them with a criminal model. However, he gives little clue as
to how this would operate. Instead, in the second part of the lecture, he tantal-
izingly refers to the possibility that, in the case of the U.K., the 'entanglement of
terrorism law in the criminal process, and in particular the use of judges and lawyers from the historically independent legal professions to make it work, may over
time transform such alien codes into something which much more closely resembles
ordinary criminal law than it does at present. Given that terrorism laws are unlikely to

disappear any time soon, this is certainly a goal worth working towards'. However, in view of the acute danger that 'terrorism law' will dilute human rights, it is deeply disappointing that Gearty does not use this occasion to develop his model, either to establish how to ensure that a criminal model complies with human rights or to show how his model can work at an international level, involving both state and sub-state actors.

It would have been helpful for Gearty at least to set out the basic human rights principles by which to steer such complex issues. It is not enough to refer to a criminal model, since criminal models can themselves breach human rights, if they define criminal action broadly or in vague terms, if they prescribe excessive or degrading punishments, or if they subject the accused to long delays, poor legal representation or other similar procedural obstacles. In this brief reply, it is only possible to state the most fundamental of values. First and foremost, the central principle of human rights is that of human dignity. At its inderogable core, human dignity entails the Kantian ideal that individuals cannot be used as a means to an end. However important or legitimate their cause, and however deep their grievance, both state and non-state bodies commit a cardinal breach of this fundamental principle when they kill and maim people as a means to further their political ends. To deliberately target civilians is immoral, unjust and in fundamental breach of human rights, whether such actions come from state actors or sub-state groups, and regardless of their objective. The innocent person shot by a soldier or a policeman has been subject to a breach of their most fundamental rights. But so has the person who is blown apart by a suicide bomb, the individual at one moment pursuing ordinary daily life, and the next minute reduced to body parts scattered over the streets. This is true in Mumbai, in Barcelona, in London and in New York no less than in Tel Aviv, in Gaza and in Baghdad. Likewise, by international law, fighters who launch missiles deliberately aimed at civilians and who locate their weapons deep inside civilian populations are committing war crimes no less than armies which respond in crass disregard of civilian life and property.

But equally, and implacably, human rights must stand up for the rights of those accused of such terrorism. Human rights cannot condone responses to violence which are themselves in breach. The fear and panic caused by arbitrary and random killings of ordinary people in the name of a higher cause have led many to argue for an exceptional approach, a justification for breaches of human rights. Not knowing who will strike next and where has led countries, concerned at the right to life of their citizens, to preventive action which gathers up in its terrified net hundreds of innocent passers-by. To counter such responses, human rights must hold the line unflinchingly. Only those who are truly guilty should be punished. Collective punishment cannot be condoned; nor can detention without proof of guilt. In fact, the basic principles of human rights require a step further, to ensure that even those who are truly guilty are not punished in a way which by its barbarity compromises the democratic and civilized values which human rights are themselves committed to.

This is clearly an enormous challenge for a human rights regime. In Britain, the Joint Committee on Human Rights has made a useful start. Recognizing both the positive duty of the state to protect its citizens from violence, and the human rights of those charged with perpetrating such violence, it attempts to define possible modifications to the criminal process which would facilitate fair trials without compromising the human rights of the defendant.[10] Ultimately, however, human rights can only operate in a framework in which all can accept that conflict must be resolved through rights. Hence it was crucial to the Northern Ireland accord that human rights and equality were central to the Good Friday agreement. Similarly, constitutional human rights have been a key part of the replacement of apartheid by a democratic settlement in South Africa. It was in South Africa too that the fundamental role of reconciliation was recognized as ploughing the soil for the cultivation of a human rights culture. As the closing paragraphs of South Africa's Interim Constitution put it in 1993, truth and reconciliation is a bridge between 'the past of a deeply divided society characterised by strife, conflict, untold suffering and injustice, and a future founded on the recognition of human rights, democracy and peaceful coexistence and development opportunities for all South Africans, irrespective of colour, race, class, belief or sex'.[11] It is difficult to break the cycle of violent response to violent acts unless all sides feel bound by a culture of human rights, and this is the daunting challenge to ourselves as human rights activists and lawyers. It is a challenge which has to be faced by moving forwards from revenge politics to reconciliation through objective and consistent application of human rights principles, both in rhetoric and reality.

Notes

1 A v. *Secretary of State for the Home Department* [2004] UKHL 56; [2005] 2 W.L.R. 87 (HL).

2 *Public Committee Against Torture in Israel* v. *State of Israel* H.C. 5100/94, H.C. 4054/95, H.C. 6536/95, H.C. 5188/96, H.C. 7563/97, H.C. 7628/97, H.C. 1043/99 (Supreme Court of Israel).

3 Alfred J. Kolatch, *Great Jewish Quotations* (New York: Jonathan David, 1996), 332.

4 www.lebaneselobby.org/Terror/Syrian%20Terrorism%20Against%20Lebanese.htm

5 Report of the International Independent Investigation Commission Established Pursuant to Security Council Resolution 1595 (2005) para. 209, at www.un.org/News/dh/docs/mehlisreport/.

6 http://web.amnesty.org/library/Index/ENGMDE240032001?open&of=ENG-SYR.

7 http://web.amnesty.org/library/eng-syr/index&start=1.

8 http://web.amnesty.org/library/index/engafr540762004.

9 Ibid.

10 Joint Committee on Human Rights Twenty Fourth Report 2006, at www.publications. parliament.uk/pa/jt200506/jtselect/jtrights/240/24002.htm.

11 Constitution of the Republic of South Africa Act 1993, s.232(4).

4 Thomas Pogge

Terrorism: reflections on harming the innocent*

The countries of the developed West are fighting a war on terror. More accurately: the governments of some of these countries are conducting a war against terrorists. This war effort was stepped up dramatically after the terrorist attack of 11 September 2001, which killed about 3,000 people in New York, Virginia and Pennsylvania. The most notable attack until then was the car bomb attack on the U.S. embassies in Dar es Salaam and Nairobi of 7 August 1998, which killed 257 people including 12 U.S. citizens. Since the 11 September attack, 202 people, including 88 Australians, have been killed in Kuta on the Indonesian island of Bali on 12 October 2002; 191 people were killed in the Madrid bombing of 11 March 2004; and the terrorist attack of 7 July 2005 in London killed 52 people.

Why wage war against these terrorists? Offhand, one might think that such a grand response to terrorism is undeserved. This thought is supported by comparisons with other threats to our life and well-being – cardiovascular disease and cancer, for instance, annually kill some 250,000 and 150,000 people, respectively, in the U.K. alone (940,000 and 560,000 in the U.S.), while traffic accidents kill over 3,000 each year (43,000 in the U.S.). In the U.K., only about one per 10,000 deaths in 2005 was due to terrorism. And even in the U.S. in 2001, the corresponding ratio was about one in 750, that is, 0.13 per cent. It would seem that even a small increase in the effort to combat cardiovascular disease, cancer, road accidents, or any of several other, similar threats would do much more to protect our survival and well-being, at lower cost, than revving up the war on terror.

This point has been made repeatedly with dramatic facts and figures.[1] Since 2001, the Global Fund to Fight AIDS, Tuberculosis and Malaria, funded by all willing governments and devoted to combating diseases that kill about 6 million people each year, has committed about $10.07 billion and spent about $5.05 billion.[2] This expenditure comes to roughly $140 per fatality. Between 2001 and 2006, the U.S. government alone has spent $438 billion on the war on terror.[3] This amount comes to roughly $146 million per U.S. fatality – over a million times more per

fatality. Many millions of deaths from extreme poverty and curable diseases could
be avoided each year, if the world's governments were willing to spend even one-
quarter as much on combating these scourges as they are now spending on their
war on terror. Such a war on poverty and disease would also avoid the substantial
human costs of the war on terror: some 5,000 coalition soldiers have been killed
and several tens of thousands wounded in Iraq and Afghanistan. Fatalities among
Iraqi and Afghan civilians have been vastly higher.

So why is terrorism being taken so seriously? This question requires nuances.
We need to distinguish reasons and causes. And we need to differentiate the various groups involved in this war.

I

I see two main explanations (sections I and II). One explanation is that public attention to terrorism serves important domestic constituencies. It serves most obviously
the news media. Their economic success depends on their ability to attract the public's attention; and it is vastly easier to attract the public to stories about terrorists
and their plans and victims than to stories about cancer and cancer victims or to
stories about traffic accidents.[4]

Public attention to terrorism also serves the interests of politicians, especially
incumbents. They can gain greatly increased attention, authority and deference from
a frightened public as well as acquiescence when they withhold information, increase
surveillance, disrespect civil liberties, and curb political opposition. Many Western
government policies – from the invasion of Iraq to the secret monitoring of citizens
and the detention of political opponents at home and abroad – have been marketed
as anti-terror measures.[5] Many non-Western governments have eagerly followed
our example, often defending severe violations of basic human rights as necessary
responses to terrorist threats.

The politicians of some countries derive a further benefit from a major war on
terror also in the international arena, namely the benefit that this war strengthens
the political power of their country. Assume simplistically that a country's political power depends on three components: military might (capacity for violence),
economic might, and international moral standing. Countries differ in regard to the
composition of their political power: Russia and the U.S. are strong militarily relative to their moral and economic strength. Japan is strong economically relative
to its military and moral strength. And Iceland's moral standing in the world is strong
relative to its military and economic strength. Now, how much each of the three
components contributes to political power depends on the regional or global environment. Military strength will be a much larger contributor to political power in
the midst of a world war than in a time of universal peace; and a country's moral
reputation will matter much more in peaceful times than in a period of war or conflict.

Therefore, governments of countries whose military strength is relatively larger than their economic and moral strengths will tend to benefit from heightened insecurity and tension by enjoying greater freedom of action due to greater acquiescence on the part of their own citizens and other countries. The political leaders of such countries with comparatively greater military strength therefore have a further incentive to foster an international climate of conflict and hostility. Such a climate stands to enhance not only their domestic standing, but also the power they wield on their country's behalf internationally.

These points are worth further thought because, by playing up terrorism in pursuit of their own ends, our media and politicians are helping the terrorists achieve exactly what they want: attention and public fear. By helping to ensure that terrorist attacks are successful in the way their perpetrators want them to be successful, the media and politicians are multiplying the damage our societies suffer from terrorism and also encouraging further terrorist attacks.

II

Those ordinary citizens in the U.K. and U.S. who have been supporting the war effort, at least tacitly, are a different matter. Why have they been so supportive of the new war? One reason is, of course, that such citizens have been persuaded that this war enhances the security of themselves and their friends and relatives from terrorist attacks. But this more prudential reason does not explain the enormous public attention paid to terrorism, nor the great cost, in terms of money and basic freedoms, that many citizens seem willing to bear to combat terrorism, because the war on terror is not a cost-effective way of protecting our health and survival. Of course, citizens are not fully informed and perfectly rational. They may not realize how small terrorism's damage has been, and how costly the countermeasures. But I think an important part of the explanation is our moral judgement that these terrorist attacks are exceptionally heinous. This judgement lends special urgency to fighting this terrorism as the effort promises not merely a reduction in the risk of harm each of us is exposed to, but also the suppression of a dreadful moral evil. Because we perceive these terrorist attacks as so exceptionally heinous, we attach to their suppression an importance that is greatly disproportional to the immediate harm they inflict.

Is it correct to consider these terrorist attacks especially heinous and thus to attach such disproportional importance to suppressing them?

Before examining this question in section III, let us address a prior concern. Some find such an examination offensive. They find it obvious that these terrorist attacks are very wrong. And they feel that the self-evidence of this proposition is denied when we examine its meaning and grounds. They feel that the question: 'What is wrong with these terrorist attacks?' suggests that these attacks are among the things about which people can reasonably disagree. And they firmly reject this suggestion.

Let me be clear then that, by asking what is wrong with these terrorist attacks, I am not suggesting that people can reasonably disagree about their wrongness, but merely that it is important to understand why these attacks are wrong. Even if we are perfectly certain they are wrong, understanding why is still important for two reasons. I will state one reason now, the other in section VII.

The first reason has to do with moral theorizing. We are often faced with moral questions or decisions that are difficult to resolve. When this happens, we engage in moral reflection. Such reflection looks at relevant empirical evidence and also at other, less difficult moral questions or decisions that may be analogous or related in some way to the problem at hand. John Rawls has analysed this ordinary method in some detail and has compared it to how we make difficult judgements in linguistics. When we are doubtful whether some particular phrase is proper English, we can hypothetically formulate grammatical rules that would forbid or allow it and then test these general hypotheses against other phrases whose status is certain. In this way, some of the rules we try out will be confirmed and others refuted. Confirmed rules can then be brought to bear on the questionable phrase to resolve our doubt.[6]

With this method, which Rawls calls reflective equilibrium, our most firmly held convictions, collectively, are the standard by which we judge difficult questions. But the method can work only if we can bring some of our most firmly held convictions to bear on the difficult question or decision we confront. This requires that we generalize from these most firmly held convictions. We can do this by hypothetically formulating more general moral principles that may then be confirmed or refuted by our firmest moral convictions, such as the conviction that these terrorist attacks are wrong. A confirmed moral principle helps us understand why these attacks are wrong, or what makes them wrong. And such a principle can then also be used to help resolve other, more difficult moral questions or decisions.

III

So what is wrong with terrorist attacks such as the five I described at the outset? As a first approximation we might say that what makes these attacks presumptively wrong is that, foreseen by the agent, they harm and even kill innocent people. I assume it is clear enough for present purposes what it means to harm or kill people. By calling a person innocent, I mean that this person poses no threat and has done nothing that would justify attacking her with lethal force. To be sure, the terrorists may have believed that some of those they attacked were not innocent in this somewhat technical sense and were thus justifiably subject to lethal attack. But they could not have reasonably believed this of the great majority of the people they attacked. They clearly foresaw that their conduct would harm and kill many innocent people. In fact, the time of day they chose for their attacks, and the lack of any prior warnings such as were often issued by the IRA and the ETA, strongly suggest that they not merely foresaw but even intended to harm and kill many innocent people.

We need not claim that it is always wrong to do what one foresees will harm or kill innocent people. It is enough that there is a firm presumption against it, which may be overcome by showing that so acting is necessary to achieve some greater good (which may consist in the prevention of some greater harm).

Justifications of this kind come in two types. Justifications of the first type assert that those who will be harmed stood to gain from the action *ex ante*. We can give this type of justification for a doctor who administers a live vaccine to 10,000 children while knowing statistically that roughly one or two of them will die from the resulting infection. This doctor's conduct is nonetheless permissible if each child's prospects of survival are expected to increase relative to no treatment and also relative to other feasible treatment options. With justifications of this type, it is enough that the expected good should outweigh the expected harm so that there is a net expected gain for each person affected. Since it is plainly false that each of the persons attacked by the terrorists stood to gain from this attack *ex ante*, we can set aside this type of justification in what follows.

Justifications of the second type assert that the harm done to innocent people is outweighed – not by some good for these same people – but by a greater good of some other kind. Some philosophers reject justifications of this second type altogether. But I find such absolutism implausible. If the brutal reign of a tyrant who is killing many thousands can be ended with a violent strike that unavoidably also kills an innocent child, then this strike seems morally acceptable, perhaps mandatory, if indeed it can save thousands from being murdered and millions from being oppressed and brutalized. Similarly, the aerial bombardment of cities may be justifiable when this is the only means of defence against a horrible aggressor state. At the opposite end of the spectrum, some philosophers hold that justifications of the second type can succeed even when the greater good just barely outweighs the harm foreseen. Such philosophers might approve of killing 19 children when this is the only way of saving 20 others. Like most, I find such an act-consequentialist standard too permissive. When the greater good an agent intends to achieve with her action will not be a good for the innocent persons this action will harm, then that good can justify the action only if it *greatly* outweighs the harm this action foreseeably inflicts. (This requirement is often thought to be especially significant when the harm to be inflicted is a means to attaining the purported good, rather than a foreseeable side effect.) For such a justification to succeed, it is further required, of course, that the harm be *necessary* for achieving the greater good in question, so that the same good could not have been achieved using any other less harmful means.

Can such a justification be provided for the terrorist attacks at issue? I believe not. To show this conclusively, one would need to run through indefinitely many candidate 'greater goods' that might be offered. This we cannot do. Instead, let us focus on three such candidate greater goods that have actually been appealed to by the terrorists or their supporters. This exercise may give us a clearer sense of how we might respond to other such justifications yet to be advanced.

One justification refers to various regimes in the Middle East – that of Saudi Arabia prominently included – which are regarded as dictatorial or un-Islamic or pro-Western. The terrorist attacks were meant to discourage the U.S. and other Western countries from supporting these regimes, especially through the station- ing of troops in their territories, and to boost the morale of those who are seeking to overthrow these regimes. A second justification appeals to the alleged good of weakening Israel by discouraging other governments from supporting it and by boost- ing the morale of Palestinians resisting the occupation of their lands. A third justification appeals to the alleged good of punishing Western countries for their past and present support of Israel and/or of dictatorial and un-Islamic Middle Eastern regimes.

To succeed, any such justification must discharge four burdens of proof. It must show that the alleged good really is a good. It must show that the terrorist attacks in question contribute to this good, at least probabilistically. It must show that the value of this contribution greatly outweighs the foreseen harms to innocent peo- ple. And, finally, any such justification must also show that all these harms were really necessary for the intended contribution to the greater good, that the same good could not have been achieved using any other less harmful means.

The quickest and clearest way of seeing that these justifications fail focuses on the fourth burden of proof. Equivalent contributions to all three candidate greater goods could have been achieved with far less harm to clearly innocent people. In fact, the manner and timing of the attacks suggest that such harm was intended. In any case, the terrorists at minimum displayed great disregard for what is often euphemistically called collateral damage. The terrorists could have attacked their U.S. targets early on a Sunday morning, for instance, when the World Trade Center area would have been nearly deserted. Such a palpable effort to spare innoc- ent people would not have reduced attention to the terrorists' cause. On the con- trary, by signalling clearly their intent to spare innocent people as far as reasonably possible, the terrorists would have made local and Western citizens less unrecept- ive to their ends and grievances, and would still have demonstrated their terrify- ing capabilities and willingness to die for their cause. Most of the harm the terrorists inflicted on innocent people was not necessary for promoting the alleged good they sought and quite possibly even counter-productive.

We might remember in this context that the disregard for the lives of innocent persons is not a defining feature of terrorism and is in fact absent from much historical terrorism. The IRA and ETA frequently issued bomb warnings before-hand in order to minimize harm to persons. And some of the 1905–6 Russian terrorists – sometimes called moral-imperative terrorists and immortalized by Albert Camus in his play *The Just* as well as in his essay *The Rebel* – were absolutely deter-mined not to harm innocents. Thus Kaliaev abandoned his first attempt to kill Sergei Aleksandrovich when he saw that the Grand Duke had his niece and nephew, two children, in his carriage.[7]

Moral justifications of the terrorist attacks fail, then, because the fourth burden of proof cannot be discharged: the attacks inflicted great harms on far more innoc-ent people than was, given the goal, reasonably unavoidable.

To this it may be objected that the terrorists and their supporters may feel that no justification is needed for their killing of innocent people. They see themselves as involved in a war in which their opponents have inflicted even greater harms upon the innocent. When one's enemy in war employs immoral methods, then it is morally permissible to employ the same methods in return.

In earlier work, I have discussed this objection under the label 'sucker exemp-tion'.[8] The basic idea is that an agent in a competitive context is not required to observe constraints that other, competing agents fail to observe. I believe that this idea can indeed be plausible, but only when the victims of an agent's constraint violations are themselves previous violators of the constraint. If you have various agreements with another person, for instance, and he turns out routinely to violate these agreements whenever it suits him, then you are not morally required to hon-our your agreements with him when it does not suit you.

The sucker exemption is distinctly implausible, however, when those whom the agent's conduct would victimize are distinct from those who have victimized her. You are not morally permitted to violate your agreements with one person be-cause some other person has violated his agreements with you. Similarly, an agent is not morally permitted to harm the friends or relatives of someone who has harmed her friends and relatives. A man is not permitted, for example, to rape the daughter of his own daughter's rapist. And likewise for the terrorists and their supporters: they are not morally permitted fortuitously to harm and kill innocent compatriots of people who have harmed innocent compatriots or associates of theirs. A person can forfeit ordinary moral protections against being harmed only through some-thing she herself has done, not through the actions of another. Therefore, what-ever wrongful harms the terrorists or their associates or compatriots may have suffered do not alter their moral relations to third parties who are not culpable for those wrongful harms.

Interestingly, Osama bin Laden has professed to share these sentiments in his early denials of any involvement in 9/11. Thus he is reported as saying, in his *Daily Ummat* interview dated 28 September 2001: 'I have already said that I am not involved in the 11 September attacks in the United States. As a Muslim, I try my best to avoid telling a lie. I had no knowledge of these attacks, nor do I consider the killing of innocent women, children and other humans as an appreciable act. Islam strictly forbids causing harm to innocent women, children and other people. Such a practice is forbidden even in the course of a battle'.[9] That bin Laden's interpretation of Islam is at least a plausible one is confirmed by various passages in the Qur'an, such as this one: 'whosoever kills a human being for other than manslaughter or corruption upon earth, it shall be as if he had killed all mankind'.[10]

IV

To show that the terrorist attacks were morally unjustifiable, I have focused on the weakest link in the purported justifications for them: any plausible purpose of the attacks could have been achieved with much less harm to innocent civilians. This focus on the fourth burden of proof should not be taken to suggest that the other three burdens can be met. I do not believe that they can. In particular, it is unclear what genuine greater good these attacks might conceivably have contributed to. Perhaps there were some people among the victims who, in the eyes of the terrorists, were sufficiently guilty to deserve death. But this is not enough for these attacks to count as successful punishment operations serving an aim of focused deterrence. The attacks were far too indiscriminate for that – both by making no effort to include specific persons perceived as guilty and by making no effort to exclude persons who were clearly innocent. 'It is better that ten guilty persons escape, than that one innocent suffer', the proverb says.[11] To justify the attacks as punishment of guilty individuals, the terrorists would have to assert something like this: 'It is better that ten innocent persons be killed than that one guilty person should continue to live'. And even then they would have to identify 337 among their victims – one in 11 for each attack – who deserved the death penalty and whose deaths would then justify the deaths of 3,365 innocent people as well as all the other collateral damage.

The attacks might be understood as collective punishments of a group, presumably a country, serving the aim of deterring this country, and others, from continuing their foreign policies relating to the Middle East. In fact, I don't know how else to make sense of the Bali bombing. But are such reprisal killings a good? Is it appropriate to punish Australia and Spain for their – let us assume: wrongful – foreign policies by killing a random selection of their citizens? Such lopsidedly distributed punishment of groups is known from history – from the Roman practice of decimating a military unit, for example, typically for cowardice or insubordination. But the moral implausibility of such punishments is no longer seriously contested. Moreover, even if such a randomly biased group punishment were a good thing, one would still need to show that this good is large enough greatly to outweigh the harm done to innocents. These innocents include most or all of the group members randomly selected, who may be children or youths or active opponents of their government's foreign policy. And they also include those outside the targeted group. In the Bali attack, about one-fifth of the victims were locals and another fifth were tourists from non-target countries. In the U.S. embassy bombings, nearly 95 per cent of victims were not from the target country.

Did these attacks, or could they reasonably have been expected to, weaken Israel or the rulers of Saudi Arabia or other disliked rulers in the Middle East, for instance by deterring Western support? The terrorist attacks have predictably increased, certainly in the U.S., sympathy and support for Israel: for Israel's secur- ity wall, settlement expansion and checkpoints in the West Bank as well as for Israel's policies of targeted assassinations and deadly reprisals against civilians in the occu- pied territories and abroad (Lebanon, most recently). The attacks have greatly increased diplomatic, financial and security support for the Middle Eastern regimes the terrorists despise and have also increased Western tolerance for, and collabora- tion with, these regimes' long-standing practices of severe repression of dissent and of Islamic dissent in particular. To be sure, the terrorists of September 11 would have welcomed the demise of Saddam Hussein's regime in Iraq, which their attacks facilitated; but they would not have welcomed the way he fell, the occupa- tion of Iraq by Western troops, or the emerging successor regime. Their attacks predictably endangered the Taliban regime in Afghanistan, leading to its replace- ment with a regime they would have found much less congenial. The terrorist attacks did accelerate Western acceptance of the first acquisition of nuclear weapons by a Muslim country.[12] But this acceptance was predicated on Pakistan's military dic- tator agreeing to a range of domestic and foreign policies that the terrorists reject as anti-Islamic and pro-Western, including active participation in the war on ter- ror. None of these Western reactions is surprising. And it is hard to see then what great good did, or could have been expected to, come out of the terrorist attacks – sufficient greatly to outweigh all the harm to innocents.

V

I have briefly presented my reasons for believing that the five terrorist attacks in focus were morally unjustifiable acts of mass homicide. This conclusion could be further disputed. Other candidate greater goods might be adduced, or modifica- tions of my account of what a successful justification would need to show might be proposed. A clever philosopher might be able to keep this game going a good while longer, and I cannot anticipate, let alone respond in advance to, all the moves such a philosopher might make.

But this is no reason for us to suspend moral judgement. These attackers and their supporters have made clear that they take themselves to be engaged in justifiable political violence. Their pronouncements are laden with moral and religious lan- guage that presents their conduct as justifiable, even noble, and urges others to follow their example. Such statements imply a responsibility to justify their attacks. They may not owe such a justification to just anyone. But they do owe a justification to their innocent victims and to the innocent friends and families of such victims. And they owe a justification also to the sincere adherents of their religion, in whose name they have attacked their targets.

Put yourself in the position of someone who is involved in planning an attack that he foresees will kill many innocent civilians. And imagine this person to be someone who takes morality seriously – understanding morality broadly here as including any religion that provides moral guidance and constraints. Such a moral person would think very hard indeed before killing large numbers of innocent people. He would not do this without having assured himself, up to a very high level of confidence, that his planned action is really justifiable – in one of the ways I have sketched or in some other way he finds compelling on reflection. For a religious person, especially when he is about to act in the name of his religion, there is the further need to make quite certain that he has really used his God-given capacities to the fullest so as to reassure himself that his planned action really accords with God's will. For a seriously religious person, what could be more terrifying than the possibility that one might not be careful enough and therefore make a mistake by killing, against God's will but in God's name, hundreds of innocent human beings?

With the cases before us, this is not a far-fetched possibility. As bin Laden has said, these attacks killed innocent human beings and Islam strictly forbids harming innocent human beings even in war. So it is – to put it mildly – not obvious that these attacks are permitted, let alone that they are God's will. Some serious thought is certainly required for a genuinely religious person conscientiously to reach the conclusion that these attacks accord with God's will.

Now suppose a genuinely religious person has conscientiously reached this conclusion. He would want to give his reasons, at least after the fact (and thus perhaps after his own death). He would feel a responsibility to explain to his innocent victims and their innocent friends and relatives why he felt compelled to harm them. He would want other Muslims not merely to follow his example, but to do so with a full appreciation of why this really is the will of God. And, perhaps most important, he would want any mistake in his understanding of Islam to be identified and corrected. A genuinely religious person seeks to live in accordance with God's will, in accordance with what his religion requires. This is distinct from seeking to live in accordance with what one *believes* to be God's will and *believes* to be required by one's religion. These two goals are distinct because of the possibility of error. To deny this possibility is to claim infallibility for oneself. This would be hubris in regard to morality, and blasphemy in any theistic religion.[13]

It is true, of course, that all we have are our beliefs. We have no belief-independent access to the truth. Still, beliefs can be more or less well founded. To the person who seeks to live in accordance with what she *believes* to be God's will, it does not matter whether her beliefs are well founded or not. To the person who seeks to live in accordance with God's will, by contrast, nothing matters more. The more pains she takes to examine and correct her understanding and beliefs, the more likely she is to get it right. And even when she gets it wrong nonetheless, she will at least have done her best to get it right by making full use of the faculties and other resources God had endowed her with.

It is then of great importance to a genuinely moral or religious person to have a full justification for an action that he knows will kill many innocent civilians, and also to present this justification, at least after the fact. Such a full justification will then be examined and discussed by others whom it will help either to follow the agent's example conscientiously, with full appreciation of the reasons why it may or should be followed, or else to avoid the error he had committed in good faith.

It is stunning how far the terrorists and their supporters fall short of the conduct of persons with genuine moral or religious commitments and scruples. They traffic heavily in the language of morality and holiness, but there is no evidence that they have seriously thought about what their religion requires of them. What they give us are simple moral colorations of the world along with fervent professions of sincerity and commitment. They do indeed seem strongly committed – after all, many of them are willing to die for the success of their attacks. But for this commitment to be a sincere commitment *to Islam*, there would need to be a serious effort substantively to connect their activities and colorations to Islamic teachings. There would need to be reflective answers to questions such as: Why is this a holy war? Who counts as an enemy in this holy war, and why? What is one allowed to do in a holy war to enemies and to the uninvolved? There is, and has been for centuries, sophisticated treatment of such questions among Islamic scholars.[14] But the terrorists and their supporters are conspicuously absent from this discourse, even though their pronouncements and actions are highly controversial within it. They seem to be quite unconcerned to rule out what I have called the most terrifying possibility for a genuine believer: the possibility that one might be mistakenly killing, in God's name but against God's will, hundreds of innocent human beings who, no less than oneself, are God's creation.

VI

I have discussed two moral failings of those involved in the five terrorist attacks. It was wrong of them to harm large numbers of innocent civilians for no compelling purpose. And they did wrong to perpetrate these attacks in the name of a religion without taking great care to work out whether their religion really justifies such attacks. Placing these two wrongs side by side, you may think that the latter pales to insignificance. But I will try to show that the latter wrong, too, is of great importance. This discussion will also bring out the second reason why it is so very important for us not merely to be certain *that* these terrorist attacks are wrong, but also to understand *why* they are wrong. We are in the same boat with the terrorists in the sense that we use moral language just as they do. Our moral judgements are fallible just as theirs are. And we have a moral responsibility, just as they do, to take great care to ensure that the important decisions we make are not merely ones that we, however sincerely, believe to be morally justifiable, but also ones that we can actually justify.

Moral language is all around us – praising and condemning as good or evil, right or wrong, just or unjust, virtuous or vicious. In all too many cases, however, such language is used only to advance personal or group interests. The speaker expresses the narrowest judgement that allows her to score her point while avoiding any further normative commitments that might encumber herself now or in the future. This is quite common in politics. Politician A criticizes politician B as unethical for accepting a free trip to a conference in Brighton courtesy of Shell Oil. Without any further explanation of what makes B's behaviour unethical, this is rather too easy a way of scoring political points. B gets tarred with the label *unethical*, while A can look good for her ethical concern without imposing any ethical constraints on her own conduct. A remains at liberty, should she be found to have accepted some free trip herself, to say that her conduct was not unethical because of its different purpose, different destination, different sponsor, or whatever.

A's conduct is not atypical in our culture. Many seek to take advantage of morality to influence the sentiments and conduct of others while avoiding any interference by morality in the pursuit of their own ends. This is a moral failing, of course, but one that may seem rather mild in comparison to horrendous crimes of violence such as those we have discussed. And yet, this common abuse of morality is of great importance, as we recognize when we consider it, as I will now do, from three perspectives: from the perspective of morality itself, from the perspective of agents, and from the perspective of our society and culture.

The imperative to take morality seriously is not a command merely of this or that morality, but one that any plausible morality – and again I include religions – must make central. Though substantive in content, this central imperative flows from understanding what it means to have, not some particular moral commitments, but any moral commitments at all.

In rough outline we might say that the central imperative to take morality seriously involves at least these three injunctions; one must try to integrate one's moral judgements, one's religious beliefs and commitments, through more general moral principles into a coherent account of morally acceptable conduct; one must work out what this unified system of beliefs and commitments implies for one's own life; and one must make a serious effort to honour these implications in one's own conduct and judgements.

Some agents who disregard the central imperative are ones who simply set aside moral considerations and moral language altogether – and typically behave badly as a result. Let us set them aside, for they are fringe groups in the contemporary world. Much more important and much more numerous are those who take no interest in morality as such – in working out its content and living in conformity with it – but nonetheless employ moral language to influence the sentiments and conduct of others. They appeal to morality in bad faith, without a sincere willingness to work out what morality requires and thus in defiance of its central imperative. In order to advance their own ends, they falsely present themselves as friends of morality, as speaking on morality's behalf. Abusing morality in this way, they are not merely bad people, behaving badly, but unjust people, behaving unjustly.[15] Such people are the analogue to judges or police officers who use the law to advance their own ends: a judge who decides in the name of the people, but on the basis of what enriches himself or what advances his sectarian ideology; a police officer who falsely arrests a young woman for his own entertainment or to prevent her from expressing political views he dislikes. Such actions are not the worst violations of the law. And yet, committed under colour of law, they are in one sense the most pernicious. Similarly, acting *under colour of morality* – misrepresenting oneself as motivated by a sincere commitment to morality in order to advance one's own ends – is not the worst violation of morality, but one that strikes at its very heart. Acting under colour of Islam or under colour of Christianity are instances of this – acts of supreme defiance where the agent puts himself in the place of God. The content of religion becomes whatever the agent declares it to be. The agent is not seeking the guidance of his religion but merely uses its moral language to colour the world as suits his separate purposes.

Imagine a society whose public culture is dominated by people of this sort – trafficking heavily in moral language without any respect for morality's central imperative. In such a culture we get endless repetitions of specific moral assertions ('The United States is the great Satan' or 'To withdraw our troops now would be a cowardly capitulation to terrorism'), and endless repetitions of unexamined generalities ('We must fight the infidels wherever they dishonour what is sacred' or 'We must defend freedom against the enemies of freedom'). Such moral appeals are made on all sides. But since they remain unexplicated and unjustified, there is no substantive moral debate. The political effect of all the moral language thrown around depends then on media access and acting skills. To have an impact, one must manage to intone, on prime-time TV, the relevant sentences with an honest face and a good show of profound conviction, conveying to the audience that one cares deeply about moral considerations and is sincerely convinced that the policy one is defending is the moral policy. And to remain unencumbered with regard to other policies one might want to defend simultaneously or in the future, one must do all this without assuming any further, possibly inconvenient substantive moral commitments.

This imagined society is not so far from what we find in the real world today. We find it in much of the Arab world. And we find it in the U.K. and in the U.S.

as well. The model also resembles current international society pretty closely. This is not to deny that there is a great deal of serious moral discourse going on, not merely in universities, but also within other (for instance religious) associations and in political fora such as in some committees of the United Nations and of various national legislatures. But the public visibility and impact of such serious moral discourse is small and diminishing, and the political fora in which it takes place are therefore increasingly shunned and marginalized. This may not seem like a calamity comparable to terrorism. And yet, such moral corruption is, in one sense, a more profound danger.

When moral language degenerates into just one more tool in the competitive struggle for advantage, then this struggle becomes ultimately unconstrained. To be sure, the power of political leaders and factions is limited by the power of other leaders and factions, and is restricted also by procedural checks and balances. But all these constraints are soft and flexible, themselves subject to indefinite modification through the use of political power. In so far as political players understand that their competitive struggle for power is always also a struggle over the rules governing this competition, they tend to be ruthless in this competition because there is no other long-term protection of their interests and values. This problem is well explicated in Rawls's discussion of a *modus vivendi*. Rawls's preferred alternative model is that of an overlapping consensus focused on firm, widely recognized social rules to which all major groups, perhaps for diverse reasons, have a principled moral commitment.[16] But even without such an overlapping consensus, there can at least be that trust among adversaries which comes from recognizing one another as genuinely moral agents who are at least committed to *their own* morality. The moral importance of avoiding a world without trust and without shared social rules gives us further moral reasons to honour morality's central imperative in our applications of moral language to both domestic and international issues.

VII

We can now appreciate the promised second reason for considering it important – even if we have not the slightest doubt – to articulate the grounds of our firm belief that these five terrorist attacks were heinous acts; to articulate our understanding of why these attacks are wrong, or what makes them wrong, as I have tried to do earlier. We must do this to honour morality's central imperative, which requires us to elaborate and extend our moral commitments to the point where they impose clear constraints on our own conduct. This is crucial for being moral persons, rather than persons acting under colour of morality. And it is crucial also for being properly recognized as moral persons, as persons with genuine moral commitments that we are willing to discuss and are determined to live up to.

There is considerable scepticism outside the affluent West about the moral fervour with which we have condemned the terrorists and prosecuted our war against them. Occasionally, such scepticism comes with sympathy for and even celebration of the terrorists. Far more frequently, however, the sceptics share our conviction that those terrorist attacks were very wrong. Their scepticism involves the judgment or suspicion that we are moralizing in bad faith, that we are interested in morality when this serves to win us support or sympathy or at least acquiescence, but that we have no interest in the moral assessment or adjustment of our own conduct and policies.

In my view, these sceptics are essentially correct. But before presenting some evidence to support their case, I should state clearly two points that I am not making and in fact strongly reject. I reject the view that wrongful conduct by our governments renders the terrorist attacks any less unjustifiable. My moral condemnation of such attacks is based on the harms they inflict on innocent civilians, who do not become permissible targets for lethal attack by wrongful policies of – even their own – governments. I also do not claim that it is impermissible for those who are doing wrong to fight the wrongs done by others. My main point in discussing our governments' conduct and policies is to show that our politicians take momentous action, in our name, without any effort to apply the morality they profess in our name to decisions that cry out for moral justification. That they can get by, comfortably, without any such effort is our fault as citizens.

Let me illustrate the point by recalling some well-known highlights of the 'global war on terror' (GWOT) as orchestrated by the U.S. and U.K. governments. Central to the GWOT as they conceive it is the doctrine that the terrorist danger justifies pervasive secrecy and disinformation towards the media and the general public, and even towards the legislature. The suggestion was, and still is, that the success of the war effort requires that most of this effort be exempt from public scrutiny and that even the scope of this exemption should not be disclosed.[17] A well-known and typical example is U.K. Attorney General Lord Peter Goldsmith threatening British media with criminal prosecution for reporting that President Bush had proposed to bomb the Al Jazeera television station in peaceful Qatar.[18]

An early episode in the GWOT was the overthrow of the Taliban regime in Afghanistan. In this initiative, our governments chose to rely heavily on the United Islamic Front for the Salvation of Afghanistan. This 'Northern Alliance' had been losing the civil war against the Taliban, but massive Western air support, funding, and U.S. teams of special forces turned the situation around in its favour. Thousands of Taliban fighters who had laid down their arms in exchange for a promise of safe passage to their home villages in an orderly surrender negotiated with the participation of U.S. military personnel, were instead crammed into metal shipping containers without air or water for several days. Between 960 and 3,000 of them died in agony from heat, thirst, and lack of oxygen. Some of the survivors were shot dead and all bodies buried in a huge mass grave.[19] The commander of the Northern Alliance forces, Abdul Rashid Dostum, later used murder and torture to intimidate witnesses to the atrocity.[20] While insisting on a full investigation of the mass graves at Srebrenica, Western governments blocked any official inquiry into the mass grave at Dasht-e Leili; and the mass murder of surrendering Taliban has now been largely forgotten in most parts of the world. Implicated also in systematic and horrific crimes against women and girls,[21] Dostum currently serves as Chief of Staff to Hamid Karzai, Commander-in-Chief of the Afghan Armed Forces.[22]

The U.S. and U.K. governments defended their 2003 invasion of Iraq, once again, as a necessary component of the GWOT. But the evidence for their claims that Saddam Hussein had weapons of mass destruction and ties to al-Qaeda was flimsy, and these claims are now known to have been false and preparations for the invasion are known to have been made well before 9/11. Hussein's regime had been responsible for horrendous human rights violations, including massive chemical weapons attacks against Iraqi and Iranian civilians. But these were most severe in the 1980s when Iraq, with Western encouragement and chemicals delivered by Western states, fought a nine-year war against Iran. At that time, our governments were on friendly terms with Saddam Hussein – though the U.S., eager to prolong the war, sold weapons and intelligence to Iran as well (the 'Iran-Contra Affair').

The U.S. and U.K. quickly took over the prisons of the regimes they had defeated and filled them with thousands of people they had taken captive in their war on terror. Labelled 'unprivileged combatants', 'unlawful enemy combatants' or 'security detainees', these people have been routinely humiliated and degraded at will by coalition personnel: stripped naked, forced to masturbate and to simulate sex acts, abused with dogs, shackled in excruciating positions, kicked and burned, beaten with electric cables, hooded and deprived of human contact for months, and tortured with electric shocks, drugs, sleep deprivation, induced hypothermia and 'water boarding' (simulated drowning).[23]

Such abuse is partly explained by the large and increasing number of 'moral waivers' that allow people with serious criminal records to join the U.S. armed forces.[24] A second contributing factor is that civilian contractors, who have played a major role in the abuse of civilians, can act with near total impunity.[25] A third important factor is that officers are virtually never prosecuted and punished, presumably to maintain the fiction that the abuse is coincidental and not related to any policies.[26] Accounts from former prison personnel make clear that, on the contrary, much of the abuse was systematic and deliberate, encouraged and condoned up the chain of command,[27] with the objective of breaking resistance to the occupation trumping any concern for protecting the innocent. This is confirmed by former U.S. Army interrogator Tony Lagouranis who, in his *Hardball* interview with Chris Matthews, estimated that 90 per cent of the people he interrogated were wholly innocent – not merely in the technical sense of innocent until proven guilty, but really innocent of any armed resistance to the occupation of Iraq or any serious crime that might conceivably justify their horrendous treatment.[28] Many were arrested for having once visited Afghanistan, for having had some association to an Islamic charity with suspected links to terrorists or their sympathizers, or even to help extract information from an incarcerated relative.

There are many facilities outside of Afghanistan and Iraq where perceived enemies of the West are held indefinitely. Best known among these is the U.S.-operated compound at Guantánamo Bay, Cuba. United Nations officials have been trying to inspect this prison since it opened in 2002, but have declined the option to visit without full access and the opportunity to conduct private interviews with detainees.[29] The U.S. Defense Department has been compelled by the judiciary to issue a list of the people it has been holding at Guantánamo Bay, and several people released from there have provided graphic accounts of how prisoners are treated.[30]

The U.S. government asserts that the prisoners it holds at Guantánamo Bay are not entitled to Geneva Convention protections[31] and intends to try them by military commissions. But the U.S. Supreme Court overruled the government on both counts, emphasizing the severe flaws of the constituted military commissions:

> The accused and his civilian counsel may be excluded from, and precluded from ever learning what evidence was presented during any part of the proceeding that either the Appointing Authority or the presiding officer decides to 'close'. . . [N]ot only is testimonial hearsay and evidence obtained through coercion fully admissible, but neither live testimony nor witnesses' written statements need be sworn.[32]

The Court concluded that trial by military commission, as envisioned, violates both the Geneva Conventions and the U.S. *Uniform Code of Military Justice*, whose article 36(b) requires that all pre-trial, trial and post-trial procedures must be uniform with those applied to crimes allegedly committed by U.S. military personnel.[33] The Court also found that trial by military commission as contemplated violates Article 3, common to all four Geneva Conventions, which requires that any punishments inflicted must be pursuant to a 'judgment pronounced by a regularly constituted court affording all the judicial guarantees which are recognized as indispensable by civilized peoples'.[34] In response to the Court's decision, the U.S. Congress has since passed the Military Commissions Act attempting to reinstate trial by military commission in a modified form.[35] Whether this legislation will survive impending Supreme Court scrutiny remains to be seen.[36]

Coalition forces have also maintained secret detention facilities around the world, reportedly in Jordan, Pakistan, Qatar, Thailand, Uzbekistan, various locations in Eastern Europe, and on the British island of Diego Garcia.[37] At these 'black sites' our governments are imprisoning so-called ghost detainees – unknown numbers of unknown persons for unknown reasons under unknown conditions. Our governments are telling us that nothing untoward is going on at such sites. But it would be irrational and irresponsible to trust that basic human rights are being respected in locations no one else has access to when such rights are not being respected in locations from which a fair amount of information is leaking out. Common sense suggests that, once persons have been caught in the secret prison system, their captors are reluctant to release them even when they become convinced of their innocence. Wholly unaccountable for their actions, these captors much prefer innocent persons to remain missing indefinitely over their resurfacing with information about conditions in the secret facilities and possibly with knowledge that might be used to identify particular torturers, interrogators, or collaborating doctors.

The U.K. is of course the main 'partner country' in this system of secret detention and torturous interrogation whose victims have no rights of any sort. U.K. officials sit with their U.S. counterparts on the Joint Detention Review Board in Iraq, U.K. officials have participated in coercive interrogations, and U.K. officials have asserted that human rights law does not bind U.K. forces in Iraq.[38] The U.S. government relied, in the first few years of the GWOT, on a 50-page memorandum signed by Assistant Attorney General Jay S. Bybee. This memorandum comments at length on the legal obligations of U.S. military personnel under the *International Covenant on Civil and Political Rights* and the *Convention Against Torture and Other Cruel, Inhuman, or Degrading Treatment or Punishment* – both ratified by the U.S. – and under implementing national legislation. Appealing to a Reagan administration precedent, Bybee reiterates nine times that the word 'torture' covers only the 'most extreme' forms of physical and mental harm which result in 'excruciating and agonizing' pain, such as 'the needle under the fingernail, the application of electric shock to the genital area, the piercing of eyeballs'[39]:

> Where the pain is physical, it must be of an intensity akin to that which accompanies serious physical injury such as death or organ failure. Severe mental pain requires suffering not just at the moment of infliction, but it also requires lasting psychological harm, such as seen in mental disorders like posttraumatic stress disorder ... Because the acts inflicting torture are extreme, there is [a] significant range of acts that though they might constitute cruel, inhuman, or degrading treatment or punishment fail to rise to the level of torture.[40]

The Bybee memo also asserts that, even when torture in this narrow sense is used, 'necessity or self-defense could provide justifications that would eliminate any criminal liability' and that judicial review of 'interrogations undertaken pursuant to the President's Commander-in-Chief powers may be unconstitutional'.[41] In plain language: most extreme forms of punishment are not extreme enough to count as torture. Even the infliction of clear-cut torture is justifiable by appeal to necessity or self-defence. And even if clear-cut torture is not so justifiable, the courts have no power to stop it when it is ordered by the president.

The Bybee memo was superseded by a memo signed by Acting U.S. Assistant Attorney General Daniel Levin on 30 December 2004, stating that 'we have reviewed this Office's prior opinions addressing issues involving treatment of detainees and do not believe that any of their conclusions would be different under the standards set forth in this memorandum'.[42] The main change from the Bybee memo is that the second and third lines of defence are now declared superfluous: because the president has directed U.S. personnel not to engage in torture, it is unnecessary to consider whether torture is justifiable and whether the courts have the authority to stop torture ordered by the president. The memo reiterates at great length that only the most extreme forms of inhuman and degrading treatment should count as torture. It thereby follows the Bybee memo in ignoring that what the U.S. has signed and ratified is a convention against torture *and other cruel, inhuman, or degrading treatment or punishment,* and in ignoring as well that the U.S. has signed and ratified the Geneva Conventions whose common Article 3 prohibits not only torture but also 'cruel treatment' and 'outrages upon personal dignity, in particular humiliating and degrading treatment'.[43] This article is common to all four Geneva Conventions, and its application can therefore not be refuted by claiming that detainees fail to qualify as prisoners of war.[44]

Among the treatments coalition partners use and officially classify as acceptable are:

Long Time Standing: This technique is described as among the most effective. Prisoners are forced to stand, handcuffed and with their feet shackled to an eye bolt in the floor for more than 40 hours. Exhaustion and sleep deprivation are effective in yielding confessions.

The Cold Cell: The prisoner is left to stand naked in a cell kept near 50 degrees F. Throughout the time in the cell the prisoner is doused with cold water.

Water Boarding: The prisoner is bound to an inclined board, feet raised and head slightly below the feet. Cellophane is wrapped over the prisoner's face and water is poured over him. Unavoidably, the gag reflex kicks in and a terrifying fear of drowning leads to almost instant pleas to bring the treatment to a halt.[45]

Another instrument in our war on terror is 'extraordinary rendition' in which persons are transferred, without any legal process, to regimes known to practice even more severe forms of torture. According to former CIA officer Robert Baer, the CIA captures individuals it suspects of ties to terrorism and puts them on a plane. 'The ultimate destination of these flights are places that, you know, are involved in torture . . . If you send a prisoner to Jordan, you get a better interrogation. If you send a prisoner, for instance, to Egypt, you will probably never see him again, the same way with Syria'.[46] Maher Arar, software engineer and Canadian citizen, was fortunate enough to be seen again. Coming from Tunis and headed for Montreal, he was detained during a stop-over at John F. Kennedy Airport and delivered to

Syria where he was held in solitary confinement and brutally tortured on a regular basis. He was released more than a year after his arrest, completely cleared of any terrorism charges by a Canadian commission of inquiry.[47] The U.S. ambassador to Canada, Paul Cellucci, commented that 'the U.S. government will continue to deport Canadian citizens to third countries if they pose a risk to American national security'.[48] Khaled el-Masri, a German citizen abducted by the CIA while vacationing in Macedonia, also resurfaced after five months of detention in Afghanistan where he was shackled, beaten, and injected with drugs. He was released somewhere in Albania when his captors realized that his abduction was a case of mistaken identity.[49]

With regard to ghost detainees and extraordinary renditions, typically no information is provided to family members of missing persons, to the general public, or even to U.S. or U.K. legislators about who is being detained, where, for how long, and under what conditions. People are being disappeared in the way people used to be disappeared in Latin America under the military dictatorships of the 1970s and 1980s. And even when the detention of specific persons by U.S. or U.K. personnel is known to their relatives and friends, the latter are often unable to obtain further information. They do not know whether their loved ones are alive or dead and, if alive, where they are being held, by whom, and how they are being treated. The pictures from coalition-run prisons such friends and relatives can see in the mass media – much more frequently abroad than in our own countries – cannot contribute to their peace of mind. And these pictures cast a terrible light on our words, such as these spoken on the occasion of the U.N. International Day in Support of Victims of Torture: 'The victims often feel forgotten, but we will not forget them. America supports accountability and treatment centres for torture victims . . . We stand with the victims to seek their healing and recovery, and urge all nations to join us in these efforts to restore the dignity of every person affected by torture'.[50]

As with regard to the terrorist attacks, we should ask whether all this barbarity, much of it inflicted on innocents, is really necessary to protect our societies from terrorist attacks. Would we be worse protected and, if so, by how much, if we did not transfer suspects to notorious torture countries? Would we be worse protected and, if so, by how much, if we allowed judicial oversight involving at the very least a public record of who has been detained as well as an opportunity for prisoners to communicate with independent doctors and lawyers? Reflection on these questions suggests that the barbarity of our response to the terrorist attacks may well be counter-productive by inciting more terrorism than it deters.[51]

VIII

What is remarkable is that our governments show so little interest in justifying, in moral terms, the great harms they are clearly inflicting on innocent persons. Of course, they traffic heavily in moral and specifically religious rhetoric, on both sides of the Atlantic. But is there any evidence that those who design and implement coalition methods in the global war on terror have thought carefully about their moral justifiability? Such serious reflection is what they would engage in if they were genuinely concerned that their conduct – or let me say, *our* conduct, for they are acting as our elected representatives in our names – be morally justifiable. And had they engaged in such serious moral reflection and convinced themselves that these methods are indeed morally justifiable under existing conditions, would they not want this justification to be publicly known so that we all can appreciate that what is being done in our names is, appearances notwithstanding, really morally justifiable?

The conduct of our politicians is better explained by their desire to act under colour of morality. This requires no more than the bald assertion that we are doing the right thing, presented in appealing tones of sincerity and commitment. What is most astonishing here again is that our politicians get away with this so easily. This is astonishing not merely in the GWOT case here under discussion, but in U.S. and U.K. foreign policy more generally.

In the 1990s, the United Nations maintained a stringent regime of economic sanctions against Iraq. These sanctions greatly reduced access to foodstuffs and medicines for poor Iraqis and further degraded Iraq's heavily damaged infrastructure, preventing the provision of electricity, water and sanitation with devastating effects on the incidence of contagious diseases. Madeleine Albright, then U.S. ambassador to the U.N., defended the sanctions regime on *60 Minutes*:

> *Lesley Stahl*: We have heard that a half a million children have died. I mean, that's more children than died in Hiroshima . . . Is the price worth it?
> *Albright*: I think this is a very hard choice, but the price – we think the price is worth it . . . It is a moral question, but the moral question is even a larger one. Don't we owe to the American people and to the American military and to the other countries in the region that this man [Saddam Hussein] not be a threat?
> *Stahl*: Even with the starvation?
> *Albright*: I think, Lesley, it is hard for me to say this because I am a humane person, but my first responsibility is to make sure that United States forces do not have to go and re-fight the Gulf War.[52]

The interviewer left it at that, and the remarks drew scant media attention in the U.S. and Europe and were not noted in Albright's Senate confirmation hearings for Secretary of State that same year. The remarks were much reported and discussed in the Arab world, however, and apparently motivated at least one of the terrorists involved in the attacks described above.[53] In her biography, Albright expresses deep regret about her remarks: 'Nothing matters more than the lives of innocent people. I had fallen into a trap and said something that I simply did not mean'.[54]

But if nothing matters more than the lives of innocent people, then why were these very severe sanctions continued without regard to their effects on Iraqi civilians? Despite considerable variation in the estimates, it was clear from the start that the sanctions' health impact on Iraqi civilians would be devastating.[55] The most careful studies I have found are Richard Garfield's, who estimates that mortality among children under 5 rose from about 40–45 per 1,000 in 1990 to about 125 per 1,000 during 1994–99 and stresses that many of the surviving children sustained lasting damage to their health.[56] Garfield estimates excess deaths among children under 5 at around 3,000 per month for the 1991–2002 period, with a confidence interval of 343,900 to 525,400 deaths for this entire period.[57]

In 1998, Denis Halliday, co-ordinator of humanitarian relief to Iraq and Assistant Secretary-General of the United Nations, resigned after thirty-four years with the U.N. Explaining his resignation, he wrote: 'I am resigning, because the policy of economic sanctions is totally bankrupt. We are in the process of destroying an entire society. It is as simple and terrifying as that . . . Five thousand children are dying every month . . . I don't want to administer a programme that results in figures like these'. [58] He added in an interview: 'I had been instructed to implement a policy that satisfies the definition of genocide: a deliberate policy that has effectively killed well over a million individuals, children and adults. We all know that the regime, Saddam Hussein, is not paying the price for economic sanctions; on the contrary, he has been strengthened by them. It is the little people who are losing their children or their parents for lack of untreated water. What is clear is that the Security Council is now out of control, for its actions here undermine its own Charter, and the Declaration of Human Rights and the Geneva Convention. History will slaughter those responsible'.[59] In 2000, Halliday's successor, Hans von Sponeck, also resigned, after thirty-two years of U.N. service, while harshly criticizing the sanctions regime as well as the dishonesty of the relevant officials in the Blair and Clinton governments.[60] Jutta Burghardt, director of the U.N. World Food program in Iraq, also resigned for the same reasons.[61]

Nothing matters more than the lives of innocent people. Most of us would agree with Albright on this point. Most of us would also agree that her, and our, first responsibility is to our own country. And most of us endorse these two commitments in such a shallow way that, like Albright, we do not even notice the tension. Then, when a choice must be made between promoting the interests of our country – our government, citizens or corporations – and those of innocent people abroad, we routinely prioritize the former without so much as examining the cost that our choices will impose on the lives of the innocent.

In this spirit, the U.S. and U.K. governments have stated that they do not track civilian deaths in the aftermath of their invasions and occupations of Afghanistan and Iraq.[62] And in the same spirit our governments press their favoured economic rules and policies upon the rest of the world. Structural adjustment programmes required by the IMF have deprived millions of African children of elementary schooling.[63] Protectionist trade barriers are unfairly depriving poor populations of a decent livelihood.[64] Loans and arms sales are keeping brutal and corrupt rulers in power in developing countries, and lax banking laws facilitate massive embezzle-ment by these countries' public officials.[65] Intellectual property rights mandated by the WTO cut off hundreds of millions of poor patients worldwide from cheap generic medicines.[66] In these cases and many more, our politicians take momentous action, in our name, without any effort to apply the morality they profess in our name to decisions that cry out for moral justification. Their bald assurances that their conduct is alright, morally, are accepted by the vast majority of citizens who are similarly inclined to avoid further thought about how our 'first responsibility' to benefit our own might be constrained by the interests of innocent people abroad. It appears that, outside a few insulated fora, the distinction between what is morally right and what is believed and proclaimed to be so has all but collapsed. This is a disastrous flaw in our public culture – one that, quite apart from its horrific effects, fundamentally undermines our ambition to be a civilization that strives for moral decency.

Notes

* This lecture was given in Oxford on 24 February 2006. I am grateful for written com-ments and suggestions I received from Kieran Donaghue, Jeff McMahan, Chris Miller, Rekha Nath, Matt Peterson, Michael Ravvin, Ling Tong, Leif Wenar and Andrew Williams.

1 See Erica Frank, 'Funding the public health response to terrorism', *British Medical Jour-nal* 331 (2005), 526–7, arguing that recent shifts of public funds into counter-terrorist efforts have a large negative impact on morbidity and mortality from natural disasters and common medical conditions, and Nick A. Wilson and George Thomson, 'Deaths from International Terrorism Compared With Road Crash Deaths in OECD Countries', *Injury Prevention* 11 (2005), 332–3.

2 The Global Fund to Fight AIDS, Tuberculosis and Malaria, 'Current Grant Com-mitments and Disbursements', 31 January 2008, available at www.theglobalfund.org/en/funds_raised/commitments.

3 Amy Belasco, *The Cost of Iraq, Afghanistan, and Other Global War on Terror Operations Since 9/11*, Congressional Research Service Report for Congress (Washington, DC: Library of Congress, 2006), available at www.fas.org/sgp/crs/natsec/RL33110.pdf.

4 This is not a pitch for censorship, of course, but for responsible and intelligent jour-nalism and reporting.

5 A considerable diversity of Western responses should, however, be noted. See Dirk Haubrich, 'Civil Liberties in Emergencies', in *Governments of the World: A Global Guide to Citizens' Rights and Responsibilities*, ed. C. Neal Tate, vol. 1 (Farmington Hills, MI: Macmillan Reference, 2006), 199–205.

6 John Rawls, *A Theory of Justice* (Cambridge, MA: Harvard University Press, 1999), §9.

7 Later, Voinarovski declares with respect to the planned assassination of Admiral Dubasov, the Governor-General of Moscow, that 'if Dubasov is accompanied by his wife, I shall not throw the bomb' (Albert Camus, *The Rebel: An Essay on Man in Revolt*, tr. Anthony

Bower (New York: Vintage, 1956), 140; Richard B. Spence, *Boris Savinkov: Renegade on the Left* (Boulder, CO: East European Monographs, 1991), 45ff.). Savinkov similarly opposes an attempt to kill Dubasov on the St. Petersburg–Moscow Express on the ground that 'if there were the least mistake, the explosion could take place in the carriage and kill strangers' (*The Rebel*, 140). Later, when escaping from a Czarist prison, the same Savinkov reportedly 'decides to shoot any officers who might attempt to prevent his flight, but to kill himself rather than turn his revolver on an ordinary soldier' (ibid.).

8 Thomas Pogge, 'Historical Wrongs: The Other Two Domains', *Justice in Time: Responding to Historical Injustice*, ed. Lukas Meyer (Baden-Baden, Germany: Nomos, 2004).

9 Interview with Osama bin Laden, *Daily Ummat* (Karachi), 28 September 2001; frequently reprinted, e.g. at www.robert-fisk.com/usama_interview_ummat.htm.

10 Qur'an 5:32.

11 In the formulation of Sir William Blackstone: *Commentaries on the Laws of England*, facsimile of 1st edn. 1765–69 (Chicago: University of Chicago Press, 1979), Book IV, 352.

12 On 22 September 2001, George W. Bush waived the so-called Pressler Amendment, which had blocked most military and economic aid to Pakistan on account of this country's nuclear weapons programme. See Robert S. Norris, William M. Arkin, Hans M. Kristensen and Joshua Handler, 'Pakistan's Nuclear Forces, 2001', *Bulletin of the Atomic Scientists* 58.1 (January 2002), www.accessmylibrary.com/coms2/summary_0286-24952646_ITM.

13 It might be objected that the possibility of error might not be a serious possibility in some cases. In the case of Moses, perhaps, when God appeared to him, or in the cases of Jesus or Mohammed or even their immediate followers or disciples. It is well to recall then that Mohammed, the final prophet according to Islamic teaching, lived some fourteen hundred years ago. So the possibility of errors in understanding the Divine will as revealed by Muhammad is certainly a real possibility in our time, as the diversity of schools and interpretations amply confirms. Exempting oneself from this possibility would be to claim the status of prophet for oneself or for some contemporary from whom one is receiving direct instruction.

14 See, for example, Khaled Abou El Fadl, 'Islam and the Theology of Power', *Middle East Report* 221 (2001), 28–33.

15 Thomas Pogge, 'Justice', in *Encyclopedia of Philosophy*, ed. Donald M. Borchert, 2nd edn. (Farmington Hills, MI: Macmillan Reference, 2006).

16 John Rawls, *Political Liberalism*, 2nd edn. (New York: Columbia University Press, 2005), lecture 4.

17 In 2005, the FBI issued 47,211 national security letter (NSL) requests requiring businesses to turn over private data about their customers. The Justice Department's public report stated that the FBI issued 9,254 NSL requests in calendar year 2005. 'The number of NSL requests we identified significantly exceeds the number reported in the Department's first public annual report on NSL usage, issued in April 2006, because the Department was not required to include all NSL requests in that report' ('A Review of the Federal Bureau of Investigation's Use of National Security Letters', Department of Justice Office of the Inspector General, March 2007, p. xix, www.usdoj.gov/oig/

special/s0703b/final.pdf). See also American Civil Liberties Union, *Hundreds of New Documents Reveal Expanded Military Role in Domestic Surveillance* (14 October 2007), www.aclu.org/safefree/nationalsecurityletters/32145prs20071014.html.

18 Kevin Maguire and Andy Lines, 'Exclusive: Bush Plot to Bomb His Arab Ally', *Mirror*, 22 November 2005, www.mirror.co.uk/news/tm_objectid=16397937&method= full&siteid=94762&headline=exclusive–bush-plot-to-bomb-his-arab-ally-name_page.html; and CNN, *Critique of Worldwide Media Coverage*, aired 26 November 2005, http:// transcripts.cnn.com/TRANSCRIPTS/0511/26/i_c.01.html. The U.S. had bombed Al Jazeera stations twice before: 2001 in Kabul and 2003 in Baghdad, killing one reporter.

19 See Babak Dehghanpisheh, John Barry and Roy Gutman, 'The Death Convoy of Afghanistan', *Newsweek*, 26 August 2002, www.globalpolicy.org/security/issues/ afghan/2002/0826memo.htm, reporting on the surrender at Konduz of 25 November 2001; Physicians for Human Rights, *Preliminary Assessment of Alleged Mass Gravesites in the Area of Mazar-I-Sharif, Afghanistan* (Boston and Washington: 2002), www.physi-ciansforhumanrights.org/library/documents/reports/report-massgraves-afghanistan.pdf, and the documentary film *Afghan Massacre: The Convoy of Death* (2002), directed by Jamie Doran, www.informationclearinghouse.info/article3267.htm.

20 Valerie Reitman, 'U.N. Probes Claims of Violence Against Afghan Witnesses: Reports of Torture and Killings are Tied to Case of Dead Taliban Fighters', *Los Angeles Times*, 15 November 2002, A13. Rory McCarthy, 'U.S. Afghan Ally "tortured witnesses to his war crimes"', *Guardian*, 18 November 2002, www.guardian.co.uk/international/ story/0,3604,842082,00.html.

21 David Filipov, 'Warlord's Men Commit Rape in Revenge Against Taliban', *Boston Globe*, 24 February 2002, A1. The rapes targeted the Pashtun community from which the Taliban had derived much of their political support.

22 Andrew North, 'Dostum Gets Afghan Military Role', *BBC News*, 2 March 2005, avail-able at www.news.bbc.co.uk/2/hi/south_asia/4308683.stm. On the evolution of the situation in Afghanistan generally, see reports by Amnesty International (www. amnestyusa.org/countries/afghanistan/reports.do) and Human Rights Watch, *Fatally Flawed: Cluster Bombs and Their Use by the United States in Afghanistan* (2002), www.hrw.org/reports/2002/us-afghanistan; *'Killing You is a Very Easy Thing for Us': Human Rights Abuses in Southeast Afghanistan* (July 2003), www.hrw.org/reports/ 2003/afghanistan0703; *'Enduring Freedom': Abuses by U.S. Forces in Afghanistan* (March 2004), www.hrw.org/reports/2004/afghanistan0304; *Afghanistan: Killing and Torture by U.S. Predate Abu Ghraib* (20 May 2005), www.hrw.org/english/docs/ 2005/05/20/afghan10992.htm. See also Uranium Medical Research Center, *UMRC's Preliminary Findings from Afghanistan and Operation Enduring Freedom* (April 2003), www.umrc.net/os/downloads/AfghanistanOEF.pdf, foreseeing 'a potential public health disaster for Afghanistan' from massive coalition use of non-depleted uranium in bombs and missiles.

23 Coalition personnel took hundreds of photographs and video clips of the abuses they inflicted on their captives; the most horrific ones were never published, but shown at closed hearings to members of the U.S. Congress. See Marian Wilkinson, 'Photos

Show Dead Iraqis, Torture and Rape', *Age*, 14 May 2004, www.theage.com.au/articles/2004/05/13/1084289818093.html; Neil Mackay, 'Iraq's Child Prisoners', *Sunday Herald* (Glasgow), 1 August 2004, www.globalpolicy.org/security/issues/iraq/attack/law/2004/0801childprison.htm, reporting over 100 children in coalition custody, subjected to rape and torture; Deborah Pearlstein and Priti Patel, *Behind the Wire* (New York: Human Rights First, 2005), www.humanrightsfirst.org/us_law/PDF/behind-the-wire-033005.pdf; Human Rights Watch, *Leadership Failure: Firsthand Accounts of Torture of Iraqi Detainees by the U.S. Army's 82nd Airborne Division* (September 2005), www.hrw.org/reports/2005/us0905 and 'U.S. Operated Secret "Dark Prison" in Kabul', *Human Rights News*, 19 December 2005, www.hrw.org/english/docs/2005/12/19/afghan12319.htm; Amnesty International, *United Kingdom Human Rights: A Broken Promise* (23 February 2006), http://web.amnesty.org/library/Index/ENGEUR450042006, and *Beyond Abu Ghraib: Detention and Torture in Iraq* (6 March 2006), www.web.amnesty.org/library/index/engmde140012006; Eric Schmitt and Carolyn Marshall, 'Task Force 6–26: Inside Camp Nama. In Secret Unit's "black room", a Grim Portrait of U.S. Abuse', *New York Times*, 19 March 2006, A1, available at http://select.nytimes.com/gst/abstract.html?res=F30617FC34550C7A8DDDAA0894DE404482. In addition to such widespread re-creational torture, there were more official torture sessions which, as recently emerged, were videotaped by the CIA. This videotaping was kept secret from the September 11 Commission, whose chairmen now feel betrayed by the CIA (Mark Mazzetti: '9/11 Panel Study Finds That C.I.A. Withheld Tapes', *New York Times*, 22 December 2007, available at www.nytimes.com/2007/12/22/washington/22intel.html). At least a few hundred hours of these video recordings were destroyed in 2005 despite various court orders requiring such evidence to be preserved (Matt Apuzzo, 'Judge wants details on destroyed CIA videotapes', *Miami Herald*, 24 January 2008, available at www.miamiherald.com/guantanamo/story/392496.html).

24 Rick Maze, 'Rise in Moral Waivers Troubles Lawmaker', *Navy Times*, 20 February 2007, available at www.navytimes.com/news/2007/02/apWaivedRecruits070213/. In 2006, 20 per cent of army recruits, over 50 per cent of marine recruits, 18 per cent of navy recruits, and 8 per cent of air force recruits needed moral waivers to enlist (Lolita C. Baldor, 'Military grants more waivers to recruits', *ABC News*, 21 April 2008, http://abcnews.go.com/Politics/wireStory?id=4695168).

25 Tens of thousands of private security contractors have enjoyed official immunity from prosecution in Iraqi courts (under Order 17, passed by the U.S.-led Coalition Provisional Authority in 2004) and de facto immunity in U.S. courts. Such contractors working for Blackwater have killed dozens of unarmed and non-threatening civilians, and contractors employed by Titan and CACI were prominently involved in the Abu Ghraib abuses, including the rape of a minor in the presence of U.S. military personnel. See Human Rights First, *Private Security Contractors at War: Ending the Culture of Impunity* (2008), at www.humanrightsfirst.info/pdf/08115-usls-psc-final.pdf. The U.S. Congress finally curtailed the de facto immunity of contractors in October 2007. The Iraqi government moved a few weeks later to end their official immunity. See the Human Rights Watch briefing at www.hrw.org/english/docs/2004/05/05/iraq8547_txt.htm.

26 The highest-ranking officer convicted was an Army Captain found guilty of kicking detainees and of staging a mock execution. He was sentenced to 45 days in jail. See Eric Schmitt, 'Iraq Abuse Trial Is Again Limited to Lower Ranks', *New York Times*, 23 March 2006, available at www.nytimes.com/2006/03/23/politics/23abuse.html. See also the chapter on investigative failures in *By the Numbers: Findings of the Detainee Abuse and Accountability Project*, at www.hrw.org/reports/2006/ct0406/.

27 *Leadership Failure* (note 23) and *'No Blood, No Foul': Soldiers' Accounts of Detainee Abuse in Iraq* (July 2006), available at www.hrw.org/reports/2006/us0706. See also Adam Zagorin, 'Pattern of Abuse', *Time*, 23 September 2005, available at www.time.com/time/nation/article/0,8599,1108972,00.htm, and especially Jameel Jaffer and Amrit Singh, *Administration of Torture: A Documentary Record from Washington to Abu Ghraib and Beyond* (New York: Columbia University Press 2007).

28 MSNBC, *Hardball: Tactics of Interrogation*, aired 16 January 2006, available at www.msnbc.msn.com/id/10895199. See also the *El Mundo* interview with former army interrogator Damien Corsetti, available in English at www.informationclearinghouse.info/article18901.htm.

29 United Nations, *Human Rights Experts Issue Joint Report on Situation of Detainees in Guantanamo Bay*, press release, 16 February 2006, available at www.unhchr.ch/huricane/huricane.nsf/view01/52e94fb9cbc7da10c1257117003517b3?opendocument. The ICRC has been visiting Guantánamo Bay since January 2002, accompanied by efforts of the American Red Cross to appease its more blindly patriotic U.S. donors: 'It seems a horror to many Americans that anyone – especially the Red Cross – would be interested in the welfare of the Afghan war detainees being held by the U.S. military in Guantanamo Bay, Cuba. However, it is our very own government that requested the International Committee of the Red Cross (ICRC) to visit with the detainees' (www.redcross.org/news/in/intllaw/guantanamo1.html). ICRC visits take place on the understanding that its reports remain confidential and are conveyed only to select U.S. authorities. One such report was leaked. Its contents are described in Neil A. Lewis, 'Red Cross Finds Detainee Abuse in Guantánamo', *New York Times*, 30 November 2004, A1, www.nytimes.com/2004/11/30/politics/30gitmo.html?ex=1259470800&en=825f1aa04c65241f&ei=5088&partner=rssnyt. See also William Glaberson, 'Red Cross Monitors Barred From Guantánamo', *New York Times*, 16 November 2007, available at www.nytimes.com/2007/11/16/washington/16gitmo.html.

30 Center for Constitutional Rights, *Report on Torture and Cruel, Inhuman, and Degrading Treatment of Prisoners at Guantánamo Bay, Cuba* (July 2006), www.ccrjustice.org/files/Report_ReportOnTorture.pdf, and *Detention in Afghanistan and Guantanamo Bay: Composite Statement of Shafiq Rasul, Asif Iqbal, and Rhuhel Ahmet* (26 July 2004), www.globalresearch.ca/articles/RAS408A.html; Moazzam Begg and Victoria Brittain, *Enemy Combatant: A British Muslim's Journey to Guantanamo and Back* (London: Free Press, 2006); Andy Worthington, *The Guantánamo Files: The Stories of the 774 Detainees in America's Illegal Prison* (London: Pluto Press, 2007). See also the extensive testimony of Jumah al-Dossari in Amnesty International, *U.S.A.: Days of Adverse Hardship in U.S. Detention Camps* (16 December 2005), http://web.amnesty.org/library/index/ENGAMR511072005 and 'The David Hicks Affadavit', *Sydney Morning Herald*, 10

December 2004, available at www.smh.com.au/news/World/David-Hicks-affidavit/2004/12/10/1102625527396.html.

31 See Mike Wiser, 'The Torture Question: Sidelining Geneva', *Frontline*, 18 October 2005, available at www.pbs.org/wgbh/pages/frontline/torture/themes/sideline.html.

32 *Hamdan V. Rumsfeld*, 548 U.S. ___ (2006), 50–1, majority opinion written by Justice Stevens, available at www.supremecourtus.gov/opinions/05pdf/05-184.pdf.

33 Ibid., 5, 59–62.

34 Ibid., 67.

35 *Military Commissions Act of 2006*, Public Law 109–366, 120 STAT. 2600 (17 October 2006), available at www.loc.gov/rr/frd/Military_Law/pdf/PL-109-366.pdf.

36 Robert Barnes, 'Justices to Weigh Detainee Rights', *Washington Post*, 30 June 2007, A1, available at www.washingtonpost.com/wp-dyn/content/article/2007/06/29/AR2007062900743.html?hpid=topnews.

37 Amnesty International, *United States of America/Yemen: Secret Detention in CIA 'Black Sites'* (8 November 2005), available at http://web.amnesty.org/library/Index/ENGAMR511772005. See also Mark Benjamin, 'Inside the CIA's Notorious "Black sites"', *Salon*, 14 December 2007, available at www.salon.com/news/feature/2007/12/14/bashmilah.

38 See 'United Kingdom' in Amnesty International, *Amnesty International Report 2005: The State of the World's Human Rights* (New York: Amnesty International, 2005), available at www.amnesty.org/en/report/info/POL10/001/2005.

39 See Jay S. Bybee, *Standards of Conduct for Interrogation under 18 U.S.C. sects. 2340–2340A*, Office of Legal Counsel, U.S. Department of Justice, 1 August 2002, 19–20, available at http://fl1.findlaw.com/news.findlaw.com/hdocs/docs/doj/bybee80102mem.pdf. Though signed by Bybee, the memorandum was apparently composed by John Yoo.

40 Ibid., 46.

41 Ibid.

42 See Daniel Levin, *Standards of Conduct for Interrogation under 18. U.S.C. sects. 2340–2340A*, Office of Legal Counsel, U.S. Department of Justice, 30 December 2004, available at www.usdoj.gov/olc/18usc23402340a2.htm, note 8.

43 Text of the Geneva Conventions at www.icrc.org/Web/Eng/siteeng0.nsf/html/genevaconventions.

44 John Yoo, a major contributor to the Levin memo, provided this defence on 2 May 2005 (http://webcast.berkeley.edu/event_details.php?webcastid=12285). In its Article 4, the Fourth Geneva Convention specifies that 'persons protected by the Convention are those who, at a given moment and in any manner whatsoever, find themselves, in case of a conflict or occupation, in the hands of a Party to the conflict or Occupying Power of which they are not nationals' – excepting only 'Nationals of a state which is not bound by the convention' (www.icrc.org/ihl.nsf/7c4d08d9b287a42141256739003e636b/6756482d86146898c125641e004aa3c5).

45 Brian Ross and Richard Esposito, 'CIA's Harsh Interrogation Techniques Described', *ABC News*, 18 November 2005, available at http://abcnews.go.com/WNT/Investigation/story?id=1322866&page=1. These techniques were used and refined by

the Nazi Gestapo, and water boarding was a technique commonly used by Pol Pot's Khmer Rouge in Cambodia.

46 BBC, *File on 4: Rendition*, aired 8 February 2005, available at http://news.bbc.co.uk/ nol/shared/bsp/hi/pdfs/15_02_05_renditions.pdf. Cf. Adrian Levy and Cathy Scott-Clark, 'One Huge U.S. Jail', *Guardian*, 19 March 2005, available at www. guardian. co.uk/afghanistan/story/0,1284,1440836,00.html: 'Robert Baer, a CIA case officer in the Middle East until 1997, told us how it works. "We pick up a suspect or we arrange for one of our partner countries to do it. Then the suspect is placed on civilian transport to a third country where, let's make no bones about it, they use torture. If you want a good interrogation, you send someone to Jordan. If you want them to be killed, you send them to Egypt or Syria. Either way, the U.S. cannot be blamed as it is not doing the heavy work"'.

47 See Commission of Inquiry into the Actions of Canadian Officials in Relation to Maher Arar, *Report of the Events Relating to Maher Arar: Analysis and Recommendations* (Ottawa: Public Works and Government Services Canada, 2006), available at www.ararcommission.ca/eng/AR_English.pdf. In another case, a British resident was rendered by the CIA to Morocco for 18 months of torture (including the cutting of his genitals with a razor blade). He was then flown to Guantánamo Bay, where he continues to be confined without charge or trial four years later. See Robert Verkaik, 'CIA Photos "Show U.K. Guantanamo Detainee Was Tortured"', *Independent*, 10 December 2007, available at http://news.independent.co.uk/world/americas/article3239372.ece.

48 See *CBC News*, 'U.S. Won't Change Policy on Deportations to Third Countries: Ambassador', 4 December 2003, available at www.cbc.ca/news/story/2003/12/04/ cellucci_passport031204.html.

49 See Neil A. Lewis, 'Man Mistakenly Abducted by C.I.A. Seeks Reinstatement of Suit', *New York Times*, 29 November 2006, A15, available at http://select.nytimes.com/ gst/abstract.html?res=F10C14FC3A5A0C7A8EDDA80994DE404482.

50 George W. Bush, 'President's Statement on the U.N. International Day in Support of Victims of Torture', 26 June 2004, www.whitehouse.gov/news/releases/2004/ 06/20040626-19.html.

51 A secret poll conducted in Iraq for the U.K. Ministry of Defence and later leaked to the media found that '45 per cent of Iraqis believe attacks against British and American troops are justified – rising to 65 per cent in the British-controlled Maysan province; 82 per cent are "strongly opposed" to the presence of coalition troops; less than 1 per cent of the population believes coalition forces are responsible for any improvement in security; 67 per cent of Iraqis feel less secure because of the occupation; 43 per cent of Iraqis believe conditions for peace and stability have worsened; 72 per cent do not have confidence in the multi-national forces' (Sean Rayment, 'Secret MoD Poll: Iraqis Support Attacks on British Troops', *Daily Telegraph*, 22 October 2005, available at www.telegraph.co.uk/news/worldnews/middleeast/iraq/1501319/Secret-MoD-poll-raqis-support-attacks-on-Bntrsh-froops.html.

52 CBS, *60 Minutes: Punishing Saddam*, aired 12 May 1996.

53 Mohamed Rashed Daoud al-'Owhali, who was given a life sentence for his involvement in the 1998 bombing of the U.S. embassy in Nairobi. See Phil Hirshkorn, 'Bomber's

Defense Focuses on U.S. Policy in Iraq', *CNN International*, 4 June 2001, available at http://edition.cnn.com/2001/LAW/06/04/embassy.bombings.02.

54 Madeleine Albright, *Madam Secretary: A Memoir* (New York: Miramax Books, 2003), 275.

55 See Campaign Against Sanctions on Iraq, *Starving Iraq: One Humanitarian Disaster We Can Stop* (March 1999), table 7, www.casi.org.uk/briefing/pamp_ed1.html, for a tabulation of the various estimates.

56 Richard Garfield, interview by *Columbia News*, 3 March 2000, available at www. columbia.edu/cu/news/media/00/richardGarfield/index.html.

57 See www.pbs.org/frontlineworld/stories/iraq/sanctions.html, also reporting Garfield's earlier estimate that the sanctions had killed 227,713 children in the 91 months from August 1990 until March 1998.

58 Quoted in John Pilger, 'Squeezed to Death', *Guardian*, 4 March 2000, available at www.guardian.co.uk/weekend/story/0,3605,232986,00.html.

59 Ibid.

60 See Hans von Sponeck, *A Different Kind of War: The U.N. Sanctions Regime in Iraq* (Oxford: Berghahn Books, 2006).

61 Burghardt's reasons (described in Anthony Arnove, 'Sanctions on Iraq: The "propaganda campaign"', *ZNET Daily Commentaries*, 1 April 2000, www.zmag.org/ZSustainers/ ZDaily/2000-04/01arnove.htm) are more fully articulated in her essay, 'The Human-itarian Situation in Iraq, the Humanitarian Program "Oil for Food", and Human Rights', *CSCA Web*, July 2001, available at www.nodo50.org/csca/english/petxalim-ddhh-eng. html.

62 'The Pentagon . . . has no plans to determine how many Iraqi civilians may have been killed or injured or suffered property damage as a result of U.S. military operations in Iraq' (Bradley Graham and Dan Morgan, 'U.S. Has No Plans to Count Civilian Casualties', *Washington Post*, 15 April 2003, A13, available at www.washingtonpost.com/ ac2/wp-dyn/A26305-2003Apr14. Jack Straw, U.K. Secretary of State for Foreign and Commonwealth Affairs, concurred, stating that 'in the conditions that exist in Iraq . . . it would be impossible to make a reliably accurate assessment . . . of the overall civilian casualties' and that, in any case, the U.K. has no obligation under international human-itarian law to make such an assessment (Jack Straw, written ministerial comment, 17 November 2004, *Hansard*, 426/57 (2004), available at www.cbc.ca/news/back-ground/iraq/casualties.html.) No credible unofficial figures exist for the civilian death toll in Afghanistan. Some of these deaths get a tiny notice in the papers, such as the fol-lowing: 'Coalition airstrike kills 9 in Afghanistan. A coalition airstrike hit a home in Afghanistan's Kapisa province, killing nine members of a family, Deputy Gov. Sayad Mohammad Dawood Hashimmi said. The military said two bombs hit a compound that armed militants were seen moving into after a rocket attack on a U.S. base. "These men knowingly endangered civilians by retreating into a populated area," said Army Lt. Col. David Accetta, a military spokesman' (www.usatoday.com/printedition/news/ 20070306/a_wobs06.art.htm). Unofficial tallies of civilian deaths in Iraq record at least 80,000 reported deaths since the 2003 invasion with the assumption that the true number is considerably larger (www.iraqbodycount.org). A recent survey estimates 654,965

excess civilian deaths between 18 March 2003 and June 2006 (with a 95 per cent confidence interval of 392,979 to 942,636), including 601,027 deaths from violence. See Gilbert Burnham, Riyadh Lafta, Shannon Doocy and Les Roberts, 'Mortality After the 2003 Invasion of Iraq: A Cross-sectional Cluster Sample Survey', *Lancet*, 11 October 2006, available at www.thelancet.com/webfiles/images/journals/lancet/s0140673606694919.pdf, 6. This survey was roundly rejected by the U.S. and U.K. governments, but found to be well grounded in internal communications within the U.K. government. See Owen Bennett-Jones, 'Iraqi Deaths Survey "was robust" ', BBC News, 26 March 2007, available at http://news.bbc.co.uk/2/hi/uk_news/politics/6495753.stm.

63 Joseph E. Stiglitz, *Globalization and Its Discontents* (New York: W.W. Norton, 2002).

64 Nicholas Stern, 'Making Trade Work for Poor People', speech at the National Council of Applied Economic Research, New Delhi, 28 November 2002, available at http://siteresources.worldbank.org/INTRES/Resources/stern_speech_makingtr-workforpoor_nov2002.pdf.

65 Raymond W. Baker, *Capitalism's Achilles Heel* (Hoboken, NJ: John Wiley, 2005).

66 See Carlos M. Correa, 'Implications of Bilateral Free Trade Agreements on Access to Medicines', *Bulletin of the World Health Organization* 84 (2006), 399–404, available at www.who.int/bulletin/volumes/84/5/399.pdf; Carlos M. Correa, 'Public Health and Intellectual Property Rights', *Global Social Policy* 2 (2002), 261–78, http://gsp.sagepub.com/cgi/reprint/2/3/261; and Thomas Pogge, *World Poverty and Human Rights*, 2nd edn. (Cambridge: Polity, 2008), chapter 9.

David Miller

Response to Thomas Pogge

Thomas has given us a challenging lecture and essay on terrorism, and the war against it. Like everything he writes, it is notable for its lucidity, directness and conviction. His criticisms cut deep, and they are directed even-handedly at both sides – at the terrorists who wantonly destroy lives without even asking themselves what could justify their deeds, and at Western governments and their agents who in the name of forestalling terror commit gross violations of human rights. Both parties, he argues, use moral language to vindicate their conduct, but they use it insincerely, because they make no serious attempt to explain how the principles they claim to stand for apply to that conduct. Nor can either side excuse itself by appeal to what the other is doing: the behaviour of Western governments, in the Middle East and elsewhere, is not sufficient to justify or excuse terrorist attacks like those that occurred on 9/11 or 7/7, but nor are these attacks sufficient to justify or excuse the treatment meted out to suspected terrorists by the U.S. and U.K. governments, among others – holding them indefinitely without trial, transferring them to countries known to practise torture and so forth.

So, a plague on both your houses: it is hard to disagree with the main charges that Thomas brings. But is he right to be quite so even-handed in his criticisms? Is there nothing that can be said in defence of the Western response to terrorism? I want to address this by looking first at how Thomas understands the particular form of terrorism that concerns him, and the reaction it has provoked among citizens in the countries where the attacks have occurred. Initially he seems inclined to explain this reaction in terms of the interests of the news media, who see terrorist attacks as attention-grabbing, and of leading politicians, who can use the new climate of fear to enhance their states' prestige and freedom of manoeuvre internationally. But he sees that there is more to it than this. Ordinary citizens regard these attacks as 'exceptionally heinous', and Thomas does not think they are wrong to believe this. But why are they so heinous? According to Thomas, because acts that inflict serious harm on people can only be justified by showing that they are necessary means to some greater good – and 'necessary' implies that all of the killing and wounding involved were unavoidable. But in the case of these attacks no attempt was made to spare the lives of innocent people – no warnings were given, there was no thought of timing the attacks so that fewer lives were lost. This is in contrast to some earlier terror campaigns, such as those of the IRA, where attempts were made to minimize harm to civilians.

One could sum this up by saying that, in Thomas's eyes, these terrorists have made a serious error in moral arithmetic. In principle, it may be justifiable to inflict harm on a small number of people for the greater good of a much larger number – even to kill the few to save many more lives, if there is no alternative (Thomas is neither a strict deontologist nor a strict consequentialist). But the terrorists made no attempt to carry out this calculation. If they had, they would have seen immediately that the end they sought did not justify the means. The same is true of the Western response to terrorism: Western governments have never seriously tried to show that internment and other anti-terrorism policies are necessary means to prevent and deter future acts of terror. They too have failed the moral arithmetic test.

But we may wonder whether this is the right way to understand, not terrorism generally, but the particular form of Islamic-inspired terrorism that has provoked Thomas's reflections. Perhaps what we are witnessing is not so much a serious failure of moral arithmetic as a rejection of the whole moral outlook that lies behind that arithmetic, in particular the idea of the equal value of all human lives. Perhaps, for the terrorists, the harms that they inflict on their victims simply don't count; so there is no need to justify the attacks in the way that Thomas assumes. The only question that needs to be asked, from their point of view, is whether the attacks serve or set back the general cause on whose behalf they are launched (forcing the U.S. to withdraw from the Middle East, forcing Israel to withdraw from Palestinian lands, etc.).

This interpretation assumes that the terrorists are acting on a certain understanding of Islamic doctrine, and what may be done in the name of Islam to unbelievers. Thomas argues that the terrorists have made no serious attempt to engage in religious discourse about what God commands in relation to killing and harming innocent human beings. This may be true, but in a way it misses the point. Even if the people who commit these acts have not immersed themselves in the study of the Qur'an and the interpretive writings that come after it, there are others who have and who are willing to offer advice. As is well known, different schools of Islam reach very different conclusions on these matters. But one influential strand, usually labelled Revivalist Islam, has developed a doctrine of jihad that allows the killing of innocent civilians when this is part of a defensive war against non-Muslims who are occupying or attacking Muslim lands. Among the arguments used are that the defence of Islam simply trumps all other considerations; and that the killing of non-Muslims is anyway a matter of moral indifference.

If these are indeed the ideas that the terrorists are acting upon, then there is a deeper sense in which their actions are 'exceptionally heinous'. They are not merely careless in their moral arithmetic, or negligent in discovering what their religious duty prescribes; they are acting consistently on a doctrine that denies that their victims have moral standing. In other words, they reject the idea that all human beings are endowed with human rights that protect them, morally, from certain kinds of harm. How should liberals react when they have to confront people who hold such views? Must they continue to treat them according to standard liberal principles? The answer is not obvious. One response is suggested by a passage from John Locke's *Second Treatise of Government* in which he considers the state of war:

> One may destroy a Man who makes War upon him, or has discovered an Enmity to his being, for the same Reason, that he may kill a Wolf or a Lyon; because such Men are not under the ties of the Common Law of Reason, have no other Rule, but that of Force and Violence, and so may be treated as Beasts of Prey, those dangerous and noxious Creatures, that will be sure to destroy him, whenever he falls into their Power.[1]

In other words: the key question is whether someone is subject to 'the ties of the Common Law of Reason', which for Locke meant recognizing human equality, and the universal reach of natural law and natural rights. If someone exempts himself from those ties, he is no better than a beast, and it is perfectly permissible to try to destroy him. He forfeits the protection of his human rights; our duty to respect such rights only extends to those who remain within the boundaries of 'the Common Law of Reason'.

Many liberals would dissent from this view. They would argue that human rights are inalienable, and therefore retained even by those who declare indiscriminate war on their fellow human beings. Perhaps they would allow that such rights can be infringed in immediate self-defence – you may kill the suicide bomber if that is the only way to prevent him from killing you and many others. But unlike Locke, they would not agree that once someone has 'discovered an Enmity to your being' you may take whatever measures are necessary to destroy him. It is not clear to me exactly where Thomas stands on this question. He is not an absolutist. He allows that people may legitimately be killed in the course of resisting a brutally aggressive state. Yet he is convinced that actions taken by Western states in the course of the war on terror, in prisons and detention centres, for example, are morally unjustified. How can he be so certain?

We should distinguish two reasons for condemning the treatment of people who are being detained and interrogated in these places. One is that many of those held are perfectly innocent, having been taken on the basis of false information, or simply the bad luck of being in the wrong place at the wrong time. Thomas at times seems to suggest that *everyone* currently being held in Guantánamo Bay and elsewhere is innocent, which is highly implausible, but he is clearly on strong ground in pointing out that the absence of proper legal procedures in these facilities has meant that many innocent people have been held for long periods in intolerable conditions. The other reason is that, regardless of what these people have done, or the risks they would represent if released, it is immoral to use the various inter-rogation techniques and other forms of treatment that he describes. Suppose, though, that some of those captured are terrorists who acknowledge no moral con-straints themselves in their dealings with infidels. Is it obvious that they are owed the same respect for their human rights as others who are genuinely innocent, or should we follow Locke and say that they may be treated as 'Beasts of Prey, those dangerous and noxious Creatures'?

Liberals often pride themselves on the fact that they are willing to treat others with respect for their human dignity even when this respect is not reciprocated. This is the moral high ground, and it is easiest to occupy when you are in no immin-ent danger yourself from the Wolves and Lyons. I do not criticize Thomas for draw-ing our attention, in such a telling way, to the violations of human rights that have been carried out in our name and for which we bear the final responsibility (since we have elected the governments that authorized them). It is important that these things are made public and that we ask ourselves how they could be justified. My question has been whether we fully realize what we are up against, and therefore whether we can always remain on the comfortable high ground – or whether we sometimes have to say 'yes, what we are doing is terrible, but it has to be done, and those we are doing it to would have no compunction about doing the same to us if the tables were turned'.

In the final part of his essay, Thomas discusses the sanctions regime that the U.N. imposed on Iraq in the 1990s, and makes it clear that he finds the defence of these measures offered by Madeleine Albright (essentially that they were the lesser evil when compared to military action against Saddam Hussein's regime) wholly unacceptable. The sanctions, he points out, predictably had a 'devastating' impact on the health of many ordinary Iraqis, especially children. In condemning these sanc-tions, he once again places himself on the moral high ground. Yet if we piece together the comments on Iraq contained in the essay, we find that Thomas is committed to the following three propositions: (a) Saddam Hussein's regime was a brutal dic-tatorship responsible for 'horrendous human rights violations'; (b) the attempt to combat it by economic sanctions imposed morally unacceptable costs on the Iraqi people – 'a policy that satisfies the definition of genocide', according to the senior U.N. official in Iraq, Denis Halliday, in a phrase that Thomas does not disown; (c) the invasion by coalition forces that deposed Saddam, and its aftermath, also involved large-scale violations of human rights. Without disputing any of these pro-positions, it is their juxtaposition that may give us pause for thought. What were we in the West supposed to do in the face of proposition (a)? Given (b) and (c), what alternatives were available? I have yet to hear a plausible answer to this question, and Thomas certainly does not offer one here. Of course, he is not required to do so. His topic is the moral hypocrisy of terrorists and Western governments. The moral high ground is a fine place to be, but sometimes it is only accessible to those who do not actually have to decide what is to be done, when confronted by horrendous regimes, or by individuals with no regard for the Common Law of Reason that distinguishes us from the beasts.

Note

1 J. Locke, *Two Treatises of Government*, ed. P. Laslett (New York: Mentor, 1965), 319–20.

5 Bat-Ami Bar On

War/terror/politics*

The initial context for this essay included the war in Afghanistan (2001–), the war in Iraq (2003–) and terrorist attacks such as those of 11 September 2001, 11 March 2004, and 7 July 2005. These events have been discursively connected by talk about 'international terrorism' and 'the war on terror', a connection hotly contested ever since it surfaced in speeches by U.S. president George W. Bush (and members of his administration) following 11 September 2001.[1] I do not here intend to contribute to the multifaceted debate about the 'war on terror', though I do align myself with the cosmopolitan democratic critique of it. My aim is to engage with the politico-conceptual difficulties of distinguishing between war and terrorism.[2] I was struggling with these issues when the 2006 war between Israel and Hezbollah broke out. Even more starkly than the wars in Afghanistan and with/in Iraq, it suggested that the line separating war from terrorism today is very thin and may be vanishing.

In the first part of this paper, I consider Mary Kaldor's distinction between 'old' and 'new' wars in an attempt to address this point; in Kaldor's view, precisely the contraction of the distinction between war and terrorism is a mark of 'new' wars. I go on to consider the merits of a free-standing conception of terrorism, that is, one independent of a relationship with war. But towards the end of the first section I argue that terrorism and war have a shared logic; they both derive from a belief in the efficacy of violence in politics and a consequent assumption that violence can therefore justifiably be relied on. In the second section, I examine this shared logic. I do so through a discussion of the 'supreme emergency exemption' usually invoked to justify the strategic targeting of civilians in war; in other words, to justify setting aside the norm that is invoked to distinguish war from terrorism. I argue that the 'supreme emergency exemption' is extremely problematic. Those who endorse it may find themselves endorsing terrorism by non-state agents too. In the third part I suggest that it is the shared logic of war and terrorism that needs to be focused on by those who like myself are concerned about the relationship of violence and politics; in order to constrain violence's place with respect to politics, the norms relating to such violence must be politicized. Such politicization is less productive today, when fear, anger and resentment are deliberately mobilized in politics. I nevertheless believe that one can do nothing better than remind people about the agency we can wield in politics, circumscribed as it may be.

I

It is hard to observe today's wars and argue unreservedly that war can be clearly distinguished from terrorism. The recent war between Israel and Hezbollah lasted 34 days; it was extensively covered, frequently in real time. Everyone could watch the war unfold. This included the spectacle of Hezbollah – considered by many to be a terrorist organization[3] – publicly announcing its intention to target Israeli civilians. In accordance, Hezbollah launched about 3,970 rockets and missiles against Israel. Because Hezbollah's Katyusha rockets cannot be calibrated effectively, many missed their targets and landed in empty fields. But some landed in populated areas, killing 41 civilians, wounding some 2,000, and leading to the internal displacement of 300,000 more. Meanwhile the spokesperson of the Israeli Defence Forces (IDF), a state-based army, was seen announcing the IDF's intention to avoid Lebanese civilian casualties. It subsequently emerged that Israel's 5,000+ air strikes and artillery bombardments had caused widespread destruction to Lebanese population centres and infrastructure, killing about 1,100 civilians, wounding about 3,600, and leading to the internal displacement of 1 million more.

These facts might be thought to speak for themselves. True, the IDF insists that it did not cross the line between war and terrorism. It asserts that the level of 'collateral damage' it inflicted was a function of Hezbollah's locating its infrastructure and fighters in densely populated areas. But the war reinforced my concerns about the thinness of the line separating war from terrorism.

Sensibilities and expectations relative to war have changed since World War I, a phenomenon now embodied in international treaties and law that suggest a conscience troubled by the costs of war, especially in human suffering.[4] Late modern wars have caused enormous suffering to civilians but since World War II civilians have become the primary casualties of war. Around 30 million civilians died in the World War II, forming about 50 per cent of all casualties. Now more civilians than soldiers die in wars. Estimates for Iraq, for example, are staggering.[5] The suffering imposed on civilians by post-modern wars like the war in Iraq is deeply troubling.[6] Moreover, the immediate exposure of this suffering by a media with global scope makes it impossible to not consider it as an essential part of any conceptualization of war.[7]

In *New and Old Wars*, Mary Kaldor suggests that the line separating war from terrorism was once thicker and more robust.[8] This was the time of 'old wars' shaped by other distinctions – many of them modern in origin, such as the distinction between the internal or domestic and external or foreign. As Kaldor points out, these distinctions are being undone and remade as a result of globalization. And the distinction between combatants and non-combatants or more generally soldiers and civilians, which warring nations are expected to respect as a matter not merely of ethics[9] but of law,[10] is also being eroded. This is the norm that terrorism in its present form is defined as violating.[11] The fading normative force of the distinction is among the markers of 'new wars'. And in Kaldor's view, today's wars are *all* 'new wars'.[12]

One solution to this problem would be to eliminate war so that terrorism could stand out in all its distinctiveness.[13] This does not mean eliminating violent conflict; it means realigning it through the formation of international forces that would become responsible for the defence of the world's population. They would function more like an international police force than an army but would be as technologically sophisticated as the military and would undergo similar training.[14] The formation of such forces would require international co-operation and a willingness to abjure a notion of sovereignty to which the right to wage war is integral. Since war in its 'old' version is almost impossible, the incentive for co-operation is quite high. Today, states entering an 'old' war will almost inevitably find themselves involved in terrorism as the 'old' war degenerates into a 'new' one.

For the time being, however, this idea is utopian. Few states will renounce so central a part of their sovereignty as the right to wage war.[15] Consequently, I turn to more plausible alternatives. Those I envisage leave the right to wage war intact. It is, after all, growing ever more meaningless because it is technically defined as the right of states to defend themselves against other states and today most violent conflicts do not take place between states. (Or perhaps I should say that they do not occur between functional states perceived as such by the majority of their populations.)[16] These alternatives include the development of a strong international legal framework that determines what counts as terrorism or aid to terrorists in international law, defines its criminality, and regulates responses. They also include strong international co-operation among police forces and enhancing the capacities of transnational bodies such as the U.N. to respond to terrorism.[17] Since some parts of this latter scheme are already operational,[18] this alternative has a chance. But it is important to emphasize that it can only work within democratic frameworks that secure a complex set of human rights and offer many avenues for accountability.[19] It is also important to reduce global injustice and address the humiliation felt by people whose rights and cultural values have been trampled on.[20]

Global injustice has grown with globalization and is among the motivations of terrorism. Humiliation is another. But not even in combination do they account for terrorism. These factors can account for individual and collective anger. But terrorism is first and foremost tactical or strategic[21] and presupposes a belief in the efficacy of and consequently the justified reliance on violence. It is, in this respect, one variant of a belief in the efficacy of and consequent justifiable reliance on coercion through violence and thus shares its logic with realist strategic thinking.[22]

Terrorism as strategy, I am suggesting, is not very different from what the realist school of international relations considers a *legitimate* strategy in the relations between political collectivities.[23] This is a strategy that most of today's states follow. Almost all of today's states, though they are signatories to international treaties and as such subject to law, put their faith in the efficacy of violence. National military spending worldwide is now about $800 billion.[24] U.S. military spending accounts for close to 50 per cent of this amount. Domestically this comes to nearly 30 per cent of the U.S. budget. This finances the U.S. strategic posture, which, especially since 2001, has been all about coercive force.[25] The Bush administration recommitted the United States to maintaining and using nuclear weapons and integrating them in flexible ways with a conventional arsenal to produce a high level of offensive capabilities. This capability is, it claims, required in order to deter threats to the U.S. and its allies in the post-Cold War world.[26] At the same time, the Bush administration has decreed that deterrence can no longer be understood in its Cold War sense but must be reformulated to include anticipatory self-defence and preventive war. Deterrence through the projection of force is, it argues, impossible in relation to non-state terrorists and states that reject internationally recognized constraints (in the Bush administration's language, these are 'rogue states').[27] Currently Iran is cited as the archetype of the rogue state. However, Iran seems to be merely playing the same game as the U.S. as it flexes its growing nuclear muscles.[28]

II

My claim about the fundamental similarity of outlook between terrorism and realism in international relations is an uncomfortable one and I should like to find a counter-argument. Terrorism – and I do not mean to demonize it – seems different. What is that difference? According to the current popular consensus, the distinctive quality of terrorism is that it targets civilians.[29] This consensus is reinforced by governments' efforts to saturate the popular imagination with certain figures of terrorism. It constructs a morally charged conception of terrorism, one that indirectly relies on the *jus in bello*[30] principle differentiating between combatants and civilians. I have already pointed out that this principle seems to belong to a different kind of war and a previous era. It is, nevertheless, used by many ethicists to mark terrorism out.[31] Thus terrorism is principally contrasted with war by both the popular consensus and the specialists. And this requires one to believe that war, despite its growing lethality to civilians and the enormous 'collateral' damage it inflicts, is profoundly different from terrorism.

But war seems not always that different. There are by now many documented cases of military operations in which disregard for the distinction between combatants and civilians was a matter of strategy. I already described the relevant aspects of the 2006 war between Israel and Hezbollah. For some, this example is undermined by the IDF's claim that it was acting with due care in a just cause, a claim which may not have been cynical. Others will believe that both sides were wrong from the very beginning, having no just cause and failing to engage with each other through diplomatic routes as required by *jus ad bellum*. I will turn, therefore, to World War II, by now a canonical example of a war that was waged justly by one side and unjustly by the other.[32]

As is well known, during World War II both sides targeted civilians.[33] Outstanding instances of deliberately wrought civilian carnage are the German Blitz; the bombing of Hamburg, Berlin and Dresden by the U.K. and U.S.; and the fire-bombing of Tokyo and nuclear bombing of Hiroshima and Nagasaki by the U.S. If terrorist acts are to be perceived as genuinely different from these and similar acts of war, one needs unambiguous norms that not only delineate when but also make sense of why it is morally acceptable to target civilians during wars.[34] These norms will have to accommodate the common moral judgements of World War II. More generally such norms would make it possible to think of some targeting of civilians as permissible, however morally troubling. But this notion seems suspicious from the outset. By now many people have culturally layered intuitions hostile to hostage-taking, the use of live shields,[35] and torture.[36] Even Israel has outlawed both hostage-taking/the use of live shields and torture in majority decisions of the Israeli Supreme Court. These decisions do not simply cite the legal grounds found in international law and Israeli domestic law; they also appeal to a notion of the conduct that befits a country subject to the rule of law and holding to basic moral values.[37] Given the moral intuitions in question, the possibility of morally justifying the permissibility of targeting civilians during a war seems highly unlikely, and this suggests, I believe, that even if violence is deemed efficacious, the tendency has been to suspect and constrain it.

Yet moral permissibility *has* been argued for cases in which civilians are intentionally targeted during war. The argument as a whole has been for a 'supreme emergency exemption' from the *jus in bello* principle of discrimination. To summarize the argument: a 'supreme emergency exemption' can be granted when

1 the targeting is undertaken by a defender (usually a politically organized community like a state) which (a) has been attacked or is about to be attacked without provocation and (b) is weaker than the aggressor;
2 the defender, if successful in attacks on civilians, will create conditions that the aggressor seeks to avoid: for example, cause the civilian population of an aggressor state to reduce its support for the aggressor state's government and military;
3 the exemption should give the defender a better chance at remedying the balance of power between the defender and the aggressor mentioned in (1b) and thus of either persuading the aggressor to end the war or of achieving victory.

Of these conditions (1) is not *too* problematic – though it is far from obvious what the term 'without provocation' in (1a) means. However, some traditional *jus ad bellum* criteria can still be used to make sense of the notion of an unprovoked attack. Thanks to historical reworking, these criteria are fairly clear and can be applied in the assessment of historical events. To take one example, the German take-over of Czechoslovakia and its invasion of Poland were clearly unprovoked.[38]

The second condition is quite speculative. It requires one to predict the kind of conduct most likely to be motivated by pain and hardship and suggests that a dual relationship holds between individual motivation and collective action on the one hand and popular action and policy on the other. These correlations are very difficult to establish empirically.[39]

The third condition is the most problematic since it assumes that the defender ought to have more than an equal chance of winning the war and therefore awards the defender something more than a right to act in self-defence.[40] The assumption might make sense if there were something morally significant about the defender that is not shared by the aggressor. In the case of individuals, the innocence of the defender with respect to an unprovoked attack has been invoked to index the defender's relevant difference.[41] However, in the case of collective defenders and states in particular, this is just one of the *jus ad bellum* criteria that have to be met to justify waging war in the first place. It cannot be used in any other way since fundamental equality is assumed to exist between sovereign polities, an understanding that dates back to the 1648 Treaty of Westphalia.[42]

John Rawls argues for the moral distinctiveness of the defender in the case of Britain's strategic targeting of civilians 'from the Fall of France in June 1940 until Russia had clearly beaten off the first German assault in the summer and fall of 1941'.[43] He is prepared to extend this justification to the end of the Battle of Stalingrad in February 1943, when the trajectory of the war was still unclear. According to Rawls, some collectivities have cultural values, practices, and social and political institutions that it is reasonable to defend. This is so because some values and institutions are better than others; their special quality is being liberal or liberal-democratic or a near approximation thereto. For Rawls, liberalism is not only the best internal political arrangement but one which enhances voluntary co-operation among political collectivities and thus reduces the chance of wars of aggression.[44] Nazism, on the other hand, exemplified values and institutions that it was unreasonable to defend. He argues that it left no space for the negotiations integral to politics; its internal no less than its external enemies were to be 'cowed by terror and brutality and ruled by force'.[45]

I sympathize with Rawls's argument because I share his conviction that liberal democracy (with a more egalitarian bent than he argues for) is a good regime and, moreover, I think that it is an important historical accomplishment. However, liberal democracy promotes certain values that are not universally shared. If one ascribes to liberal democracy a special worth, this ascription is not value-neutral.[46] The case for the *special* merit of liberal democracy is value-laden or pragmatic and usually both.[47] This does not detract from Rawls's assessment of Nazism. The evidence on the subject is quite uncontroversial.[48] As odious as I find Nazism (and its more recent avatars), I do not think that my valuation of liberal democracy confers a special right on liberal democracies: the right to a 50/50 or better chance of success in its own self-defence. If one cannot confer such right, one cannot make sense of the 'supreme emergency exception' and its licence for intentional targeting of civilians during war. Being 'on the side of the angels' does not confer a right to victorious self-defence, independent of the means used to achieve it.

Michael Walzer has recently reassessed his own arguments in favour of the 'supreme emergency exemption'.[49] He now argues that the 'supreme emergency exemption' presupposes an understanding of communities as self-perpetuating over time. He believes that a serious threat to the 'ongoingness' of a community constitutes a 'supreme emergency' and as such overrides the values and principles that otherwise restrain strategies of war. As a result, he cannot help but admit that terrorism might be justified in a 'supreme emergency'.[50]

Walzer believes that he can avoid excessive appeals to the 'supreme emergency exemption' by insisting that it is very restrictive. I am more doubtful about this.[51] I note that Walzer finds a way to argue for the rightness of the Mutual Assured Destruction (MAD) nuclear strategy adopted by the superpowers during the Cold War. Ideas play an important role in the shaping of practice and his position on MAD reinforces realist perspectives rather than the moral ones he elsewhere recommends.[52]

Norms and their relative strength at any given time can determine a state's choices and conduct. The turn towards strategic targeting of civilians by both sides during World War II can be understood, as Ward Thomas shows, to demonstrate that the norms requiring a careful distinction between combatants and civilians had been weakened.[53] The 'supreme emergency exemption', as Walzer, Rawls and others have stated it, may contribute to this weakness. Where faith in the efficacy of force prevails, reliance on it is likely to follow; weaker norms make it easier to contemplate war and terrorism alike.

III

The norms requiring that belligerent parties discriminate between combatants and civilians during war have been strengthened and weakened since World War II. International treaties and laws have attempted to defend civilians while adjusting to new technological capabilities.[54] Legal and ethical training for officers and cadets may have enhanced the effectiveness of these norms.[55] But they have been undermined by the willingness of the Cold War superpowers to use the world's population and indeed the planet itself as hostages of their strategy of nuclear deterrence.[56] They have also been weakened by the superpowers' willingness to support tyrannical regimes and fight proxy wars.[57] The unqualified support by some on the Left for terrorism deployed in anti-colonial and liberation struggles, beginning with Algeria, has had a similar effect.[58] They are currently being still further weakened by neo-conservatives who believe that the only appropriate response to terrorism is complete licence for those combating it.[59]

There is a tendency to think that the strengthening of norms such as the *jus in bello* principle of discrimination requires more ethical training for military and other security personnel. No doubt this helps. But it cannot be sufficient when beliefs about and reliance on the efficacy of violence are so strong. More important is the politicization of the norms that restrain violence and the reliance on it. By politicization, I mean critical engagement with these normative understandings in multiple political settings. This might take many forms. Norms can be protested, debated and professed. Stories can be told about them. They can be enacted and embodied in art as a demonstration of their value or as a contestation. The more often violence-constraining norms are articulated and contested in the public sphere, the greater people's awareness of and stake in them, independent of the position from which one enters the political contestation. And if norms are to function as a vital social force, people must be aware of and have a stake in them. When policy and the norms of warfare are contested, they cease to be obscure and come further and further under public scrutiny.

Politics is the alternative to violent coercion as a means of attaining all political ends, including the security of individuals and collectivities, a more just distribution of resources and burdens, the recognition of cultural uniqueness, and a greater share in the possibility of a good and flourishing life. Politicization can change habits. More especially, it can undermine the prevailing trust in the efficacy of violence as a justifiable means to political ends. Coercion-free politics may be impossible but, in my understanding, politics and violence are, nonetheless, distinct.[60] Of course, they have much in common: at their core is conflict in which two or more sides manoeuvre for control.[61] Since political defeat brings with it a temptation to reject the rules of the political game, conflict is also a source of potential coercion in politics. Coercion, though, is tolerable in politics when the political culture, public sphere and political institutions facilitate people's participation in determining the policies that affect their lives – in political entities where people can, in general, reach workable temporary compromises that many will seek to remake. I favour liberal-social-democratic politics with a populist or participatory bent because I think that it meets this requirement. But there are other political arrangements in which people get an effective say about what is important to them and have a chance of reaching acceptable compromises.[62]

However politics cannot function as an alternative to violence when it becomes infused with fear, anger or resentment. These feelings tend to make bridging between people and groups almost impossible. And bridging is indispensable to the political compromises that yield workable results; it cushions loss and helps the defeated to wait for another chance rather than reject the rules of the game. The United States offers a telling example. Fear, anger and resentment settled into place after 11 September 2001 and have led to pervasive support for the Bush administration's isolationist nationalism and unilateralism.[63] The result has been expensive wars in Afghanistan and Iraq, additional small military operations in a variety of other places such as the Philippines,[64] imprisonment without due process of people branded by the Bush administration 'enemy combatants' (most famously in the detention centre in Guantánamo Bay),[65] domestic policies of suspicion enshrined in the Patriot Act,[66] and resort to torture as a means of intelligence gathering (despite the outcry about the abuse of prisoners at Abu Ghraib).[67]

Wendy Brown offers an analysis of resentment in politics[68] that can, I think, be applied to fear and anger as well. According to Brown, resentment involves an identity-forming attachment to a trauma. When resentment enters politics, it does so in the form of an identity politics focused on the victimization of one's group and one's self. In practice this reinforces one's attachment to the initial trauma and the feelings that accompany it. Such groups become increasingly self-centred and eventually reject political negotiation. This failure can be best understood via Chantal Mouffe's distinction between antagonism and agonism.[69] Both refer to conflict. Antagonists are hostile to each other and seek each other's ruin. Agonists struggle to win political power and define the political agenda while accepting certain rules within which their struggle for hegemony is to take place. A politics permeated by fear, anger and resentment is antagonistic rather than agonist.

For a declining world power like the United States, mobilizing people around a politics of fear, anger and resentment can help to maintain its hegemony – which is now that of an antagonist counting on its destructive capabilities.[70] Problematic as this is for current international affairs, it is not unique. These feelings are being mobilized all over the world and not only in the United States. It is hard to explain the current Holocaust denial in Iran and its popularity on other grounds. It is hard to make sense of Palestinian crowds cheering during missile attacks on Israel during the Gulf War on other grounds. And the mobilization of fear, anger and resentment is one explanation for the attractiveness of terrorism in certain quarters. In terrorism, antagonism finds a fitting expression. Both war and terrorism give free rein to destructiveness.

IV

But there remains an important difference between terrorism and war. Even when norms are weakened and war is increasingly entangled with terrorism, there is, at least in liberal democracies, a chance for politics; and where politics has a chance, violence can be brought to account, including the violence of war. Politicians, military strategists, military officers and soldiers can all be held accountable by the people. Terrorists cannot. Perhaps in the future some transnational space can be created so terrorists too can be held accountable but this is not yet a viable route.

The importance of such accountability is that it is political. Political ends are best achieved without violence in the public sphere even when politics is permeated with acrimony. Looking into the question of Nazi responsibility in the aftermath of World War II, Hannah Arendt wrote that a clue for the practice of post-war politics could be found in a Jewish 'Yom Kippur' prayer and practice:

> Perhaps those Jews, to whose forefathers we owe the first conception of the idea of humanity, knew something about that burden when each year they used to say 'Our Father and King, we have sinned before you', taking not only the sins of their own community but all human offences upon themselves. Those who today are ready to follow this road in a modern version do not content themselves with the hypocritical confession, 'God be thanked, I am not like that', in horror at the undreamed of potentialities of the German national character. Rather in fear and trembling, have they finally realized of what man is capable – and this is the precondition of any modern political thinking.[71]

To enter politics in order to reform the norms that keep violence in check and do so knowing what people are capable of requires an existential courage for which Arendt does not and cannot give a recipe. But I believe that courage of this kind can still be found in everyday life and therefore continue to trust politics as the space of responsibility.

Notes

* I want to thank the organizers of the Oxford Amnesty Lectures for their invitation, Chris Miller for carefully editing my paper, and Lisa Tessman for reading drafts of it and generously commenting on them.

1 Al Jazeera suggests that the phrase 'war on terror' was first used in the late nineteenth century by the Russian police with reference to Russian anarchists. It was reused in the late 1940s by the British police in Palestine to describe its response to Jewish terrorists and in the mid-1980s by President Ronald Reagan. (*Aljazeera.Com*, 01.01.2003, accessed June 2006 at www.aljazeera.com)

2 Not all terrorism has political goals. Its goal may be economic gain, as for example in Sierra Leone. See John Perkins's *Confessions of an Economic Hit Man* (San Francisco: Berrett-Koheler, 2002). Terrorism with political goals is normally called 'political terrorism'. I reject this term, agreeing with Hannah Arendt that violence and politics do not mix. See Hannah Arendt's *On Violence* (New York: Harcourt Brace, 1970).

3 Hezbollah is a complex organization: a political party, a social-service organization and a well-trained militia. It rejects the intentional targeting of civilians other than Israeli civilians.

4 See Michael Howard's discussions in *War and the Liberal Conscience* (New Brunswick: Rutgers University Press, 1978).

5 See www.iraqbodycount.org (accessed January 2007).

6 For a panorama of civilian suffering in the twentieth century, see Eric Hobsbawm's *The Age of Extremes: A History of the World, 1914–1991* (London: Michael Joseph and Pelham Books, 1994).

7 See Michael Ignatieff's *Virtual War: Kosovo and Beyond* (New York: Picador, 2000).

8 Mary Kaldor, *New and Old Wars: Organized Violence in a Global Era* (Stanford: Stanford University Press, 1999), 13–30. Kaldor develops her initial understanding of the difference between 'old' and 'new' wars following observations she made regarding Bosnia. There are some disputes regarding the distinctions Kaldor draws. See in this regard Stathis N. Kalivas's ' "New" and "Old" Civil Wars: A Valid Distinction?', *World Politics* 54 (2001), 99–118. However, the distinction has enough conceptual merit to be taken seriously.

9 In the traditional ethics of war, the principle of discrimination between combatant and non-combatant proscribes intentional harm to civilians.

10 This is part of 'International Humanitarian Law' and a current priority of the United Nations. See the U.N. website at www.irinnews.org/webspecials/civilprotect/sec1cp1.asp#pround (accessed February 2006).

11 On the historical changes undergone by terrorism, see Walter Laqueur's *Terrorism: A Study of National and International Political Violence* (Boston: Little Brown, 1977) and *No End to War: Terrorism in the Twentieth Century* (New York: Continuum, 2003).

12 See Mary Kaldor's analysis of the war in Iraq in 'Iraq: The Wrong War', at the Open Democracy website: www.opendemocracy.net (accessed September 2005). Kaldor's position is unintentionally supported by General Rupert Smith's *The Utility of Force: The Art of War in the Modern World* (New York: Alfred A. Knopf, 2007).

13 Some do argue that terrorism is not distinctive. See Samuel Scheffler's 'Is Terrorism Morally Distinct?', *Journal of Political Philosophy* 14.1 (2006), 1–17.

14 Kaldor hints at a solution of this sort.

15 On the importance of such sovereignty for today's states see Norrin M. Ripsman and T.V. Paul's 'Globalization and the National Security State: A Framework for Analysis', *International Studies Review* 7 (2005), 199–227 and Hauke Brunkhorst's 'The Right to War: Hegemonial Geopolitics or Civic Constitutionalism?', *Constellations* 11.4 (2004), 512–26.

16 This is an extension of the notion of 'democratic peace'; at least since 1945, neighbouring democracies have tended not to fight each other. But see the challenge to this position by Joanne Gowa in *Ballots and Bullets: The Elusive Democratic Peace* (Princeton: Princeton University Press, 2000). There remains some reason to believe that the functionality of a state and its being perceived as such by its population is a factor in peacefulness. See Thomas P.M. Barnett, *The Pentagon's New Map: War and Peace in the Twenty-First Century* (New York: Berkley Books, 2004).

17 See *Confronting Terrorism*, vol. II of the Club de Madrid Series on Democracy and Terrorism. The volume was developed in a summit that took place 8–11 March 2005 in Madrid. It is available at www.clubmadrid.org/cmadrid/index.php?id=1 (accessed September 2005). In 2002, Daniele Archibugi and Iris Marion Young developed similar suggestions. See their 'Toward a Global Rule of Law', *Dissent* 48 (Spring 2002) 27–32. One can find suggestions of this sort throughout the literature on terrorism by liberal/left-leaning advocates of global democracy.

18 See for example the U.N. action at www.un.org/terrorism (accessed September 2006) and the European Union action at www.coe.int/t/e/legal_affairs/legal_co-operation/ Fight_against_terrorism (accessed September 2006).

19 The United States' recent experience offers an example of the danger of operating against terrorism in a manner that breaks with the traditions of liberal democracy. See David Luben's 'The War on Terrorism and the End of Human Rights', *Philosophy and Public Affairs* 22.3 (2002), 9–14, and Russell Hardin's 'Civil Liberties in the Era of Mass Terrorism', *Journal of Ethics* 8 (2004), 77–95.

20 See *Addressing the Causes of Terrorism*, vol. I of the Club de Madrid Series on Democracy and Terrorism (note 17).

21 Most standard definitions of terrorism call attention to its means, ends and logic and therefore define terrorism as a strategy or tactic. In 'Terrorism Without Intention', *Ethics* 114 (2004), 752–71, David Rodin argues that terrorism cannot be understood only with reference to intentions and therefore as a strategy or tactic. But he does so because he is interested in a moral definition of terrorism that includes negligent or reckless uses of violence against non-combatants by both states and non-state agents.

22 On standard strategic thinking see Paul Roger's *Losing Control: Global Security in the Twenty-First Century*, new edn. (London: Pluto, 2002).

23 I am simplifying: realists come in several stripes (classical, neoclassical, structural and liberal). But, with the exception of the liberals who prioritize diplomacy, they share certain assumptions about the priority of brute force in the relations between states.

24 For some sense of what benefits the moneys currently spent on military action could buy, see http://costofwar.com/index.html. I access it periodically in order to measure the daily sacrifice everyone is making in order to finance the Iraq War alone.

25 Comparison of Clinton and Bush administration Reports to Congress regarding U.S. security is striking. They clearly diverge in their approaches to international relations. Clinton seems to have belonged to the liberal realist school. Bush's neo-conservatism has been criticized by some traditional conservatives as idealist rather than realist. But from the outset the Bush administration insisted that its version of foreign policy was realist and it does seem to be a version of 'hegemonic' realism.

26 See summary and excerpts of the 2002 Nuclear Posture Review at www.globalsecurity. org/wmd/library/policy/dod/npr.htm (accessed December 2005).

27 See President Bush's speech at West Point on 1 June 2002 at www.whitehouse.gov/ news/releases/2002/06/20020601-3.html (accessed December 2005).

28 For interesting analyses of Iran see OpenDemocracy at www.OpenDemocracy.net (accessed December 2005).

29 One need not think of civilians as 'innocent'. It suffices that they are not in a position to respond to an attack in the way combatants are. See Charles Townshend's discussion of this in his *Terrorism: A Very Short Introduction* (Oxford: Oxford University Press, 2002).

30 The just war framework is traditionally divided into two distinct parts: one deals with the justification for war (*jus ad bellum*) and one with acts during a war (*jus in bello*). This distinction is respected by most theorists but seems counter-intuitive. For arguments that build on alternative intuitions, see Jeff McMahan's 'The Ethics of Killing in War', *Ethics* 114 (2004), 693–733. I do not endorse just war theory as such. It has many weaknesses. McMahan addresses some. See the interesting discussion of other

weaknesses by David Rodin in *War and Self-Defense* (Oxford: Oxford University Press, 2002).

31 C.A.J. Coady, for example, does so in his entry on 'Terrorism' in the *Encyclopedia of Ethics*, ed. Lawrence C. Becker and Charlotte C. Becker, 2ⁿᵈ edn. (New York: Routledge, 2001), 1,697. Several feminist ethicists have also invoked this principle. See, for example, Claudia Card in 'Questions Regarding a War on Terrorism', *Hypatia* 18.3 (2003), 164, and Alison M. Jaggar in 'Responding to the Evil of Terrorism', *Hypatia* 18.3 (2003), 176. Among the exceptions is Virginia Held's 'Terrorism and War', *Journal of Ethics* 8 (2004), 59–75.

32 See two works in particular on this point. Michael Walzer, 'World War II: Why Was This War Different?' *Philosophy and Public Affairs* 1 (1971), 3–21 and Studs Terkel, *The Good War: An Oral History of World War II* (New York: Knopf, 1984).

33 There are World War I examples of the intentional targeting of civilians. But they were not for the most part enactments of strategy on a par with those of World War II and the technology available was not so devastating, so the scope for destruction was much smaller. Still, ideas about the strategic targeting of civilians first began to emerge during World War I.

34 On the subject of normative lines, see Michael Walzer's *Just and Unjust Wars: A Moral Argument with Historical Illustrations* (New York: Basic Books, 1977), 259–68.

35 Some discussion of these issues took place with respect to nuclear strategy especially in its Mutually Assured Destruction (MAD) version. But moral intuitions on these do vary. See, for example, a defence of hostage-taking/use of live shields by Jonathan Schonsheck in 'The End of Innocents: An Array of Arguments for the Moral Permissibility of a Retaliatory Nuclear Strike', *Journal of Social Philosophy* 18 (1987), 14–25.

36 Lately torture has been defended by Alan Dershowitz. See http://edition.cnn.com/2003/LAW/03/03/cnna.Dershowitz/ (accessed June 2005).

37 The Israeli Supreme Court decided against torture in 1999 in HCJ5100/94 and against various uses of civilians as hostages, live shields and the like in 2005 in HCJ3799/02. HCJ3779/02 built on HCJ5100/94 suggesting that a similar logic operates in both cases. Both decisions can be downloaded at http://elyon1.court.gov.il/eng/verdict/framesetSrch.html (accessed February 2005). The 1999 torture decision has been criticized as not strong enough. There have been few criticisms of the 2005 decision.

38 I am obviously taking sides here in the *Historikerstreit* and similar discussions.

39 In *The Evolution of Nuclear Strategy* (New York: St. Martin, 1981) Lawrence Friedman notes that the World War II bombing strategy of intentionally targeting civilians simply borrows from ordinary strategic thinking the idea that morale is important, generalizing it in such a way that instead of 'combatant' morale, 'civilian' morale is the target. There was little factual evidence to support this strategic extension. (4–9)

40 Self-defence as a collective right as distinguished from an individual right is often assumed but is not easy to make sense of, as David Rodin shows in *War and Self-Defense* (note 30).

41 For an example see Phillip Montague's 'Self-Defense and Choosing Between Lives', *Philosophical Studies* 40 (1981), 207–19.

42 An English translation of the treaty can be found at www.yale.edu/lawweb/avalon/westphal.htm (accessed April 2005). For a discussion of problems with the appeal to a

defender's innocence, see Cheyney Ryan's 'Self-Defense, Pacifism, and the Possibility of Killing', *Ethics* 93 (1983), 508–24.

43 See John Rawls's *Law of Peoples* (Cambridge, MA: Harvard University Press, 1999), 98. Rawls builds on Walzer's discussion of 'supreme emergency' in *Just and Unjust Wars* (note 34), 251–68. I have addressed other aspects of Rawls's position in 'Just (Decent?/ Mere?) War' in *Feminist Interventions in Ethics and Politics: Feminist Ethics and Social Theory*, ed. Barbara S. Andrew, Jean Clare Keller and Lisa H. Schwartzman (Lanham, MD: Rowman and Littlefield, 2005), 201–12.

44 Rawls develops most of this in the first part of *Law of Peoples* (note 43), reworking Emmanuel Kant's position in 'Perpetual Peace' (1795) in *Political Writings*, ed. H.S. Riess (Cambridge: Cambridge University Press, 1991), 93–115.

45 *Law of Peoples* (note 43), 99.

46 Rawls's argument in favour of liberalism has many critics. See Chantal Mouffe's 'Rawls: Political Philosophy Without Politics' (1990) in *The Return of the Political* (London: Verso, 1993), 41–59. For a strong critique of the methodology more generally see Charles Mills, ' "Ideal Theory" as Ideology', *Hypatia* 20.3 (2005), 165–84.

47 My tendency is towards a pragmatic argument that I think does not escape a commitment to some values. I am not alone in this predicament. See, for example, Robert A. Dahl's *On Democracy* (New Haven: Yale University Press, 2000), 44–61.

48 I find Hannah Arendt's analysis of totalitarianism (which Rawls does not mention) quite convincing in this regard. See *The Origins of Totalitarianism*, 2nd edn. (New York: Harcourt Brace, 1958), especially part 3 on totalitarianism.

49 Walzer, Michael, 'Emergency Ethics' (1988) in *Arguing About War* (New Haven and London: Yale University Press, 2004), 33–50.

50 Walzer, Michael, 'Terrorism: A Critique of Excuses', ibid., 54.

51 I join my concerns to those of C.A.J. Coady in 'Terrorism, Morality and Supreme Emergency', *Ethics* 114 (2004), 772–89, though Coady comes at the problem differently.

52 Walzer believes that realism stands in opposition to moral judgements and spends the first chapter of *Just and Unjust Wars* (note 34) attempting to convince his readers to adopt a moral rather than a realist position. But see Ward Thomas, *The Ethics of Destruction: Norms and Force in International Relations* (Ithaca: Cornell University Press, 2001) for an attempt to combine realism and morality.

53 *The Ethics of Destruction* (note 52), especially 87–146.

54 See the two 1977 additions to the Geneva Convention at www.ohchr.org/english/law/ protocol1.htm and www.ohchr.org/english/law/protocol2.htm (accessed August 2005).

55 For an example see descriptions of Philosophy studies at the U.S. Air Force Academy at www.usafa.af.mil/df/dfpy/?catname=dean%20of%20faculty (accessed August 2005).

56 There are many studies of the superpowers' nuclear strategies. But see the papers edited by Henry D. Sokolsky in *Getting MAD: Nuclear Mutual Assured Destruction, Its Origins and Practice* (2004) at the U.S. Army War College Strategic Studies Institute at www.strategicstudiesinstitute.army.mil/pubs/display.cfm?pubID=585 (accessed September 2005).

57 The U.S. role in Iran and Iraq and its involvement in the Iran-Iraq War exemplify this especially well. For an analysis of the Iran-Iraq War and U.S. involvement see Dilip Hiro's *The Longest War: The Iran-Iraq Military Conflict* (New York: Routledge, 1991).

58 The most famous position in defence of terrorism was offered by Jean Paul Sartre in his preface to Franz Fanon's *Wretched of the Earth* (New York: Grove, 1965 [French, 1961]). Also see Ted Honderich's *Political Violence: A Philosophical Analysis of Terrorism* (Ithaca: Cornell University Press, 1976).

59 For examples see various publications at the Center for Security Policy at www.center-forsecuritypolicy.org/ (accessed December 2006).

60 Hannah Arendt offers the strongest argument regarding the difference between politics and violence. See *On Violence* (note 2). Arendt, though, seems to search for a coercion-free politics, which I find utopian. Jane Mansbridge criticizes Arendt and others on this point in 'Using Power/Fighting Power: The Polity', in *Democracy and Difference: Contesting the Boundaries of the Political*, ed. Seyla Benhabib (Princeton: Princeton University Press, 1996), 46–66.

61 I tend to an agonistic view of politics. See Chantal Mouffe's *On the Political* (London: Routledge, 2005) for an articulation of an agonistic position. I am more Arendtean in my tendencies than Mouffe.

62 I disagree with John Rawls's position regarding liberalism and its others. See his *Law of Peoples* (note 43).

63 For analyses see The Brookings Institute at www.brook.edu/ (accessed September 2005).

64 For a sense of the U.S. current and future military plans see Brigadier General Mike Milano's 2006 document 'The Army in Transition' which can be downloaded via a link at www.comw.org/tct/terrorism.html#6 (accessed December 2006).

65 See reports and current information at Amnesty International (www.amnesty.org) and Human Rights Watch (www.hrw.org).

66 See American Civil Liberties Union (ACLU) on the Patriot Act at www.aclu.org (accessed May 2005).

67 News about Abu Ghraib broke in May 2004. In June 2005 the U.S. submitted a report to the U.N., admitting torture at various detention centres in Afghanistan and Iraq, and in Guantánamo Bay, a fact widely reported. Information about U.S. reliance on torture by third parties has been given relatively little coverage.

68 Wendy Brown, 'Wounded Attachments', in *States of Injury: Power and Freedom in Late Modernity* (Princeton: Princeton University Press, 1995), 52–76. See also Judith Butler *'Precarious Life': The Powers of Mourning and Violence* (London: Verso, 2004).

69 Chantal Mouffe introduces the idea as she begins to engage with Carl Schmitt's work. See her *The Return of the Political* (note 46) and the *Democratic Paradox* (London: Verso, 2000), as well as *On the Political* (note 61).

70 See Giovanni Arrighi and Beverly J. Silver's *Chaos and Governance in the Modern World System* (Minneapolis: University of Minnesota Press, 1999).

71 Hannah Arendt, 'Organized Guilt and Universal Responsibility', *Jewish Frontier* (1945), 23. I refer to Arendt's very impressive statement in my *The Subject of Violence: Arendtean Exercises in Understanding* (Lanham, MD: Rowman and Littlefield, 2002), 58. See also Larry May's discussion in 'Socialization and Institutional Evil', in *Hannah Arendt: Twenty Years Later*, ed. Larry May and Jerome Kohn (Cambridge, MA: MIT Press, 1996), 83–105.

Thomas Dublin

Response to Bat-Ami Bar On

Bat-Ami Bar On offers a thoughtful treatment of similarities and differences between war and terrorism as both have evolved in the contemporary world. She emphasizes the difficulty of accepting the most common criterion for distinguishing between war and terrorism: their different treatment of civilians and non-combatants. Drawing on the work of Mary Kaldor and on discussion of the recent Israeli-Hezbollah War, she shows how difficult it is nowadays to accept the frequently cited distinction that warfare attempts to minimize civilian casualties while terrorism specifically targets the civilian population.

Having acknowledged the blurring of the boundaries between 'new' war and terrorism, Bar On concludes by arguing for one significant difference: that warfare as waged by modern, liberal democratic states has at least the merit of being susceptible to control by the political process. As conducted by states, warfare is subject to state policies, which in turn may be supported or reversed by political action. Spying a modest silver lining in an otherwise distinctly cloudy setting, Bar On concludes that 'an existential courage . . . can still be found in everyday life'. She continues 'to trust politics as the space of responsibility'.

Bar On's analysis certainly forces readers to think about the place of violence in the contemporary world. By remaining on the level of abstract analysis, however, she seems to me to gloss over a crucial dimension of these issues. For historians, and that is the perspective I bring to this discussion, the devil is in the details. And as I think about the application of this analysis to the current United States war in Iraq, I am painfully aware of the divergence between her conceptual analysis and recent history. In democratic states, leaders are accountable for acts of aggression committed under their leadership, she argues; non-state actors are not accountable to any constituency. Is her argument justified in the light of the American and British invasion of Iraq in 2003? The concept of accountability that she invokes has proven a thin reed that has done and is doing very little to constrain the actions of the American presidency.

Consider for a moment the various sorts of accountability that might have operated in the circumstances. First, international agencies were significant players in relation to the international demand that Iraq submit to monitoring and supervised disarmament, but George W. Bush insisted on circumventing the established multilateral mechanisms operating under the umbrella of the United Nation. He clearly felt no need for their authorization. He therefore refused to be bound by the collective judgement of members of the Security Council. In addition, neither the American Congress nor the British Parliament was able to muster the courage and independence required to deny their nations' executives the authority to launch the war. Both administrations fabricated the case for war and their legislatures failed to hold them accountable – to require an honest and convincing argument for going to war as a final resort. This failure to hold the war-makers accountable occurred despite massive, worldwide popular expression of opposition to war. Anti-war protests on the weekend of 15–16 February 2003, during the build-up towards war, drew between 6 and 10 million protestors in sixty countries.[1] Neither popular opposition nor the lack of United Nations sanction deterred the Bush administration in its determination to displace Saddam Hussein.

Still, one could argue that democratic societies engaging in the 'new' warfare are accountable retrospectively; that as the consequences of their actions become evident, democratic governments are necessarily responsive to subsequent elections. Yet developments in the United States dissuade one from an overly optimistic application of this principle. First and foremost, a democratic nation at war often rallies to its leaders whether or not the war is justified; this phenomenon was seen with Margaret Thatcher's controversial Falklands/Malvinas War and with George Bush's re-election in 2004 in an election contested largely on the grounds of foreign policy and 'national security'. But the November 2006 elections in the U.S. provided a clear statement of popular opposition to the war in Iraq. In the House of Representatives, Democrats, running largely on their opposition to the war, gained 31 seats and took control of that body. In the Senate only a third of the seats were contested, but still the Democrats emerged with a one-vote majority. What was the result? Despite controlling both houses of Congress, the Democrats have proved unable in the half year they have held a measure of power to effect any change in American policy on Iraq. In fact, during that period, the President implemented a plan to increase the number of American troops deployed there, calling this a 'surge' rather than an 'escalation'. American deaths in the war have indeed surged as has sectarian civil war in that country. Opinion polls find President Bush's popularity at all-time lows, but neither Congressional efforts nor popular opinion have succeeded in holding the president accountable. American policy seems unlikely to change significantly until the election of a new president in November 2008.

The failure of mobilized public opinion to change the course of the war is due in part to the generally craven behaviour of the mass media in the United States. Having spent the 2006–7 academic year in Oxford, I had occasion to see a much more robust and critical media at work. American newspaper and television news have given George W. Bush a free ride for the most part. Criticism has tended to be seen as 'unpatriotic'

– a confusion the Bush administration has done much to encourage. American reporters 'embedded' in the corps that went into Iraq have relied overwhelmingly on Defense Department briefings while, by their reporting on presidential speeches and news conferences, journalists have frequently served as mouthpieces for the administration. No American reporter displays a hard-hitting opposition to government policy akin to that of Robert Fisk of the *Independent* in Britain. The response in the U.S. to Michael Moore's films demonstrates that there is a public eager for the critical independence Moore demonstrates. But to say that there is an occasional opposition voice in the wilderness of a largely sycophantic media is not to say that the American media are able to hold President Bush accountable.

Another measure of the administration's *un*accountability has been the failure of the judiciary to stop the resort to torture, to compel the administration to abide by the Geneva Conventions, or to guarantee a measure of due process in the trials of 'enemy combatants' still detained at Guantánamo Bay. With torture, extraordinary rendition, and the virtually unlimited detention of prisoners without true due process, the Bush administration has demonstrated itself beyond the law. Periodically, individual judges have made rulings that challenge the administration's blanket assertions of unlimited power, and the Supreme Court has forced the administration to backtrack and secure Congressional authority for its handling of Guantánamo prisoners, but continued revelations call into question the fairness of the military tribunals operating at Guantánamo. In more than five years, with more than 600 detainees held at the camp, only a single case has moved to trial, an Australian who eventually pleaded guilty in an agreement that permitted him to serve an additional nine months' sentence in his homeland. Neither international public opinion nor court intervention has been able to assure due process to these prisoners of war whom the administration refuses to treat as such. The United States is a functioning democracy but its handling of individuals seized during the war in Afghanistan resembles the behaviour of unaccountable hostage-takers.

This discussion suggests some of the difficulties involved in drawing too sharp a distinction between the war-making of states and the terrorism of non-state actors on the grounds of political accountability. Until democratic societies such as the United States and Great Britain succeed in ensuring a greater accountability to public opinion, democratic institutions, and national and international law in the making of foreign policy and the waging of war, there will remain more blurring in any discussion of war and terror than many of us will be comfortable with. These realities in the relations between war, terror and politics undercut the measured upbeatness of Professor Bar On's conclusion. I only wish she were right!

Note

1 BBC News Online, 17 February 2003 at http://news.bbc.co.uk/2/hi/europe/2765215.stm.

6 Jeff McMahan

War, terrorism and the 'war on terror'

What terrorism is

Most of us agree that terrorism is always, or almost always, wrong, which is hardly surprising, since the word is generally used to express disapproval. If an act of which we approve has features characteristic of terrorism, we will be careful to deny that it is in fact an act of terrorism. For example, those who believe that the bombings of Hiroshima and Nagasaki were morally justified tend to deny that they were instances of terrorism. So while we agree that terrorism is almost always wrong, we sometimes disagree about what it is we are condemning.

To avoid misunderstanding, I will say at the outset what I understand terrorism to be. Acts of terrorism are intentional efforts to kill or seriously harm innocent people as a means of affecting other members of a group with which the immediate victims are identified.[1] Usually the aim is to terrorize and intimidate the other members as a means of achieving some political or broadly ideological goal, though the aim might be different: it might, for example, be to punish or achieve vengeance against the group as a whole. Although the group against which terrorism is directed is usually political in nature, it need not be. It might, for example, be the group of doctors who perform abortions.

Because the term 'terrorism' is normatively loaded and therefore tends to be used by people to describe their enemies whatever their enemies may do, there is no definition that can capture all the many ways in which the term is ordinarily used. But the definition I have offered seeks to identify the core descriptive features of terrorism, while also explaining why terrorism, in its paradigm instances, is morally so abhorrent. Many of the definitions currently on offer in the literature stipulate that the agents of terrorism must be 'non-state actors' (thereby conveniently ruling out even the conceptual possibility that states can be guilty of terrorism; the most that states can do is to 'sponsor' terrorism), or that the targets of terrorist action must be non-combatants rather than, as I suggest, innocent people (thereby raising the question why violent police action does not count as terrorism), and so on. I think that these and other proposed restrictions on the notion of terrorism are distortions that derive either from the dominant state-centred paradigm of international relations or from the theory of the just war which claims that combatants are legitimate targets while non-combatants are not.

The claim that terrorism involves intentional attacks upon the innocent raises a number of questions. I will discuss two. First, what is the relevant sense of 'innocence'? As I will use it here, 'innocent' has two senses, one formal, the other substantive. In the formal sense, a person is innocent when he has done nothing to lose his right not to be attacked or otherwise harmed – that is, when he has done nothing to make himself morally liable to attack. The substantive sense of the term gives a criterion of liability to attack. According to the regnant version of the theory of the just war, the criterion of liability to attack is posing a threat to another. On this view, the substantive sense of 'innocent' is 'unthreatening'. Another common sense is 'defenceless'. For reasons that I will not elucidate here, I believe that neither of these is the appropriate substantive sense with which to fill out the formal notion, for neither is correlated with a plausible criterion of liability to attack.[2] The appropriate sense, in my view, is 'morally innocent', by which, in this context, I mean 'not morally responsible for a wrong in a way that makes one morally liable to attack as a means of preventing or correcting that wrong'.

A second important question about innocence is whether a terrorist act is to be understood as an intentional attack on a person who is in fact innocent, or whether it is better understood as an attack on a person whom the attacker *believes* to be innocent. If we insist that a killer must believe his victim or victims are innocent in order for his act to count as terrorism, we will have to concede that there are fewer terrorists than we thought. Because many of those who are uncontroversially terrorists are morally motivated, it would be surprising if they believed that their victims were innocent in the relevant sense. Many appear, on the contrary, to accept some doctrine of collective guilt that allows them to believe that all the members of the group against which their action is directed are collectively inculpated. So an act can be a terrorist act even if the agent believes the victims are not innocent. (It can, however, matter *why* the agent believes the victims to be non-innocent. There can be mistakes of moral status and mistakes of identity. An attacker who correctly identifies his victims but mistakenly believes that they are non-innocent is a terrorist. But suppose a combatant fighting in a just war attacks a group of people whom he mistakenly believes to be enemy combatants, and attacks them intending in part to terrorize other enemy combatants. He is intentionally attacking people who are in fact innocent with the intention of terrorizing other members of their group. But because his mistake is factual rather than moral, he is not a terrorist.)

It is worth stressing that it is a necessary feature of acts of terrorism not just that they must be intended to kill people who are in fact innocent but also that the killing must be intended as a means of affecting others. Consider, for example, a person who bombs an abortion clinic intending only to prevent the killings of foetuses that would otherwise occur there. If this person does not intend to terrorize other abortion providers, he is not a terrorist, even if he would welcome it as a side effect if others were frightened into closing their clinics. If an act of killing is *purely* defensive, in that it is intended *only* to prevent the victim from causing harm, it is not terrorism even if the victim is innocent. Yet an act may be both defensive and punitive and still be terrorism. If, for example, the clinic bomber intends both to defend foetuses and to punish the particular abortionists he kills, he is nevertheless a terrorist if he also intends to terrorize and intimidate other doctors who perform abortions.[3]

Terrorism and unjust war

If what I have said is right, whether an act of killing counts as terrorism depends in part on what the killer's intentions are. What most people think of as legitimate acts of war also kill innocent people, and often on a scale much larger than that which contemporary terrorists have so far reached. The difference is that while terrorists intend to kill people who are innocent as a means of affecting others, legitimate acts of war kill innocent people only as a side effect – as 'collateral damage', in military jargon.

   It is perhaps surprising that a distinction as important as that between terrorism and just warfare could be a matter of what an agent's intentions are rather than a matter only of what he causes to happen in the world. Indeed, many philosophers now argue that the intention with which an act is done does not affect the permissibility of the act. These philosophers have adopted a variety of positions on the distinction between terrorism and just war. Some have argued that there is an important difference between the two that does not involve intention: for example, that the moral principles that govern the conduct of war are different from those that govern the use of violence in other contexts, that the prohibition of killing the innocent can be overridden in order to destroy a military target as a means of advancing a just cause but not in order to terrorize people as a means of advancing a just cause, that it matters whether the killing of innocent people is a causal means to the achievement of a good or an effect of the achievement of the good, and that violence in war typically has appropriate political authorization, whereas in terrorism it does not.[4] Other philosophers who reject the relevance of intention to permissibility have been led by their rejection of terrorism in the direction of pacifism, while still others have openly endorsed the permissibility of terrorism in a wider range of cases than most of us are willing to recognize.[5]

   I will not consider here whether the intention with which an act is done can affect the permissibility of the act. Nor will I explore the moral difference between terrorism and just warfare. But I will, as a means of understanding the moral and legal status of terrorists, examine the moral difference between terrorism and *unjust* war.

A war can be unjust for various reasons. It might be fought for a just cause but be unnecessary for the achievement of that cause, or disproportionately destructive relative to the importance of the cause. Usually, however, wars are unjust because they are fought for a goal, or cause, that is unjust. I will refer to combatants who fight for an unjust cause as 'unjust combatants' and to combatants who fight in a just war as 'just combatants'.

Unjust combatants pose a problem for the understanding of terrorism that I have offered. When unjust combatants attack just combatants, they are attacking people who are morally innocent, since those who merely defend themselves and others against wrongful attack are not thereby guilty of a wrong that makes them liable. If unjust combatants attack just combatants intending not only to eliminate the threat they pose but also to elicit fear in other just combatants, hoping thereby to deter them from fighting, then by the definition I have given, those unjust combatants are terrorists. Even if they mistakenly believe that their cause is just and thus that their adversaries are not innocent, that should not exclude their being terrorists, just as the abortion clinic bomber's mistaken belief about the status of his victims does not prevent him from being a terrorist, if his act is intended in part to intimidate other abortionists.

In practice this may not mean that many unjust combatants count as terrorists, since most presumably do not specifically intend for their acts of war to intimidate other enemy combatants. But those unjust combatants who do have that intention seem to be counter-examples to my definition, since no one believes that they are terrorists. Indeed, most people believe that unjust combatants do not act wrongly at all, provided they obey the rules of engagement, even if they intend for their acts of war to frighten and deter other enemy forces.

It is, however, hard to discern relevant differences between an unjust combatant and the abortion clinic bomber who intends to terrorize abortionists generally, and whom most will agree is guilty of terrorism. The unjust combatant is, of course, an agent of the state and does not act illegally, whereas the bomber is a private individual who violates the law. But these differences do not seem to constitute the difference between permissible killing and terrorism. The unjust combatant is, after all, the agent of a state that is acting illegally through his action.

I suspect that our tendency to treat the clinic bomber but not the unjust combatant as a terrorist derives from our correct sense that terrorists deliberately attack illegitimate targets together with the mistaken but widely accepted view that all combatants are legitimate targets. Our unreflective acceptance of the just war theory's identification of the distinction between combatants and non-combatants with the distinction between legitimate and illegitimate targets has, if I am right, distorted our understanding of terrorism. (Many people do, however, consider certain attacks against military targets as terrorism. Many Americans, for example, describe the bombing of the Marine barracks in Lebanon in 1983 and the attack on the *USS Cole* as acts of terrorism. They defend this classification by noting that the U.S. was not formally at war and the attackers were not agents of a state. Yet the attackers could claim to be legitimate agents of national liberation acting against hostile forces unjustly occupying their homeland.)

There are, however, morally significant differences between recognized terrorists and unjust combatants who confine their attacks to military targets. What are they?

Unjust combatants by definition fight in support of ends that are unjust. Terrorism, by contrast, is defined by its use of wrongful means. It is possible to use terrorism, or terrorist tactics, in support of ends that are just. For example, the British bombings of German cities in World War II that were intended as a means of demoralizing the civilian population were acts of terrorism wrongfully committed in pursuit of a just cause in a just war. (The bombings of Hiroshima and Nagasaki were also terrorist acts perpetrated in a just war, though their immediate aim – unconditional rather than conditional surrender – was not just.) So a comparison between terrorists and unjust combatants solely in terms of the ends they pursue seems initially to suggest that the acts of unjust combatants are, if anything, more seriously objectionable than those of terrorists. But contemporary theorists of the just war generally claim that the conditions in which unjust combatants fight absolve them of responsibility for the aims of their war. And the goals that terrorists pursue are often unjust.

Perhaps, then, what distinguishes terrorists from unjust combatants is a matter of the means they use to achieve their aims. It might be argued that terrorists necessarily use wrongful means to achieve their aims, whereas unjust combatants do not, provided they obey the rules of war. If unjust combatants are absolved of responsibility for the aims of the war in which they fight, they may not be guilty of any wrongdoing at all. This is in fact the common view.

But this understanding of the action of unjust combatants is mistaken, despite its widespread acceptance. Unjust combatants are instruments of injustice. Even if they confine their attacks to military targets, they still do not serve their country's unjust ends by permissible means. This is because for them, with rare exceptions, there simply are no legitimate targets. Unless they are fighting in a war in which both sides are in the wrong, unjust combatants engage in combat against just combatants. And, unless the just combatants pursue their just aims by wrongful means, they are innocent in the relevant sense, for they do not make themselves liable to attack, or lose their moral right not to be attacked, simply by defending themselves and other innocent people against a wrongful attack. Most of us accept that it is normally wrong to kill innocent people as a means of achieving a goal that is *just*.

How, then, could it be permissible to kill innocent people as a means of achieving goals that are *unjust*?

With these observations as background, reconsider the comparison between unjust combatants and terrorists. Terrorists by definition use unjust means, while unjust combatants by definition serve unjust ends. Terrorists often but not necessarily pursue unjust ends. Except perhaps in wars in which no one has a just cause, unjust combatants almost invariably use unjust means – that is, means that wrong their victims. With respect to ends and means, therefore, there is so far no reason to suppose that what terrorists do is morally worse than what unjust combatants do. Yet unjust combatants are almost universally believed to enjoy various privileges and immunities, such as exemption from punishment for killing just combatants, that no one believes that terrorists are entitled to. Is this belief justifiable? Or should we accept that what unjust combatants do is typically wrong to roughly the same degree as what terrorists do? Or should we perhaps conclude that what terrorists do is in general morally objectionable only to the degree that we think that what unjust combatants do is objectionable?

There are three morally significant differences between unjust combatants and terrorists. Among these I do not include the fact that, unlike the just combatants killed by unjust combatants, the victims of terrorism are unthreatening and defenceless. As I noted earlier, that just combatants pose a threat does nothing to make them legitimate targets, since they are justified in posing a threat. And the murder of innocent people would be no less wrong if terrorists were to give them a sporting chance of defending themselves.

The first of the three significant differences between unjust combatants and terrorists is that even when both use unjust means to achieve unjust ends, unjust combatants in general have a greater range of excuses that mitigate their culpability and may even exculpate them entirely. Unjust combatants, for example, are often compelled to fight, whereas most terrorists are volunteers. (There are of course exceptions, such as child soldiers who have been abducted, brutalized, drugged, and sent to conduct a terrorist massacre in a village.) There are also epistemic differences. Unjust combatants tend to believe, often understandably and sometimes even reasonably, that what they do is justified. They may have limited access to information, they may have been lied to by their government, they regard the order to fight as morally and legally authoritative, and there is a long history of general acceptance of the idea that a combatant does not act wrongly if he confines his attacks to enemy combatants. Terrorists, by contrast, systematically violate a prohibition against intentionally attacking people who are merely going about the ordinary business of life – bystanders – that has been recognized in virtually all cultures for thousands of years, and is, indeed, recognized even in their own cultures. If, for example, Baruch Goldstein had been acting as an authorized agent of the Israeli state when he massacred 29 Muslims at prayer in 1994, this would have been recognized even by Palestinian terrorists as morally different from the killing of Palestinian civilians as a side effect of an attack on a launch site for missiles aimed at Israel. And it is reasonable to hold such terrorists accountable for failing to recognize the inconsistency between the belief that terrorist acts by their enemies would be specially heinous and the belief that their own terrorist acts are permissible. In general, therefore, there is less epistemic justification for terrorists than for unjust combatants to believe that what they do is morally permissible.

Yet the appeal to excuses cuts both ways, for some of the excuses that are often cited on behalf of unjust combatants also apply to *some* terrorists. Many suicide bombers, for example, are credulous and uneducated young people who have been repeatedly assured by the moral, political and theological authorities in their culture that the killing of randomly chosen members of a population they regard as their enemy is supremely meritorious and will gladden the heart of the deity. From the nature of their action we may infer that they strongly believe that what they do is right – more strongly, presumably, than most unjust combatants believe in the rightness of what they themselves do. So, if we accept that unjust combatants do wrong but, because of the epistemic limitations under which they act, are not to be condemned or punished, we should also accept that the same may be true, though perhaps to a lesser degree, of some terrorists.

There is, moreover, a further reason for thinking that the excuses available to unjust combatants do not provide a significant ground of moral differentiation between them and terrorists. The claim that a person's action is excused presupposes that the person has acted wrongly. Yet what most people believe is not that terrorists and unjust combatants both act wrongly but that unjust combatants are excused while terrorists are not; it is, rather, that terrorists act wrongly while unjust combatants act permissibly, provided that they obey the rules of engagement.

The second important difference is that whereas unjust combatants who attack just combatants usually intend only to eliminate an obstacle to the achievement of their goals, terrorists who kill innocent people *use* their victims strategically as means to their ends. Common sense intuition tends to distinguish between these modes of agency, and to regard the opportunistic use of the innocent as the more seriously objectionable of the two.[6] It is important to note, however, that this does not distinguish all unjust combatants from terrorists. Those who intend the killing of just combatants as a means of terrorizing the enemy also use their victims opportunistically.

The third and perhaps most important difference between unjust combatants and terrorist, is that unjust combatants who obey the rules of engagement thereby respect and preserve laws and conventions designed to limit the violence of war. Even though unjust combatants act wrongly when they attack just combatants, we nevertheless grant them *legal* permission to do so. This legal permission is endorsed by morality because of its pragmatic utility. Morality is in effect compelled by current conditions to allow, and indeed to require, that certain wrongful acts be impunible under the law.

The explanation for this is ultimately traceable to the epistemic constraints under which combatants act. For a variety of reasons, some of which I gave in citing excusing conditions that commonly apply to the action of unjust combatants, most unjust combatants believe that the war in which they are fighting is just. Given the absence of any authoritative and epistemically reliable judicial body empowered to pronounce on matters of *jus ad bellum*, whatever is legally permitted to the just will therefore be done by the unjust in the belief – often genuine but sometimes feigned – that they are among the just. If, therefore, our aim is to make it more likely that unjust combatants will adhere to certain restrictions that ought to apply to them, we will have to subject just combatants to those restrictions as well, even if the restrictions ought not to apply to them. At present, this means that the principles governing the conduct of war must be neutral between just and unjust combatants. Since a neutral rule prohibiting killing in war by both just and unjust combatants would be not only ineffective but also unjust, since it would deny the permissibility of defence by the just against the unjust, the only feasible option is a rule permitting both just and unjust combatants to fight.

But there is no similar necessity for legally or conventionally permitting anyone to engage in terrorism. Because terrorism involves intentionally killing the innocent, it can be morally justified, if at all, only in conditions of extremity, and even then only for those with a just cause. Such conditions are rare enough that terrorism can be legally prohibited without, in general, unduly burdening the just in conflicts with the unjust. This is why participation in an unjust war, though morally impermissible, should be legally permissible, at least in the current institutional context, while terrorism must be legally impermissible in addition to being virtually always morally impermissible.[7]

This, then is the most significant difference between unjust combatants and terrorists: that even though both act wrongly, unjust combatants act under a legal permission that is justified morally by its utility in constraining the violence of war, while terrorists deliberately breach the barriers between war and ordinary life, thereby undermining the laws and conventions that have been devised precisely to insulate ordinary life from the violence and disruption of war.

Are terrorists combatants?

I have argued that unjust combatants are legally and conventionally permitted to act in ways that are morally impermissible. Part of what this means is that we agree not to punish or condemn them for participating in an unjust war, even if in doing so they kill people who are innocent in the relevant sense. I have claimed that terrorism should remain illegal – that is, that it should be legally forbidden even to those with a just cause and that it should always be punishable under the law. But doubts can arise about this. At least in certain cases, it can be and has been debated whether terrorists have, or ought to have, combatant status. Terrorists themselves often claim to be combatants, particularly when they are captured, since they would like to be accorded prisoner of war status. And, perhaps surprisingly, the Bush administration also claims that terrorists are enemy combatants in its 'war on terror'. Are terrorists combatants?

The concepts 'terrorist' and 'combatant' are not mutually exclusive. Given the definition of terrorism I have proposed, it is clearly possible for regular, uniformed military personnel to use terrorist tactics in the course of a war. These would be combatants who had also become terrorists. Their use of terrorist tactics would make them war criminals.

Consider, though, whether terrorists who are not members of any regular army or militia, and who do not openly distinguish themselves as combatants, are nevertheless entitled to combatant status. In the immediate aftermath of 9/11, Bush vowed that he would bring the surviving terrorist plotters to justice. But this is not what one does to enemy combatants.[8] The rhetoric soon shifted, however, and terrorists were declared to be enemy combatants. This is perhaps surprising because it appears to accord to terrorists a kind of legitimacy that they lack. But the reasons for the shift are transparent. Under international law, combatants may be attacked and killed at any time, anywhere, by enemy combatants. Thus, by declaring that terrorists are combatants, the administration invested itself with the right to hunt them down and kill them anywhere in the world without making an attempt to capture them.

There are, however, disadvantages, from the Bush administration's point of view, to declaring that terrorists are combatants. For those with combatant status are legally granted rights and immunities as well as liabilities. It is because combatant status carries certain rights and immunities that captured terrorists seek to be classified as combatants. Combatants who are captured have prisoner of war status, which means that they may not be interrogated and must be treated humanely and be repatriated at the conclusion of hostilities. Enemy combatants also have the legal right to attack military targets, such as military, police, and government personnel and facilities. If the terrorists of 9/11 were combatants, those who flew planes into the World Trade Center were guilty of war crimes. But if the others had worn uniforms and had flown an otherwise empty plane into the Pentagon, their action would not have been a war crime; it would not have been illegal at all. They would have been acting within the legal rights accorded to combatants.

How could the Bush administration invest itself with legal rights to do all that it wanted – that is, how could it claim the right to hunt down terrorist suspects and kill them while also denying them both the legal right to attack U.S. military personnel as well as legal rights against interrogational torture and punishment in the event that they are captured? The solution on which the administration settled was to designate terrorist suspects as 'unlawful combatants'. This is a notion that had its origin in a case in 1942 in which German military personnel infiltrated the U.S. disguised as civilians in order to sabotage facilities that were important to the American war effort.[9] The crime of which these saboteurs were guilty, and for which most of them were executed, is that they were combatants who disguised themselves as non-combatants to facilitate the conduct of military operations. In the words of Chief Justice Harlan Fiske Stone, who wrote the judicial opinion on this case after the executions had already been carried out, 'enemy combatant[s] who without uniform come . . . secretly through the lines for the purpose of waging war . . . are generally deemed not to be entitled to the status of prisoners of war, but to be offenders against the law of war subject to trial and punishment by military tribunals'.[10] There are various reasons why it might be thought that unlawful combatants should be treated differently from combatants who are guilty of war crimes involving intentional attacks against non-combatants – for example, that their action threatens to diminish respect for the distinction between combatants and non-combatants by undermining the adversary's assurance that people who appear to be non-combatants pose no threat. In any event, this case established the precedent for the concept of an 'unlawful combatant' to which the Bush administration has appealed.

According to the administration, unlawful combatants are like lawful combatants in that they may be attacked at will without an attempt to capture them. Yet they lack the rights and immunities of lawful combatants and thus may be tried by either civil or military courts for harms they may cause, even to opposing combatants. The administration also claims, though this is even more controversial than its other assertions about the status of unlawful combatants, that they are subject to indefinite detention without trial and lack rights against harsh techniques of interrogation.

My concern in this essay is with morality rather than law. Yet because the laws and conventions of war have been designed to serve moral purposes, we cannot determine how we ought morally to treat terrorists and terrorist suspects without taking account of their legal status. I will therefore explain why it is doubtfully coherent to suppose that terrorists who do not act as distinguishable members of a regular military organization either have or could have combatant status.

The laws of war are not direct adaptations of the principles of morality to the circumstances of war.[11] They are human creations designed to serve certain purposes. The main purpose they are intended to serve is the separation of war from other human activities. They are designed to insulate ordinary civilian life from the destructive and disruptive effects of war. Combatant status is a legal artefact that has a crucial role in the achievement of this overriding purpose. The granting of combatant status involves a tacit bargain. Those to whom it is granted are thereby guaranteed humane treatment and eventual release if they are captured, as well as immunity to legal prosecution even if the war in which they fight is wrongful and illegal. In exchange for these rights and immunities, they are required to observe certain constraints on the conduct of war. They are required, in particular, not to conduct intentional attacks against civilians. Combatant status is conditional on reciprocity: one is entitled to the benefits only if one restricts one's action in the required ways.

Terrorists, however, subvert the central purpose of the laws of war in at least two ways. First, and most obviously, they intentionally attack civilians. It is their intention to expose ordinary civilian life to the violence characteristic of war. Second, those terrorists who are not already uniformed members of a regular military force in wartime carry out their missions clothed as civilians, thereby eroding the ability of those who would uphold the laws of war to distinguish between those who are threatening and those who are not. It is, in short, the essence of terrorism to do precisely what the laws of war have been devised to prevent. And combatant status is, in effect, a reward offered as an incentive not to do precisely what terrorists do. It would be pointless to grant the rewards for refraining from engaging in terrorism to terrorists themselves.

Even if it is true that people are *entitled* to the protections afforded by combatant status only if they obey the restraints imposed by the laws of war, it is possible that there could be reasons to accord the same protections even to those who systematically subvert the restraints. There might be contingent or pragmatic reasons to grant to terrorists protections to which they have no claim as a matter of right. It is, however, hard to imagine what those reasons might be.

I have argued that terrorists cannot have combatant status. Yet combatants who commit terrorist acts in their role as combatants remain combatants and therefore seem to be terrorists who have combatant status. This is actually not as puzzling as it may seem. When someone in the role of a combatant commits an act recognized as terrorism, he becomes a war criminal and forfeits the privileges of combatant status. He is, to put it paradoxically, a combatant who lacks combatant status.

Still, the legal status of a combatant who has committed a terrorist war crime is different from that of a terrorist who is guilty of the same act but has not acted as a member of a regular military organization. If the law accords some privileges to the former that it denies to the latter, does this mean that the law does, in some instances, what I claim would be pointless – namely, grant at least some of the rewards for refraining from terrorism to terrorists? Recall that terrorists undermine the aims of the laws of war in two ways: by intentionally attacking innocent civilians and by posing as civilians, thereby making it more difficult for their adversaries to respect the distinction between combatants and non-combatants. When a uniformed combatant intentionally kills the innocent for terrorist purposes, he is at least not guilty of the second of these offences. It may therefore make sense to accord him certain legal privileges just for that, while denying those privileges to those who both kill the innocent *and* blur the distinction between combatants and non-combatants.

Terrorists as criminals

In law, the alternative to assigning terrorists combatant status is to treat them as criminals – people with no special protected status whose acts violate domestic or international law. On this view, anti-terrorist action is a species of police action or law enforcement; thus, the treatment of terrorists comes within the scope of the legal and conventional norms governing police work rather than those governing the conduct of war. This explains why the Bush administration did not persist with its initial characterization of the terrorists of 9/11 as criminals, despite the fact that criminal status would deny them whatever legitimacy might be implied by combatant status. For the norms of law enforcement require that criminals be arrested and tried in civilian courts, but the administration prefers 'manhunts' (the term favoured by former Secretary of Defense Rumsfeld), killing, and – for the survivors – indefinite detention with interrogational torture.

Note that I have written that treating terrorists as criminals is *the* alternative, rather than *an* alternative, to treating them as combatants. This is because at present we have only two bodies of conventional and legal norms that might plausibly govern co-ordinated, large-scale responses to the threats of violence that terrorists pose: the norms of war and the norms of law enforcement. Because I have argued that terrorists cannot be classified as combatants, I conclude that at present they have to be regarded as criminals – that is, people who are guilty of criminal acts and criminal conspiracies – and that terrorist suspects are criminal suspects.

It is, of course, possible to hold that the treatment of terrorists need not be governed by the norms devised by or for any institutionalized practice, such as war or law enforcement. One might, for example, hold that anti-terrorist action should be directly governed by moral principles of self- and other-defence, unmediated by any institutional framework. On this view, terrorists might permissibly be killed by anyone, provided that the conditions of legitimate self- or other-defence were satisfied – that is, if killing them were a necessary, discriminate and proportionate means of averting a threat of unjust (and, some would insist, imminent) harm that they posed to innocent people.

Obviously, however, it would be unwise to allow the threat of terrorism to be addressed by individuals acting in their capacity as private citizens. The threat requires an institutional response and, as I suggested in the previous section, institutions cannot operate solely on the basis of the fundamental principles of morality. The principles that regulate and guide the functioning of large-scale social institutions must be designed to be responsive to pragmatic considerations such as problems in the co-ordination of collective action and differences in the likely consequences of promulgating and attempting to follow certain principles in different social and political conditions.

At present the only types of institution we have that are capable of addressing the threat of terrorism are military institutions, whose activities are governed by the war convention and the laws of war, and institutions for law enforcement, which are governed by the norms for police action. Of these, only the norms for police action can be appropriately applied to anti-terrorist action.

This is a conclusion I accept only with reluctance. For while terrorists are not combatants, they are also unlike ordinary criminals. Criminals are seldom motivated by the kinds of ideological concern that motivate terrorists, and their goals and the means they use to achieve them tend accordingly to be rather limited. Because many terrorists are morally, politically, and perhaps theologically motivated, and because their goals tend to be ambitious, embracing the lives of a great many people, they often seek to terrorize and intimidate entire political communities, and the level of destruction they seek to inflict is correspondingly large. Thus far their achievements have usually fallen well short of their aspirations. In some cases they may even see terrorism as a second-best option to be pursued only because genocide is unattainable.

There are other general differences between terrorists as a class and ordinary domestic criminals that tend to make anti-terrorist action rather different from domestic police action. These differences will be the focus of much of the remainder of this essay. They suggest the desirability of forging a new set of norms and conventions for anti-terrorist action that would be intermediate between the norms for police action and the norms governing the practice of war. While my remarks will be relevant to determining what the content of those norms should be, I will not presume to offer suggestions for specific norms, conventions or laws. That is a task better left to people whose expertise in the formulation of social and political policy is greater than mine.

The requirement of arrest

One important element of the norms governing police action that distinguishes them from the norms and conventions governing the practice of war is what I will call the 'requirement of arrest'. This is the requirement that police seek to arrest criminal suspects so that they may be brought to trial rather than immediately attacking or killing them. Police action is in general only derivatively or secondarily defensive. Social defence against criminals proceeds indirectly through arrest, trial and detention rather than directly through immediate preventive violence. Killing is permitted only as a last resort, or as a matter of necessity. The police are permitted to kill a criminal suspect only when that is necessary to incapacitate him when he resists arrest and poses a serious and immediate threat to others.

Many people think that the requirement of arrest is excessively constraining in anti-terrorist action. They think that it is permissible to go after terrorists by military means even if terrorists are not themselves combatants. Is this right, or should anti-terrorist agents be required to try to capture terrorists rather than kill them?

To answer this question, it is necessary to understand the rationale for the requirement of arrest. Suppose that a man has committed a series of murders and remains dangerous. From the point of view of the police and the courts, he must of course remain a criminal *suspect*. But it is a presupposition of the example that he is in fact an actual criminal, a murderer. Although this is by hypothesis objectively true, the police are still required to try to arrest him and bring him to trial. This is so even if they *know* that he has committed a series of murders and remains dangerous (that is, even if their belief that he is a dangerous murderer is both epistemically justified and true). The critical question for our purposes is whether the requirement that the police arrest rather than kill him derives from *his rights*? Does he have a basic, non-derivative moral right to be arrested and tried rather than attacked and killed?

I think not. Given that he has in fact murdered innocent people and poses a wrongful threat to the lives of others, he is morally *liable* to be attacked or even killed if that is the most effective means of defence against him. If, for example, he were lurking in the park late at night and a private citizen, knowing the facts, could kill him as he approached his victim, it would be permissible and desirable for the citizen to do so. In killing him in defence of the potential victim, the citizen would neither wrong him nor violate his moral rights. The murderer has no moral right not to be killed while he continues to threaten the lives of others.

The reason we insist that the police must try to arrest him rather than kill him derives not from his moral rights but from the rights of other people – *innocent* people. It is simply too dangerous to the lives and liberties of innocent people to allow the police to kill rather than capture people they believe to be dangerous criminals. To give the police licence to attack or kill criminal suspects without first attempting an arrest would inevitably and perhaps frequently result in the killing of innocent people, either through mistake or abuse. The requirement of arrest is a norm we accept as a concession to the fallibility of the agents charged with the defence of the innocent.

Parallel claims apply to anti-terrorist action. Actual terrorists – people who are in fact trying to kill innocent people as a means of achieving their political ends – are morally liable to defensive killing if that is the most effective way to prevent them from killing their potential victims. An actual terrorist would not be wronged by being killed to prevent him from killing innocent people. This is a clear implication of uncontroversial principles of self- and other-defence. Yet for various reasons, the assumption that terrorists are liable to defensive action cannot serve as a guide to action in strategies for combating terrorists. For that would expose innocent people to unreasonable levels of risk at the hands of those assigned to their defence.

Perhaps the most significant risk is the risk of misidentification. In domestic law, the principal, though by no means only, reason we insist that criminal suspects be arrested and tried is to ensure that the innocent are not punished by mistake. For mistakes are easy to make when criminals try as well as they are able to evade identification. In this respect both domestic police work and anti-terrorism are quite different from war. For in war combatants are required to wear uniforms to distinguish themselves both from civilians and from combatants of other countries. But no one wears a uniform to identify himself as a criminal or a terrorist.

The risks of misidentification are considerable even in domestic anti-terrorist action, as was shown recently when British police killed a Brazilian man whom they mistook for a terrorist shortly after the terrorist bombings in London in 2005. But the risks of misidentification are exacerbated when anti-terrorist action has to be conducted in foreign countries, and especially when it has to be carried out without the co-operation of the government of the country in which it is conducted. In 1973, for example, agents of Mossad, the Israeli intelligence and counter-terrorism agency, killed an innocent Moroccan waiter in Norway in the mistaken belief that he was the leader of the Palestinian 'Black September' terrorist group that had massacred Israeli athletes at the 1972 Munich Olympics. This case provoked an international scandal, but in general the incentives to exercise reasonable care in identifying and attacking foreign terrorists are weaker than those for exercising care in domestic police work or anti-terrorist action. Governments will naturally take greater precautions to avoid killing their own citizens by mistake.

Another reason for insisting on the requirement of arrest in anti-terrorist action is that terrorists seldom offer the opportunity to attack them in isolated areas. If one attempts to kill them preventively, one generally must attack them where other people live, thereby imposing grave risks on the innocent. This objection to hunting down and killing terrorists is often expressed by saying that the harm caused to the innocent by the attempt to kill terrorists may be *disproportionate* to the harm that such acts might be expected to avert.

While there are thus good reasons grounded in the necessity of avoiding harming the innocent to impose a requirement of arrest on anti-terrorist action, there are also reasons to believe that the requirement of arrest must sometimes be suspended in anti-terrorist action. These reasons derive from the various ways in which anti-terrorist action frequently differs from domestic law enforcement.

May the requirement of arrest sometimes be suspended in anti-terrorist action?

There are three features that together tend to distinguish anti-terrorist action from ordinary police work. The most important of these is, of course, that the threats posed by terrorists are often substantially greater than those posed by ordinary criminals. As I noted earlier, they often seek to coerce an entire people through terror by inflicting the greatest levels of death and suffering of which they are capable. So the harms to be averted through anti-terrorist action are in general significantly greater than those that ordinary police work seeks to prevent. When this is true, I will say that the 'threat condition' is satisfied.

Second, efforts to capture terrorists may be less effective as a means of defence than attempting to kill them. (When this is true, I will say that the 'effectiveness condition' is satisfied.) This difference in likely effectiveness is more pronounced in anti-terrorist action than in domestic law enforcement, especially when anti-terrorist action must be conducted abroad. When terrorists who threaten one country reside in another, the government of the country in which they live may, for a variety of reasons, including a concern for its own political survival, provide only limited, token support for the work of foreign anti-terrorist agents. Or it may provide no support at all, or may even engage in active obstruction of efforts to arrest terrorist suspects. Also, and for obvious reasons, terrorists tend to choose to live in areas where they enjoy the support of the local population. In these cases, terrorists often have sentinels who will alert them to the approach of anti-terrorist agents, assist them to evade capture, and obstruct their removal or extradition in the event that they are captured.

Third, efforts to arrest terrorist suspects are often more dangerous to anti-terrorist agents than killing them would be. (When this is true, I will say that the 'danger condition' is satisfied.) It is, of course, also true of domestic police work that killing criminal suspects would often be safer for the police than trying to arrest them. But the difference in the degree of risk between the options of capture and killing is much greater in the case of anti-terrorist action. This is in part because terrorists are more likely than ordinary criminals to fight to the death in resisting arrest. Not only are the penalties terrorists would face if convicted in general greater, but also terrorists are more highly motivated and may indeed regard the opportunity to kill anti-terrorist agents before dying a martyr's death as more desirable than being arrested and punished. But if terrorists can reliably be expected to resist arrest with maximum violence, it could be imprudent to forfeit the element of surprise by attempting an arrest rather than simply attacking them with the intention of capturing any who might be induced to surrender.

Another reason why anti-terrorist action is more dangerous, particularly in foreign areas, is related to one of the reasons why arrest may be less effective than killing as a method of defence. When terrorists have sentries who can warn them of the approach of strangers, as well as local supporters who are willing to protect them, anti-terrorist agents face the prospect of ambush both in trying to capture the terrorists and, if they succeed, in trying to extract them for trial elsewhere. Killing, by contrast, may often be accomplished from a safe distance.

The dangers of attempting to capture determined and well-organized terrorists are illustrated by the events that culminated in the killing in November 2002 of six people whom the U.S. described as al-Qaeda militants. They were killed by a Hellfire missile fired from a Predator drone aircraft while they were driving in a van in the Yemeni desert. This instance of 'targeted killing' by the U.S. was much criticized (perhaps on good grounds, though objective evaluation is difficult because the primary source of information about the incident is the government that carried out the attack), but the relevant point here is that 14 soldiers had earlier been killed in an attempt to capture one of the people who was killed in the strike.[12]

I concede that the three respects I have cited in which anti-terrorist action may differ from domestic police work are not respects in which anti-terrorist work *always* differs from ordinary police work. The threat, effectiveness and danger conditions are less likely to obtain when anti-terrorist action takes place in a domestic rather than foreign setting, and are less likely to obtain even in a foreign setting when the foreign government is co-operative and competent.

My claim is only that when the three conditions do obtain, or even when only the first and second obtain, there is good reason to suspend the requirement of arrest. For when the threat that terrorists pose is grave, when killing them would be more likely to avert the threat than trying to capture them, and when trying to capture them would be riskier than killing them, we may then owe it to the terrorists' potential victims – both the innocents they would otherwise kill and the agents whose responsibility it is to protect those innocents – to try to kill them rather than to try to capture them. If the choice that terrorists have forced on us is between killing them and allowing the innocent to remain at risk of being killed by them, justice may demand that they, rather than the innocent, bear the costs of their own wrongful action.

The three conditions that may justify suspension of the requirement of arrest in anti-terrorist action may also be satisfied in some cases of domestic law enforcement. If a criminal suspect is highly dangerous to those around him, if killing him would be more effective in eliminating the threat he poses than an effort to arrest him, and if attempting to arrest him would be significantly more dangerous for the police than killing him, the requirement of arrest may yield to moral principles of self- and other-defence, making it permissible to kill him. The most obvious case in which these conditions may obtain is when a criminal suspect resists arrest through violence. The reason it is permissible to attack a suspect in such a case is that his use of violence both makes him liable to attack and also suggests that the risks to the police and others of continuing to try to subdue him have become excessive. But if, *in advance* of attempting an arrest, there is good evidence that a person has already acted in a way that makes him liable to defensive action and the risks of attempting to arrest him are *as great as* or even *greater than* those in a typical case in which a suspect violently resists arrest, it seems that the requirement of arrest ought, as a matter of consistency, to be suspended in this case as well.

The problem of liability

Both in domestic law enforcement and in anti-terrorist action, the obvious objection to bypassing the requirement of arrest and resorting directly to defensive action is that this involves treating a person as a criminal, and harming him in the process, without first demonstrating his guilt. The person who is attacked rather than arrested is denied the presumption of innocence.

This, however, is a necessary feature of all action that is defensive rather than punitive, *ex ante* rather than *ex post*. And sometimes police action does have to be purely defensive. For example, on the day on which I am making revisions to this essay – 16 April 2007 – police in Blacksburg, Virginia, have just engaged in defensive action against a murderer who killed 32 people on the campus of Virginia Polytechnic University – though if their action succeeded at all, it was apparently only by inducing the murderer to kill himself.

The difference between this kind of case and most instances of anti-terrorist action, however, is that terrorists seldom present themselves as targets while they are in the process of committing a terrorist act. Suicide bombers, an increasingly common species of terrorist, act only once and cannot be punished after the fact. If one has sufficient knowledge to be able to attack them before they can detonate their explosives, and if an attempt to arrest them would risk an immediate detonation among innocent people, it could be justifiable to attack them pre-emptively. But there could also be cases in which *preventive* attack, before the threat becomes imminent, would offer the best prospect of effective defence. If the threat, effectiveness and danger conditions are met, could preventive attack against a terrorist suspect be justified?

There are, of course, various objections to preventive defence. But many of the familiar objections to preventive *war* – for example, that recognition of the permissibility of preventive war could provide a legal rationale for virtually any war that a country might be tempted to fight – do not apply, at least not very strongly, to preventive defence against individual terrorists, or terrorist suspects. Yet one important objection may apply, at least in many cases. This is that preventive defence may involve attacking a person who has as yet done nothing to make him morally liable to attack. To attack someone who is not liable to attack is to attack someone who is innocent in the relevant sense. In general, it is unjust to subject a person even to preventive *detention*; how much worse, then, to subject him to preventive *execution*. We simply may not kill those who we think, even on very good grounds, will later become terrorists. Justified defence, like justified punishment, requires that the person acted against be doing something, or has done something, that makes him morally liable to what is done to him.

This objection to preventive anti-terrorist action should be distinguished from the objection based on the possibility of misidentification, though they are related and perhaps overlapping. The problem of misidentification is that anti-terrorist agents may mistakenly attack people who have no association with terrorism of a sort that would make them dangerous to others. The problem of liability is that anti-terrorist agents may attack people who *are* associated with terrorism in ways that may make them dangerous but who as yet have done nothing to forfeit their rights against attack. In terrorism, as in crime, there are many people who are dangerous, in the sense that they are significantly more likely than most other people to commit terrorist or other criminal acts, but who have so far not acted in a way that would make them liable to preventive action. Such people would be wronged if they were attacked to prevent them from posing a threat in the future.

The problem of liability is not an objection to preventive defence *in contrast* to arrest. For it would also be unjust to arrest a person if one has no reason to believe that he has done anything to make himself liable to punishment. The problem of liability is instead a general problem for any anti-terrorist action that is preventive in character, as most action against suicide terrorists – and indeed most action against all other first-time terrorists – must be.

The problem is not serious when there is compelling evidence that a person has been actively engaged in planning and preparing for a terrorist attack. In these cases we can follow the law of attempts by claiming a right of intervention against an uncompleted attempt, or the law of conspiracy in claiming that the preparatory actions are themselves a ground of liability to preventive measures, including arrest and even, if the conditions for the suspension of the requirement of arrest obtain, preventive attack.

Liability to preventive action

But what about people who have recently joined a terrorist organization and are currently performing non-violent functions within the organization while training for possible future missions, yet are not planning, preparing for, or participating in any actual mission? Are such people liable to preventive attack?

To answer this question, it may help to consider a parallel problem in war. Suppose that our intelligence services discover decisive evidence that the leaders of another country are planning a war of unjust aggression against us. At this point, however, the ordinary rank-and-file soldiers of the country know nothing about their leaders' plans. Suppose we can defend ourselves against the planned aggression only by attacking now, preventively. Are the unmobilized soldiers of our potential adversary liable to attack, even though they are not attacking us and even though there is at present no war between them and us? Most people believe that they are indeed liable, simply by virtue of their membership in the military. Anyone who wears their uniform is considered by most people to be a legitimate target of attack. Even if our surprise, preventive attack were illegal, the law holds that our own rank-and-file combatants who carried it out would not be guilty of war crimes. They would not be guilty of killing the innocent, provided they confined their attacks to the soldiers on the other side.

But how could merely wearing a uniform constitute a ground of liability to attack? To judge a person liable to attack merely by virtue of his membership in a certain group, such as a military organization, is, as I suggested earlier, the way in which terrorists rationalize their attacks against the innocent. Yet there may be grounds for holding unmobilized soldiers liable to preventive attack that do not presuppose a repellent doctrine of collective liability that makes mere membership in a group a basis of liability.

The argument for liability appeals to the idea that when a person enlists in the military, or when he allows himself to be conscripted into the military, he has become an instrument of the will of his superiors. The norms of military institutions are such that when a person becomes a member, he effectively commits his will to obedience. If his leaders begin to plan and prepare for an unjust war, he will have been made into an unjust threat by their action – assuming that he will in fact obey, as virtually all soldiers do. He may have been converted into a threat even if he is unaware of his leaders' plans, and so is unaware of having become a threat to others. Since it was foreseeable when he joined the military that this might happen, he is responsible for having become a threat. This is the basis of his liability.

One may object that while sometimes a person may be at fault for joining the military – for example, if the military organization he joins is known to be likely to fight in an unjust war – many people who join the military do so for good moral reasons, and act admirably when they do. How, one may ask, can morally permissible and indeed admirable action be a basis of moral liability to preventive force? The answer is that fault is not necessary for liability in this kind of case. When a person joins the military and surrenders his will to his leaders, he thereby becomes *strictly* liable to preventive force in certain conditions. He knows, or should know, the moral risk he runs in surrendering his autonomy to his leaders, and if he has bad luck in having leaders who convert him into a threat without his knowledge, he rather than his potential victims must pay the cost of his earlier choice.

This argument for the liability of unmobilized soldiers to preventive force may be restricted in scope in two ways. First, there are rare instances in which active duty soldiers do disobey. But even those who engage in conscientious refusal are usually committed at the outset and renege on the commitment only later when they discover exactly what they have been committed to. It seems plausible to suppose that they remain liable to preventive force as long as their wills are committed. There may, of course, be a few who manage to preserve their autonomy by remaining uncommitted to future obedience, deciding whether to obey each order only when it is given. These individuals may not be liable to preventive force; but they are nevertheless responsible for misleading others by their presence in the military to believe that they *are* committed to obedience; they therefore may have no justified complaint if they are treated by others as if their wills were committed to future obedience.

Second, the argument for liability presupposes that all those in the military entered it voluntarily. But this is false. I concede this objection: a person cannot be liable to preventive force by virtue of having joined the military if his becoming a member was genuinely involuntary. Exactly what the conditions of voluntariness are is a contentious issue. For present purposes, perhaps it will do to say that a person's membership in the military is voluntary when he could reasonably have avoided it. When people enlist in the military voluntarily, or when they allow themselves to be conscripted into the military when the penalties for conscientious objection are mild, we can say that their being in the military is voluntary and they may be held accountable for their choice. By contrast, those who acquiesce in conscription only because the penalties for conscientious objection are draconian may be said to serve involuntarily. The argument for liability may not apply to them.

The argument I have given for strict liability among military personnel provides, I believe, the best defence of the common belief that even unmobilized soldiers can, on rare occasions, be legitimate targets of preventive attack. Most people who would accept this argument would also think that it applies unrestrictedly to all members of all legitimate military organizations. I think, however, that it is subject to one further, highly significant restriction. I believe that it applies only to those soldiers whose leaders are planning and preparing for an *unjust* attack. But I will not discuss or defend this restriction here. For the point of the argument is to suggest that those who believe that members of the military – including those who are unmobilized – may be legitimate targets of preventive attack should also accept that members of terrorist organizations may be liable to preventive attack for the same reason. Indeed the argument for strict liability is stronger in the case of members of terrorist organizations than in the case of military personnel. This is so for several reasons. First, most terrorists are enthusiastic volunteers. There are people who are compelled to become terrorists – for example, child soldiers in Africa who commit massacres in villages as a means of terrorizing and intimidating the larger population – but they are atypical. Second, it is scarcely possible to join a terrorist organization permissibly and for morally admirable reasons. For a terrorist organization is by definition committed to the intentional killing of innocent people as a matter of policy. This is not, however, a necessary feature of military organizations and is not even contingently a feature of most actual military organizations.

Earlier I proposed three conditions that together could justify the suspension of the requirement of arrest in anti-terrorist action. I will now suggest two further conditions that, if satisfied, could justify *preventive* action against terrorists or terrorist suspects. The first is that the person is an active member of an organization that uses terrorist tactics *as a matter of policy*. Such an organization is dedicated to killing innocent people; its members may therefore be liable to preventive measures on the ground that they are guilty of conspiring to kill the innocent. Yet there are some organizations which comprise many branches that perform different functions, some of which are legitimate while others are terrorist. It is therefore important to insist on a second condition, which is that preventive action should be reasonably expected to make a proportionate contribution to the prevention of terrorist action. Preventive action may not be taken against a member of an organization that is involved in terrorism unless there is reason to believe that this will actually serve to protect the innocent. In this respect the restrictions on anti-terrorist action are more stringent than those conventionally imposed on military action in war. For in war the killing of enemy combatants is conventionally permitted even when there is no evidence that killing them will make any contribution to the achievement of the aims of the war. (My own view is that this is a mistake and that acts of killing in war should likewise be subject to a requirement of necessity.)

In cases in which these two conditions are satisfied *and* the threat, effectiveness and danger conditions are satisfied as well, terrorists or terrorist suspects may be liable to preventive attack. The five conditions together are sufficient to make a person presumptively liable to preventive attack even if he has so far never engaged in actual terrorist action and, perhaps, even if he is not currently engaged in preparing for a specific terrorist action. In cases in which the two conditions are satisfied but the three conditions justifying the suspension of the requirement of arrest are not, terrorist suspects may be liable to preventive arrest even in the absence of evidence that they have previously participated in terrorist action or are actively preparing for a specific terrorist action. The grounds for liability to preventive arrest are similar to the grounds for arrest in the law of conspiracy, except that in these cases the ground of liability would have to be *complicity* in a conspiracy to commit terrorist acts rather than active individual preparation for specific terrorist action.

Proportionality in police action, anti-terrorist action and war

I noted earlier that one important reason for imposing the requirement of arrest on anti-terrorist action is that attacks on terrorists do not and cannot take place on remote battlefields but must in general be conducted in areas where other people live, thereby exposing innocent people to grave risks of harm as a side effect. Some people who agree that terrorists are not combatants and that anti-terrorist action is not governed by the norms and conventions of war contend that the proportionality constraint on anti-terrorist action is more restrictive than that which applies to action in war. They believe, in other words, that anti-terrorist action must not expose innocent people to levels of risk as high as those to which it may be permissible to expose them in the course of war. Michael Walzer, for example, claims in a recent article that 'justice demands . . . that the army take positive measures, accept risks to its own soldiers, in order to avoid harm to civilians. The same requirement holds for anti-terrorists – holds *more strongly*, I think, insofar as it is mostly police rather than soldiers who are at work in this "war" (or, the soldiers are doing police work), and we impose much higher standards of care for civilians on the police than we do on armies in combat'.[13]

There is a sense in which this is true. As a general matter, the requirement of due care for the safety of bystanders is stronger in the case of police work than it is in war; but this is only because the goals of police action are in general less important. Many criminal suspects, including some actual murderers, will not pose a serious threat to others even if they are not arrested. We seek to arrest, try, and punish criminals for a variety of reasons other than to defend ourselves against them: for example, retribution, redress, reform, deterrence of others, and so on. Such aims are usually less important, or less certain of achievement through punishment, than preventing a criminal from further harming the innocent. But in those cases in which the primary aim of law enforcement is defence rather than punishment – for example, when a murderer is on a rampage and threatens to kill a great many people – the requirement of due care for the safety of bystanders to which the police are subject may be less demanding, since more is at stake.

Indeed, there is one reason why the proportionality constraint may on such occasions be *less* demanding than the corresponding requirement that applies in war and foreign anti-terrorist action. This is that those who would be endangered by domestic police action in these cases may already be at considerable risk from the criminal, so that it may be on balance safer for them if the police take more aggressive measures against the criminal. The risk of inadvertent harm to the innocent from the action of the police may be outweighed by the extent to which police action reduces the threat that the criminal poses to the innocent. Unless we think that there is some reason why it is better to be at greater risk from a criminal than to be at lesser risk of accidental harm by the police, the requirement of due care, or proportionality, should be relaxed in these cases.

There is, in fact, no difference in stringency between the proportionality constraint on acts of war and the proportionality constraint on police action. They are the same constraint. A state of war does not have the effect of weakening or compromising the rights of innocent people. Their right not to be harmed as a side effect of an act of war is no less strong than their right not to be harmed as a side effect of police action. It is just that in war the harms to be prevented are generally greater; therefore the harms that it can be permissible to risk or to inflict as a side effect of averting those harms can be correspondingly greater and still be proportionate.

There is, however, one reason why anti-terrorist agents could be justified in some instances in adhering to a weaker standard of due care for bystanders. There may be instances in which anti-terrorist agents know that many of the people among whom terrorists are living are supporters who shelter and assist them in various ways.

These people are not themselves terrorists. Their action does not make them liable to intentional attack. But those who voluntarily allow terrorists to live in close proximity to them in order that they may shelter and support them can have no legitimate complaint if they are harmed as a side effect of action taken against the terrorists to which there would otherwise be no objection. Such people make themselves liable to the risks they run by collaborating with people who are themselves legitimate targets of attack. They cannot claim a right not to be harmed even unintentionally when acknowledgement of such a right would enable them to provide a moral shield for terrorists.

It is of course almost never true that all the bystanders who would be at risk of being harmed by an attack against terrorists are supporters who aid and abet terrorist activities. But it can nevertheless make a difference if *some* are. Here is a hypothetical example based on a recent and all-too-real episode. In the summer of 2006, members of Hezbollah in southern Lebanon fired thousands of missiles into northern Israel. Many of the warheads were packed with metal pellets that on detonation spewed out in all directions. At the explosion sites I saw a few months later (one a children's playground), all surfaces within about a 100-foot radius – houses, trees, walls, sidewalks, pavements – were densely riddled with deep pock-marks from these pellets. (The pellets themselves had long since been collected by neighbourhood children.) The nature of the missiles, combined with the fact that they were not aimed at military targets, indicates that the intention of those who fired them was to kill as many people as possible. It did not matter who these people were as long as they were Israelis. These were therefore terrorist attacks. Many of the missiles were fired from within villages in southern Lebanon. Israel was criticized, with some justification in my view, for causing disproportionate civilian casualties in its defensive strikes against the missile sites. But suppose that Israel had chosen to make a more restrained and measured military response, making precision strikes against only a small number of carefully chosen missile sites. Suppose that all the sites from which missiles had been launched were within villages and that Israeli tactical planners had to choose between attacking one launch site within a village known for its allegiance to Hezbollah and attacking another site within a village known for its opposition to Hezbollah's terrorist tactics. I think it would clearly be wrong to attack the latter, if other factors were equal, since it would be reasonable to expect that a higher percentage of the unintended casualties in the other village would befall people whose support for terrorism had made them liable, at least to some degree, to suffer the side effects of anti-terrorist action. They would, at a minimum, have weaker grounds for moral complaint at being harmed by action directed against terrorists whom they had sheltered and assisted. If this is right, it suggests that the proportionality constraint on anti-terrorist activity *may* be more stringent if terrorists are attacked in a neutral area than if they are attacked in an area in which they are known to be sheltered and assisted.

It is worth stressing, however, that if the standard of care may sometimes be less stringent in foreign anti-terrorist action than in domestic law enforcement, that is *not* because the people among whom terrorists live matter less because they are members of another society. People who are wholly innocent – who are in no way responsible for the threats terrorists pose – have the same right not to be attacked or harmed whatever their nationality.

This means that the proportionality constraint in war and in anti-terrorist action abroad is actually more stringent than most people suppose. If we want to determine whether it would be acceptable to kill a certain number of innocent people as a side effect of some act of war, or of some anti-terrorist action, we should ask ourselves if it would be permissible to proceed *if* the innocent people who would be killed were our compatriots rather than foreigners. If we think that it would be wrong to sacrifice our compatriots in those circumstances, then we ought not to proceed. Suppose, for example, that the only way to eliminate the threat from a certain terrorist is to fire a missile at the hotel room in which he is staying. If it would be wrong to fire the missile if the hotel were in New York or London, then it would be wrong to fire it if the hotel were instead in Baghdad, or Kabul.

I will conclude by asserting two liberal pieties that, though familiar and even platitudinous from the point of view of the political left, nevertheless seem to me to be both true and profoundly important. One is that attacks against terrorists or terrorist suspects that kill the innocent, either by mistake or as a side effect, are often not only disproportionate but also counter-productive. By inflaming the hatred of those related to the victims by nationality or religion, these acts may recruit more terrorists than they eliminate. The second, related point is that the most important part of anti-terrorist action is not military action, police action, or even interdiction of terrorist attacks. It is to give justice, and to show generosity and magnanimity to oppressed, exploited, humiliated or merely disadvantaged peoples whose grievances – some unreasonable but many legitimate – are the ultimate sources of terrorism.[14]

Notes

1 For the sake of brevity, I will refer only to killing rather than to killing or harming.

2 For a critique of the criterion of liability found in the dominant version of the just war theory, see Jeff McMahan, 'The Ethics of Killing in War', *Ethics* 114 (2004), 693–733.

3 Here I assume that those who perform abortions do not thereby make themselves liable to attack. If they did, the clinic bomber would be relevantly analogous to a hypothetical bomber of the SS quarters at a pre-war Nazi concentration camp, intending to intimidate SS officers at other camps. This person would not be a terrorist, since his victims would be liable to attack.

4 See Judith Jarvis Thomson, 'Self-Defense', *Philosophy and Public Affairs* 20 (1991), 283–310; Thomas Scanlon, *Moral Dimensions: Permissibility, Meaning, Blame* (Cambridge, MA: Harvard University Press, 2008), chapters 1 and 2; Frances Kamm, *Morality,*

Mortality Volume II: Rights, Duties, and Status (New York: Oxford University Press, 1996), especially part II; and Lionel McPherson, 'Is Terrorism Distinctively Wrong?' *Ethics* 117 (2007), 524–46.

5 One who moves in the direction of pacifism is David Rodin, 'Terrorism Without Intention', *Ethics* 114 (2004), 752–71. Two who defend terrorism are Jonathan Bennett, *The Act Itself* (Oxford: Clarendon Press, 1995), 218; and Uwe Steinhoff, *On the Ethics of War and Terrorism* (Oxford: Oxford University Press, 2007), especially chapters 3 and 5.

6 See Warren Quinn's remarks on 'eliminative' and 'opportunistic' agency in his 'Actions, Intentions, and Consequences: The Doctrine of Double Effect', *Philosophy and Public Affairs* 18 (1989), 344.

7 For elaboration on the moral and legal status of unjust combatants, see Jeff McMahan, 'The Morality of War and the Law of War', in *Just and Unjust Warriors: The Legal and Moral Status of Soldiers*, ed. David Rodin and Henry Shue (Oxford: Clarendon Press, 2008), 19–43.

8 Bush declared: 'Make no mistake, the US will hunt down and punish those responsible for these cowardly acts'. One would think it would be preferable to condemn terrorist mass murderers for what they really are, but apparently the macho code requires that one insult them as cowards, even if what they have done is to fly a plane into a building. On the distinction between war and criminal justice, see George Fetcher, *Romantics at War: Glory and Guilt in the Age of Terrorism* (Princeton: Princeton University Press, 2002), 3–9.

9 *Ex parte Quirin*, 317 U.S. 1 (1942). For a good discussion of this case and its implications for the policies of the Bush administration, see *Romantics at War* (note 8), chapter 5. Also see Shlomy Zachary, 'Between the Geneva Conventions: Where Does the Unlawful Combatant Belong?', *Israel Law Review* 38 (2005), 378–417.

10 *Quirin* (note 9).

11 For discussion, see 'The Morality of War and the Law of War' (note 7).

12 For information on the attack, see http://archives.cnn.com/2002/WORLD/meast/11/04/yemen.blast/index.html. For discussion, see Michael Walzer, 'Terrorism and Just War', *Philosophia* 34 (2006), 10–11.

13 'Terrorism and Just War' (note 12), 9–10 (emphasis added).

14 I am deeply grateful for comments on an earlier draft of this essay to Marcia Baron, Saba Bazargan, Yitzhak Benbaji, C.A.J. Coady, David Enoch, David Estlund, Mark Greene, Michael Gross, Frances Kamm and the students in her graduate seminar at Harvard, Larry May, David Mellow, Chris Miller, Gerhard Øverland, Derek Parfit, Melinda Roberts, David Rodin, Saul Smilansky, Daniel Statman, Alec Walen, Daniel Wikler and Col. Daniel Zupan.

David Rodin

Response to Jeff McMahan

What moral norms should regulate our response to terrorism? Should terrorists be considered combatants under the laws and ethics of war? Or should they rather be regarded as dangerous criminals, so that our response ought to be governed by the norms of police action? These are the questions at the heart of Jeff McMahan's original and closely argued essay. His compelling answer is that terrorists must be treated as criminals, not combatants. In this I wholly agree, though I will suggest that there are important political reasons for this conclusion that stand alongside the elegant moral argument provided by McMahan.

But what follows from treating terrorists as criminals rather than combatants? In particular is there a duty to arrest terrorists rather than simply kill them outright? McMahan concludes that there is a strong, though defeasible, presumption in favour of arrest. Here I think McMahan underplays the strength of the conclusion. The reasons underlying the obligation of arrest go beyond those considered by McMahan and this has important consequences for his account of the defeasibility conditions that follow.

McMahan's approach to the requirement of arrest is to focus not on the rights of suspects (which he thinks can be forfeit in certain circumstances), but on the need to protect the innocent from the risks of mistaken forceful action by the police. This is clearly a relevant consideration. But in fact the requirement to minimize mistake in police action, however important, is peripheral to the underlying reason for the requirement of arrest. This reason has more to do with rights than McMahan allows – both the rights of the suspect himself, and of other members of society – and with the societal role played by arrest and punishment.

It is important to remember that the function of arrest is not simply to remove potentially dangerous individuals from society. Arrest is the first stage – the necessary preliminary – to a broader process of morally just criminal law enforcement. This process consists in the familiar elements of arrest and evidence gathering (a police function); trial (a judicial function); and punishment and related outcomes (a function of the prison and probation services, ideally supported by rehabilitation, psychiatric, educational and community services). When thinking about the requirement to arrest terrorist suspects, we must think about the whole process of law enforcement, and especially the possibility of conducting a fair trial, not simply the immediate act of capture.

Once the issue is couched in these terms it is much harder to ignore the fact that important rights are at stake. As Amnesty International has tirelessly stressed throughout its history, every human has a basic right not to be subject to the coercive power of the state without a just and transparent legal process.[1] Moreover this right is possessed by the guilty as well as the innocent. When a criminal has been convicted of a crime we do not then say that he had no *genuine* right to be tried, but only an *apparent* right prior to the establishment of his guilt. Rather, conducting a fair and transparent trial, with appropriate opportunities for appeal, is a necessary condition for punishment to be just. Without it there can be no punitive *authority*, and punishment, even of the guilty, without proper authority is always unjust.

What can account for the peculiar importance and strength of the right to arrest and trial? Part of the answer lies in the fact that the right to trial is not simply a right of the suspected criminal alone, it is a right of *all* members of society: we all have a right that suspects be arrested and tried. This shared right stems from two kinds of consideration. First is what we might call the 'public truth' function of criminal justice. By recording evidence and exposing criminal acts to public scrutiny, judicial trials ideally perform several important social-moral functions. They expose criminals to a kind of 'epistemic shame' (the shame of having others 'know') which is quite different from punitive shame. They can facilitate emotional closure and healing for victims. They allow society to publicly reaffirm and develop shared values within a rational system of law governed by rules of precedent. It is these functions of the trial that 'truth and reconciliation' councils attempt to replicate without the punitive element.

The social functions of trial are important, but there is a second, more important reason underlying the obligation to arrest and conduct trials. We all have a right that suspects be openly tried because this is a fundamental protection (perhaps *the* fundamental protection) against abuse by the power of the state. Much political philosophy in the social contract tradition has emphasized the fear of anarchy – the 'state of nature' – as the prime motivation of political ethics. The state is rightly viewed as fulfilling an essential moral function by curtailing anarchy and enabling co-operative social goods. Yet, as thinkers like Hannah Arendt and Judith Shklar have emphasized, another fear – fear of the abusive and predatory side of state power – is of equal importance for any account of political rights and justice. The fact remains that states possess an unparalleled power to harm and abuse citizens. The twentieth century's grim history of genocide and massacre, disappearances, torture, arbitrary detention, forced marches and ethnic cleansing reminds us how terrible the power of the state can be when not constrained by just laws and judicial institutions. We risk a kind of historical myopia if we view terrorism as posing a unique threat to our rights and security. States have historically demonstrated a power to harm and commit injustice that terrorist groups can so far only dream of.

The right not to be subject to the coercive power of the state without fair trial is our first, and (in a well-functioning judicial system) our best, defence against tyranny and arbitrary state power. This rationale is different to McMahan's worry about mistake in police violence (though it shares with it a concern with protecting a broader set of rights than those of the suspect alone). It is not simply the fear of mistaken violence, but the fear of deliberate violence without accountability that lies at the foundation of the right to arrest and trial. Nor is this an idle fear. The experience of detainees at Guantánamo shows how quickly even liberal democratic states can fall into abusive practices without appropriate legal oversight.

On the view I am advocating, the provisions of just law enforcement – including the rights governing arrest, trial and punishment – serve a dual function. They are at once an enabling component of state power, and a limit on the exercise of that very same power. They are a means for the state to stop criminals on our behalf, and they are our means to prevent the state from itself becoming criminal.

So important is the moral foundation of the right to arrest and trial, that we may wonder how it could ever be justified to kill suspects without trial in the course of police action. In fact the answer to this question is logically embedded in the very same right. For a suspect's right to arrest and trial is also a duty – and the right and duty operate reciprocally. When one is suspected of a crime, one has a duty to submit to a fair trial, if required to do so on appropriate grounds, by agents of the state. But if one fails to observe this duty by resisting arrest then one thereby becomes liable to reasonable police force (including, if necessary, lethal force).

McMahan considers the right to use force against those resisting arrest as a sub-species of self-defence: the point for him is that the police have the right to use force against those who *violently* resist.[2] This is of course true, but it misstates the basic moral mechanism at work. Imagine a suspect who resists arrest by locking himself in a 'safe room' to which no one has access. The police would be justified in using force to break into this room, even at considerable risk to the life of the suspect, though the suspect has threatened no violence in resisting arrest. The reason is that the suspect has made himself liable to police force by spurning a meaningful opportunity to surrender and submit to a fair trial. The police use of force must be proportionate (both to the nature of resistance and the gravity of the accused offence) but it can certainly be lethal.

Of course the police sometimes need to use force in self-defence or the defence of others. But it is against the context of the overriding importance of the composite right and duty of arrest and trial that self-defence must be understood. Self-defence is in many ways an aberration within a law-governed society. Self-defensive violence is sometimes necessary to protect the rights of innocent persons, but it threatens the moral presumption that violence should never be inflicted without legal oversight. Self-defensive violence engages the two elemental fears that lie at the core of political philosophy: permitting self-defensive violence involves the risk of anarchy by multiplying opportunities for the private use of force, and it risks tyranny by providing opportunities for the extra-legal use of violence by agents of state. The conditions for using defensive force have been formulated with these risks very much in mind and traditionally the conditions have been very restrictive indeed. Defensive force must be necessary, proportionate and in response to a threat that is imminent. It is limited, in other words, to necessary action against grave threats that wear their injustice and immediacy clearly on their face. To borrow a formulation from international legal jurisprudence, self-defence is restricted to cases in which there is 'necessity of self-defence, instant, overwhelming, leaving no choice of means, and no moment for deliberation'.[3]

McMahan contests the requirement of imminence, in cases where the threat to innocent people from potential terrorist attack is high. He argues that if five carefully specified tests are met, then a terrorist suspect may be liable to preventive force – in other words he may be killed before he poses an imminent threat to the innocent. The five tests involve the risk posed by the suspect, the effectiveness of the preventive killing compared with arrest, the danger posed to enforcement officers by attempting arrest, active membership of a terrorist organization and that the killing make an actual contribution to protecting innocent persons.

I am sceptical that we can become liable to preventive force in this way. But let us assume that we accept these five tests as correctly stating objective criteria for liability to preventive force. We must still ask how appropriate these tests would be as operational principles for real state officials. As we have seen, the norms that govern arrest and the permissibility of defensive violence are not determined only by the liability or immunity of suspects. They are also responsive to the need to protect all of us from arbitrary state power. In this context we must interrogate the proposed criteria carefully: who will be applying the criteria? On the basis of what evidence? With what oversight? Are we willing to grant the conditional right of preventive killing to officials of our own state, knowing what we know of their mode of operation and the reliability of their intelligence? Would we be willing to extend these rights to our allies in the 'war on terror' such as the Russian, Pakistani, Turkish or Moroccan secret service agencies?

There is moreover an important additional restriction on defensive force, codified within most legal systems. We insist on subjecting defensive action to a *post hoc* judicial review, in order to determine whether the conditions of self-defence have really been met. Those who act in self-defence are therefore required to undertake a significant legal and moral risk: they assume the presumption of wrongful homicide and are forced to plead the exceptional legal defence of self-defence in order to achieve exoneration. The requirement of *post hoc* review applies to the defensive acts of both private individuals and state officials, though the review process takes different forms and reflects different burdens of evidence. By means of *post hoc* review the potentially anarchic violence of self-defence is brought within the purview of legal regulation, albeit in a retrospective manner.[4]

But it might seem that the requirement of *post hoc* review actually strengthens McMahan's argument for preventive police action. If all putatively defensive violence must be subject to the requirement of *post hoc* judicial review, then surely this will act as an effective check on arbitrary state power. Appropriate preventive action can be used to avert potentially devastating terrorist threats and any problems with abuse of the preventive defence power by state officials can be sorted out by the careful *post hoc* application of McMahan's five tests.

The problem with this proposal is that the tests are poorly suited to the task of regulating defensive action, either *post hoc* or *ex ante*, because they are indeterminate. Consider the 'effectiveness condition', a centrally important test. This states that the requirement of arrest can be overridden only if killing a terrorist suspect would be more effective in preventing a future terrorist attack than arresting him. But how are we to judge whether this condition is satisfied in a particular case? It may be true, as McMahan says, that killing a suspected terrorist without first attempting an arrest may bring some tactical advantages through maintaining the element of surprise.

But against this must be balanced several competing considerations of effectiveness. By killing a suspect one gives up all possibility of interrogating him and thus gaining potentially valuable information that could prevent future attacks. One must also consider the effect that our actions have on the recruitment of future terrorists. One of the great advantages of a well-ordered public trial is that it can expose the true character and motivation of culprits. Terrorists under trial are often revealed to be lonely and marginalized individuals, with a readiness to murder infidels and fellow believers alike and whose philosophical and religious beliefs are extreme (even within their own traditions) and often incoherent. Persons exposed in this way are far less likely to serve as models for terrorist recruitment than the heroic martyr killed by the apparently unaccountable iron fist of the oppressor, perhaps by the 'cowardly' means of a remote missile attack.[5]

One may be tempted to conclude on the basis of the interrogation and recruitment considerations that the effectiveness condition will never, or almost never, be met in practice. This would mean that McMahan's account of preventive self-defence will collapse into the traditional account requiring imminent threat. But the deeper point is that we just can't know if that is the case or not. The causal chains between the potential harm averted by the killing of one terrorist suspect, the harm caused by the potential incitement of other terrorists, and the failure to avert harm by killing potential sources of intelligence are long, complex, and dependent on many unknowable counter-factual assumptions. It is highly unlikely that general argument or specific evidence will settle the question of preventive effectiveness conclusively one way or the other.

In the hypothetical examples of philosophical argument, we can simply stipulate that conditions such as effectiveness and necessity are met, and this makes for seductive conclusions. Who would not want to take effective preventive action against terrorist atrocities, if we know the person killed is really liable to defensive force? But in the real world evidence is always ambiguous and problematic. The traditional, restrictive conditions for self-defence are precisely tailored to this ambiguous reality. They operate in a way that is symbiotic and supportive – when an attack is imminent it is much easier to be sure of the necessity and proportionality of the response, and of the unjust nature of the threat. But as soon as one departs from this traditional context of imminent self-defence, the ambiguity and indeterminacy of the conditions become radically amplified. How can we know that the future attack 'prevented' by the police killing of a terrorist suspect would ever have occurred? The evidential void created by expanded conceptions of self-defence will most often be filled by violent action that is arbitrary or politically motivated.

In my view then there are just two appropriate contexts for police violence against suspected criminals. The first is the ordinary right to use necessary proportionate force in defence against an imminent threat. The police share this right with all persons.[6] Second, the police have the right to use proportionate force against those who resist a properly mandated attempt at arrest, after having been given a reasonable opportunity of surrender. Of course the crucial question here is: what constitutes a 'meaningful opportunity to surrender'. In Hollywood shows the police officer always shouts out – 'you are under arrest, come out with your hands up!' This may not be appropriate to complex and dangerous terrorist operations, and other more cautious protocols may need to be developed. But many police forces around the world have experience in conducting arrests of well-organized and well-armed mafia and drug gangs. This experience must be supplemented by comprehensive ethical and jurisprudential debate to establish an appropriate set of powers and protections.

This seems like a restrictive account of police powers – and it is. But I believe that it follows from the premise of treating terrorists as criminals. One risk of drawing this conclusion, of course, is that it will only serve to cast doubt on the premise. If the requirement to arrest suspected criminals is really as strong as I have suggested, perhaps one should after all treat them as combatants. But the reasons for treating terrorists as criminals rather than combatants are political and strategic as much as they are moral.

Since 2001 we have learned the hard way that traditional military force is poorly suited to combating global terrorist movements. Admittedly the occupation of Iraq was executed with mind-boggling incompetence, and it is in any case unclear whether this operation should be regarded as part of the 'war on terrorism'. But even the war in Afghanistan, conducted with comparative success and legitimacy, has failed to root out terrorist activity there. Terrorist groups – small, agile, geographically mobile, informally organized, and often virtually invisible – make a maddening opponent for our armed forces configured, as they are, to smash the armies of nation states. As many leaders, including George Bush, have recognized, terrorism will ultimately be defeated by superior values – the much repeated mantra of winning 'hearts and minds'. Yet if one recognizes this, it seems an act of perversity to elevate terrorists to the presumptively legitimate status of enemy combatant rather than dangerous criminal.

Of course one of the reasons for choosing war rather than criminal law as the primary forum of response to al-Qaeda in 2001 was the fact that policing and judicial institutions with global reach were weak in comparison with military institutions. The United States is a military colossus, and, as the old saying goes, 'to the man with a hammer every problem looks like a nail'. Yet one cannot help wondering how differently things might have turned out if the resources dedicated to the wars in Iraq and Afghanistan had instead been utilized to develop a dedicated international police and judicial capability with a remit to arrest and try terrorists. Those two wars have cost the U.S. government $570 billion as of August 2007 according to the Congressional Research Service, and some estimates suggest that the final cost could be as high as $3 trillion. In comparison the annual operating budget of the international police agency Interpol is just $60 million.

A fair, open and transparent criminal justice system is one of the jewels in the crown of the Western system of values. The challenges in bringing this system to bear on global terrorist movements should not be underestimated, but they do not seem insurmountable given sufficient resources and political will. If the struggle against terrorists and violent extremists is really a battle of values, then we in the West need to deploy our own basic values with more consistency and confidence.

Notes

1 It is interesting to note, however, that combatants in war do not have this right under current international law. They may be killed by agents of the enemy state without trial, irrespective of whether they are fighting in a war of aggression or of defence. They may also be detained without trial for the duration of the conflict as prisoners of war (though they also receive a set of countervailing rights and protections).

2 McMahan, p. 175.

3 The phrase is from the famous 'Caroline Doctrine' formulated by U.S. Secretary of State Daniel Webster in a dispute with the British Crown in 1842 (quoted in Y. Dinstein, *War, Aggression and Self-Defence* (Cambridge: Grotius Publications, 1988), 227).

4 This, incidentally, explains why preventive killing raises profoundly different issues to preventive arrest. The difference lies in the *post hoc* potential for remedying mistake:

those subject to wrongful preventive arrest can be compensated (to some extent); those subject to wrongful preventive killing cannot.

5 It must however be acknowledged that the process of arrest and trial poses its own challenges. The policy of raiding civilian houses in Iraq and Afghanistan to search for suspected terrorists and insurgents has caused considerable resentment among the local population. Moreover, public trials can be used by suspects to grandstand and gain additional publicity.

6 One difference is that while all persons have the *right* to use force in self- and other-defence, the police arguably also have the *duty* to defend others.

7 Khaled Abou El Fadl

Islamic law, human rights and neo-colonialism

My lecture will focus on the interface and tensions between the human rights tradition and the Islamic tradition, particularly Islamic law. What is the 'Islamic tradition' and, more particularly, the Islamic legal tradition? Islamic law stands in a paradoxical position vis-à-vis the human rights tradition. Western scholars have argued that the roots of the human rights tradition are to be found in Judaeo-Christian Natural Law, and more specifically, in the Natural Rights tradition.[1] In my view, after post-Enlightenment Christian thought, the Islamic legal tradition has contributed most to the emergence of the human rights tradition.[2] Today, however, Islamic law is often invoked against the universality of human rights. Many Muslims and non-Muslims believe that Islamic law is fundamentally at odds with modern human rights.[3] They contend that the two systems of thought and institutions cannot be reconciled.

Saudi Arabia, for instance, often specifies that it will comply with a human rights treaty only in so far as it is consistent with Islamic law. Western commentators suggest that these reservations make such treaties meaningless; Saudi Arabia claims that without such reservations, Islamic law is nullified.[4] The issue is whether either system is assumed to be immutable. If Islamic law is expected to accommodate the ever-increasing 'territorial' claims of human rights regimes, will it necessarily lose its integrity? If the space in human life occupied by Islamic law is all-encompassing, does this make human rights marginal and irrelevant?

For the purposes of this presentation, when I refer to the human rights tradition I am not referring to international human rights treaties, which are vehicles for generating positive legal commitments. Nor am I referring to statements of aspiration by sovereign states such as those made in the Universal Declaration. A human rights commitment is an intellectual conviction given reality by protecting and serving the well-being, dignity and autonomy of human beings – simply because they are human. It is important to distinguish civil from human rights. Recognizing only the rights of the citizens of a particular democracy is a form of civil rights commitment.

Recognizing only the rights of particular groups distinguished by race, ethnicity, religion or national affiliation does not amount to a human rights commitment. Human rights are not contingent on the attitude of a majority. On the contrary, only if the majority decides to honour the rights of all human beings is it considered to have acted morally. This is the anti-majoritarian thesis.

A human rights commitment entails a belief in the universality of rights. Attribution of these rights is not contingent on the values that a particular group adhere to. Those who make a human rights commitment are duty-bound to honour the human rights of all people. Reciprocity of conduct or treatment has no bearing on the binding nature of that commitment. People who have made that commitment will not resort to torture even if they have themselves been maltreated or tortured.

And people cannot be coerced into making human rights commitments. The very logic of human rights precludes coercing people into changing their habits, customs and social practices. Social practices cannot be coerced without traumatic social upheaval. More importantly, the use of coercion against socio-cultural convictions is inconsistent with the individual and collective right to self-determination.

Coercing governments raises different ethical questions. For example, attempting to coerce governments to comply with the convention prohibiting genocide or the Geneva Conventions on armed conflicts is in many cases morally defensible. However, attempting to coerce governments to force their citizens to alter their socio-cultural practices is in most cases not morally defensible.

If my analysis thus far makes sense then the idea of universalism versus relativism is a false paradigm. Those who commit themselves to human rights must believe in universal standards but must also respect the right of others to be different; they might be offended by the practices of particular cultures, but feeling revulsion is one thing; failing to respect the right to be different is quite another. The variability of rights raises the same type of challenge and requires a similar response. Proponents of a particular scheme of human rights are bound to believe that at a minimum all human beings must be afforded the set of rights propounded by that scheme. They should not oppose people being afforded more rights than those supported by their own scheme. But any additional rights are then treated as privileges and not universal rights.

I

These abstractions mean very little unless backed up by a conviction firmly embedded in the individual conscience. But the level at which such commitments produce recognizable results is not law but culture. Many laws honouring human rights are mere rhetoric. Political systems, particularly constitutional democracies, may be necessary for the implementation of human rights commitments but do not engender them. It is at the socio-cultural level that individual commitments turn into a collective sense of entitlement, denial, or outrage. Before becoming effective laws, human rights are embedded in individual consciences and expressed as cultural practices. By emphasizing the role of culture as a foundation for human rights practices, I do not mean to marginalize the role of doctrine. Theories of universal human rights are in perpetual dialectic with cultural practices. But this does not mean that human rights paradigms are endlessly negotiable. For example, the growing acceptance in the United States of preventive detention in secret prisons and of the use of torture in the war against terrorism is fundamentally inconsistent with any human rights scheme. I will say more on this point later.

What is or has been the impact of human rights practices on Islamic beliefs and doctrines? It would be fallacious to speak of a single Islamic socio-cultural practice. But any commonality can be ascribed to Islamic doctrines, which originate in textual sources such as the Qur'an and in theological beliefs. Of particular interest to me is the unifying impact of Islamic law on Muslim cultures and particularly on the possibility of Islamic human rights commitments. For most Muslims, Islamic law is *the* normative system to which they willingly defer. There are also countries like Saudi Arabia or Iran, where a particular interpretation of Islamic law enjoys mandatory authority. In these states, governments perform a considerable amount of socio-cultural engineering under the pretence of applying God's law.

II

What is the Islamic legal system? In modern times – especially in the colonial and post-colonial eras – it has been consistently misrepresented. The massive corpus that represents the Islamic legal system – the cumulative determinations of diverse interpretive communities through many centuries; the encyclopaedic reference sources of the different schools of thought; the judicial hornbooks; the collections of *responsa* (*fatawa*), the texts documenting judicial precedents and notable judgments, the many texts on legal reasoning, philosophy and hermeneutics, the large number of texts on ethics (*akhlaq*), morality, principles of governance, administrative law – these have been essentialized into a very simplistic image. Such views often result from treating the Islamic legal system as a politicized symbol. (Of course, no legal system can avoid being manipulated and exploited as a political tool but there is a difference between respecting the integrity of a legal system and ignoring its integrity in order to serve political interests.) No set of legal determinations authoritatively represents the Islamic legal system. It is a cumulative system of juristic investigations by interpretive communities into the Divine Will and the public good. It is represented by several competing schools of jurisprudential thought. These schools diverge on legal methodology and hermeneutical approaches but all of them are considered equally authoritative. When we speak of Islamic law we are speaking of a vast micro-history that presents a rich and complex picture. I emphasize this to counter the stereotypical portrayals of Islamic law as an immutable, code-based system. But I do not want to give the impression that Islamic law is entirely fluid. A specialized linguistic and methodological practice unites the various schools under a single systematic tradition.

It is ironic that with all this diversity the most uniform determinations in the Islamic legal tradition are those most *inconsistent* with contemporary human rights. These are the laws of *hudud*, dealing primarily with the punishment of criminal offences. Because they are adopted by the majority of the different schools, they pose the most formidable philosophical challenge to Muslims who wish to make a commitment to human rights. Most human rights advocates would consider the severing of the left hand of thieves or the stoning of adulterers to be serious human rights violations – at least as serious as the use of torture.

Paradoxically, the laws of *hudud* are the most difficult to apply. From the time of the Prophet, *hudud* penalties have been permitted only under the strictest procedural requirements, limiting the application of these measures. Moreover, the Qur'an also sets up ethical barriers to *hudud* penalties by persistently exhorting Muslims to be merciful and forgiving.[5] The practice of the Prophet indicates that where there is any doubt, the *hudud* penalties cannot be enforced. For most of Islamic history, the *hudud* penalties have had a very limited impact on the socio-cultural practices of Muslims. This serves to illustrate the methodological error committed by cultural fundamentalists Muslim or non-Muslim, who tend to conflate Islamic law with Muslim cultures – or do the exact converse. They assume that all components of Muslim cultures (such as honour-killings or female genital mutilations) are dictated by Islamic law. The example of *hudud* penalties suggests how politicized discourses about the role of Islamic law have become. This politicization has had a devastating affect on efforts to seek a proper balance between the two formidable normative systems of Islamic law and human rights.

III

Today, fundamentalist groups often treat *hudud* penalties as the symbolic embodiment of the Divine Law. They have become a symbol of cultural autonomy and resistance to Western hegemony. Consequently, Islamic activists are often suspicious of any attempt to understand these penalties in their socio-historical context. In this regard, the penalty for apostasy, one of the *hudud* punishments, is an ideal example. Although the Qur'an explicitly provides that there should be no duress in religion, most medieval Muslim jurists argued that an apostate, after being given a chance to repent, ought to be put to death.[6] In the medieval context, this was unremarkable. Among the Abrahamic religions, Jewish law punished rebels and apostates with death while Papal law and procedure prescribed the burning or execution of heretics and apostates.[7] The followers of the nascent religion of Islam experienced a rude awakening when the leaders of the Christian Byzantium Empire arrested the chieftains of Arab tribes from Judham, Ghassan, Kalb and Kinda and had them crucified, mutilated, and eventually executed for the crime of converting to Islam. Not surprisingly, this context impacted on medieval Muslim jurists, who could not transcend the limitations of their time.[8] In the modern age Islamic activists have tended to treat any effort to re-examine the socio-historical dynamics of this law as assaults on the integrity of the Shari'a; they are viewed as disingenuous attempts to appease the West at the expense of the Divine Law.[9]

Through this dynamic the many universalistic and inclusivist orientations within Islamic law and theology have been superseded by a defensive cultural particularism. Of course, this new theology selectively reinvents much of the Islamic intellectual tradition. Other doctrines are ignored or maligned. In some cases, the offending historical material has simply been destroyed. Exclusivists maintain the pretence of being devout and conservative protectors of the one and only true Islam: they alone (they claim) have the will to withstand the cultural onslaughts of Western colonialism and imperialism.[10]

But this approach ignores Islam's substantial humanitarian tradition and aborts any potential for the emergence of human rights schemes founded on the Islamic legal and intellectual tradition. Exclusivists re-engineer the classical legal tradition in response to the onslaught of Colonialism and the ideological aggression of the proponents of human rights. They construct Islamic law such that it becomes a symbol of opposition to Western interventionism.[11]

Muslim cultures have not proven themselves to be uniquely resistant to human rights. Many Christian or simply non-Muslim societies have been no less resistant. But is the obstacle contemporary Islamic beliefs, not least those relating to Islamic law? Or is the West's promotion of a suppositious culture of liberty and human rights one of the main contributors to the rejection of a human rights culture outside the Western world? Has the 'war on terror' helped to promote human rights cultures?

IV

Recently, a number of prominent Saudi jurists shocked the Muslim world when they issued *responsa* (pl. *fatawa*, sing., *fatwa*) declaring that it is sinful for Muslims to believe in the illegality of slavery; that the abolition of slavery was a Western heretical innovation (*bid'atun fasida*) which it is incumbent on Muslims to reject. They also declared that the many Muslim jurists living and dead who condemned slavery as consistent with Shari'a thereby forfeited their status as Muslims. They concluded by acknowledging that all Muslim countries have become signatories to and ratified the Convention on the Abolition of Slavery, but have done so only because they were coerced by the West.

The timing of these *responsa* was disconcerting. They coincided with allegations by Amnesty International and Human Rights Watch that boatloads of children taken from disaster- and poverty-stricken areas such as Pakistan, Bangladesh and Indonesia had been taken to Saudi Arabia and other Gulf countries and sold into slavery.[12] Of course, this created a strong suspicion that the *responsa* were issued to legitimate a gruesome social practice. It is deeply troubling to entertain this possibility.

A *fatwa* issued by a qualified jurist is a non-binding legal opinion. Unless enacted into law – when it becomes a *hukm* or a *tashri'* – a *fatwa* invites Muslims to submit to the Divine Will as it applies to the case at hand.[13] Islamic *responsa* have played an important and complex role in Islamic history. The slavery *responsa*, however, are not likely to have much influence outside Saudi Arabia and the Gulf. What makes these *responsa* interesting is that they attempt to reopen an issue long settled in Islamic law. It has always been an affirmative objective of Islam to end slavery as an institution. The Qur'an and classical Islamic law had for centuries promoted the manumission of slaves. But in the second half of the twentieth century, Muslims accepted that stamping out slavery was a moral objective of the Islamic faith. It was therefore unlawful for Muslims to own or deal in slaves.[14]

The attempt to reopen the issue of slavery clearly illustrates a certain kind of dynamics between Islamic law and human rights. This is not a cultural and ethical divide between Muslims and the West. Abolition was initiated by Western states but the Muslim environment was very receptive. When these *responsa* were issued the United States was pushing for the liberalization of the Saudi political system and for religious reforms. These efforts generated considerable resentment among the Saudi clerical class. American efforts to compel the overhaul of the religious educational institutions of several Muslim countries by exerting pressures on the governments of these countries reinforced their sense of disempowerment. The American government was perceived as attempting to engineer an Islamic faith that served American political interests. This American pressure has undoubtedly had its effect; in a number of Muslim countries, for the first time since the colonial era no courses on Islam are taught. Islam has been replaced in school curricula with courses on *akhlaq* (good conduct).[15] The Saudi *responsa* on slavery exemplified a strategy of resistance to American hegemony in the region.

V

As a religious tradition, Islam shares with the human rights tradition its emphasis on the sanctity of human life. The Qur'an, the teachings of the Prophet Muhammad (the Sunna), and the interpretive communities of Islam all place a high value on human life. Humans are considered viceroys (*khulafa' fi al-ard*); they are said to have entered into a symbolic covenant (*amana*) with God by which creation is entrusted to their care. All human beings are bearers of the Divine trust. But Muslims have the additional duty of bearing witness for God (*shuhada' li-Allah*). They are expected not only to safeguard God's creation but to defend the moral and ethical principles of Islam. They must all times enjoin the good and forbid the evil (*al-amr bi al-ma'ruf wa al-nahy 'ann al-munkar*).[16]

The law (the set of Divine directives)[17] is a sacred trust at the core of this covenantal obligation. Muslims have an obligation to establish justice (*'adl*). This includes the upholding of equity (*'ihsan*), compassion (*rahma*), fairness and equality (*musawa*) and principles such as the presumption of innocence (*bara'at al-dhimma*) and the prohibition against the use of coercion or compulsion (*man' al-ikrah*).[18] As early as the eighth century, diverse interpretive communities maintained that the moral obligation of any Muslim state – and the objective of the Shari'a – is to promote the people's welfare or well-being. Of course, such concepts are highly negotiable. The Muslim classical age,[19] however, refined this concept. The juristic interpretive communities agreed that the protection of dignity (*al-karama*), rationality (*al-'aql*), personality (reputation) (*qiwama*) and privacy (*al-satr*) were among the core values for human well-being. Life, property, dignity and reputation enjoyed a level of sanctity (*'isma*). Classical jurists also developed legal doctrines rejecting practices such as the mutilation of corpses, torture (*al-ta'dhib, al-mithla, al-musabara*), defamation (*al-qadhf*), collective punishment, excessive taxes (*mukus*), and the killing of non-combatants during rebellions or wars.

Although these doctrines had clear humanitarian overtones, they did not constitute significant contributions to the formation of a human rights culture. Compared to other (non-Muslim) legal cultures, they afforded an advance in the degree of respect afforded human beings. But they did not constitute a developed system of ethical reasoning or a coherent set of ideological convictions.[20] Of course, it would be anachronistic to fault Muslim jurists of the tenth or twelfth centuries for failing to articulate coherent humanitarian ideologies.[21] But one wonders why later generations of Muslims did not develop these legal orientations into doctrines that could support a cultural commitment to human rights.

The Arabic word for a moral or legal right is: *haqq*. As early as the ninth century, Muslim jurists recognized the idea or concept of a right. They classified rights as belonging (1) to God; (2) to humans or (3) shared by God and human beings.[22] Rights were recognized as protected spheres and most jurists agreed that the spheres protected by law were life, intellect, lineage, honour and property.[23] Classical Muslim jurists recognized that there was a significant bifurcation between the moral consequences of actions in the Hereafter and the legal consequences of actions on this earth. The rights of God were vindicated by God in the Hereafter while the rights of people were to be vindicated by the legal system on this earth.[24] Furthermore, according to the classical juristic tradition, rights belonging to human beings could not be abrogated by the state or even God.[25]

The classic discourses on *huquq* (rights), in combination with Islam's emphasis on the sanctity of human life, afforded promising orientations. Indeed, some
Muslim commentators cite the *huquq* discourses to proclaim that Islam developed
a Natural Rights tradition like that developed by the West. This claim is problematic at many levels. The *huquq* tradition, unlike that of Natural Rights, was not
primarily focused on exploring inalienable immunities or entitlements. But these
discourses are very similar to the early European debates on natural law; *huquq*
too referred to what properly belongs to God as opposed to what is left to human
jurisdiction.

I ought to note another important classical jurisprudential discourse in Islam.
As early as the ninth century, Muslim theologians and jurists developed a field of
ethics comprising the investigation of good and evil (*al-husn wa al-qubh*) and the
obligation to do good and refrain from doing evil (*al-ilzam*). The most promising
insights into the natural entitlements of human beings are found in this field. The
classical discourses on *husn* and *qubh* investigated the extent to which right and
wrong is rationally derived or defined by revelation. They also investigated imperatives born of ethical values such as justice and compassion.[26]

A few examples: a tradition attributes to Ali, the Prophet's cousin and fourth
Caliph of Islam, the saying: 'If I heard a voice from the sky announce that lying is
good, I would not lie', meaning that lying is inherently evil. The import of this tradition is that no text can render human enquiry into right or wrong superfluous.
However, the implications of this saying remained unexplored except by the Rationalist
schools, which developed interpretive communities exploring the notion that
moral obligations do not begin or end with the revealed text.

Another example more directly pertinent to human rights: according to a very
well-known tradition, Umar bin al-Khattab, close companion of the Prophet and
the second Caliph of Islam, criticized the inequitable conduct of one of his appointed
governors with the words: 'By what right do you enslave people (through oppression and injustice) when they were born free!' This statement too left little imprint
outside the writings of the Rationalist jurists. Exploring its implications, the Qadi
'Abd al-Jabbar, a tenth-century Mu'tazili scholar and author of a remarkable multi-
volume work titled *al-Mughni*[27] (which rivals Aquinas's *Summa* in size, sophistication and insight), reached the conclusion that slavery is inherently immoral (*huwa
qubhun li dhatih wa laysat min makarim al-akhlaq*). This was true even when retali-
ating against the enslavement of Muslims during a war. The Qadi was no outsider
to the Islamic tradition. Islamic jurisprudence and theology have long emphasized
the desirability of manumitting slaves out of charity or repentance.[28] But Rationalists
such as Ibn Rushd (Averroes) or much later, Muhammad bek Shafiq, in many ways
went beyond the literal words of the Qur'an in condemning the institution of
slavery as immoral and therefore un-Islamic (*tunafi makarim al-akhlaq wa hiya
ithmun wa fasad fa laysat min al-Islam*).[29]

The Rationalists of Islam made substantial contributions to human thought – to the ethical legacy of humanity and not just of Islamic culture. They did not conceive of the religious text as supplanting reason but as a firm moral foundation that propels ethical investigation. In doing so, they contributed to the idea of a universal truth both accessible and accountable to human beings and binding upon them. They made Islamic civilization part of a historical progression from Greek philosophy to the European Renaissance and the Age of Enlightenment.[30] Ibn Rushd (Averroes), not Thomas Aquinas, was the first to argue systematically that the a priori principle of moral obligation is to enjoin the good and avoid wrong.[31] This was also Aquinas's First Principle – often credited with opening the door to the Natural Rights tradition. And Aquinas was quite familiar with the thought not just of Averroes but with that of prominent Muslim Rationalists such as Ibn Sina (Avicenna), Ibn Baja (Avempace), and al-Ghazali.[32] In his *Summa*, evincing his familiarity with the micro-discourses of the Muslim Rationalist scholars, Aquinas frequently takes sides with one Muslim philosopher against another.

My point is not to make the typically apologetic and historically inaccurate claim: Muslims did it first! Quite the opposite. Although the Islamic classical tradition was rich with ideas well suited to a cultural trajectory favouring human rights, it did not bear this fruit. In the West, in part by co-opting Islamic intellectual achievements, the Natural Law tradition eventually gave birth to the Natural Rights tradition, which in turn was instrumental in developing the revolutionary idea of universal human rights.[33] And it should be emphasized that the human rights culture is not secular in origin. Many Western historians tend to ignore the fact that Natural Rights emerged from deeply religious (notably Christian) perspectives.[34] The most prominent jurists of the Natural Rights tradition from William of Ockham and Jean Gerson through Pufendorf, Vitoria, Suárez and Grotius to Locke and Rousseau and more recently Karl Barth, Germain Grisez or John Finnis were all deeply religious people. Christian ethics influenced their commitments, choices and priorities.[35] Until the end of the nineteenth century, Natural Rights theorists continued to invoke the Divine as the ultimate source of obligation; even if rights are said to exist in nature, it is the Divine that is the source of obligation.

In Islam, the classical Natural Rights thesis was philosophically developed by Rationalist jurists such as the Andalusians: Ibn Baja (d. 1138), Ibn Aqil (d. 1185), Ibn Rushd (d. 1198), and Ibn Tufayl (1185).[36] The same thesis was treated by Rationalists such as Sadr al-Din al-Shirazi (aka Mulla Sadra) (d. 1641), Ibn al-Hasan al-Tusi (d. 1067), Nasir al-Din al-Tusi (d. 1274), Ibn Aqil (d. 1119), al-Suhrawardi (d. 1191, founder of the school of Illumination), Abu Bakr al-Razi (d. 925), and Fakhr al-Din al-Razi (d. 1209). The Rationalists had a profound impact on the foundations of Islamic jurisprudence but their influence on Islamic civilization as a whole waned after the twelfth century. This was a pivotal point; Islamic civilization, under siege by the Christian West, had now to defend itself against renewed waves of

Crusaders. It suffered the loss of Andalusia[37] and the sacking of Baghdad, the capital of the Abbasid Caliphate, by the Mongols in 1258. Defensive, conservative orientations tend to thrive in times of socio-economic and political unrest. But from the twelfth century onwards a fateful and ironic exchange seems to have taken place – as Rationalist forces retreated in the Islamic civilization, these same intellectual orientations started on their laborious progress in the West.

VI

Rationalist scholars made genuinely original contributions to the classical Natural Rights thesis during the Ottoman and Safavid periods in both Sunni and Shiʿi Islam. But for the most part their works were isolated achievements. The growth of con-servatism and anti-Rationalist theological orientations eventually culminated in the ultra-conservative and uncompromisingly anti-Rationalist Wahhabi movement in contemporary Islam. This was due to a variety of historical reasons that cannot be adequately described in this essay. In brief, the more than a dozen Crusades waged against the Muslim heartland, after assuming a secular veneer, culminated in the humiliating colonial experience, which methodically undermined the institutions of Islamic law.[38] More significant than the military occupation by the West of most of the Muslim world were the economic and cultural concessions forced on Muslims. The abolition of the Caliphate in 1922 and the wholesale adoption of Kemalist secularism in Istanbul, the former capital of the Ottoman Empire and symbol of Muslim unity, was an act of unprecedented historic significance. Of course, long before it was formally abolished, the Ottoman Caliphate's legitimacy was seriously undermined; it had ceased to offer effective governance; its governors were often intolerably oppressive; towards the end of its existence, it was unable to protect its provinces. But the abolition of the Caliphate marked the end of an institution sym-bolizing the idea of Islam not just as a religion but as a civilization. Muslims had succumbed to the new reality of nation states. For centuries the Turks had played a critical role in defending different parts of the Muslim world from invasion and forcible conversion. The Turkish counter-offensive led to the siege of Vienna in 1683. But the Treaty of San Stefano, signed in 1878, extracted humiliating concessions from the Ottomans. The Ottoman Empire might have been the 'sick man of Europe',[39] but its allegiance and identity were clear. Despite the many Arab rebellions, often supported by Western colonial powers, the Turks were allied with Muslim polit-ical causes and, at least in principle, Muslims as a whole remained united against Western colonialism.

But Atatürk's Turkey did not just secularize; it switched sides. It rejected Muslim culture and law as inferior to that of the West. Atatürk actively sought to Westernize every aspect of Turkish life. Turkey declared itself a European coun-try. The Turks also decided to stay out of the ongoing conflict between Muslims

and Christian colonial powers.[40] Like many reform-minded nationalists, Atatürk legitimated the colonial fantasy of the 'White Man's Burden' – the disingenuous idea
that Western powers colonized Muslim countries for their own good. Western col-
onizers claimed to help the colonized rid themselves of traditional social systems
by establishing representative systems of governance. Far more significant were
the economic and political structural realities within which both the colonizer and
colonized were forced to function.

This structural reality was the challenge of modernity and the Turkish response
seemed to confirm a painful reality: that the Muslim *umma* (the united Muslim nation
mentioned in the Qur'an and the traditions of the Prophet Muhammad) had
moved from the realm of inspirational ideal to superstition. The whole Muslim world
was undergoing a massive socio-political transformation that altered the nature and
role of religious beliefs and practices. For only the second time in Muslim history,[41]
the status of Shari'a was openly challenged. But many Muslims contended that while
the renegotiated status of religion in the West was the product of historical processes and needs, the debates in the Muslim world took place within the coercive
contexts of colonialism and a Western-defined modernity. At the heart of all these
debates was a basic anxiety as to whether surrendering to the demands of modernity in effect meant the end of the Muslim tradition. The dominant role of Western
educated elites in Muslim societies exacerbated this anxiety. Modernity has forced
a nationalistic culture on all Muslim states. Citizenship status has come to define
the political treatment likely to be afforded a person – the miserable fate of state-
less Palestinians has amply demonstrated this. Modernity also imposed a de facto
secularism on Muslim societies since secular modern epistemology defined the devel-
opmental aspirations of the Third World.[42] The logic of development purportedly
displaced the authority of religion. Traditional societies, it was claimed, disintegrate
when humans realize that divine sovereignty is fundamentally at odds with their
own sovereign will. Human perceptions of their well-being and needs are shaped
by the aspirations created by Western technologies.

These ideas – and the anxieties that persistently accompany them – continue
to have serious consequences on human rights discourses. The nation state was a
defining component of the world order in the post-colonial era. And after gaining
independence, most Muslim states ended up with secular political orders. From the
eighteenth century on, Western culture and its institutions continued to replace
the institutions of Muslim culture.

One of the most profound changes was the systematic displacement of Islamic
law. This was achieved through a long process of forced commercial concessions,
special privileges for foreign nationals, the right of intervention on behalf of non-
Muslim minorities, courts of special subject-matter jurisdiction, mixed courts such
as the Anglo-Muhammadan courts in India, scholarship programmes for members
of the ruling class to study in European law schools, the construction of secular law

schools that increasingly monopolized the legal market, and the implementation of numerous legal reforms. The end result was the replacement of Islamic law, in most cases, with the Civil Legal system. The institutions that had once supported the development of Islamic jurisprudence became entirely marginal. Most schools of Islamic law were closed primarily due to the shortage of clientele. The death warrant of Islamic law was the co-optation by the state of the private endowments that funded the largest and oldest institutions for the study of Islamic law.[43] A paradoxical duality developed in Muslim cultures: from the age of colonialism to this day, Muslims have mostly been governed by the French legal system. At the same time, the very experts who implemented foreign legal systems would write books exalting the superiority of the Islamic system. In effect, modern Muslims transformed Islamic jurisprudence from a dynamic living system to a relic admired but never used. The reality today is that modern Muslims have been completely deracinated from their own legal tradition. Muslim legal experts are woefully ignorant about the institutions and epistemologies that informed Islamic jurisprudence. As a final irony, Western scholarly discourses on the Islamic legal tradition nowadays have considerable authority in Muslim secular academies.[44]

Some countries attempted to Islamize their legal systems in the 1970s and 1980s by implementing specific measures mostly derived from the *hudud* laws. But these politicized measures were not geared to providing legal solutions to existing problems but to reinforcing the appearance of Islamicity; such campaigns were high on propaganda but did little more than strengthen the perception that Islamic law is fundamentally at odds with the Natural Rights of human beings. Consider the obscene examples paraded before the world: Pakistani and (later) Nigerian rape laws. The unflattering views of Islamic law in the contemporary age are hardly surprising. In part, the sensationalism and apologetics that plague the field of Islamic law are explained by the feeling throughout the Muslim world of being under siege. Given Western interventionism, this was probably unavoidable.[45] This sense of being under siege, combined with an intense sense of alienation from modernity, generated sharply reactive tendencies including the conservatism and intolerance of the Wahhabis. Clinging to idealized prototypes ('the Golden Age') led to a superficial Islamicity that was fundamentally rejectionist.

The discussion thus far explains why Muslims failed to develop the full potential of the Natural Rights strain in their own tradition. Contrary to prevalent stereotypes, the Muslims of today do not reflect the normative systems of their forefathers. Wahhabism, the dominant creed of Saudi Arabia (founded on the intolerant theological views of Muhammad bin Abd al-Wahhab, d. 1791), has popularized the most anti-Rationalist and despotic trends within the Islamic tradition. Ironically, Wahhabis would agree with the secularists that there is no place for human autonomy in the light of God's sovereignty; they would go on to argue that whatever limited rights humans may earn are contingent on the fulfilment of their religious duties.[46] From the eighteenth century to this day, the Wahhabis have formed an alliance with the Al Saud family and rule over Mecca and Medina. And throughout its history, the Wahhabi-Saudi alliance has depended on Western aid and protection, first British then American, for its very survival. Moreover, since the formation of the alliance, Wahhabi militants have slaughtered thousands of Muslims as, with British support, they fought against the Ottoman Caliphate, then turned to massacring Shi'i populations in south Arabia and southern Iraq. Since the founding of the Saudi state in 1932, Saudi governments and Wahhabi theologians have exploited Islam to defend one of the worst human rights records in the world. Wahhabi-Saudi Islam, far from being authentically native, is a fanatic aberration raised and sustained by Western colonialism. The Islamic law applied in Saudi Arabia today is a bizarre blend of nationalistic, pragmatic, empiricist and amoral influences. In another context, I have argued that Wahhabi Islam is effectively a secularized faith in which religion is confined to a peripheral role.[47] And the Saudi legal system belongs to neither the Islamic tradition nor the Western tradition; it is a mangled deformity born of the worst elements of both traditions.

VII

Here we come to an important point. The fact that Muslims have become disconnected from their own legal tradition and failed to develop the Natural Rights potentialities existing in the Rationalist orientation does not explain why human rights cultures have not developed in any case in Muslim countries. With the waning of colonialism, the 1948 Universal Declaration of Human Rights arguably represented a transitional moment in history. Muslim states could have developed human rights cultures on the basis of (1) the Natural Rights tradition represented by the Universal Declaration; or (2) the consensual model that governed human rights conventions. It is true that representatives of some Muslim countries such as Egypt and Indonesia and part-Muslim countries such as Lebanon played an active role in the passage of the Universal Declaration. (Saudi Arabia was the only Muslim country not to vote in favour of the Declaration on the grounds that some provisions were fundamentally inconsistent with Islam.) But at the very point when the Universal Declaration was issued by the General Assembly, most Muslim countries were still subject to colonial rule. Egypt, which had taken such an active role, had not yet gained full independence from Great Britain. The issue of self-determination was complicated not just by de-colonization (some Muslim countries gained their independence only in the 1960s) but by the partition of Palestine. The individual-rights portions of the Declaration were championed in Muslim countries by a Western-educated elite, indifferent or hostile to religion in general. The U.N. Charter placed effective powers in the hands of the Security Council, giving a majority of the world's countries a mere advisory role. No Muslim country is a permanent

member of the Security Council. This reinforced the perception that the Charter
marked a continuation of Western hegemony. The power of veto enjoyed by the
permanent members (especially in the context of the Cold War) greatly diluted the
impact of the Universal Declaration.

In the 1950s, 1960s and 1970s, Muslim countries signed many human rights instruments of the consensual positivist model. But (as we have seen), the signature of
treaties by authoritarian governments does not necessarily reflect the cultures
of those peoples. Moreover, these conventions and treaties were signed as a means
of gaining favour with the superpowers during the Cold War. The U.S. could
refuse to sign major human rights treaties with impunity but few Muslim countries
dared do the same. Instead, some Muslim countries signed but entered reservations; they would comply with the provisions only to in so far as they were consistent with Shari'a,[48] thus allowing them to interpret Islamic law in any way that
they wished. In repeated declarations, such as the Cairo, Doha and Casablanca
Declarations,[49] Muslim governments affirmed their commitment to human rights.
But the governments most active in passing these declarations were the ones with
the worst record of human rights abuses. None of the countries affirming the
incompatibility of international human rights with Shari'a actually enforced the Islamic
legal system.

Because of the limited effectiveness of worldwide conventions, the 1980s witnessed the enactment of regional human rights conventions such as the European,
African and American conventions.[50] It is often argued that regional conventions
were designed to reflect the customs of the regions that enacted them. But this really
holds true only of regions where governments represent the normative choices of
their people. Far from affirming the integrity of international human rights, regional
conventions represented concessions to particularism and cultural relativism.

VIII

The moral and ethical logic informing human rights treaties did not influence the
normative commitments of Muslims. From the Muslim point of view, the whole
field seemed somewhat farcical. Even if superpowers such as the United States agreed
to be held accountable, they often zealously backed governments with abysmal human
rights records, such as that of Iran under the Shah. The U.S. was willing to pretend
that friends like Israel and South Africa did not engage in discrimination. It verb-
ally condemned but in effect ignored human rights abuses by countries such as Saudi
Arabia. Inconsistency, hypocrisy, or multiple standards infected the foreign policies of the supposed champions of rights.[51] Muslims have swung back and forth between the idealism and realism of the West. If Muslims had identified ethical goals and
anchored them in their own intellectual heritage, the effect of Western double
standards might have proved negligible. But one reason why Muslims have not

developed a human rights culture is undoubtedly that they have never experienced them as a living reality.

How *have* they experienced human rights? What has been the impact of human rights in the life of the common Muslim? Here we must return to the *fatwa* issued by the Saudi jurists. They claimed that believing in human rights is so heretical as to render a Muslim an apostate. Who was their intended audience? What induced them to construct a *fatwa* apparently designed to antagonize and offend? Answer: they were flouting the perceived sanctities of the West. However, the intended assault on Western sanctities is done at the expense of Islamic tradition. This repulsive *fatwa* had more to do with cumulative political frustrations than any authentic Islamic tradition. A partial list of those frustrations would include the presence of American troops on Saudi soil; the Saudi government's execution of 160 reputable Wahhabi jurists who dared sign a petition opposing the presence of American forces on Saudi land and the United States' silence about the massacre; the occupation of Iraq and the shocking conduct of the U.S. forces and government in the 'war on terror', in Abu Ghraib and Guantánamo.

This pattern of politicization is a microcosmic example of the Muslim experience with the paradigm of human rights, which has been advocated by, first, colonial powers and then one superpower. These powers preached human rights but what they practiced were civic rights. They acted as if observing civic rights meant upholding human rights and then assumed that this authorized them to preach human rights to the Muslim world. But the problem goes much deeper. Colonialism systematically destroyed local Muslim initiatives to develop the kinds of institutions theoretically recommended by the West – unless such initiatives derived from the colonial power. One example: the 1906 Iranian Constitutional Revolution was pioneered by Shi'i jurists and was remarkably liberal. It was thwarted by a British-Russian agreement threatening that an invasion would follow the first session of its newborn parliament.[52] The lesson imparted by colonialism was clear: human rights is an exercise in hypocrisy; rights and democracy are completely subservient to *realpolitik*; and national norms trump moral norms. Instead of rehabilitating the human rights paradigm, everything that followed colonialism tended to reinforce these negative impressions.

I have already commented on the impact of the Cold War. The CIA aborting the second Iranian Constitutional Revolution in 1953;[53] the 1956 invasion of Egypt; the humiliating 1967 defeat;[54] Kissinger diplomacy and the 1973 war;[55] the Israeli invasion of Lebanon in 1985; the Russian invasion of Afghanistan: was this environment conducive to the development of human rights cultures in the Muslim world? However, the period of real possibilities was the 1990s. The Cold War had ended. Local NGOs emerged on a very large scale. Some of these NGOs in the Muslim world ran huge risks to generate substantive doctrines of human rights and substantive commitments to them. True, these NGOs were for the most part founded by Western-educated elites. But there were encouraging indications that on issues such as torture and due process, they were building a discourse shared with the societies in which they worked.

Alas, the end of the Cold War coincided with the beginning of the Bush era. And the parallels between the Bush era and the colonial age are unsettling. As in the colonial age, we find lip-service given to Islam but a profound alarmism about the living tradition; Islam can be as patriarchal and ritualistic as it likes, as long as it does not challenge the existing power structures. This is why the Bush adminis- tration is comfortable with Saudi Wahhabism; in all political matters, Saudi Wahhabi theology is entirely pragmatic. Saudi Wahhabism (as opposed to the Wahhabism of Bin Laden for instance) makes obedience to rulers, however unjust, a theolo- gical duty. As in the colonial era, at the social and cultural levels religious tolerance tends to disappear. In Western societies, there is a tendency to equate Islam with reactionary historical forces. This tends to legitimate culturally led religious bigotry. In the colonial era, Islam was regularly caricatured. In the United States of today, the flood of bigoted literature and films has risen in proportion to the aggressive- ness of U.S. foreign policy. Few weeks go by without one or more Islamophobic books appearing on the *New York Times's* best-sellers list.

Islamophobia is a necessary adjunct to a foreign policy of social and cultural engineering. The Bush administration and its neo-con ideologues believe that Islam needs social engineering to save Muslims from themselves. This was clearly in evidence in the invasions of both Afghanistan and Iraq. In both instances, think- tanks and lobbying organizations felt free to discuss whether the new constitutions should identify the country as Islam; allow a role for Shari'a; be obligated to grant Christian missionaries visas or not. They knew that the Bush government believed it had the right to directly influence the choices of Muslims; it regarded the incor- poration of Shari'a law as inherently dangerous.[56] Like the old colonialists, the neo- cons felt free to shape how and what is taught about Islam in Muslim countries' school systems. The Bush administration did this in Afghanistan and Iraq. Egypt, Jordan, and the Yemen all revised their secondary-school curriculum in response to pressure from the U.S. Today, in the heart of Mecca, no imam would dare give a sermon about jihad; this is not permitted by the Saudi government because talk of jihad makes the American government nervous.

The policies of the Bush era are similar to Colonialism's in two other respects: exceptionalism and protectoratism. The Bush administration is convinced of its moral superiority; it believes that this superiority justifies abhorrent violations of human rights. Neo-cons act as if the killing and torturing of innocent people is qualitatively different when performed by the U.S. government. The logic of exceptionalism has made what was unthinkable a few years ago if not acceptable then at most a regret- table technocratic infraction. Before the occupation of Iraq, the U.S. government was already engaged in the practice of proxy torture – the 'rendition' of suspected terrorists to countries where they are tortured. It perceives resistance to American occupation as reactionary and this attitude serves to remove moral and legal inhibitions. It was therefore not long before the U.S. government moved from proxy torture to practising torture not just at Guantánamo and Abu Ghraib but at special U.S. detention centres in Iraq, the Arab world, Europe and South America.[57] Predictably, it refused to allow the Red Cross to inspect those detention centres. The U.S. has also engaged in the abduction of Muslim dissidents from several countries including, most notoriously, Italy and the Netherlands. It has performed extra-judicial killings. France won infamy as a colonial power because it had killed one to two million; according to several (non-U.S.) estimates, between the occupation of Afghanistan and Iraq, the U.S. and its allies have killed over one million Muslims. Of course, this figure is not comprehensive; it does not, for example, include the half-million lives, mostly children, lost in Iraq as a result of the U.S.-led embargo.[58] Few Americans can even conceive of the level of violence inflicted on the countries of the Middle East in the name of bringing democracy. By the United Nations' estimates, because of the U.S.-led occupation of Iraq and other U.S. policies involving the use of force, there are currently 8–10 million refugees in the Arab world alone (this does not include Afghanistan, Pakistan, or Iran).[59] The trauma inflicted on the region does not simply concern the victims of occupation and violence. Trauma also creates collective memories, narratives of suffering and humiliation, which generate the rehabilitation of mythologies of past heroism. These are steps in a polarizing process, which is unlikely to aid the acknowledgement of universalities. Bin Laden and those who dream of taking vengeance against the West are, like the neo-cons, believers in the 'clash of civilizations' thesis. Like the neo-cons, they are also firm believers in exceptionalism; they claim to espouse the values of Islam, but commit the most heinous acts. Bin Laden and other radical Islamists are hostile towards human rights advocates, whom they consider agents of foreign powers;[60] but nothing could have undermined the cause of human rights as much as the exceptionalist policies of the U.S. and its allies.

Consider 'the Yamama deal'. The United Kingdom and Saudi Arabia struck a secret agreement involving a $70 billion arms deal allegedly conditional on the British government surrendering two prominent Saudi dissidents, Sa'd al-Din al-Faqih and Muhammad al-Mis'iri, both naturalized British citizens and well-known human rights activists who have exposed the numerous abuses of the Saudi government. Relying solely on evidence provided by the Saudi government, the British government arrested both and charged them with supporting terrorism. The purpose of the proceedings was to denaturalize al-Faqih and Mis'iri as a prelude to surrendering them to the Saudi government, though there can be no doubt that once surrendered to Saudi Arabia both men would have been tortured and killed.[61] The pragmatism of a deal like this leads to cynicism about the very paradigm of human rights. It taps into collective Muslim memories of Western exceptionalism and selectivity. Even the most basic and fundamental human rights are not, it seems, *always* applicable. This is the theory of the occasionality of rights[62] and it never seems to be invoked in *favour* of Muslims.

The harm that befalls Muslims from this politically oriented manipulation of human rights is immeasurable. Very often it affects the Muslim sense of dignity and honour. Protectoratism is a particularly humiliating form of the occasionality of rights and a mirror image of the colonial practice of special privileges. Acting like a traditional or colonial power, the U.S. has privatized significant sectors of the Iraqi oil industry and then granted itself special oil concessions in Iraq. This comes after all Muslim countries, Iraq included, had begun nationalizing their oil industries during the 1950s and 1960s in what was then celebrated as a major step towards self-determination. And again, consistent with colonial practices, American soldiers who raped a young girl and killed her family were not tried in an Iraqi court but prosecuted by an American tribunal. This behaviour replicates the policies of colonial powers in refusing to submit their own citizens to the jurisdiction of native courts. American military tribunals have given out disproportionately lenient sentences to soldiers convicted of torture, rape and murder. If these soldiers were to commit the same offences on American soil or if they were tried under Iraqi law their punishments would have been much more severe.[63]

Even more troubling is the return to a dangerously imperialist form of protectoratism, with the idea that certain ethnicities or religious minorities must be protected by the U.S. I was appointed by President Bush to the U.S. Commission on International Religious Freedom. Having served as a commissioner for three years, I became extremely concerned that there was a strong orientation towards the colonial practice of *wisaya* – the placing of non-Muslim religious minorities under the protection of Western powers. In May 2006, American Copts held a convention in New York City calling attention to the purported persecution of Copts in Egypt. The convention received a letter from President Bush stating the protection of Copts in Egypt was a matter of U.S. national security. The letter did not explain why the protection of Copts, as opposed to, let us say, Muslims living in Israel, is a matter of U.S. national security.[64] Clearly, the U.S. is following the age-old rule of 'divide and rule', replicating the colonial practice of Balkanization by playing off the Muslim world's religious, sectarian and ethnic divisions.

All of the practices discussed above – exceptionalism, occasionality, the civilizing mission and so on – are means to something much more important. This is to provide the U.S. with its claim to high moral ground. It enables Americans to see their interventions as by definition benevolent and to react with shock and contempt when their interventions are resented. A narrow range of words is used to articulate this objective: freedom-loving people, God-given rights, and God-given liberty. Symbolically, this language differentiates between the good and bad – it distinguishes friend from foe. It is a partly secularized version of the historical 'God-fearing people' versus 'savage heathens'. Muslims are told that in order to become 'freedom-loving' they must accept democracy, human rights, and liberal values, institutions considered by the neo-cons to be the product of the Judaeo-Christian tradition. When Muslims adopt liberal values, does this mean that Islamic civilization has been defeated? Are Muslims being invited to join a universal humanitarian culture? (If so, the U.S. hardly seems fit to extend such an invitation.) Or are Muslims being asked to recognize the victory of Judaeo-Christian over Islamic civilization? A recent Rand Corporation report is rather instructive. It argues that liberal Muslims, even if committed to the ideals of human rights and democracy, are not natural allies of the U.S. and the West because they remain committed to an Islamic identity.[65] The U.S. ought therefore only to support secularized Muslims because they are more easily convinced of the value of U.S. strategic goals. The report then goes on to list secular Muslims deemed acceptable to the U.S. Every single person on this list is either an Islamophobe or a self-hating Muslim. Examples include Salman Rushdie, a principled spokesman against Islamic convictions, Wafa Sultan, a proud atheist, and Ayan Hirsi Ali, the author of the best-selling book: *I, the Infidel*.[66] The report bolsters the suspicion that the current so-called civilizing mission is not a mission but a crusade. Cultures of human rights and democracy cannot grow in coercive contexts. There can be no true sense of dignity when a people live under foreign occupation. Cultures of occupation lead to endless cycles of resistance and repression that are hostile to human rights.

The U.S., like its colonial predecessors, has been keen on building parliamentary institutions. Superficially, such institutions legitimate the occupier; elections may pre-empt revolutionary movements. But the imposition of democratic institutions does not create a democratic system. Neither authoritarian local rulers nor colonial powers have felt secure enough to forego power and thus allow the emergence of democratic constitutionalism. Institutions constructed under these conditions typically lack durability. Students of colonialism will not be surprised if the electoral institutions of Iraq and Afghanistan crumble as soon as the U.S.-led occupation departs. The neo-cons seem unaware that this is not because of a lack of American power but because of its excessive use.

My point is to emphasize the counter-productiveness of policies that betray their own declared ideals. Understandably, the Muslim world is increasingly being asked to take responsibility for itself and to stop blaming the West for its own failures. But one cannot ignore the impact that the West has had on Muslims. In terms of historical memory, colonialism does not belong to the distant past. Western countries have continued to be intimately involved with numerous aspects of the Muslim world especially the Middle East. Western politicians have resisted the idea that Muslims could be simultaneously committed to an Islamic identity and democracy and human rights. They have therefore adopted a policy of silent acquiescence in the repression of every Islamic movement that has successfully competed in fairly held elections (Algeria, Jordan) and the pre-emptive repression of Islamic activists or groups who seemed well placed in provincial elections (Egypt, Jordan);

they have remained quiet about the escalating levels of repression in countries where Islamic groups were believed to be particularly strong (Tunisia, Mauritania, Yemen, Bahrain); and failed to take decisive stands when popularly elected governments with Islamic proclivities have been overthrown by secular military juntas (Pakistan, Turkey). The same bias is responsible for wasted opportunities in dealing with liberal but Islamic orientations in Sudan and Iran and has led to the immoral practice of persuading one country to invade another either to bring the downfall of a purportedly Islamic government or to prevent such a government from coming into power, as in the invasions of Iran by Iraq and Somalia by Ethiopia. Part of the price tag for attempting to overthrow the Islamic Republic of Iran was a decade-long silence on Saddam's intolerable human rights record and his infamous genocide against the Iraqi Kurds.

In short, it is difficult to ignore the reality of Western anxiety concerning Islam in power. It is difficult to explain to Muslims the ease with which Western countries deal with extremist Hindu parties coming to power in India or fundamentalist Jewish parties coming to power through coalition in Israel. Compare this with the attitude of Western states towards any Islamic political party regardless of its profession of democratic values: the Muslim Brotherhood in Egypt and Jordan, and the Islamic Renaissance Party in Tunisia.[67] It is hardly surprising that the Muslim laity responds to these inconsistencies by tapping into its not too distant historical memory; its experience with the West supports arguments about double standards, hypocrisy, and religious hostility.

The despotic secular governments of Muslim countries certainly believed they had understood the nature of the game – they could avoid being pressured by Western governments about their abysmal human rights records if they limited their repression to Islamists, who just happened to be their most formidable foes. With the end of the Cold War, there was euphoria about the possibility of a new era for human rights. But in the Middle East this sense of hopefulness was shared only by a few secular thinkers. Almost all Islamists took a pessimistic view of this new period. During the Cold War, Western governments sought tactical advantages in supporting some Islamist movements – alas, not always the most humanistic or enlightened movements. With the end of the Cold War this incentive no longer existed. It is important to remember that most of the governments of the Muslim world are not only staunchly secular but have a well-founded fear of anything Islamic that they cannot control. Some governments, such as the Moroccan, Sudanese, Libyan, Pakistani, and other states, wear a thin Islamic veneer in the belief that this bolsters their legitimacy, coupled with zero tolerance towards any competing claim to Islamicity. This intolerance is even more severe in the case of Saudi Arabia, whose proclaimed *raison d'être* is its guardianship of the two holy sites of Mecca and Medina and of authentic orthodox Islam. A dissenting Islamist in Saudi Arabia is guaranteed to meet a grimmer fate than that of a dissenting secularist.

The intensification of Western repression against Islamic thinkers or activists has at times been coupled with policies that seemed designed to change the religious trajectory of society – policies that ranged from banning the wearing of the veil in schools, universities and governmental institutions to liquidating Islamic financial institutions, banning the use of loud speakers in the call for prayers, prohibiting unauthorized individuals from public preaching, or sharply decreasing the amount of religious programming in state-regulated television. These policies were undertaken in the hope of changing the popular basis for political legitimacy in Muslim countries. They only succeeded in convincing Muslims of the foreignness of their own governments. Predictably, the repression of Islamists led to the sense that there was a sustained effort designed to exclude Islamic values from the lived public space of Muslims. Thus at the end of the Cold War, when Western theorists enthusiastically predicted a new world order,[68] the experience of most Muslims, especially in Middle Eastern countries, was one of alienation. This was a direct outcome of the intolerable despotism of most Muslim governments, which had become alien entities holding on to power through brute force.

IX

The ultimate consequence of this process was to create the setting for the irrational polarization that has taken place in the Bush era. The West's tacit approval of the human rights abuses committed against Islamists contributed to a disastrous process of disinformation about the relationship between the West and Islam. Polarization leads to the dehumanization of the other, which is a necessary prelude to the breakdown of moral barriers to the use of force. The ideas of the neo-cons represented a true paradigm shift. Since 2001 there has been an elitist plutocracy that rules the world with a hegemonic power not seen in my opinion since the Roman Empire defeated Carthage. The world has regressed: a superpower or empire, in the name of a religious truth (very much like the vulgar Natural Law tradition), demands personal allegiance from the leaders of weaker states and treats such states as satellites. Nations are given a draconian choice: you are either with us or against us. This bears a painful resemblance to historical fundamentalist divisions such as the abode of Islam or Christendom versus the Pagans or Infidels. These new plutocrats believe that God is pleased with what they do.[69] Of course, the Bin Ladens of the world believe the same. What is completely lost between the two moralizing but immoral camps is inalienable human rights.

Conclusion

Why have Muslims not built polities in which human rights are upheld and respected? If my analysis is correct, the question ought to be: How could Muslims have possibly done so?! Human rights constitute a rare and remarkable development in human history. As Muslims entered the modern age, none of the political paradigms forming part of their reality afforded convincing human rights models. The superficially promising post-Cold War period set the stage for the Bush era – an era that turned back to the paradigms of colonialism. In the field of human rights, Western civilization – the dominant civilization of this age – has neither led by example nor exerted a positive influence on Muslim cultures. One way to see the experience through Muslim eyes is to consider the number of Muslims who have been killed or injured or made into refugees in the twentieth and twenty-first centuries as a direct result of Western policies in Algeria, Palestine, Egypt, Syria, Lebanon, Iraq, Iran, Libya, Somalia, Nigeria, Afghanistan, the Philippines, Indonesia, and other countries. The calculation must be made in the millions.

There is no alternative to developing human rights cultures through a cumulative process of education and internally generated pressure. Every society has its own epistemological and ontological sources; in the case of Muslim societies the most persuasive sources are those of Islam. But Muslims have been uprooted from their own tradition. The puritanical Wahhabi movement has, under the sponsorship of the Saudi state, succeeded in convincing many Muslims and non-Muslims alike that its intellectual and moral impoverishment represents the sum of what Islam has achieved. It has played a devastating role, perhaps surpassed only by colonialism, in obscuring the richness, diversity and humanity of Islamic tradition. Now the Bush policies have returned Muslims to the alienating policies of colonialism and boosted the legitimacy of Wahhabism.

Muslims must make their own way to human rights; they must do so by anchoring themselves in the elements in Islam that could have led to firm commitments in favour of human rights, and could still do so. The challenges appear insurmountable. But a true believer knows that God is capable of doing anything. Every observing Muslim knows the teaching: 'If a people chooses to be with God, God chooses to be with them'. What better way of choosing to be with God than to celebrate God's creation by recognizing the inherent value of each of his viceroys on earth?

Notes

1 See *Stanford Encyclopaedia of Philosophy*, James Nickel and Betsy Lamm, s.v. 'Human Rights', http://plato.stanford.edu/entries/rights-human/ (accessed 1 August 2007). See also Jack Donnelly, 'Human Rights and Human Dignity: An Analytical Critique of Non-Western Conceptions of Human Rights', *American Political Science Review* 76 (1982), 303 (stating 'most non-Western cultural and political traditions lack not only the practice of human rights but the very concept. As a matter of historical fact, the concept of human rights is an artifact of modern Western civilization'.).

2 See George Makdisi, *The Rise of Humanism in Classical Islam and the Christian West* (Edinburgh: Edinburgh University Press, 1990). See also Mehdi K. Nakosteen, *History*

of Islamic Origins of Western Education (Boulder: University of Colorado Press, 1984) and Joel Kraemer, *The Culture Bearers of Humanism in the Renaissance of Islam* (Tel-Aviv: Tel-Aviv University, 1984).

3 See Muhammed Sa'id Al-'Ashmawi, 'Reforming Islam and Islamic Law', in *Islam in Transition*, ed. John J. Donohue and John L. Esposito, 2nd edn. (New York: Oxford University Press, 2007), 181–3.

4 Ann Mayer, *Islam and Human Rights: Traditions and Politics* (Boulder: Westview Press, 1991), 13–14.

5 See Khaled Abou El Fadl, 'The Death Penalty, Mercy and Islam: A Call for Retrospection', in *Religion and the Death Penalty*, ed. Erik C. Owens, John D. Carlson and Eric P. Elshtain (Grand Rapids, MI: W.B. Eerdmans, 2004).

6 See K. Abou El Fadl, 'Law of Duress in Islamic Law and Common Law: A Comparative Study', *Arab Law Quarterly* 2 (1991), 121 and *Islamic Studies* 30 (1991), 305.

7 See Khaled Abou El Fadl, *Rebellion and Violence in Islamic Law* (New York: Cambridge University Press, 2001).

8 During the formative period of Islamic law (the first three Islamic centuries or the seventh to the tenth centuries AD), the charge of apostasy was typically invoked in cases in which the authority of a state legitimated by religion was challenged by seditious conduct that included collective abdication of the Islamic faith. In the pre-modern era as a whole, charges of apostasy were rarely brought against private individuals. Before the colonial period of Islamic history there are very few documented cases of individuals prosecuted on charges of apostasy and executed. For a more detailed discussion, see *Rebellion and Violence* (note 7).

9 See Abid Ullah Jan, 'The Limits of Tolerance', in *The Place of Tolerance in Islam*, ed. Joshua Cohen and Ian Lague (Boston: Beacon Press, 2002), 42–50.

10 See Abou El Fadl, *The Great Theft: Wrestling Islam from the Extremists* (New York: Harper, 2005).

11 Ibid.

12 See the Central Intelligence Agency's World Factbook report on Saudi Arabia: 'Saudi Arabia is a destination country for workers from South and Southeast Asia who are subjected to conditions that constitute involuntary servitude including being subjected to physical and sexual abuse, non-payment of wages, confinement, and withholding of passports as a restriction on their movement; domestic workers are particularly vulnerable because some are confined to the house in which they work and are unable to seek help … *tier rating*: Tier 3 – Saudi Arabia does not fully comply with the minimum standards for the elimination of trafficking and is not making significant efforts to do so'. As reported by UNICEF, the tsunami created a substantial and significant possibility of increased human trafficking from South and Southeast Asia; see UNICEF, 'Press Release on the Tsunami Disaster', www.unicef.org/media/media_24721.html (accessed 1 August 2007). These problems were also widely reported in the Asian press. See Channel News Asia Report, 'Criminals and Opportunists Take Advantage of Tsunami Tragedy', www.channelnewsasia.com/stories/afp_asiapacific/view/125654/1/.html (accessed 1 August 2007). The convergence of these reports suggests that the tsunami disaster greatly increased the number of slaves trafficked to Saudi Arabia and other countries in the Middle East.

13 It is perfectly possible for a jurist to find no convincing evidence that God has any will concerning the situation at issue. In these situations, jurists are supposed to rely on mandatory legal presumptions such as: Unless there is specific evidence of a prohibition, permissibility should be assumed, or: Every person is presumed to be free of obligation or liability unless there is evidence to the contrary, or: Individual harm cannot be presumed to constitute a public harm, but public harm is evidence of impermissibility. For a more detailed discussion, see Khaled Abou El Fadl, *Speaking in God's Name* (Oxford: Oneworld, 2005), 9–169. For a more detailed discussion of the Fatwa and the Islamic legal process in general, see Khaled Abou El Fadl, *The Authoritative and the Authoritarian in Islamic Discourses*, 3rd printing (Alexandria: Al-Saadawi Publications, 2002).

14 See *Islam and Human Rights* (note 4).

15 In the wake of the genocide against Muslims in Bosnia the United States did not react by demanding that educational curricula in Serbia or Croatia be revised to remove bigoted teachings about Islam. Likewise, the United States never admits the existence of racially prejudiced or religiously bigoted portrayals of Arabs and Islam in Israel. Moreover, the American government itself has not been open to having conversations either with Muslim states or NGOs about the way that Islam is taught in public schools in the U.S. These facts are well known in the Muslim world and contribute to the sense of disempowerment felt by many Muslims.

16 All Islamic sects and schools of thought agree that enjoining the good and forbidding the evil is a solemn ethical obligation on Muslims. There was, however, some theological disagreement as to whether this obligation was a sixth pillar of the faith. All Muslims are in agreement that there are five pillars that define the Islamic faith: (1) the testament of faith; (2) five daily prayers; (3) fasting the month of Ramadan; (4) paying alms to the poor (the obligation of *zakat*); and (5) Hajj or pilgrimage to Mecca once in a lifetime for those capable of doing so. The Rationalist school of thought (historically, known as the Mu'tazila) contended that the duty to enjoin the good and forbid the evil was a sixth pillar of the Islamic faith. See *The Great Theft* (note 10), 122–4.

17 The term 'law' here does not necessarily mean a detailed set of positive commandments; the law means the fundamental and basic Divine directives to human beings, directives not subject to the vagaries of time and place. The Covenantal Law is absolute, immutable, eternal, and inherently good (Shari'a). What is derived from the Covenantal Law is contingent, contextual, revisable and experimental (*fiqh*). On the distinction between Shari'a and *fiqh*, see *Speaking in God's Name* (note 13), 30–40; Irshad Abdal-Haqq, 'Islamic Law: An Overview of Its Origin and Elements', in *Understanding Islamic Law*, ed. M. Ramadan (Lanham, MD: AltaMira Press, 2006), 3–42.

18 See *Speaking in God's Name* (note 13), 27–8.

19 There are various definitions of the Islamic classical age, but in this context I use the expression to refer to the period from the time of the death of the Prophet to the ninth/ fifteenth century.

20 Modern-day Islamists retort that the Qur'an provides a coherent ethical framework for a humanitarian ideology. This often-heard argument ignores the distinction between the potentially perfect realization of the Qur'an and a cultural realization of it. The Qur'an

may indeed embody the most perfect ethical and humanitarian message but this does not mean that Muslims today have fully understood its message.

21 On humanistic orientations in medieval Islam and on their likely impact on the development of European humanism, see the works by Makdisi, Nakosteen and Kraemer cited in note 2.

22 See Khaled Abou El Fadl, *Islam and the Challenge of Democracy* (Princeton: Princeton University Press, 2004), 23–30.

23 Ibid.

24 The important exception to this rule is the *hudud* penalties. See below.

25 See also *Understanding Islamic Law* (note 17) 50–7; and Wael B. Hallaq, *Islamic Legal Theories* (New York: Cambridge University Press, 2004), 85.

26 See generally Khaled Abou El Fadl, *The Search for Beauty in Islam* (Lanham, MD: Rowman & Littlefield, 2006).

27 He also wrote a much shorter set of works known as the five epistles that in many ways are even more significant for the fields of natural law, natural rights, and ethics than *al-Mughni*, which is an encyclopaedic opus documenting in great detail the arguments of al-Basri's opponents.

28 The Qur'an itself repeatedly urges Muslims to manumit slaves. Classical Muslim jurists almost always dedicate a chapter of their writings to discussion of the legal issues relating to the manumission of slaves, notably the rules concerning the possible right of a slave to buy back his freedom from the owner and the rights of a slave to own money or property (without which discussing the right of a slave to buy his/her freedom is otiose.) These writers rarely dedicate a chapter to the topic of purchasing slaves.

29 See Ibn Rushd, *The Distinguished Jurist's Primer*, tr. Imran Ahsan Khan Nyazee (Reading: Garnet, 2000).

30 Most Western (and even Muslim) scholars writing on the European heritage of faith and reason specify their purported Hebrew origins before going on to the Greek tradition, the Greco-Roman world, Christian Scholasticism, Humanism, Thomism, Renaissance, the so-called Cartesian revolution, the Protestant Reformation – including the Lutheran revolt and Calvinism. Then, if they are fair-minded, they proceed to the Catholic Reformation and thence to the birth of the Enlightenment and the reason-based progression to the age of modernity and secularism. This is somewhat inconsistently called the Judaeo-Christian heritage. In the absence of the Islamic connection, this tradition would be discontinuous yet the 'Muslim link' is mostly ignored. The Rationalist orientations within Islam not only influenced numerous Christian theologians and philosophers but had a considerable impact on Jewish thinkers such as Maimonides.

31 See *The Culture Bearers* (note 2).

32 Although al-Ghazali was associated with the Ash'ari theological school of thought, he also wrote a very well-known refutation of the philosophical methods of speculative theology. In the later phases of his life his thought was marked by a distinctive blend of aesthetic rationalism or perhaps rational aestheticism. Al-Ghazali influenced a considerable number of Western thinkers: from Thomas Aquinas to Ramón Marti, author of *Pugio Fides*, and all the way to Pascal.

33 A number of scholars contend that the Western civilization and all its ethical achievements, including human rights, originated from a uniquely Christian or Judaeo-Christian foundation. For instance see, Thomas Woods, *How the Catholic Church Built Western Civilization* (Washington DC: Regnery Publishing, 2005), 197–215.

34 I am aware that this is a controversial claim and that there are scholars (typically of the positivist orientation) who believe that universal human rights developed only when rights theorists freed themselves from the shackles of religion. In fact, some have argued that in an effort to make their theories accessible, accountable, and legitimately universal, Natural Rights theorists, in effect, got rid of God, and attempted to base their theories on reason alone or rationally justified basic goods. But it is argued that, in doing so, Natural Rights theorists entirely undermined their own coherence or plausibility. This is sometimes dismissively referred to as 'the crisis of Natural Rights theory' but criticisms of modern Natural Rights theories invariably seem to go back to the so-called 'Naturalistic Fallacy'. For instance, see Pauline Westerman, *The Disintegration of Natural Law Theory: Aquinas to Finnis* (Leiden: Brill, 1998), especially 231–85. I cannot deal with this here. But note that the argument that rights theory made sense only after it had discounted the divine as an authoritative frame of reference is obviously a normative and not a historical claim.

35 See Elizabeth Bucar and Barbara Barnett, eds., *Does Human Rights Need God?* (Grand Rapids, MI: Edermans Publishing, 2005) especially the article by Max Stackhouse, 'Why Human Rights Needs God: A Christian Perspective', 25–40.

36 The author of *al-Hayy bin Yaqdhan*, a book that became widely influential in both the Islamic and Latin-language worlds. Eventually, this tale was plagiarized into the famous Robinson Crusoe story.

37 The loss of Muslim Spain was gradual and protracted; not until the mid-fourteenth century was all of Muslim Spain (with the exception of Granada) conquered by the Christian Kingdoms. Granada was captured in 1492.

38 Reportedly, the French general who led the military campaign against Syria made a point of visiting the grave of Saladin in July 1920 to declare: 'Here Saladin! We have returned, but this time we are here to stay!' See Robert Fisk, *The Great War for Civilisation* (New York: Alfred A. Knopf, 2005) and Karen Armstrong, *Holy War* (London: Macmillan, 1988).

39 This meant that the competing colonial powers impatiently awaited the death of the Ottoman Empire so that they might rush in and grab its possessions.

40 Many intellectuals from various parts of Muslim world, such as the well-known jurist Rashid Rida, argued that Atatürk's reforms were intolerable to a Muslim people such as the Turks and that it was therefore only a matter of time before the Turks rose in rebellion against Atatürk's policies.

41 In my view, the first time was when Shari'a established itself as the authoritative moral and legal point of reference for all Muslims in the first century of Islam, shortly after the death of the Prophet. Of course, many Western scholars would take issue with this claim, and insist – without much evidence – that Shari'a only established its authority several centuries after the Prophet's death.

42 This approach is quite widespread. It suggests that empiricism, realism and individualism are the dominant philosophies of the developed world because they are necessitated by the logic of modernity.

43 *The Great Theft* (note 10), 26–45.

44 This is demonstrable, for instance, in the often-repeated jargon about closing the gates of *ijtihad* in the tenth century and in the transplanting of Western discourse asserting that al-Shafi'i founded the field of *usul al-fiqh* – a position now uncritically accepted in Muslim scholarship.

45 See generally *The Great War for Civilisation* (note 38).

46 For a fuller account of Wahhabi theology, see generally *The Great Theft* (note 10).

47 See generally, Khaled Abou El Fadl, *And God Knows the Soldiers* (Lanham, MD: University Press of America, 2001).

48 See *Islam And Human Rights* (note 4).

49 See 'Cairo Declaration on Human Rights in Islam', art. 17(c), 5 August 1990, *Organization of the Islamic Conference* A/CONF.157/PC/62/Add.18 (1993), available at www.religlaw.org/interdocs/docs/cairohrislam1990.htm. See also WTO, 'Doha Declaration', *Doha WTO Ministerial 2001*, Ministerial Declaration adopted on 14 November 2001, available at www.wto.org/english/thewto_e/minist_e/min01_e/mindecl_e.htm. See also, 'Casablanca Declaration', released at the Middle East/North Africa Economic Summit, Casablanca, Morocco, 30 October – 1 November, 1994, *U.S. Department of State, Dept. of State Dispatch*, 7 November 1994, available in LEXIS, GENFED Library, DSTATE File.

50 See Inter-American Commission on Human Rights, 'American Declaration of the Rights and Duties of Man', art. 13 (1948), available at www.cidh.org/Basicos/basic2.htm. See also 'African Charter on Human and People's Rights', art. 5, 27 June 1981, O.A.U. Doc. CAB/LEG/67/3 rev. 5, reprinted in 21 *I.L.M.* 58 (1982) and the 'European Convention for the Protection of Human Rights and Fundamental Freedoms', 4 November 1950, *European T.S.* no. 5.

51 See Kenneth Anderson, 'Secular Eschatologies and Class Interests', in *Religion and Human Rights*, ed. Carrie Gustafson and Peter Juviler (Armonk, ME: Sharpe, 1999), 115. See also, Richard Falk, *Human Rights Horizons: The Pursuit of Justice in a Globalizing World* (New York: Routledge, 2000).

52 See Helen Chapin Metz, ed., 'Iran: A Country Study', *Country Studies/Area Handbook Series* (Washington, DC: Library of Congress, 1987). Similar cases of the European powers actively aborting any movement towards constitutionalism and democracy occurred in Egypt and Tunisia. See Helen Chapin Metz, ed., 'Egypt: A Country Study', *Country Studies/Area Handbook Series* (Washington, DC: Library of Congress, 1990) for a discussion of British attempts to prevent the emergence of any type of constitutional or democratic government in Egypt in the nineteenth and twentieth centuries, and Encyclopaedia Britannica, 'Entry on Tunisia: The Growth of European Influence', www.britannica.com/eb/article-46620 (accessed 17 July 2007) for an account of how Tunisia's newly formed constitutional government – the first in the region, which established equal rights before the law for all Tunisian subjects – was undermined by European intrigues and interests and finally terminated by the French invasion of 1881.

53 For an extensive discussion of how the bloody CIA-sponsored coup that ended the Mossadeq era in Iran killed off the liberal constitutionalist trends in Iran and directly

led to the birth of Khomeni's illiberal theory of the *vilayat al-faqih* (the rule of the jurist-counsel) see Mark Gasiorowski, *U.S. Foreign Policy and the Shah: Building a Client State in Iran* (Ithaca: Cornell University Press, 1991).

54 The humiliating 1967 defeat is said to have killed off pan-Arab nationalism, and severely damaged the cause of liberalism in the Arab world. However, defeat alone is not the issue here so much as the war crimes committed during and immediately following that defeat. Much as the later American-led war to liberate Kuwait involved a proverbial turkey-shoot of retreating Iraqi soldiers, so Israeli soldiers not only shot withdrawing Egyptian soldiers in 1967 but massacred a large number of surrendered Egyptian soldiers and prisoners of war. Despite Egypt's vocal and repeated complaints that Israel had committed war crimes by killing POWs, the accusations were dismissed out of hand by the U.S. However, a number of reports have emerged during the last ten years that strongly suggest that the murder of Egyptian POWs by Israeli soldiers did in fact occur and was probably approved by the Israeli Army's command structure. See Lisa Beyer, 'A Soldier's Confession: Admitting to Killing Egyptian POWs in 1956, a Veteran Stirs a Nation's Conscience', *Time Magazine*, 28 August 1995 (vol. 146, no. 9). See also Katherine M. Metres, 'As Evidence Mounts, Toll of Israeli Prisoner of War Massacres Grows', *Washington Report on Middle East Affairs*, February/March 1996, 17, 104–5.

55 Christopher Hitchens, *The Trial of Henry Kissinger* (New York: Verso, 2002).

56 See Angel Rabasa, Cheryl Benard, Lowell H. Schwartz and Peter Sickle, 'Building Moderate Muslim Networks', *RAND Center for Middle East Policy Report* (Santa Monica, CA: Rand Corporation, 2007).

57 Remarkably, the Bush administration obtained a 50-page memorandum from the office of Legal Council at the Department of Justice asserting that the president, notwithstanding the Convention Against Torture (CAT), could authorize the use of torture without violating international law – although CAT does not permit any derogations (exceptions). See Karen J. Greenberg and Joshua L. Dratel, eds., *The Torture Papers* (New York: Cambridge University Press, 2005).

58 The precise number of deaths caused by the embargo is a matter of debate but the half-million estimate cited above is probably on the low side. A number of academic studies have found that 350,000–500,000 Iraqi children died between 1991 and 2000 as a result of the embargo. See Mohamed Ali, John Blacker and Gareth Jones, 'Annual Mortality Rates and Excess Deaths of Children Under Five in Iraq, 1991–98', *Population Studies* 57 (2003), 217, which finds that 400,000–500,000 children under the age of five had died as a result of the embargo by 1998. See also David Cortright, 'A Hard Look at Iraq Sanctions', *The Nation* (3 December 2001), which cites two earlier academic studies on the subject, indicating that approximately 227,000 children had died by 1998, and 350,000 children by 2000, as a result of the embargo.

59 www.unhcr.org/cgi-bin/texis/vtx/statistics/opendoc.pdf#zoom=100 (UNHCR Report on Refugees in the Middle East.

60 In two statements made on 21 October 2001 and 6 October 2002, Bin Laden mocked the Western commitment to democracy and human rights, describing it as hypocrisy, and predicted that his war with the West would send both institutions 'to the guillo-

tine' as his war led the West to show its true inhumane face. See Bruce Lawrence, ed., *Messages to the World: The Statements of Osama Bin Laden* (London/New York: Verso, 2005), 113 ('guillotine') and 170; and Khaled Abou El Fadl, 'The Crusader; Why We Must Take Osama bin Laden's Writings Seriously', *Boston Review*, March/April 2006.

61 See www.guardian.co.uk/world//sep/27/bae.saudiarabia; www.publications.parliament. uk./pa/cm199596/cmhansrd/vo960124/debtext/60124-51.htm.; http://findartides.com/ p/articles/mi_qn4158/is_19960224/ai_n14035752; www.telegraph.co.uk/htmlcontent. jhtml?html=/archive/1996/04/18/ndis/8.html. At the time of writing, both men are still resident in Britain. Dr. Faqih is currently litigating to have his name removed from the UN 1267 Committee list of terrorists.

62 For an extensive discussion of the issues surrounding American exceptionalism and selectivity, see Michael Ignatieff, ed., *American Exceptionalism* (Princeton: Princeton University Press, 2005).

63 See Richard Falk, Irene Gendzier, Robert Jay Lifton, eds., *Crimes of War: Iraq* (New York: Nation Books, 2006).

64 Further, the Commission's most recent report similarly focuses on the alleged persecution of Copts in Egypt while completely neglecting the human rights abuses committed against Muslims in Israel. See Nina Shea, Congressional Task Force on Religious Freedom, 'Religious Freedom in Egypt: Recent Developments', *Congressional Testimony by USCIRF Vice Chair*, 23 May 2007. The Commission's report is at complete odds with the State Department Report, which paints a far rosier picture regarding the position of Copts in Egypt, pointing out that five of the twenty-five appointed members, as well as the president, of the quasi-governmental (Egyptian) National Council for Human Rights are Copts and that a significant portion of the Coptic population have been able to travel to Israel. See State Department Report, 'Human Rights and Labor; Entry on Egypt', *International Report on Religious Freedom*, Bureau of Democracy (2006).

65 In effect, the report registers the fact that even liberal Muslims object to Muslim countries being made into Western colonies. Of course, the report does not speak in those terms. Nor does it differentiate between Western/American and Muslim interests. See 'Building Moderate Muslim Networks' (note 56).

66 The RAND report also includes individuals such as Ibn Warraq, the polemical, secularist author of *Why I am Not a Muslim* and *Leaving Islam: Apostates Speak Out*, who have explicitly denied being Muslims at all, and overtly non- or anti-Muslim secularist websites, such as nosharia.com, based in Canada and Europe. Further, even though the report was written for the Center for Middle East Public Policy, barely half of the individuals and groups named in the chapter on secular Muslims are even originally from the Middle East. In fact, based on region of origin, the majority of individuals named in the report are either Western-born or emigrants from Southeast Asia (i.e. Bangladesh, Pakistan and India). In short, the report suggests supporting individuals who no longer consider themselves Muslim, live outside of the Muslim world, and are not even from countries in the Middle East, as a mode of changing Muslim and Middle Eastern political and religious culture from within.

67 For an excellent discussion of the West's knee-jerk intolerance towards any form of Islamic political party – even when that party's particular platform is overtly liberal and

democratic – see Mumtaz Ahmad, 'Islam And Democracy: The Emerging Consensus', *Journal of Turkish Weekly*, 20 June 2005. For a discussion of the Muslim Brotherhood and the cost of the West's near-irrational distrust towards it as a potential ally in curbing the influence of Islamic Puritans and Radicals in the Muslim world, see Robert S. Leiken and Steven Brooke, 'The Moderate Muslim Brotherhood', *Foreign Affairs*, March/April 2007. For a discussion of the Islamic Renaissance Party and the West's acquiescence in the oppression of the party's leaders in Tunisia despite its relatively liberal political platform, see Linda G. Jones, 'Portrait of Rashid al-Ghannoushi', *Middle East Report*, July/August 1988, 19.

68 See Abdullahi Ahmed An-Na'im, ed., *Human Rights in Cross-Cultural Perspectives* (Philadelphia: University of Pennsylvania Press, 1992). See also, John S. Nurser and David Little, *For All Peoples and All Nations: The Ecumenical Church And Human Rights* (Geneva: WCC Publications, 2005) and C.G. Weeramantry, *The Lord's Prayer: Bridge to a Better World* (Liguori, MO: Liguori/Triumph, 1998).

69 See Alexander Cockburn and Jeffrey St. Clair, *Imperial Crusades: Iraq, Afghanistan, and Yugoslavia* (New York: Verso, 2004). See also, Jim Wallis, 'Dangerous Religion', *Sojourner Magazine*, September/October 2003.

Shaykh Muhammad Afifi al-Akiti and Dr. H.A. Hellyer

Response to Khaled Abou El Fadl

Professor Khaled Medhat Abou El Fadl, an ardent champion of the Muslim ration-alist tradition, provides a significant service to students and jurists alike in this essay relating Islamic law and the human rights tradition in the West. He explores the historical connections for the emergence of human rights schemes within the Islamic intellectual tradition – but makes it clear that the Islamic world ultimately failed to develop an indigenous natural rights discourse. His analysis points to political reasons for this underdevelopment and argues that Muslims must develop their own human rights culture. Here, we will focus on one of the tensions between the two systems, a tension inherent in the legal tradition.

El Fadl rhetorically asks, 'What is the "Islamic tradition" and, more particularly, the Islamic legal tradition'? It is helpful to limit the question to the Islamic legal tradition, as the Islamic tradition as such (*al-turath al-islami*) comprises a number of sciences each with their own definition. All of them follow a particular pattern that has ensured their integrity through the centuries. The institutionalization of authoritative pedigree (*isnad*) enabled the Muslim scholarly class to combine uni-formity and diversity, providing for conclusive agreement (*ijma'*) on issues that had to be decided and a respectful diversity of opinion (*ikhtilaf*) in others.

With regard to law, this developed through the creation of legal paradigms that coalesced into the celebrated schools of law (*madhahib*; sing. *madhhab*). These in turn allowed Islamic law to remain a living tradition while observing recognized methodologies of interpretation and jurisprudence. This *madhhab*ist representa-tion – 'under a single systematic tradition' – is identified as the 'classical tradition' of Islamic law.

El Fadl draws attention to one issue that emphasizes the dynamism of Islamic legal interpretation (*fiqh*): slavery. Classical Islamic law, like all pre-modern law sys-tems, made provision for slavery and established the slave as a recognized legal entity with specific rights. It should be noted, however, that the meaning of the term slave (*raqiq*) in Islamic law is very different from its sense in other legal systems. The

Islamic tradition insisted on the religious benefit of emancipating slaves, legalized intermarriage between slaves and free persons, and provided material support from public funds to purchase a slave's own freedom. These protections were enshrined in Islamic law. The name of the branch of law covering this system of ownership is *'itq* (lit. emancipation). Consider, too, the name of the Mamluke dynasty that ruled Egypt from the twelfth to the sixteenth century: Mamluke literally means 'owned'. They were slaves who legally belonged to the state, 'government servants' in the most literal sense. These two facts testify to the ambiguity of Islam's recognition of slavery.

True, Muslim jurists were slow to legislate against the institution of slavery as such. But they did eventually outlaw slavery. The provisions concerning slave-ownership thus became irrelevant and the new norm (*al-'ada*) was easily justified from within the legal corpus – through the schools of law and not independently of them, in a spirit of respect for the past comparable to the *stare decisis* of Western legal tradition. As with any economic institution – and slavery was an economic institution as much as anything – abolition was not immediately effective; certain sectors of society benefited from slavery. Now that all Muslim states have signed up to the international treaties outlawing slavery, the proscription of slavery has become a covenant that Muslims must abide by, since Islamic law regards the upholding of contracts as a sacred bond. A similar reassessment occurred with the recognition of the nation state by Muslim jurists. This was arguably a much greater conceptual departure from pre-modern norms.

On the matter of slavery, then, disagreement on the part of 'exclusivists' and 'Islamists' is merely a sign that they are, as Abou El Fadl says, not jurists but political agitators seeking public support for a 'politicized symbol'. Jurists posit Islamic law as the expression of God's Law on earth for the benefit of His Creation and not merely as a political tool vis-à-vis the West.

El Fadl also raises a very pertinent question when discussing the conflicts between universalism and relativism. He correctly notes 'Those who commit themselves to human rights must believe in universal standards but must also respect the right of others to be different; they might be offended by the practices of particular cultures, but feeling revulsion is one thing; failing to respect the right to be different is quite another'.

In an intra-Muslim discussion, this has its own ramifications. The juridical corpus is vast and allows for much difference of opinion. Indeed, one of Islam's legal maxims states that objections should never be raised in matters where jurists disagree but only where they are agreed in rejecting a particular position. Thus, a follower (*muqallid*) of a certain school of law should not, as far as possible, be penalized by a judge (*qadi*) who belongs to another school. Judges were known to advise plaintiffs to seek judgements from other judges when the alternative ruling might prove easier to implement than their own. The open nature of Muslim judges in general vis-à-vis non-Muslim religions and their religious laws is also well known.

Such openness cannot be taken for granted in our age. And, more importantly, it cannot be imposed. It reflects a healthy societal attitude towards diversity that is sustainable only when it comes from within.

This is especially relevant with respect to the provisions for capital punishment (*hudud*) in the Islamic tradition. A majority of pre-modern jurists agreed that these punishments should form part of the law but accepted that the execution (or suspension, commutation or revocation) of these punishments was the prerogative of the supreme political authority. They also insisted on the extremely strict standards of evidence and procedure required for conviction. However, they could never reject the principle of capital punishments: to do so would have implied that their legislative predecessors, including the Prophet, had been mistaken. No Muslim jurist would or could do that. Thus provision of the death penalty for a capital crime enjoys a wide consensus; and in classical legal doctrine, only considerations extrinsic to the crime itself, such as the intervention of the state, constitute any impediment (*mani'*) to the prescribed punishment. The 'capital' nature of the crime itself is unalterable. The dynamism of the tradition allows for an essential continuity that can accommodate a changing world. This kind of essentialism may remind us of the English constitution.

In the search for a common language for the human family – an ethical lexicon – there are therefore more than sufficient resources within the Muslim tradition to contribute to contemporary philosophical ethics. Islamic institutions within the Muslim world, such as the Aal al-Bayt Institute (Jordan), the International Institute of Islamic Thought and Civilization (Malaysia), Nahdhatul Ulama (Indonesia) and the Tabah Foundation (Abu Dhabi), are leading the way in this regard. It is still early days, but the signs are promising, particularly with the growth of a scholarly class conversant with Western traditions. They have taken a long time to reach this point, it might be said. But by the same token, the yoke of colonialism and imperialism was also of long-standing. Change does not often come quickly and cannot have permanent results unless it comes from within the tradition.

The loss of the caliphate – a previously unthinkable event – left an indelible mark on the development of the Islamic intellectual and juridical traditions. Western hegemony led to the degradation of the schools of law. Imperialism, colonialism, and then nationalism realigned priorities in public education and downplayed the importance of a sound religious education. It is not surprising that, in such a system, many who favoured the 'open exploration' recommended by al-Ghazali[1] no longer went into religious studies but became engineers and doctors.

And today we are seeing the results of this redefinition of educational priorities. When 'Islamization' came about, it was informed by identity politics rather than a real philosophical impetus towards the creation of a modern Islamic nation state. 'Islamicity' was the watchword in a political showdown between secularists and religious conservatives. The dynamism of classical Islamic law served not the public sphere but a brutalized ideology of resistance. How could it be otherwise? The Islamist movements reflected populist dissatisfaction with their own governments and the prevailing New World Order. Neither they nor the people had experienced a truly open political system in the modern and post-modern age. And a society torn apart by contested identities is not a fertile source of intellectual renewal.

We have seen the effect of this process many times over. El Fadl refers to one of its most recent manifestations: the Wahhabi movement's stance against human rights. But why would the Wahhabis view the human rights discourse of the West as anything but a Western imperialist tool? How often have Muslims benefited from the rights supposedly accorded by the Western human rights tradition? When we look at the record of the relevant countries and at Western tolerance of their government's repressive policies (whether based on political pragmatism or convenient alliance), the answers to these questions are clear enough.

The provision of legal solutions to contemporary problems need not constitute a break with classical tradition. It can be done either by making traditional legal doctrines relevant to the contemporary world, or, more exceptionally, by re-evaluating certain established practices, as occurred with the abolition of slavery. The issue for the classical scholarly establishment is not *whether* such re-evaluation should take place but *how*, a point in large measure dependent on whether those who argue for it have the juridical training required. The Islamic legal tradition has a long history of continual redevelopment – but on its own terms. This means a spirit of open exploration coupled with scholarly scruple rather than superficial 're-formation exercises' or 'politicized measures'. The immediate prospects for such intellectual development are not good. There are crises enough occupying the Islamic mind. But if an authentic Islamic renaissance (*tajdid*) is to occur, it must embrace the legal tradition rather than grossly simplifying or jettisoning it. Recognizing – as Abou El Fadl does – the dynamic aspects of the tradition will help contemporary Muslim jurists to find their *own* way of engaging with human rights discourse.

Note

1 The Muslim jurist and theologian at the turn of the sixth Islamic century, Abu Hamid al-Ghazali (d. 1111), notes confidently in his *Summa Islamica*, the *Ihya' 'Ulum al-Din* (*Revivification of the Religious Sciences*), the enlightened attitude that is needed by scholars if they are to further the spirit of open exploration: 'The one who is in the pursuit of truth is like the one who is searching for a lost item: it makes no difference whether it is found by his hand or by someone who can support him'.

8 Joanna Bourke

The threshold of the human: sexual violence and trauma in the 'war on terror'

I

Ameen Sa'eed Al-Sheikh was arrested on 7 October 2003 and taken to the now-infamous Baghdad Correctional Facility (Abu Ghraib). 'Do you believe in anything?' an American interrogator asked. 'I believe in Allah', Al-Sheikh replied, and the interrogator responded: 'But I believe in torture and I will torture you'.[1] The threshold of humanity has become the torture chamber. As legal philosopher Costas Douzinas says, it 'takes inhumanity to define humanity by separating out the non-human. The extreme strategy of bio-power is precisely to demarcate the human through extreme acts of inhumanity inflicted on bare animal life'.[2] The cold-blooded violence of torture is the site of that extremity. In the words of Assistant Attorney General Jay Bybee in August 2002, torture is defined as 'extreme acts', which

> must be of an intensity akin to that which accompanies serious physical injury such as death or organ failure . . . Because the acts inflicting torture are extreme, there is [a] significant range of acts that though they might constitute cruel, inhuman, or degrading treatment or punishment fail to rise to the level of torture.[3]

This definition, later rescinded, influenced American policy for a defined period. And so we have it: an act might be 'cruel, inhuman, or degrading', but so long as it does not involve 'death or organ failure', it does not constitute torture. Yet Bybee's formulation is in excess of the normal requirements, as he and everyone else knew. If torture is what renders the victim non-human, the non-humanity in question is not simply that of death. Torture does indeed define the threshold of the human: it is the attempted destruction of an individual; rendering that being 'non-human' through infliction of pain and through systematic exposure of the body. And what we have seen and are seeing in the 'war on terror' is a politics in which humanity is defined through the actions of the inhuman (torturer) on the non-human (victims). As another Abu Ghraib prisoner put it:

They stripped us naked as a newborn baby. Then they ordered us to hold our penises and stroke it . . . They started to take photographs as if it was a porn movie. And they treated us like animals not humans . . . No one showed us mercy. Nothing but cursing and beating. Then they started to write words on our buttocks, which we didn't know what it means. After that they left us for the next two days naked with no clothes, with no mattress, as if we were dogs.[4]

II

Of course, as historians always remind us, we have seen earlier versions of this dehumanization: in the lynching photographs of the American South; in the ears and fingers necklaced together by British and American service personnel during the two World Wars; and in the rape orgies of the wars in Korea and Vietnam. Even during the previous war in Iraq (the First Gulf War) few of us were fooled by the sanitized spectacle on our television screens. However, in the current 'war on terror', not only have victims, their extended families, and their communities become witnesses to their own humiliation, but those rituals of degradation have been broadcast around the world, globalizing torture as a strategy of demarcating humanity.

In a number of troubling ways, we have all participated in these attempts to create a hierarchy of humanness. Indeed, the Abu Ghraib images might make us wonder whether Jean Baudrillard's argument about the First Gulf War did not apply equally to this 'war in Iraq'.[5] Everything is as it was: the war never happened; Saddam's torturers never left Abu Ghraib. This new generation of Western torturers simply employed more sophisticated technologies to enable the abuse – and fear of abuse – to reach every corner of the earth.

Former conflicts have given rise to a universalized tongue frequently put to use in speaking of the 'war on terror'. It is one that effaces individual histories and specific geographies. The 'barbarism' which we hear such a lot of is part of the dehumanizing patois. Talk of barbarism returns us to the stark oppositions that got us into trouble in the first place: Us versus Them; good versus evil; God versus Satan; Civilization versus Barbarism. These are the rhetorical figures that have always justified holy wars, jihads, apocalypses. And talk of the banality of evil also misses the point – though cruel deeds of such magnitude do indeed infuse every banal nuance of the society from which they are born. Deeds of brutality are never meaningless. Dehumanizing deeds attempt to efface the significance of the individual on whom they are committed. But that is just a preliminary. For perpetrators of violence, it is never enough merely to inflict suffering: those causing pain insist that their victims ascribe a meaning to their pain, a meaning of the torturer's choice. Like rapists in civilian contexts, perpetrators of violence in the 'war on terror' do one of two things: they either eroticize pain or give primacy to the spoken word by demanding a bogus recital of their 'deserving it' or 'asking for it'. Such language attempts to justify what is always unjustified: the infliction of suffering.

By creating a trauma-aesthetic and sorting perpetrators, bystanders and victims into positions of hierarchy, we are complicit with this language and recognize degrees of responsibility in the victim, thus in some sense ourselves justifying the infliction of pain.[6] When the pitiless actions of some perpetrators are presented as more 'comprehensible' than others (more on this later), we, too, sort victims into a hierarchy of suffering. Indeed, we aestheticize not only the pain of the victims but our own responses to their pain. The very process of discussing injustice inevitably promotes the distancing process that we so loudly lament. The debate invites us to assess what becomes a spectacle of pain and to do so aesthetically, contemplatively. Like it or not, vision is an act of aggression, a disciplining activity. As one of Iraq's greatest female poets, Nazik al-Mala'ika, put it in her poem about the torture by the French of an Algerian resistance fighter:

> The details of your torture were on every tongue,
> And that hurt us, it was hard for our sensitive ears to bear.

Going on to add:

> Did we not use her suffering to give meaning to our poetry?
> Was that a time for song?[7]

Simone de Beauvoir – an ardent opponent of torture during the French-Algerian War – reminds us of an important fact: we get accustomed to other people's pain. As she acknowledged, 'in 1957, the burns in the face, on the sexual organs, the nails torn out, the impalements, the shrieks, the convulsions, outraged me', but by the 'sinister month of December 1961' she was saying: 'like many of my fellow men, I suppose, I suffer from a kind of tetanus of the imagination ... One gets used to it'.[8]

Are we so numb? In an article published over ten years ago but even more relevant today, historian Eric Hobsbawm observed that people have 'got used to' terror. 'I don't mean we still can't be shocked by this or that example of it', he observed, 'On the contrary, being periodically shocked by something unusually awful is part of the experience'.[9]

III

The international shock caused by the Abu Ghraib photographs suggested that 'something unusually awful' had happened. The horror was not because of the torture as such, since that was well known, and continues to be endorsed at the highest levels. Of course, there were those in whom the photographs elicited patriotic celebration rather than distress. Republican senator James Inhofel, speaking to a Senate Armed Services Committee hearing, was, he said, 'outraged' by the outrage everyone seems to have about the treatment of these prisoners ... I am also outraged by the press and the politicians and the political agendas that are being served by this ... I am also outraged that we have so many humanitarian do-gooders right now crawling all over these prisons looking for human rights violations while our troops, our heroes, are fighting and dying.[10]

Later that day he reiterated his protest: 'A lot of the American people don't know what animals these people are'.[11]

But there was something new about the photographs: something that both shocked and titillated. Here we had *female* perpetrators of sexual abuse on *men*. Lynndie England was intriguingly attractive as the dominatrix of the American dream.[12] The photographs that came out of Guantánamo Bay or even the photographs of the Basra abuses had none of the power of the Abu Ghraib ones. We had already become inured to images of terror unless they were tied to our mass media's obsession: sex. Big Brother became boring, so we introduced the possibility of a sex romp; reports of torture were humdrum until we did the same. And there, in that sentence, is the obscenity: Big Brother and torture casually 'bedded' in the same sentence.

The issue of female involvement permeated discussions of the torture at Abu Ghraib, and the torture images were rapidly assimilated into a society already saturated with spectacle. Thus, one of the most popular radio show hosts could say,

You know, if you look at – if you, really, if you look at these pictures, I mean, I don't know if it's just me, but it looks like anything you'd see Madonna or Britney Spears do onstage. Maybe I'm – yeah. And get a NEA [a National Endowment for the Arts] grant for something like this. I mean, this is something that you see onstage at Lincoln Center from an NEA grant. Maybe on *Sex and the City* – the movie.[13]

On the internet, civilian men and women posted photographs of themselves 'doing a Lynndie'. Detailed internet instructions on 'doing a Lynndie' start with the phrase 'Find a victim who deserves to be "Lynndied"'; then, 'Make sure you have a friend nearby with a camera ready to capture the 'Lynndie', 'Make a hitchhiking gesture with your right hand and extend your right arm so that it's in roughly the same position as if you were holding a rifle. Keeping your left arm slightly bent, point in the direction of the victim and smile'.[14] The smile was important: the individuality and agency to which it testified were in direct contrast with the status of the degraded and objectified 'victim'.

With the language of rights under pressure from the mantras of dehumanization and commodification inherent in pornography, we have to remember – and the current 'war on terror' reminds us – that there is no natural 'human', no amorphous 'Other'. The techniques involved in creating the non-human were embedded in everyday policies, attitudes and practices. Thus, when James Schlesinger, chair of Bush's Independent Panel to Review DOD Detention Operations at Abu Ghraib, chides the International Committee of the Red Cross for failing to 'adapt itself to the realities of conflict, which are far different from the Western European environment from which the ICRC's interpretations of the Geneva Conventions [is] drawn', he alerts us to the fact that the 'human' in his conception is Western.[15] When the military does not even deign to record Iraqi deaths, we are bound to reflect on the construction of a racial and religious enemy that is evidently not as human as 'us'.

Four main anthropogenetic strategies help draw the line between the human, the inhuman, and the non-human: torture, religion, human rights, and trauma narratives.

IV

First: torture. The shock of the current 'war on terror' resides particularly in the way acts of inhumanity have focused on the sexualized body. In the contemporary crisis, the emphasis on *sexual* abuse is not (as some critics may wish to insist) a deviation from hardnosed considerations of all-pervading state power and seemingly unassailable military muscle. Where discrepancies of power between protagonists are so disproportionate as to render systems of law (national or international) hollow, and where individuals from forty different nations can languish in the liminal space of Guantánamo Bay, a place of doubtful legal status ('in' but not 'of' Cuba, a country with which the U.S. has no diplomatic ties), politics operates on the body. This body has been extraordinarily sexualized.

It is surprising, therefore, that although sex has been used cynically and relentlessly in the 'war on terror', there has been little analysis of a sexualized dimension. Descriptions of rape as a weapon of war and as a technology of dehumanization were successfully applied in the cases of Bosnia and Rwanda (both dubbed primitive, warring nations), but commentators remain reluctant to draw similar conclusions about reports of the behaviour of American and British troops – even after digital culture provided us with an avalanche of abusive images, a visual glossolalia of sexual horror.

This occurred despite the fact that the full extent of the abuse has been concealed. After all, when the Abu Ghraib scandal broke, members of Congress were shown 1,800 other photographs and videos, some of which were – and still are – considered far too revolting to be broadcast.[16] In particular, photographs of female victims of abuse have been deemed far too politically explosive to be placed in the public domain. The emphasis laid on abuse by female perpetrators, with its implication that this was particularly injurious to Islamic men, has been allowed to overshadow the equally heinous but more 'conventional' abuse of women, for which the Bush government seems to have escaped responsibility.

For many principled feminist, pacifist, and human rights campaigners, it has been difficult incorporating the existence of *female* perpetrators into their analyses of sexual abuse. Although there were women abusers in former conflicts – from Buchenwald to the Balkans – they were easily marginalized, both descriptively and theoretically. But in the case of the war in Iraq, some of the most visible architects of suffering are women. The focus has generally been on Private Lynndie England, Private Megan Ambuhl and Specialist Sabrina Harman. But let's not forget those other women: Brigadier General Janis Karpinski (the General directing Abu Ghraib at the time of the abuses), Major-General Barbara Fast (most senior American intelligence officer in Iraq and the officer responsible for reviewing the status of detainees), and Dr. Condaleezza Rice (responsible since October 2005 for managing the occupation).

When faced with female perpetrators of inhuman violence, what narratives have been employed? Indisputably, the most common approach is simply to deny any significance in the presence of women on the other (wrong) side of the baton. Larry (England) is effortlessly substituted for Lynndie. At best, the practice among writers on sexual abuse seems to be to acknowledge in a footnote that women sexually abuse men, then to proceed to develop a theory premised entirely on male perpetrators. Face-to-face with images of female perpetrators and powerful female leaders implicated in torture (including sexual torture), theories premised on the assumption that it is the male of our species who are 'rapists, rape fantasists, or beneficiaries of a rape culture'[17] become (at best) wishful thinking.

A less craven approach involves rewriting the genealogy of violence to include women in the 'active' frame. This takes many forms. Evolutionary psychologists proffer evidence of female (lower) animals and non-human primates who are aggressive.[18] But I, for one, fail to be convinced by arguments reducing the complexity of human society and history to a connection with our primate ancestors.[19]

Others situate female abusers in terms of so-called natural roles: in other words, rape by women is a continuation of other female roles, particularly that of mother. One prominent version draws attention to an instinct unique to the female sex. Linked to an evolutionary perspective that sees male violence as originating in the pugnacious instinct, female aggression is deemed to arise from the maternal instinct: the arousing of the 'primitive cave-woman' to defend her (male-led) clan. And because (according to this view) the maternal instinct is unconstrained by culture (being entirely based on timeless biological urges), the female soldiers' involvement in torture was (in the words of one commentator on the Abu Ghraib abuses) 'yet another lesson in why women shouldn't be in the military . . . Women are more vicious than men'.[20] This approach encourages an emphasis on Lynndie England's pregnancy and the alleged fact that the female perpetrators were 'smitten with [Charles] Graner', the man most frequently seen in the photographs.[21]

A more sociologically infused perspective posits that female perpetrators of sexual violence expose the folly of a world that deprecates femininity and views bodies (particularly female ones) as commodities. Women come to adopt the same attitude toward, all bodies. As women become similar to men in social, economic and cultural terms, inhuman behaviour carried out by women is sure to rise (so this story goes). In an increasingly democratic military, 'the American woman is given the phallus' and 'invited to participate in the militarised masculine aesthetic along with the men, to become the one who penetrates the racialized other'.[22] The shared militarization and masculinization of feeling dissolves conventional gender divisions.

For the political elite and moral Right, it is a convenient response, enabling them (yet again) to bind the 'war on terror' into the moral crusade of Family Values. In Churches throughout the West, Abu Ghraib has been used to call the flock back to a more conservative morality. It is interesting to remember that the main male perpetrator, Charles Graner, was originally charged not with abuses but with *adultery* (with Lynndie England). The National Coalition for the Protection of Children and Families put it bluntly when it declared that the torture photographs were 'liberalism taken to its natural and logical conclusion', drawing attention particularly to the 'tangled web of licentious behaviour, sexual perversion, infidelity, and promiscuity' within the military. It should 'serve as a warning to those who continue to advance so-called sexual freedom beyond its intended boundaries of lifelong, natural, and monogamous marriage'.[23] In this line of argument, responsibility is neatly diffused. As Frank Rich entitled an article in the *New York Times*: 'It Was Porn That Made Them Do It'. He noted that

> If porn or MTV or Howard Stern can be said to have induced a 'few bad apples' in one prison to misbehave, then everyone else in the chain of command, from the commander-in-chief down, is off the hook. If the culture war can be cross-wired with the actual war, then the buck will stop not at the Pentagon or the White House but at the Paris Hilton video, or 'Mean Girls', or maybe 'Queer Eye for the Straight Guy'.[24]

Pornography creates torturers? Or maybe inhumanity has been sponsored by the feminist movement? Phyllis Schlafly certainly thinks so, predicting that the photograph of Lynndie England holding a man on a leash would 'soon show up on the bulletin boards of women's studies centers . . . that picture is the radical feminists' ultimate fantasy of how they dream of treating men'.[25]

Setting aside Phyllis Schlafly's send-up of feminists (which portrays women as emotionally brutalized rather than overly fond of mimicking men), this explanation of female perpetration implies a male norm, into which women passively fall. Yet, in a culture still permeated with assumptions of compulsory heterosexuality, men and women stand in different relations to sexual intercourse. After all, one of the most powerful aspect, of the female perpetrators of Abu Ghraib is that the (penisless) women trumped male power, not only in the sense that these women claimed omnipotence in relation to the male prisoners, but also because they had no need to use a penis to do so. The penis is, after all, a deeply flawed instrument of power and one with none of the resilience and fortitude of, for instance, the fist or (fire-) arm. In talking about weapons of torture, Elaine Scarry refers to the way in which 'in converting the other person's pain into his own power, the torturer experiences the entire occurrence exclusively from the non-vulnerable end of the weapon'. But in those forms of sexual abuse employing the penis, the perpetrator's attention begins to 'slip down the weapon toward the vulnerable end', contesting its power.[26] The cruel triumph of the female perpetrators resides in the fact that they tortured without consciousness of that form of self-vulnerability.

Finally, some attempts to understand female perpetrators at Abu Ghraib ask: might sexual violence 'masculinize' torturers who happen to be biological female, while 'feminizing' victims who happen to be biologically male? In studies focusing on sexual violence in war and in prison contexts, this is a popular argument. Male victims are said to become 'social women'; male perpetrators have their masculinity enhanced; female perpetrators become 'social men'. On this account, cruelty is synonymous with virility and the female abuser is 'really' a man. Thus, Lynndie England is described as a 'phallic female', 'tomboyish', a 'leash-girl', who turned out to be 'something other than a natural lady'.[27]

At first sight, this is a simple way out of the dilemma: nothing much changes – just a few labels. The female is erased and coded as male. There is an easy logic to the argument. And there is no doubt that both male and female perpetrators taunted victims with degraded words used to refer to femaleness. In Abu Ghraib, for instance, male prisoners were goaded for being 'girls' and were forced to wear female underwear. There is also no doubt that perpetrators of both sexes take strength and power, as well as pleasure, from their actions. But to say this turns female perpetrators into 'social men' is both to imply an essential link between manliness and violence, and to reinforce the dichotomies male-active and female-passive. The gendered notion of masculinity and femininity as active/passive confuses social imaginary with lived history, placing women outside the symbolic order.

Moreover, what we have seen in Iraq (and elsewhere) is not women participating in masculine rituals, but women using conventional tropes of their gender to shame and subjugate. While male guards in Abu Ghraib stomped on male prisoners with boots, threatened to bugger the men in the showers, and poked phosphoric lights up their arses, the women threw menstrual fluid and slowly strip-teased. We have to take seriously the idea that female perpetrators are not simply imitating men, but living out their own fantasies about power and sexuality. Sharon Marcus put it succinctly when she pointed out that taking 'male violence or female vulnerability as the first and last instances in any explanation of rape is to make the identities of rapist and raped pre-exist the rape itself'.[28]

This was what made much of the world recoil in horror when the Abu Ghraib photographs were released: female rapists as agents of extreme sexual cruelty. These women were regarded as much worse than their male comrades in atrocity: they were not merely inhuman, but monstrous. Even when women were engaging in abuses that were not explicitly sexual, the very womanliness of the perpetrators enabled their actions to be sexualized: by definition, female performance was pornographic.

Outrage was also sparked by the fact that the most widely reported victims of sexual abuses in Abu Ghraib, Basra, and elsewhere in the 'war on terror' were not the 'usual victims' (women),[29] but men. The photographs were a stark reminder of an uncomfortable detail: not only the female body, but the male body as well, is violable, penetrable. For many heterosexual men, it is a hard detail to accept, particularly in wartime when the military encourages the notion of the invulnerable male body. For the armed forces, the 'warrior' has to be portrayed as 'cold steel'; in the current panic over female combatants, this man needs to be protected from the vulnerabilities that even military women in 'hot' combat zones might embody.

The tortured body, in particular, transcends 'straight' gendered inscriptions. It is not only the female body 'whose borders cannot be defended'[30] – recall the use of a broom handle by the NYPD cops to sodomize Abner Louima, a Haitian immigrant; witness the naked skirmishing and sodomization linked with 'hazing' incidents in the British Navy and Army which are periodically publicized. The tortured male body is both phallic and a receptacle. If the male victim does not 'perform' (erection and even ejaculation), he is laughed at as being deficient. One prisoner recalls being sexually abused by American guards:

> He said to me, 'Are you married?' I said, 'Yes'. They said, 'If your wife saw you like this, she will be disappointed'. One of them said, 'But if I saw her now, she would not be disappointed now because I would rape her'.[31]

On the other hand, involuntary erections also confirm a debility in manhood: an absence of masculine will, coupled with the suggestion of homosexuality. Neither tumescence nor detumescence can guarantee patriarchy; both here become a show of weakness. During sexual torture the male victim's body is always lacking.

All bodies are permeable and appropriable by the in-human. By contrast, the in-human presents itself as possessing a surfeit of humanness. After all, it is the in-human – the torturers and their masters – who define the human. Theirs is the humanizing *episteme* and theirs the culture that employs the most sophisticated technologies invented by humanity (everything from fighter jets to techniques of psychological torture) in his or her mission. However, the in-human is also presented in terms of a universal humanity devoid of (indeed, transcending) gender. Neither masculine nor feminine: simply all-powerful in-humanity.

The suffering subject, on the other hand, is defined as lacking 'true' humanity, burdened with an excess of *body*. Bunching these bodies by gender – one portion of the great trilogy (the other two are class and ethnicity) – inevitably leads to a universal femaleness: the woman effaced in religious dogma as inherently inferior is also eradicated in conventional human rights discourse because that discourse is premised on the heterosexual white male. Not only does such a 'bunching' enforce the association of 'woman' with 'victim', but it also serves to relegate one group (male victims of women's sexual violence) to a dismissive footnote. In creating a hierarchy of suffering, we are thus again reduced to endorsing abuse.

The sexualization of torture is only one way in which the 'war on terror' has delineated who is (and who is not) human. Religion, human rights, and trauma narratives are three other mechanisms for rationalizing suffering.

V

Religion remains a powerful site for disciplining bodies. Indeed, in the politics of the corporeal, Christianity is central. 'Do you pray to Allah', the American interrogators screamed at a prisoner, hooded and tortured in the 'correctional facility'. When he replied 'yes', they yelled, 'Fuck you' and 'Fuck him'. After threatening to rape him and his wife, they forced him to eat pork, drink alcohol, and curse Islam. 'They ordered me to thank Jesus that I'm alive', he recalled, 'And I did what they ordered me'.[32] In this way, bodies became disposable because 'the one and only true God' is on the side of the torturers. Bush's love of the anti-Babylonian prophet Ezekiel, the administration's frequent use of millenarian rhetoric, and the strong sacrificial undertones of much contemporary Protestantism (when the Abu Ghraib photographs were released, audiences were watching entranced as Jesus was tortured in Mel Gibson's *Passion of Christ*), have provided a convincing religious lens through which to 'read' torture.[33] Abdou Hussain Saad Faleh, the hooded man on the pedestal, thus becomes a devotional icon, his very innocence making him more (not less) appropriate as sacrificial victim.

Messianic Protestantism, predicated on the Book of Revelations and infused with evangelical moralism, encourages a notion of unending war on evil and the Anti-Christ – without any sense of accountability. And like psychoanalysis, that other 'talking cure', prayer affords purification from those irrepressible violent urges. Was this the hope of the nine-year-old American girl from 'Our Lady of Peace', a Catholic school? It seems not: she sent members of an interrogation unit in Iraq a drawing of aeroplanes dropping bombs on small figures wearing turbans. The caption read, 'We are praying for you and saying the rosary in class for you today'.[34]

Even more noticeable is the use of the secular religion of our times (that is, human rights) to justify suffering by deciding who stands outside the threshold of the human.[35] Jamal Al Harith, a British former detainee of Guantánamo Bay, recognized the bond between languages of rights and torture, noting that

> They actually said that – 'You have no rights here'. After a while, we stopped asking for human rights – we wanted animal rights. In Camp X-Ray my cage was right next to a kennel housing an Alsatian dog. He had a wooden house with air conditioning and green grass to exercise on. I said to the guards, 'I want his rights' and they replied, 'that dog is member of the U.S. army'.[36]

The languages of human rights here cross over into the animal rights movement (though, historically, the inspiration probably went in the opposite direction, with burgeoning interest in human rights borrowing languages from nineteenth-century societies for the prevention of cruelty to animals).[37] And, because of the cultural link between animality and femaleness, it is no coincidence that the *male* rendered non- or sub-human is more shocking than the female similarly reduced.

The questions for those employing the languages of human rights have always been: who is this 'human'; what are his or her 'rights'? In recent years, both the notion that 'human' is self-explanatory and that 'rights' are natural and eternal, have taken a direct hit. Innumerable, hidden particulars have been laid bare: the 'human' of traditional human rights speech is swathed in a white skin, a Western body. More to the point, he has tended to be a heterosexual male. This is one of the reasons why it has taken so long to get the rape of women understood as a mainstream *human* rights issue, as opposed to an issue of discrimination. When we look at the right to bodily integrity – the right not to be tortured or raped, for instance – the question becomes: does this right apply to the (suspected) terrorist? Or to any individual who might have been picked up on the streets of Iraq or Afghanistan and incarcerated in one of our Correctional Facilities?

Innumerable commentators say not – including, most notoriously, Alan Dershowitz. Here is his lawyerly dodging of the prohibition on 'cruel and unusual punishments' on page 135 of *Why Terrorism Works*:

> Constitutional democracies are, of course, constrained in the choices they may lawfully make. The Fifth Amendment prohibits compelled self-incrimination, which means that statements elicited by means of torture may not be introduced into evidence against the defendant who has been tortured. But if a suspect is given immunity and then tortured into providing information about a future terrorist act, his privilege against self-incrimination has not been violated . . . Nor has his right to be free from 'cruel and unusual punishment', since that provision of the Eighth Amendment has been interpreted to apply solely to punishment after conviction.

Dershowitz is not alone – Michael Ignatieff shocked many people when he, too, defended the use of sleep deprivation and 'keeping prisoners in hoods'.[38] Assistant Attorney General Jay S. Bybee's definition of torture (which introduced this chapter) not only gave legal legitimacy to extreme acts, but also legitimated acts inflicted only to obtain information and with the intention to cause only short-term harm. For an act to be defined as torture, the perpetrator had to specifically *intend* to cause significant and long-term bodily injury. Although Bybee's memo was later rescinded (in December 2004), it had profound influence on policy. For instance, Bybee's views were echoed in Lieutenant Diane Beaver's legal brief to Joint Task Force 170 at Guantánamo Bay. She advised that a public official would not have violated the Eighth Amendment

so long as the force used could plausibly have been thought necessary in a particular situation to achieve a legitimate governmental objective, and it was applied
in a good faith effort and not maliciously or sadistically for the very purpose of
causing harm . . . The federal torture statute will not be violated so long as any of
the proposed strategies are not specifically intended to cause severe physical pain
or suffering or prolonged mental harm.

In the event that public officials might be punished under the Uniform Code of
Military Justice (Article 128 of which decreed that poking a person in the chest or
placing a wet towel or hood over a detainees head constituted assault), Lieutenant
Diane Beaver recommended that 'it would be advisable to have permission or immunity in advance from the convening authority, for military members utilizing these
methods'.[39] Yet Vice-President Cheney was able to respond to Amnesty International's 2005 report condemning various American practices with the dismissive
line, 'For Amnesty International to suggest that somehow the United States is a
violator of human rights, I frankly just don't take them seriously'. President Bush
merely dismissed the report as 'absurd'.[40] In the fight to bring democracy to the
Iraqis, torture was, it seems, inevitable. Democracy itself is used to make sense of
suffering: if only the Iraqis were more democratic and less terroristic, 'we' would
not need to do this to them. If only they had told the truth, 'we' would not need
to torture them thus. In the words of a flag on the front door of Megan Ambuhl's
(an Abu Ghraib abuser) home: 'Freedom isn't Free'.[41]

VI

This is hardly new to the current 'war on terror'. In at least three contexts, acceptance of torture can be seen as mainstream. These contexts fan out from the U.S.
prison complex, to the detainees in Guantánamo Bay and, finally, to the international colonial project. From the 1970s, the American penitentiary system has become
an extraordinary example of carceral totalitarianism within a nation formally obsessed
with principles of liberty. What happened in Abu Ghraib is inextricably linked to
everyday prison practices in America, particularly within the supermax units where
all prisoners are viewed as violent threats thus requiring extreme repression. In such
places, prisoners may be confined for indefinite periods and subjected to conditions so harsh that they violate international law as well as U.S. constitutional safeguards.[42] Actions amounting to torture continue to be practised within these
institutions. Systematic humiliation, the use of dogs to intimidate, sleep deprivation,
and physical brutality are frequently experienced by prisoners. The fact that many
of the abusers at Abu Ghraib were former guards in civilian life is no coincidence.
In a letter written to his family in 2003, Staff Sgt. Ivan Frederick, one of the perpetrators of the abuses in Abu Ghraib, admitted the usefulness of his work-experience
at Buckingham Correctional Center in Virginia. 'I was placed in [Abu Ghraib]', he

observed, 'because of my civilian background working as a correctional officer . . . The [commander] wanted it run like a prison in the US'.[43] Specialist Charles Graner was also a product of this environment, having served as a guard at Pennsylvania's Greene State Correctional Institute. He was at that prison during the 1990s, when evidence of extreme brutality and torture reached such horrendous levels that it could no longer be ignored. According to the attorney of a prisoner at the Greene State Correctional Institute, prisoners were regularly blungeoned by a prison guards. His client even had the letters 'KKK' painted on his back with his own blood. 'What they are running [at Greene] is a concentration camp', this attorney noted, adding, 'It's like an Alcatraz mentality. It's horrible. In my 22 years as an attorney, I have never seen such a place as Greene. I have never seen such bigots in my life'.[44] Though he did not explictly refer to sexual violence, there is abundant evidence showing that rape too is endemic in American prisons. The most reliable estimates suggest that between 5 and 9 per cent of all male prisoners incarcerated in American prisons have been sexually assaulted.[45] However, other commonly cited estimates range from anything between 1 per cent and 22 per cent.[46] Finally, even the existence of detention without trial is not uncommon in America. According to the best analysis, before 9/11 there were more than 20,000 immigrants (many unable to speak English) being held in custody in the U.S.A. for long periods of time.[47] Since 9/11 the number of detainees held without charge in American prisons is estimated at over 50,000.[48] Abuse is home-grown.

The legal status of Guantánamo Bay may seem doubtful but does, in fact, arise out of the legacy of Insular Cases decided by the Supreme Court between 1902 and 1922. According to these cases, the United States can rule over distant peoples without constitutional restraint. A territory can 'belong to' but 'not be part of' the United States. Granted indefinite control over the territory, yet freed from duties arising from sovereignty, the U.S. government can act independently of any human rights treaties and constitutional restraints. In other words, rather than being aberrant, Guantánamo resides at the centre of American imperial traditions.[49]

More to the point, with regard to colonial peoples in the past, languages of rights and democracy have been fundamental in rendering torture customary. As was seen during the French-Algerian War, France's need to propagate its doctrines of human rights went hand in hand with its 'ideology of the *mission civilisatrice*'. As Rita Maran astutely observed (and she could have been speaking of the current war),

> The civilizing mission was an ideology simultaneously drawn from and undercutting the doctrine of the 'rights of man'. Those operating in its aura ignored or were oblivious to its inherent contradiction that restricted who might qualify for full status as 'man'. The shared understanding was that France's presence in Algeria was philanthropic, bringing civilization to Algerians through education, roads and bridges, hospitals, an array of modern technical achievements, and last but not least, through notions of rights. When this process was disrupted by the Algerian

revolution, the government, acting through its military and civilian agents took the position that unusual means were justified to restore order. By this logic, torture, one of the unusual means, was justified.

Notions of France's 'civilizing mission' became both a 'rationalization (in advance of torture)' and 'a justification (after the torture)'.[50] In the words of Omar Rivabella in *Requiem for a Woman's Soul*, they 'torture in the name of justice, in the name of law and order, in the name of the country, and some go so far as pretending they torture in the name of God'.[51]

In the name of justice, law, order and God, designating individuals 'terrorist' enables them to be placed outside the human. One of the main agents in this process is that pre-eminent power engaged in defining human rights – the United States. After all, in an increasingly globalized world, characterized by rapid changes induced by mass media, technology, emigration and immigration, and global capitalism, the key question becomes: how do we decide which rights are universal (that is, able to transcend cultural peculiarities) and which are local (and, by implication, peripheral)? The question is crucial because globalization is primarily an issue of struggle – of the ability of one group to define its own local values or characteristics as 'global' while designating other groups' values as 'local'. The group with most clout decides. In other words, designating certain values or characteristics 'local' denies significant agency in its adherents. For instance, claims that the Middle Easterner's culture is anti-secular (and thus 'behind the times'), governed by appeals to absolute (religious) authority, and regulated by 'cultural' factors deprive the Middle Easterner 'both of a formative role in the global arena and, conversely, of reasons for behavior that might have international origins'. But there is no need to assume that secular institutions are more 'universal' than religious ones, nor that 'differences in secular institutions are mere variations on a universal system whereas the differences between, say, Judaism, Christianity, and Islam, are distinctions between particulars'. In much human rights speech, however, 'secular' has been designated the dominant and universal, while 'religious' is dismissed as representing the particular and local.[52] This enables the pre-eminent power (U.S.A.) to operate what legal sociologist Boaventura de Sousa Santos dubbed a kind of 'globalised localism'.[53] Globalization always depends upon localization (in this case, designating local American mores the universal ones). It is the 'global localism' of the Bush administration that decides who is the 'human' in the 'human rights' equation, and which rights that 'human' is entitled to.

VII

Finally, pathologizing some forms of sexual violence (such as the rape of men by women) has enabled other forms to be normalized. Debate about the rape of *women* in prisons (including Abu Ghraib) in Iraq is muted, for instance, as is analysis of

enforced prostitution and (a shrewd oxymoron) 'forced consent' or sexual intercourse as a way to obtain food or shelter. The *U.S. News and World Report* even
blamed the Abu Ghraib torture on 'the lack of a reliable local brothel where male
soldiers are able to unwind. Experts [unnamed] have long appreciated the fact that
sexual activity can often be a way of relieving the anxiety of war'.[54] The 'beast in all
men', exacerbated in the crucible of war, is here being used to justify the abuse of
women through legalized prostitution. Again, we have seen this before, in occupied Japan immediately at the end of World War II when the euphemistically named
'Recreation and Amusement Association' was set up to cater for the sexual needs
of the Allied occupying forces after mass rapes had come to international attention.

There are innumerable other examples drawn from previous conflicts. In the
context of the war in Vietnam, Gavin Hart's study of 718 combatants is typical. At
one stage in his article entitled 'Sex Behavior in a War Environment', Hart noted
that over 10 per cent of the men had 'suffered penile trauma' on one occasion during their military service and 5 per cent had done so more than once. The cause
of penile trauma? According to Hart, it was due to the refusal of some women to
consent to certain sexual acts. In his words:

> Failure [of the women] to indulge in fellatio at this stage often proved traumatic.
> Not infrequently, refusal caused the angry prostitute to violently wrench the erect
> penis causing severe preputial tears.

This discussion of forced sex is positioned as if it constituted a natural aspect of
wartime sexuality. The 'unacceptance' of women to engage in particular acts was
(according to Hart) in itself, unacceptable. Hart does mention sexual ethics:

> History continually relates how ethical and moral codes change radically under con-
> ditions of war. These altered standards together with absence from homeland and
> family, and ethical codes they represent, are conditions which favor promiscuity.[55]

The forced sexual acts carried out by soldiers are placed in the context of 'promiscuity'. Ethics were firmly positioned with the context of 'homeland and family' –
the humans 'at home'. In other words, pathologizing some acts of sexual violence,
particularly those against a racially different enemy, but also those against certain
classes of women ('prostitutes' as opposed to 'women'), normalized sexual violence.
Those who questioned this were themselves aggressively threatening the nation's
manhood in a time of crisis. To such arguments, a common Iraqi expression might
be posited: 'An excuse uglier than the guilt'.

Hart was writing at the time of the war in Vietnam. When he used the word
'trauma', he was referring to physical damage to men's intimate bodies. Since then,
narratives of trauma have gained power by fusing body and soul. Psychological
'trauma', inscribed on the body, has become the slogan of our time. As historian
Alfred McCoy has painstakingly documented, U.S. techniques of torture have

been practised (with executive knowledge) by the CIA since the Cold War: so-called 'no touch torture' (or psychological methods) has garnered the largest proportion of funding precisely on the grounds of its efficiency in accelerating breakdown.[56]

VIII

Today, even more than at the time Hart was writing, the language of psychological trauma has been co-opted by *perpetrators* of violence. The invention of post-traumatic stress disorder in the 1980s was precisely a mechanism that allowed individuals who had tortured and raped Vietnamese women and men to be portrayed (and to portray themselves) as victims. The diagnosis of PTSD was given to servicemen who had suffered the 'trauma' of raping and slaughtering other individuals. In the contemporary 'war on terror', psychological trauma experienced by service personnel in Iraq is also being used to justify abuse. In the words of Rush Limbaugh (a popular talk show host) speaking about the perpetrators of the Abu Ghraib abuses on CBS News, 'You know, these people are being fired at every day ... you ever heard of emotional release? You of heard [sic] of need to blow some steam off?[57]

The use of the trauma trope has had three main effects. In terms of the *victims*, one effect has been to create a universal suffering subject outside of history. It is to reduce the individual to his or her animal substructure, to an undifferentiated identity as a body-in-pain. Instead of historical specificities, we have an ahistorical narrative based on supposedly biological and psychological constants. Instead of history, we have a universalist notion of the body. The danger of this approach is that it blinds us to the fact that terror is always local. To universalize it is to remove the specifics of an individual's history; it is to situate torture in the realm of moral edification. The role of history is to demystify this category of the universal – revealing the fundamental undecidability of the human in the material world and specifying the 'what, who and wherefore' of all judgements of universality. The specificities of the past enable us to imagine a future in which there is no 'inevitable'.

While suffering has been universalized, the abusers have been individualized. As General Mark Kimmitt, Deputy Director of Coalition Operations in Iraq, told *60 Minutes II*, 'So what would I tell the people of Iraq? This is wrong. This is reprehensible, but this is not representative of the 150,000 soldiers that are over here. I'd say the same thing to the American people. Don't judge your army based on the actions of a few'.[58] 'Rotten apples' have been identified; the putrid barrel, ignored. In the context of the election of 2000, the use of distorted and false intelligence to justify the pre-emptive invasion of Iraq, the Patriot Act, the dramatic restrictions on civil liberties, the construction of a network of secret prisons or 'black sites' around the world, and the 'rendering' of suspects to countries known to employ torture, it takes a feat of remarkable self-delusion to continue to regard what happened at Abu Ghraib as somehow an aberration from 'American' practices. But that is precisely what has happened. Broader structural forces are overlooked. Only those prosecuted got their hands dirty. Those who practice systematic and instrumental cruelty (as promoted by the most powerful agents within political institutions) are left alone. The guilty ones are those seen to have revelled in the carnivalesque aspects of violence. In the words of the CIA document of 1963, *KUBARK Counterintelligence – July 1963*, coercion is 'simply a method for obtaining correct and useful information'.[59] Cool and calculated cruelty is acceptable. So long as the guidelines are followed and torture is conducted in a dispassionate, instrumental way, all is well. What individuals like Lynndie England and Charles Graner did wrong was to abandon the guidelines. They took obvious pleasure in their duties. The carnival got out of hand.

The final effect of the trauma narrative has been to insist that the perpetrators are not the only ones 'traumatized' in the 'war on terror': so too are the witnesses and bystanders. Our so-called trauma at hearing what American and British troops are doing in Iraq has trumped the wrong done to Iraqis. In the end, then, torture is about us. Even the argument about the need to adhere to the Geneva Conventions regarding prisoner treatment is framed in terms of helping 'our own armed forces sustain their difficult role' by providing 'moral sanction to the difficult imperative of killing'.[60] As Senator Joseph Biden told the Senate Foreign Relations Committee hearings, adherence to the laws of war was crucial to protect American service personnel. In the context of the Abu Ghraib photographs, this tendency was even more pronounced, with the media being profoundly interested in the photographers, not the photographed. The chief questions focused on us: what *effects* would the abuses have on *our* security; would the photographs increase *our* risk? The Iraqi victims ceased to 'be' after the camera-flash. They stepped out of history.

IX

The Bush administration may have become one of the most secretive in modern history, but the result has been a proliferation of talk. The 'war on terror' has, on the surface, been preoccupied with censorship and silence. The (Iraqi) dead are not counted; the (American) dead are quietly returned to American soil. It is government policy to censor images of coffins returning from Iraq. When the images from Abu Ghraib were first brought to public attention, leading politicians urged Americans to avert their eyes from the photographs. Donald Rumsfeld even refused to read the Taguba report (the official military inquiry conducted in 2004 into the Abu Ghraib abuses) for as long as he could.

But the unspeakable has become the unsilenceable. The mass circulation of these images has dulled their political impact. They rapidly entered art galleries – as art. High fashion photographers (such as Steven Meisel in the September 2006 Italian issue of *Vogue*) adopted poses from this 'war on terror', including ones drawn explicitly from the torture in Abu Ghraib. On the internet, real and fake photographs claiming to emanate from Iraq were published. Viewers were unable to distinguish between the two. Specifically dedicated 'Real Rape' internet sites purportedly based in Iraq rapidly appeared. The images were fetishized, released from historical context and the specifics of the interaction between torturer and tortured.

Being steeped in notions of trauma and seduced by apocalyptic fantasies, it is easy to forget that the seemingly unrestrained tyrannical desire of abusers is always contested. Even the tortured can forge ethical meaning in the midst of the inhuman. One example would be men like Nori Samir Gunbar Al-Yasseri, hooded and tortured in Abu Ghraib in the presence of three male and two female American guards. In his words:

> When we were naked he ordered us to stroke, acting like we were masturbating and when we start to do that he would bring in another inmate and sit him on his knees in front of the penis and take photos which looked like this inmate was putting the penis in his mouth. Before that, I felt that someone was playing with my penis with a pen. After this they make Hashim . . . stand in front of me and they forced me to slap him on the face, but I couldn't because he is my friend. After this they asked Hashim to hit me, so he punched my stomach. I asked him to do that, so they don't beat him like they had beaten me when I refused to hit Hashim.[61]

This was a gift: a gift not as contract, commodity, or even social exchange: there was no bond of obligation established (indeed, it was purposefully refused) and no debt was bestowed with obligations attached. Asymmetrical and non-reciprocal, it was an act of corporeal generosity.

In contrast, our security – and, since the bombs in London, our suffering – have become the main ways we justify inflicting misery on others. The torture photographs generated shock throughout much of the world but, paradoxically, caused ethical debate to fossilize into discussions about the skewed morals of individual perpetrators as opposed to the biopolitics of the war in general. Dehumanized bodies are our abjection, the visible border that designates subject from object, human from non-human. The 'human' does not emerge whole from the natural world. Attempts to insist upon a universal humanity posited upon a shared corporeality are doomed to fail, undermined by those states of power that construct our bodies according to different graduations of humanness. We cannot escape complicity: as Costas Douzinas reminds us, our humanity is defined through the torments the inhuman visits on the non-human. But we should not despair. Human rights do not arise out of timeless moral truths. Nor is there a universalist definition of the human. The pursuit of human rights is itself a historical and cultural process, operating through social action, and providing a language not only for dignity but also for rebelliousness. If, as Pierre Bourdieu put it, human rights are 'nothing other than the most universal gains of previous struggles',[62] then perhaps Nori Samir Gunbar Al-Yasseri's striving to be more than human can point to a new way of defining basic humanity.

Notes

1 Mark Danner, ed. *Torture and Truth: America, Abu Ghraib and the War on Terror* (London: Granta Books, 2005), 219.

2 Costas Douzinas, *Human Rights and Empire: The Political Philosophy of Cosmopolitanism* (Abingdon Routledge-Cavendish, 2007), chapter 5.

3 Memorandum: Jay S. Bybee to Alberto R. Gonzales, 1 August 2002, cited in *Torture and Truth* (note 1), 155.

4 *Torture and Truth* (note 1), 228. Also see Adam Zagorin and Michael Duffy, 'Inside the Interrogation of Detainee 063', *Time*, 20 June 2005, 29–30.

5 Jean Baudrillard, *The Gulf War Did Not Take Place* (Bloomington: Indiana University Press, 1985).

6 For the best discussion, see Allen Feldman, 'Memory Theatres, Virtual Witnessing, and the Trauma-Aesthetic', *Biography* 27.1 (winter 2004), 186.

7 Nazik al-Mala'ika, 'Jamilah and Us', in *Iraqi Poetry Today*, ed. Saadi A. Simawe (London: Modern Poetry in Translation, 2003).

8 Simone de Beauvoir, *La Force des Choses*, vol. 2 (Paris: Gallimard, 1963), 124–265.

9 Eric Hobsbawm, 'Barbarism: A User's Guide', *New Left Review* 206 (July/August 1994), 44.

10 James Inhofel, cited in Henry A. Giroux, 'What Might Education Mean After Abu Ghraib: Revisiting Adorno's Politics of Education', *Comparative Studies of South Asian Africa, and the Middle East* 24.1 (2004), 7.

11 'Notebook', *The New Republic*, 24 May 2004, 10.

12 Richard Goldstein, 'Bitch Bites Man!', *Village Voice*, 10 May 2004, in www.villagevoice.com/generic/show_print.php?id=53375&page=goldstein2&issue.

13 Quoted in 'Notebook' (note 11), 11.

14 See http://badgas.co.uk/lynndie/.

15 James Schlesinger, Harold Brown, Tillie K. Fowler, Charles A. Horner and James A. Blackwell, Jr., *Final Report of the Independent Panel to Review DOD Detention Operations* (Washington: U.S. Department of Defense, 2004), viewed 6 May 2006, www.globalsecurity.org/military/library/report/2004/d20040824finalreport.pdf.

16 John Barry, Michael Hirsch and Michael Isikoff, 'The Roots of Torture', *Newsweek*, 24 May 2004, 28.

17 There are innumerable examples of this logic, but a typical one is Adriene Sere, 'Man and the History of Rape', at http://holysmoke.org/fem/fem0126.htm.

18 For example, see Jacquelyn W. White and Robin M. Kowalski, 'Deconstructing the Myth of the Nonaggressive Woman: A Feminist Analysis', *Psychology of Women Quarterly* 18 (1994), 175–89.

19 For a critique, see my study, *Rapists: A History* (London: Virago, 2007).

20 Ann Coulter, cited in Gary Younge, 'Blame the White Trash', *Guardian*, 17 May 2004.

21 Tony Gutierrez, 'Lynndie England Convicted in Abu Ghraib Trial', *U.S.A. Today*, 26 September 2005, in www.usatoday.com/news/nation/2005-09-26-england_x.htm. Also see Michelle Cottle, 'G.I. Jane', *New Republic*, 24 May 2005, 38.

22 Bonnie Mann, 'How America Justifies Its War: A Modern/Postmodern Aesthetics of Masculinity and Sovereignty', *Hypatia* 21.4 (fall 2006), 159. Mann is writing from a feminist perspective and accepts that military women remain the 'lesser partner'.

23 National Coalition for the Protection of Children and Families, 'Abu Ghraib: Lessons in S-xual [*sic*] Morality', www.nationalcoalition.org/culture/articles/ca050523.html.

24 Frank Rich, 'It Was Porn That Made Them Do It', *New York Times*, 30 May 2004, AR1 and AR16.

25 Phyllis Schlafly, 'Equality for Women in our Army', *Eagle Forum*, 19 May 2004, in www.eagleforum.org/column/2004/may2004/04-05-19.html.

26 Elaine Scarry, *The Body in Pain: The Making and Unmaking of the World* (New York: Oxford University Press, 1985), 59.

27 'Bitch Bites Man!' (note 12).

28 Sharon Marcus, 'Fighting Bodies, Fighting Words: A Theory and Politics of Rape Prevention', in *Feminists Theorize the Political*, ed. Judith Butler and Joan W. Scott (London: Routledge, 1992), 391.

29 It has already been noted that there were plenty of female victims, whose privacy the U.S. government is somehow inclined to protect.

30 Moira Gatens, *Imagining Bodies: Ethics, Power and Corporeality* (London: Routledge, 1996), 33.

31 Ameen Sa'eed Al-Sheikh in *Torture and Truth* (note 1), 217.

32 Ameen Sa'eed Al-Sheikh, ibid., 219.

33 Hugh Urban, 'The Secrets of the Kingdom: Spiritual Discourse and Material Interests in the Bush Administration', *Discourse* 27.1 (winter 2005), 141–66.

34 Chris Mackey and Greg Miller, *The Interrogators' War: Inside the Secret War Against Al Qaeda* (Boston: Little, Brown, 2004), 182.

35 For the best discussion, see Costas Douzinas, *The End of Human Rights* (Oxford: Hart Publishing, 2000).

36 www.mirror.co.uk/news/allnews/content_objectid=14042696_method=full_siteid=50143_headline=-MY-HELL-IN-CAMP-X-RAY-name_page.html.

37 See Hannah Arendt, *The Origins of Totalitarianism* (San Diego: Harvest Books, 1979), 292 and Karen Halttunen, 'Humanitarianism and the Pornography of Pain in Anglo-American Culture', *American Historical Review* 100.2 (1995), 303–34.

38 Michael Ignatieff, 'Lesser Evils', *New York Times Magazine*, 2 May 2004, 86.

39 Lieutenant Diane Beaver, 'Legal Brief on Proposed Counter-Resistance Strategies to Department of Defense, Joint Task Force 170', 11 October 2002, in *Torture and Truth* (note 1), 175.

40 Cheney Offended by Amnesty Criticism', CNN.com and 'Bush: Amnesty Report "Absurd"', CNN.com.

41 Christian Davenport and Michael Amon, 'Accused Soldiers a Diverse Group', *Washington Post*, 9 May 2004, 18, in www.ccmep.org/2004_articles/general/050904_wp.htm.

42 For the best discussion, see Michelle Brown, '"Setting the Conditions" for Abu Ghraib: The Prison Nation Abroad', *American Quarterly* 57.3 (September 2003), 973–97.

43 Max Blumenthal, 'America's Rape Rooms: From the War on Drugs to the War on Terror', viewed 6 May 2006, www.buzzflash.com/contributors/04/05/con04209.html.

44 Ibid.

45 For estimates, see Alan J. Davis, 'Sexual Assaults in the Philadelphia Prison System and Sheriff's Vans', *Trans-Action* (December 1968) and Wayne S. Wooden and Joy Parker, *Men Behind Bars: Sexual Exploitation in Prison* (New York: Plenum Press, 1982), 99.

46 For lower estimates, see Peter L. Nacci and Thomas R. Kane, 'Inmate Sexual Aggression: Some Evolving Propositions, Empirical Findings, and Mitigating Counter-Forces', *Journal of Offender Counseling, Services, and Rehabilitation* 9 (1984), 10–11. For higher estimates, see Cindy Struckman-Johnson and David Struckman-Johnson, 'Sexual Coercion Rates in Seven Midwestern Prisons for Men', *The Prison Journal*, 379 (2000), 379–90.

47 Michael Welch, *Detained: Immigration Laws and the Expanding I.N.S. Jail Complex* (Philadelphia: Temple University Press, 2003), 23.

48 *Final Report of the Independent Panel to Review DOD Detention Operations* (note 14).

49 Amy Kaplan, 'Where is Guantánamo?', *American Quarterly* 57.3 (September 2005), 831–58. Also see Christina Duffy Burnett, 'A Note on the Insular Cases', in *Foreign in a Domestic Sense: Puerto Rico, American Expansion, and the Constitution*, ed. Christina Duffy Burnett and Burke Marshall (Durham, NC: Duke University Press, 2001), 389–92.

50 Rita Maran, *Torture: The Role of Ideology in the French-Algerian War* (New York: Praeger, 1989), 188.

51 Omar Rivabella, *Requiem for a Woman's Soul* (New York: Penguin, 1986), 86. Also see Adolfo Pérez Esquivel, *Christ in a Poncho* (Maryknoll, NY: Orbis, 1984), 13.

52 Kevin Dwyer, 'Beyond a Boundary?: "Universal Human Rights" and the Middle East', *Anthropology Today* 13.6 (December 1997), 14.

53 Boaventura de Sousa Santos, *Toward a New Common Sense: Law, Science and Politics in the Paradigmatic Transition* (London: Verso, 1995), 263.

54 Marianne Szegedy-Maszak, 'Sources of Sadism', *U.S. News and World Report* 136.18 (24 May 2004), 30.

55 Gavin Hart, 'Sexual Behavior in a War Environment', *Journal of Sex Research* 11.3 (August 1975), 223.

56 Alfred W. McCoy, 'Cruel Science: CIA Torture and U.S. Foreign Policy', *New England Journal of Public Policy*, 19.2 (winter 2005), 209–62.

57 'Rush: MPs Just "Blowing Off Steam"', CBS News, 2 May 2004, in www.cbsnews.com/stories/2004/05/06/opinion/meyer/main616021.shtml. Also see Jack Hitt, 'The Diddly Award', *Mother Jones*, September/October 2004, in www.motherjones.com/news/feature/2004/09-401.html.

58 'Court-Martial in Iraq: U.S. Army Soldiers Face Court-martials for Actions at Baghdad's Abu Ghraib Prison', *60 Minutes II*, 28 April 2004, in http://globalresearch.ca/articles/CB405A.html.

59 *KUBARK Counterintelligence: July 1963*, in www.gwu.edu/~nsarchiv/NSAEBB/NSAEBB122/CIA%20kubark%201-60.pdf.

60 William S. Shepard, 'International Law and the War on Terrorism', *Mediterranean Quarterly* 16.1 (winter 2005), 89.

61 *Torture and Truth* (note 1), 229.

62 Pierre Bourdieu, *Méditations pascaliennes* (Paris: Seuil, 1997), 146.

Avner Offer

Response to Joanna Bourke

Joanna Bourke attempts to capture the experience of torture through the lens of
cultural theory. Until art itself (literature and poetry more than the visual arts) probes
this experience, we have to make do with the mediation of critics. Her essay sets
up torture as an erotic spectacle, leaving no doubt as to how deeply revolting she
finds it. In vivid word-images and quotations she exposes the spectacle of degradation, and in the same breath blames us (and herself) for being complicit in it.
That experience of arousal, combining voyeurism and outrage, is partly cathartic
but perversely aesthetic. It invites us to blame ourselves for the very abuse that it
condemns. That is the reflexivity which is the staple of cultural criticism. This ambiguity (we are forced to admit) is a feature of our post-modern condition. It is a subtle,
troubling account of the kaleidoscopic experience of on-looking from various
aspects – gender, class, ethnicity are those she underlines. A fine intelligence is at work
there, and cannot help imparting the (disturbing, but also pleasing) glow of insight.
But where does that leave our moral selves? Has art subverted reality here? The
abrasive, brutal, lonely, terrifying experiences of pain and torture are tamed by clever
analysis. This is not to blame the analyst – we need to meditate on evil as best we
can, with the blinkers we have. We need to numb ourselves a little in order to cope.
It is no criticism of criticism to say that art is likely, eventually, to do it better.

The erotic here is the erotic of sadism. It falls within the domain of the per-
verse and the abnormal, though (as the author points out) that often gets normalized
in the discourse of the permissive society. Extensive quotes from American military and legal directives and manuals are shown to license torture in various forms.
They underline the means of torture, but not its ends. The precautionary principle is invoked by officials and their advocates but the careful attention to means
of torture is not matched by any clear justification of its purpose. There is an implication in these texts that torture might be expressive rather than instrumental. What
they convey to the attentive reader is a barely hidden relish to discard the rules of
civilization.

What is that notion of civilization? Where does it come from? I offer an additional take, grounded in my own discipline of economic history, to complement the cultural one so strikingly presented by Bourke. Victorian liberalism was presented by its advocates as an alternative to militarism and empire. In the nineteenth century, at least, this distinction had some merit.[1] In economic theory, as in economic exchange, trade may be adversarial, opportunistic, strategic – but it is not permitted to be violent. Unequal power (the unequal ability to walk away from a deal) is mediated, softened, legitimized through money and contract. In the service of trade, it is forbidden to maim and kill. Why is that? In a doctrine as dependent on such a primitive notion of human nature as economics, why is grabbing what you can not allowed? The reason is that trading is a form of reciprocity based on consent. For markets to work their magic, transactions have to be voluntary. Each one becomes a link in a chain. Traders hope to continue to deal with each other. Expectations are based on repetition and gradually build up reputations for probity. Probity engenders trust, and trust makes trading easy. Nineteenth-century liberals even hoped that trade might trump warfare altogether.

The Victorian and Edwardian efforts to tame war were part of the same liberal vision.[2] Two great international legal conferences in the Hague, in 1899 and in 1907, underscored two vital distinctions in international treaties, which lie at the basis of 'humanity in warfare'. These were first, the distinction between combatants who are legitimate targets of violence, and non-combatant civilians, who have immunity from violence under protection of the law. The second, related distinction, is between combat and surrender. Once arms have been laid down, the erstwhile combatant is granted immunities similar to those of other non-combatants. It is these late-Victorian and Edwardian treaties which provided the basis for the better-known and subsequent Geneva Conventions.

The same Hague conferences also strove to set up immunities for commerce in wartime. The main issue was the right of neutrals to continue to trade in wartime, under the principle (stated and promoted primarily by the United States), of 'the freedom of the seas'. This liberal regime of commerce, together with the restatement of the laws of war, of *jus in bello* (justice in warfare), were an effort to insulate non-combatants, whether neutral merchants or non-bearers of uniforms and arms, from the violence of war. Violence appeared to be containable. Europe had experienced peace and rising prosperity, almost unbroken, for almost a century.

Commerce is impersonal – everyone is welcome if they have something to offer. Hence the acceptability of ethnic, cultural and religious outsiders, of Chinese, Indians, Quakers, Huguenots, Venetians, Jews. Commerce was indifferent to their identity, even as the support of their communal identity was crucial to their capacity to trade. In a world of business based fundamentally on trust, repeated transactions established reputations, identities and acceptance of protagonists, at least at the personal level. Indifference to identity was transformed by repetition into reliance on identity.

That Victorian world could not contain its tensions and hostilities, and it took more than half a century, until the 1960s, to restore the project of an open world governed once again by the imperatives of commerce. The hostile Soviet bloc (an ideological enemy of markets and commerce) collapsed and gave way to this ideal in 1989, and one neo-liberal (Fukuyama) famously proclaimed it as the End of History. The theory of comparative advantage, a new freedom of the seas under the flag of neo-conservative globalization, was meant (once again) to dissolve antagonisms and anxieties, to flatten the earth, to integrate the Lexus and the Olive Tree. That, at any rate, was the proclaimed purpose of the 'Washington Consensus'.

But many of the putative beneficiaries did not see it that way. The reason they failed to appreciate the benefits was that a global dollar hegemony undermined their own existing local hegemonies. The prospect of rising standards of living was no compensation for loss of local identity and authority. Across the various global peripheries the spread of globalization (in its commercial or military forms) menaced those who had held sway there before as domestic generals, chieftains, politicians and priests. The British Empire in its day (and its French, Belgian, Spanish, Portuguese and American contemporaries in the nineteenth century) often used force to subjugate local supremacies. Between the wars, Britain used air power extensively to intimidate village chieftains. But the firepower, economic power, and 'soft' power of cultural persuasion (though often destructive) were less than those of the U.S.A. today. Across cultures it has generally been accepted that a challenge to identity is a mortal threat that relaxes the prohibition on killing. A challenge to selfhood, to the honour of the family, to the integrity of the nation and its symbols, to the icons of religion, justifies discarding restraint and resorting to violence.

One interpretation to the outrage of 9/11 was that this was the long-delayed revenge of the wretched of the earth. In response, it was rightly pointed out that the perpetrators of terror were often well educated and well off. Bin Laden was the rich son of a rich construction mogul; Mohamed Atta had professional training in a German university. Even Ayatollah Homeini or Mullah Omar belonged to their countries' elites. Their sources of their authority were local, not universal: the secular nationalist development dictatorship of a Saddam Hussein, Assad, Mubarak or Mugabe; the nationalism of Pushtun warlords in Afghanistan; the religious fundamentalism and Arab nationalism of Bin Laden; the divine authority of Ayatollahs, Mullahs, and Taliban. However powerful on the spot, these local elites could not compete in the dollar game. But they had a measure of immunity as well. No one has claimed the reward for Bin Laden yet. They were bound to be beaten in the globalized game of commerce. The challenge of dollar globalization has elicited a broad range of evasive and defensive responses, across the globe. For some fractions of the elites, the threat to identity appeared to brook no compromise. Bin Laden smashed his planes into the World Trade Center, the aptly named, assertive, self-styled symbolic edifice of the compelling, irresistible power of globalization.

The insult of 9/11 provided America with a licence to abandon the ethics of commerce. In the American creed, Protestant religion, individualism expressed as 'freedom', and market capitalism form a distinctive entity. Although the nation was scaled up out of a mosaic of ethnicities, its patriotism was cemented by fear and loathing of the world beyond. America has a tradition of brutality with adversaries, up to and including extermination: as experienced by Indians, blacks, workers. This tradition of violence possibly harks back to the adversarial traditions of Northern Irish Protestant religion.[3] At the heart of the American creed is an intense individualism, underpinned by a sense of divine mission. This creed is potentially in conflict with the benign liberal/utilitarian calculus of co-operative advantage. The ego, by definition, brooks no restraint. No rules in self-love and war – it comes to the same thing. David Hume sarcastically expressed this priority: 'It is not contrary to reason to prefer the destruction of the whole world to the scratching of my little finger'.[4]

Long before 9/11, through the proxy conflicts of the Cold War, that dour individualist stream had muddied the waters of globalization with a creed of military dominance. The response to the insult of 9/11 was to veer away from commercial values and into the warrior role of violence and unbridled dominance. The definition of the enemy as intangible ('terror') and the choice of disinhibited means ('war') licensed the rejection of civility and a civilian response. There were no uniforms or licensed combatants to respect. That armed civilians sheltering in the population resisted the occupations of Iraq and Afghanistan weakened further the self-imposed restraints of bourgeois warfare. Casting the enemy as a demon was a licence to demonize the self. It was a rejection of the restraint and self-control of the prudent businessman and a surrender to the atavistic celebration of cruelty that Bourke provides a glimpse of.

We should resist the temptation to follow it by normalizing such drives – and seek any anchor we can find in the traditions of civility, of humanity, primarily those set up for the practice of warfare by our bourgeois predecessors. The defences of civility and humanity are thin, while the argument from necessity is often compelling. Once this argument becomes legitimate, there are those, the opposite of squeamish, ready to push restraint to one side, to inflict pain, destruction and death on anyone who stands in the way. For many of us the temptation of barbarism is always there, and we need to cling to the formalities of conventions, law and custom, to the thin civilities of commerce, to protect us from the worst aspects of ourselves.

Notes

1 D.C.M. Platt, *Finance, Trade and Politics in British Foreign Policy 1815–1914* (Oxford: Clarendon Press, 1968); Avner Offer, 'Costs and Benefits, Prosperity and Security 1870–1914', in *The Oxford History of the British Empire, vol. III. The Nineteenth Century*, ed. A. Porter (Oxford: Oxford University Press, 1999), 690–711.
2 G.F.A. Best, *Humanity in Warfare: The Modern Law of Armed Conflicts* (London: Weidenfeld & Nicolson, 1980).
3 Anatol Lieven, *America Right or Wrong: An Anatomy of American Nationalism* (London: HarperCollins, 2004).
4 David Hume, *A Treatise of Human Nature (1839–40)*, ed. David Fate Norton and Mary J. Norton (Oxford: Oxford University Press, 2003), Bk. 2, pt. 3, p. 267.

9 Shaykh Muhammad Afifi al-Akiti

Defending the transgressed by censuring the reckless against the killing of civilians[1]

I Introduction and *Taqrīẓ* – Shaykh Gibril F. Haddad

In the name of God, the All-Beneficent, the Most Merciful.

Gentle reader, Peace upon those who follow right guidance!

I am honoured to present the following *fatwā* or 'response by a qualified Muslim Scholar' against the killing of civilians written by the Oxford-based Malaysian jurist of the Shāfiʿī School, my inestimable teacher, Shaykh Muhammad Afifi al-Akiti, and entitled *Defending the transgressed by censuring the reckless against the killing of civilians*.

The Shaykh authored it in a few days after I had asked him to offer some guidance on the issue of targeting civilians and civilian centres by suicide bombing in response to a pseudo-*fatwā* by a deviant U.K.-based group, which advocates such crimes.

Upon reading Shaykh Afifi's *fatwā*, do not be surprised if you have never before seen such clarity of thought and expression together with breadth of knowledge of Islamic Law applied (by a non-native speaker) to the definition of key Islamic concepts pertaining to the conduct of war and its jurisprudence, its arena and boundaries, suicide bombing, the reckless targeting of civilians, and more.

May it be the best possible start to true education on the impeccable position of Islam, which is squarely against terrorism, in anticipation of the day when all its culprits are brought to justice.

Dear Muslim reader, *al-Salāmu ʿalaykum wa-raḥmatuLlāh*:

Read this luminous *Fatwā* by Shaykh Muhammad Afifi al-Akiti carefully and learn it. Distribute it, publicize it, and teach it. Perhaps we will then be counted among those who do something to redress wrong, not only with our hearts as we should always do, but also with our tongues, in the fashion of the inspired teachers and preachers of truth.

I have tried to strike the keynote of this *Fatwā* in a few lines of free verse, mostly to express my thanks to our Teacher but also to seize the opportunity represented by this long-hoped-for response to remind myself of the reasons why I embraced Islam in the first place.

A *TAQRĪẒ* – HUMBLE COMMENDATION

Praise to God Whose Law shines brighter than the sun!
Blessings and peace on him who leads to the abode of peace!
Truth restores honour to the Religion of goodness.
Patient endurance lifts the oppressed to the heights
While gnarling mayhem separates like with like:
The innocent victims on the one hand and, on the other,
Silver-tongued devils and wolves who try to pass for just!

My God, I thank You for a Teacher You inspired
With words of light to face down Dajjāl's advocates.
Allāh bless you, Ustādh Afifi, for **Defending the transgressed
by censuring the reckless against the killing of civilians!**
Let the powers that be and every actor-speaker high and low
Heed this unique Fatwā of knowledge and responsibility.

Let every lover of truth proclaim, with pride once more,
What the war-mongers try to bury under lies and bombs:
Islam is peace and truth, the Rule of Law, justice and right!
Murderous suicide is never martyrdom but rather perversion,
Just as no flag on earth can ever justify oppression.
And may God save us from all criminals, East and West!

By permission of Shaykh Afifi I have done some very light editing having to do mostly with style, spelling or punctuation such as standardizing spacing between paragraphs, providing in-text translations of a couple of Arabic supplications, adding quotation marks to mark out textual citations, and so forth.

I have also provided an alphabetical glossary of Arabic terms not already glossed by the Shaykh directly in the text.

May Allāh *Subḥānahu wa-Ta'ālā* save Shaykh Muhammad Afifi here and hereafter, may He reward him and his teachers for this blessed work and grant us its much-needed benefits, not least of which is the redress of our actions and beliefs for our safety here and hereafter.

Blessings and peace on the Prophet, his Family, and all his Companions, *wal-Ḥamdu liLlāhi Rabb al-'Ālamin.*

Gibril F. Haddad
Day of Jumu'a after 'Aṣr
1 Rajab al-Ḥaram 1426
5 August 2005
Brunei Darussalam

II Fatwa – Shaykh Muhammad Afifi al-Akiti

Defending the transgressed by censuring the reckless against the killing of civilians

مدافع المظلوم بردّ المهامل

على قتال من لا يقاتل

A *fatwā* according to the *Madhhab* of Imām al-Shāfiʿī
by Shaykh Muhammad Afifi al-Akiti

The original question:

If you have time to address this delicate issue for the benefit of this mercy-bound[2] *Umma* which is reeling in *fitna* day in and day out, perhaps a few blessed words might use a refutation of the following text as a springboard?

I would like you to read the following article which highlights some of the problems we are facing and [shows] why young Muslims might turn to extremism. The article was issued by *Al-Muhajiroun*, which is headed by Omar Bakri Mohammed; whatever our reservations about the man, it is the content I am more concerned about, and it is these types of writings which need to be countered.

Excerpt from an article by Al-Muhajiroun:[3]

'AQD AL-AMĀN: THE COVENANT OF SECURITY
The Muslims living in the west are living under a covenant of security, it is not allowed for them to fight anyone with whom they have a covenant of security, abiding by the covenant of security is an important obligation upon all Muslims. However for

those Muslims living abroad, they are not under any covenant with the *kuffār* in the west, so it is acceptable for them to attack the non-Muslims in the west whether in retaliation for constant bombing and murder taking place all over the Muslim world at the hands of the non-Muslims, or if it an [*sic*] offensive attack in order to release the Muslims from the captivity of the *kuffār*. For them, attacks such as the September 11th Hijackings is [*sic*] a viable option in *jihād*, even though for the Muslims living in America who are under covenant, it is not allowed to do operations similar to those done by the magnificent 19 on the 9/11. This article speaks about the covenant and what the scholars have said regarding Al-'Aqd Al-Amān – the covenant of security. [. . .]

Shaykh Muhammad Afifi al-Akiti's reply:

بسم الله الرحمن الرحيم

الحمد لله الذي يحُدُّ الحربَ ولا يُحِبُّ المعتدين والصلاة والسلام على قائد الأمة الذي هو
أصبر على أذى الأعداء بقُتُوَّةٍ كاملة ومُرُوَّةٍ شاملة وعلى آله وأصحابه وجيشه أجمعين

[In the name of God, the Merciful and Compassionate. Praise be to God Who sets
the boundaries of war and does not love transgressors! Blessings and peace on the
General of the Community, the most patient of men in the face of the harm
inflicted by enemies, imbued with perfect chivalry and complete manliness, and upon
all his Family, Companions, and Army!]

This is a collection of *masā'il*, entitled: *Mudāfi' al-maẓlūm bi-radd al-muhāmil 'alā qitāl man lā yuqātil* [Defending the transgressed by censuring the reckless against the killing of civilians], written in response to the *fitna* bewildering this mercy-bound *Umma*, day in and day out, a *fitna* partly caused by those who, wilfully or not, interpret the legal discussions of the subject of warfare (for which the technical *fiqh* terminology varies according to *bāb: siyar, jihād,* or *qitāl*) outside their proper context and use these interpretations to justify their evil actions. May Allāh open our eyes to the true meaning [*ḥaqīqa*] of *ṣabr* and to the fact that only through it can we successfully endure the struggles we face in this *dunyā*, especially during our darkest hours; for indeed He is with those who patiently endure tribulations!

There is no *khilāf* that all the Shāfi'ī *fuqahā'* of today and other Sunni specialists in the Sacred Law from the Far East to the Middle East reject outright [*mardūd*] the opinion cited above from *Al-Muhajiroun* and consider it not only an anomaly [*shādhdh*] and very tenuous [*wāhin*] but also completely wrong [*bāṭil*] and a misguided innovation [*bid'a ḍalāla*]: the *'amal* can never be adopted by any *mukallaf*. It is regrettable too that the article above was written in a legal style at which any doctor of the Law should be horrified and appalled (since it is an immature yet persuasive attempt to cloak a misguided personal opinion in authority from *fiqh* and an effort to hijack our Law by invoking just one of the many *qaḍāyā* of this *bāb* while recklessly neglecting others). It should serve to remind the students of *fiqh* of the importance of legal analysis and awareness of the *thawābit* and the *ḍawābiṭ* when reading a *furū'* text, in order to ensure that the principal rules have not been breached in any given legal case.

The above opinion is problematic in three legal particulars [*fuṣūl*]:

1 the target [*maqtūl*]: without doubt, civilians;
2 the authority for carrying out the killing [*āmir al-qitāl*]: as no Muslim authority has declared war, or if there has been such a declaration there is, at this time, a ceasefire [*hudna*]; and
3 the way in which the killing is carried out [*maqtūl bih*]: it is either *ḥarām* – and cursed, since it is a form of suicide [*qātil nafsah*] – or at the very least so doubtful [*shubuhāt*] that it must be avoided by those who are religiously scrupulous [*wara'*].

Any sane Muslim who believed otherwise and thought the above was not a crime [*jināya*] would be both reckless [*muhmil*] and deluded [*maghrūr*]. Whether he realizes it or not, by adopting this view or acting on it he would be hijacking rules from our Law that are meant for the conventional (or authorized) army of a Muslim state and are addressed to those with authority over it (such as the executive leaders, the military commanders and so forth) and not to individuals who are unconnected to the military or who lack the political authority of the state [*dawla*].

The result in Islamic jurisprudence is: if a Muslim carries out such an attack voluntarily, he becomes a murderer and not a martyr or a hero and he will be punished for it in the Next World.

Faṣl I. The target: *maqtūl*

The proposition: 'so it is acceptable for them to attack the non-Muslims in the west', where 'non-Muslims' can be taken to mean – and clearly does, in the document, mean – non-combatants, civilians, or, in the terminology of *fiqh*, 'those who are not engaged in direct combat' [*man lā yuqātilu*].

This opinion violates a well-known principal rule [*ḍābiṭ*] from our Law:

لا َيَجوزُ قَتْلُ نسائِهم ولا صِبْيانهم إذا لم يُقاتِلوا

[It is not permissible to kill their (i.e., the opponents') women and children if they are not in direct combat.]

This is based on the Prophetic prohibition on soldiers killing women and children, from the well-known Ḥadīth of Ibn 'Umar (may Allāh be pleased with them both!) related by Imāms Mālik, al-Shāfi'ī, Aḥmad, al-Bukhārī, Muslim, Ibn Mājah, Abū Dāwūd, al-Tirmidhī, al-Bayhaqī and al-Baghawī (may Allāh be well pleased with them all!) and other Ḥadīths.

Imām al-Subkī (may Allāh be pleased with him!) made the scholarly understanding of this prohibition unequivocally clear. The standard rule of engagement deduced from it is that: '[a Muslim soldier] may not kill any women or any child-soldiers unless they are in combat directly, and they can only be killed in self-defence'.[4]

It goes without saying that men and innocent bystanders who are not direct combatants are also included in this prohibition. The nature of this prohibition is so specific and well defined that there can be no legal justification or legitimate shar'ī excuse for circumventing this convention of war and targeting any non-combatants or civilians whatsoever. Moreover the ḥukm shar'ī of killing them is not only ḥarām but also a Major Sin [Kabīra] and contravenes one of the principal commandments of our way of life.

Faṣl II. The authority: āmir al-qitāl

The proposition: 'so it is acceptable for them to attack the non-Muslims in the west whether in retaliation for constant bombing and murder taking place all over the Muslim world at the hands of the non-Muslims', where it implies that a state of war exists with a particular non-Muslim state on account of its being perceived as the aggressor.

This opinion violates the most basic rules of engagement from our Law:

أَمْرُ الجهاد مَوْكولٌ إلى الإمام واجتهادِه ويلزم الرعيَّة طاعتُه فيما يراه من ذلك

[The question of declaring war (or not) is entrusted to the executive authority and to its decision: compliance with the authority's decision is the subject's duty.]

and:

وللإمامٍ أو أميرٍ خيارٌ بين الكفّ والقتال

[The executive or its subordinate authority has the option of whether or not to declare war.]

In a Muslim state, decisions on questions relating to ceasefire ['aqd al-hudna], peace settlement ['aqd al-amān] and the judgment of prisoners of war [al-ikhtār fī asīr] can only be taken by the executive or political authority [imām] or by a subordinate authority appointed by the former authority [amīr mansūbin min jihati l-imām]. This is something Muslims take so much for granted from the authority of our naql [scriptures] that none will reject it except those who act counter to their own 'aql [intellect]. The most basic legal reason ['illa aṣliyya] is that this matter involves the public interest, and consideration of it thus belongs solely to the authority:

لأنّ هذا الأمرَ من المصالح العامَّة التي يختَصُّ الإمامُ بالنظرِ فيها

All of this is based on the well-known legal principle [qāʿida]:

تَصَرُّفُ الإمامِ على الرَّعِيَّة منوطٌ بالمصلحة

[The decisions of the authority on behalf of the subjects are determined by the public good.]

and:

فيفعل الإمامُ وجوباً الأحَظَّ للمسلمين لاجتهاده

[So the authority must act for the greatest advantage of (all) Muslims in making its judgment.]

Naṣīḥa

Uppermost in the minds of the authority during their deliberation over whether or not to wage war should be the awareness that war is only a means and not an end. Hence, if there are other ways of achieving the aim and the highest aim is the right to practice our religion openly (as we can in today's Spain, for example, in contrast with medieval *Reconquista* Spain), then it is better [awlā] not to go to war. This has been succinctly expressed by Imām al-Zarkashī (may Allāh be pleased with him!):

وجوبُه وجوبُ الوسائلِ لا المقاصدِ

[Its necessity is the necessity of means, not ends.]

The upshot is – whether one likes it or not – that the decision and discretion and right to declare war or *jihād* for Muslims lie solely with the various authorities as represented today by the respective Muslim states; they do not lie with any individual, even if he is a scholar or a soldier (and not just anyone is a soldier or a scholar); in the same way that an authority (such as the *Qāḍī* in a court of law: *maḥkama*) is the only one with the right to excommunicate or declare someone an apostate [murtadd], whose killing would otherwise be extra-judicial and unauthorized.

Even during the period of the Ottoman caliphate, there were multiple Muslim authorities: for example, another Muslim authority outside the Ottoman territories – such as one in the Indian subcontinent – might have been engaged in a war when at that time the Khalifa's army was at peace with the same enemy. This is how it has been throughout our long history, and this is how it will always be, and this is the reality on the ground.

Faṣl III. The method: *maqtūl bih*

The proposition: 'attacks such as the September 11th Hijackings is [*sic*] a viable option in *jihād*', where such attacks employ tactics – analogous to the Japanese kamikaze missions of the Second World War – that have been described as self-sacrificing or martyrdom or suicide missions.

There is no *khilāf* on this question from any *qāḍī*, *muftī* or *faqīh* that this proposition and those who accept it are breaching the scholarly consensus [*mukhālifun lil-ijmāʿ*] of the Muslims since the 'Hijackings' resulted in the killing of non-combatants; moreover, the proposition is an attempt to legitimize the killing of indisputable non-combatants.

As for the kamikaze method and the tactic by which the attack was carried out, there is a difference of opinion with some jurists as to whether or not it constitutes suicide, which is not only *ḥarām* but also cursed. On this, we must enter into detail. (Note that in all of the following cases it is formally assumed that the target is legitimate – i.e., a valid military target – and that the action is carried out during a valid war when there is no ceasefire [*fī ḥāl al-ḥarb wa-lā hudnata fīh*], as was the case with the Japanese kamikaze attacks.)

Tafṣīl I

If the attack involves a bomb placed on the body or placed so close to the bomber that when the bomber detonates it he or she is certain [*yaqīn*] to die, then the More Correct Position [*Qawl Aṣaḥḥ*] according to us is that it does constitute suicide. This is because the bomber, being also the *maqtūl* [the one killed], is unquestionably the *qātil* [the immediate and active agent that kills] = *qātil nafsah* [self-killing, i.e., suicide].

FURŪʿ

If the attack involves a bomb (the lobbing of a grenade and the like) but the attacker thinks that when the bomb is detonated, it is uncertain [*ẓann*] whether he will die in the process or survive the attack, then the Correct Position [*Qawl Ṣaḥīḥ*] is that this does not constitute suicide, and were the bomber to die in this selfless act, he becomes what we properly call a martyr or hero [*shahīd*]. This is because the attacker, were he to die, is not the active, willing agent of his own death because the *qātil* is not necessarily the *maqtūl*.

An example [*ṣūra*] of this is: when in its right place and circumstance, such as in the midst of an ongoing battle against an opponent's military unit, whether ordered by his commanding officer or on his own initiative, the soldier makes a lone charge and as a result of that initiative manages to turn the tide of the day's battle but dies in the process (and not intentionally by his own hand), then that soldier dies as a hero (and this circumstance is precisely the context of becoming a *shahīd* – in Islamic terminology – as he died selflessly). If he survives, he wins a Medal of Honour or at the least becomes an honoured war hero and is remembered as a famous patriot (in our terminology, becoming a true *mujāhid*).

This is precisely the context of the *mas'ala* concerning the 'lone charger' [*al-hājim al-waḥīd*] and the meaning of 'putting one's life in danger' [*al-taghrīr bil-nafs*] found in all of the *fiqh* chapters concerning warfare. The *Umma's* Doctor Angelicus, Imām al-Ghazālī (may Allāh be pleased with him!) provides the best impartial summation:

If it is said: What is the meaning of the words of the Most High:

$$\text{وَلَا تُلْقُوا بِأَيْدِيكُمْ إِلَى التَّهْلُكَةِ}$$

[*and do not throw yourself into destruction by your own hands!*]?[5]

We say: There is no difference [of opinion amongst scholars] regarding the lone Muslim [soldier] who charges into the battle-lines of the [opposing] non-Muslim [army that is presently in a state of war with his army and is facing them in a battle] and fights [them] even if he knows that he will almost certainly be killed. The case might be thought to go against the requirements of the Verse, but that is not so. Indeed, Ibn 'Abbās (may Allāh be well pleased with both of them!) says: [the meaning of] '*destruction*' is not that [incident] but the failure to provide [adequate] supplies [*nafaqa*: for the military campaign; in the modern context, the state should provide the arms and equipment and so forth necessary for the purpose for which all of this is done] in obedience to God [as in the first part of the Verse which says: وَأَنْفِقُوا فِي سَبِيلِ اللهِ (*And spend for the sake of God*)[6]].

That is, those who fail to provide such equipment will destroy themselves. [In another *Ṣaḥābī* authority] al-Barā'a ibn 'Āzib [al-Ansārī (may Allāh be well pleased with them both!)] says: [the meaning of] '*destruction*' is [a Muslim] committing a sin and then saying: 'my repentance will not be accepted'. [A *Tābi'ī* authority] Abū 'Ubayda says: it [the meaning of '*destruction*'] is to commit a sin and then not perform a good deed after it before he perishes. [Ponder over this!]

In the same way that it is permissible [for the Muslim soldier in the event described above] to fight the non-Muslim [army] unto death, such acts [to that extent and with that consequence] are also permissible [i.e., for the enforcer of the Law, since the '*ā'id* (antecedent) here goes back to the original pronoun (*ḍamīr al-aṣl*) for this *bāb*: the *muḥtasib* or enforcer, such as the police] in [matters of] law enforcement [*ḥisba*].

However, [note the following qualification (*qayd*):] were he to know [*zannī*] that his charge will *not* cause harm to the non-Muslim [army] – for example, were a blind or weak person to charge the [enemy] battle-lines – then his action is prohibited [*ḥarām*], and is included under the general meaning ['*umūm*] of '*destruction*' from the Verse [for in this case, he will be literally throwing himself into destruction].

It is only permissible for him to advance [and suffer the consequences] if he knows that he will be able to fight [effectively] until he is killed, or knows that he will be able to demoralize the non-Muslim [army]: by their witnessing his courage and by their conviction that the rest of the Muslim [army] is [also] selfless [*qillat al-mubāla*] in their willingness to sacrifice themselves for the sake of God [the closest modern non-Muslim parallel would be 'to die for one's country']. Thus the will to fight [*shawka*] of the non-Muslim army will be shaken [and this may cause panic and the collapse of their battle-lines].[7]

It is clear that this selfless deed, which any modern soldier, Muslim or non-Muslim, might perform in battle today, is not suicide. It may hyperbolically be described as a 'suicidal' attack: but to endanger one's life is one thing and to die by one's own hand during the attack is obviously another. And as the passage shows, it is possible even under these circumstances for either situation to arise: an attack that is *taghrīr bil-nafs*, that is, not prohibited; and an attack of the *tahluka*-type, which is prohibited.

Tafṣīl II

If the attack involves ramming a vehicle into a military target and the attacker is certain to die, as with the historical Japanese kamikaze missions, then our jurists have disagreed over whether it does or does not constitute suicide.

QAWL A

Those who consider it suicide argue that there is the possibility [*ẓannī*] that the *maqtūl* is the same as the *qātil* (as in *Tafṣīl I* above) and would therefore not allow of any other qualification whatsoever, since suicide is a cursed sin.

QAWL B

Whereas those who consider otherwise, even when the *maqtūl* may be the same as the *qātil*, will allow some other consideration such as the possibility that by carrying out this action the battle of the day could be won. There are further details in this alternative position, such as that the commanding officer does not have the right to command anyone under him to perform this dangerous mission, so that, were it to be legitimate, it could only be legitimate when it is not performed under anyone else's orders and is the sole initiative of the soldier concerned (for example, an initiative taken in defiance of the standing orders of his commanding officer).

The first of the two positions is the Preferred Position [*muttajih*] among our jurists. The second is the Rarer Position because of the vagueness of the precedents; because its legal details are fraught with difficulties and ambiguities and because its dissenting position [*muqābil*] involves such significant consequences (namely, the consequences that follow from suicide, for the *Ijmā'* is that one who commits suicide will be damned to committing it eternally).

In addition to this juristic preference, the first position is also better and preferable since it is the original or starting position [aṣl] and because in relation to it we invoke the well-known and accepted legal principle:

الْخُروجُ مِنَ الخِلاف مُسْتَحَبٌّ

[To avoid controversy is preferable.]

Finally, the first position is religiously safer, since, given the ambiguity of the legal status of the person performing the act – whether it will result in the *maqtūl* being also the *qātil* – there is doubt [*shakk*] and uncertainty concerning the second position. Therefore this case falls under the category of doubtful matters [*shubuhāt*] of the kind [*nawʻ*] that should be avoided by those who are religiously scrupulous [*waraʻ*]. And here, the wisdom of our wise Prophet (may Allāh's blessings and peace be upon him!) is illuminated by the Ḥadīth of al-Nuʻmān (may Allāh be well pleased with him!):

فمَن اتَّقى الشُّبُهَاتِ اسْتَبْرَأَ لِدِينِهِ وَعِرْضِهِ

[He who saves himself from doubtful matters will save his religion and his honour.][8]

Wa-Llāhu aʻlam biṣ-ṣawāb! [God knows best what is right!]

Fāʼida

The original ruling [*al-aṣl*] for using a bomb (the medieval precedents are Greek fire [*qitāl bil-nār* or *ramy al-naft*] and catapults [*manjanīq*]) as a weapon is that it is *makrūh* [offensive] because it kills indiscriminately [*yaʼummu man yuqātilū wa-man lā yuqātilū*], unlike rifles (medieval example: a bow and arrow). If the indiscriminate weapon is used in a place where there are civilians, it becomes *ḥarām* except when used as a last resort [*min ḍarūra*] (and of course, only then when used by military personnel authorized to do so).

Ḥāṣil

From consideration of the foregoing three legal particulars, it is evident that the opinion expressed regarding the *ʻamal* in the article cited is untenable by the standards of our Sacred Law.

As to those who may still be persuaded by it and suppose that the action can be excused on the pretext that there is scholarly *khilāf* on the details of *Tafṣīl* II from *Faṣl* III above (and that therefore, the *ʻamal* itself could ultimately be legitimated by invoking the guiding principle that one should be flexible with regard to legal controversies [*masāʼil khilāfiyya*] and should agree to disagree); know then there is no *khilāf* among scholars that its rationale does not stand, since it is well known that:

لا يُنْكَرُ الْمُخْتَلَفُ فيه وإنما يُنكر الْمُجْمَعُ عليه

[The controversial cannot be rejected; only (breach of) the unanimous can be rejected.]

This *qā'ida*, which is very terse in expression, means that an action about which there is *khilāf* may be excused while an action that contravenes *Ijmā'* is categorically rejected.

Since it is agreed (at very least) by all scholars that killing non-combatants is prohibited, the *'amal* overall is unquestionably outlawed.

Masā'il mufaṣṣala

Question I

If it is said: 'I have heard that Islam says that the killing of civilians is allowed if they are non-Muslims'.

We say: On a joking note (but ponder over this so your hearts may be opened!): the authority is not with what 'Islam says' but with what Allāh (Exalted is He!) and His Messenger (may His blessings and peace be upon him!) have said!

But seriously: the answer is absolutely *no*; for even a novice student of *fiqh* would be able to see that the first *ḍābiṭ* above (*Faṣl* I) concerns a non-Muslim opponent in the case of a state of war having been validly declared by a Muslim authority against a particular non-Muslim enemy, even when that civilian is a subject or in the care [*dhimma*] of the hostile non-Muslim state [*Dār al-Ḥarb*]. If this is the extent of the limitation to be observed with regard to non-Muslim civilians belonging to a declared enemy state, how much higher will the standard be in cases where there is no valid war or when the status of war is ambiguous? Keep in mind that there are more than one hundred Verses in the Qur'ān commanding us at all times to be patient in the face of humiliation and to turn away from violence [*al-i'rāḍ 'ani l-mushrikīn waṣ-ṣabr 'alā adhā al-a'dā'*], while there is only one famous Verse in which war (which does not last forever) becomes an option (in our modern context: for a particular Muslim authority and not an individual), when a particular non-Muslim force has drawn first blood.

Question II

If it is said: 'What about the verse of the Qur'ān which says *kill the unbelievers wherever you find them* and the *ṣaḥīḥ* Ḥadīth which says "I have been ordered to fight against the people until they testify"?'

We say: It is well known among scholars that the following verse,

فَاقْتُلُوا الْمُشْرِكِينَ حَيْثُ وَجَدْتُمُوهُمْ

[*kill the idolaters wherever you find them*]⁹ is in reference to a historical episode: it refers to those among the Meccan Confederates who breached the Treaty of Ḥudaybiyya [*Ṣulḥ al-Ḥudaybiyya*] that led to the Victory of Mecca [*Fatḥ Makka*],¹⁰ and consequently, no legal rulings, or in other words, no practical or particular implications, can be derived from this Verse on its own. The Divine Irony and indeed Providence from the last part of the Verse, '*wherever you find them*' – which many of our *mufassirs* understood in reference to place (i.e., attack them whether inside the Sacred Precinct or not) – is that the victory against the Meccans happened without a single battle taking place, whether inside or outside the Sacred Precinct; on the contrary, there was a general amnesty [*wa-mannun 'alayhi bi-takhliyati sabīlihi* or *nahā 'an safki d-dimā'*] for the *Jāhilī* Arabs there. Had the Verse not been subject to a historical context, then you should know that, since it is of the general type ['*āmm*], it will therefore be subject to specification [*takhṣīṣ*] by some other indication [*dalīl*]. In lay terms, even assuming we did not know that it related to the *Jāhilī* Arabs, it could only refer to the case of a valid war when no ceasefire is in force.

Among the well known exegeses of '*al-mushrikīn*' from this Verse are '*an-nākithīna khāṣṣatan*' [specifically, those who have breached (the Treaty)];¹¹ '*al-ladhīna yuḥāribūnakum*' [those who have declared war against you];¹² and '*khāṣṣan fī mushrikī l-'arabi dūna ghayrihim*' [specifically, the *Jāhilī* Arabs and not anyone else].¹³

As for the meaning of 'people' [*al-nās*] in the well-related Ḥadīth cited above, it is confirmed by *Ijmā'* that it refers to the same '*mushrikīn*' as in the Verse of Sūra al-Tawba above and therefore refers only to the *Jāhilī* Arabs [*mushrikū l-'arab*] during the closing days of the Final Messenger and the early years of the Righteous Caliphs and not to any other non-Muslims.

To sum up, we are not in a perpetual state of war with non-Muslims. On the contrary, the original legal status [*al-aṣl*] is a state of peace, and making a decision to change this status is the right and responsibility of a Muslim authority that will in the Next World answer for its *ijtihād* and decision. (Moreover, this decision is not divinely entrusted to any individuals as such, not even to soldiers or scholars.) How can one believe that we are in a perpetual state of war with non-Muslims when there is a well-known rule in our Law that a Muslim authority can seek help from a non-Muslim under certain conditions, for example from non-Muslim allies on condition they are of goodwill towards Muslims:

لا يستعين بمشركين إلا بشروطٍ كأن تكونَ نيَّتُه حسنة للمسلمين

Question III

If it is said: 'I have heard a scholar say that "Israeli women are not like women in our society because they are militarized". By implication, this means that they fall into the category of women who fight and that this makes them legitimate targets if only in the case of Palestine'.

We say: No properly schooled jurists from any of the Four Schools would say this as a legal judgment if they faithfully followed the juridical processes of the ortho-dox Schools relating to this *bāb*; for if it is true that the scholar made such a state-ment and meant it in the way that you imply, then not only does this violate the well-known principal rule above (*Faṣl* I: 'It is not permissible to kill their women and children if they are not in direct combat'), but the supposed remarks also show a lack of sophistication in the legal particulars. If this is the case, then it has to be said here that this is not among the *masā'il khilāfiyya*, about which one can afford to agree to disagree, since it is outright wrong according to the principles and the rules from our *uṣūl* and *furū'*.

Let us restate the *ḍābiṭ* again, as our jurists have succinctly summarized its rule of engagement: a soldier can only attack a female or (if applicable) child soldier (or a male civilian) in self-defence and only when *she herself* (and not someone else from her army) is engaged in direct combat. (As for male soldiers, it goes without saying that they are considered combatants as soon as they arrive on the battlefield even if they are not in direct combat – provided of course that the remaining con-ventions of war have been observed throughout, and that all this arises during a valid war when no ceasefire is in force.)

Not only is this strict rule of engagement already made clear in our secondary legal texts, but it is also obvious from the linguistic analysis of the primary proof-texts used to derive this principal rule. Thus the form of the verb used in the scrip-tures, *yuqātilu*, is of the *mushāraka*-type, so that the verb denotes a direct or personal or reciprocal relationship between two agents: the minimum for which is one of them making an effort or attempt to act upon the other. The immediate legal implication here is that one of the two can only be considered a legitimate target when there is a reciprocal or direct relationship.

In reality [*wāqi'*], this not what happens on the ground (since the bombing missions are offensive in nature – they are not targeting, for example, a force that *is attacking* an immediate Muslim force; but rather the attack is directed at an overtly non-military target, so the person carrying it out can only be described as attack-ing it – and the target is someone unknown until seconds before the mission reaches its end).

In short, even if these women are soldiers, they can only be attacked when they are *in direct combat* and not otherwise. In any case, there are other overriding particulars to be considered and various conditions to be observed throughout, namely, that it must be during a valid state of war when there is no ceasefire.

Question IV

If it is said: 'When a bomber blows himself up he is not directing the attack towards civilians. On the contrary, the attack is designed to target off-duty soldiers (which I was told did not mean reservists, since most Israelis are technically

reservists). The innocent civilians are unfortunate collateral damage in the targeting of soldiers'.

We say: There are two details here.

TAFṢĪL A

Off-duty soldiers are treated as civilians.

Our jurists agree that during a valid war when there is no ceasefire and when
an attack is not aimed at a valid military target, a hostile soldier (whether male or
female, whether conscripted or not) who is not on operational duty or not wearing a military uniform and when there is nothing in the soldier's outward appearance to suggest that the soldier is in combat, is considered a non-combatant [*man
lā yuqātilu*] (and in this case, must therefore be treated as a normal civilian).

A valid military target is limited to either a battlefield [*maḥall al-maʿraka* or *saḥat
al-qitāl*] or a military base [*muʿaskar*; medieval examples are citadels or forts;
modern examples are barracks, military depots, etc.]; and anything else such as a
restaurant, a hotel, a public bus, the area around a traffic light, or any other public
place can *never* be considered a valid military target, since first, these are not places
and bases from which an attack would normally originate [*maḥall al-raʾy*]; second,
there is certain knowledge [*yaqīn*] that the targeted persons are intermingling
[*ikhtilāṭ*] with non-combatants; and third, the non-combatants have not been
given the option to leave the place.

As for when the soldiers are on the battlefield, the normal rules of engagement
apply.

As for when the soldiers are in a barracks or the like, there is further discussion
on whether the soldiers become a legitimate target, and the *Qawl Aṣaḥḥ* [the More
Correct Position] according to our jurists is that they do, albeit to attack them in
such places is *makrūh*.

TAFṢĪL B

Non-combatants cannot at all be considered collateral damage except when they
are in or at a valid military target, where they may be so deemed, depending on
certain extenuating circumstances.

There is no *khilāf* that non-combatants or civilians cannot at all be considered
collateral damage at a non-military target in a war zone and that their deaths are
not excusable by our Law and that the one who ends up killing one of them will
therefore be sinful as in the case of murder, even though the soldier who is found
guilty of it would be excused from the ordinary capital punishment [*ḥadd*] unless
the killing was found to be premeditated and deliberate:

أو أتى بمعصيةٍ تُوجِب الحدَّ

If the killing was not premeditated, the murderer's punishment would be subject to the authority's discretion [ta'zīr] and he would in any case be liable to pay the relevant compensation [diya].

As for a valid military target in a war zone, the Shāfi'ī School has historically considered the possibility of justifying collateral damage, whereas other schools have held it to be outlawed in all cases. The following are the conditions stipulated for allowing this controversial exception (in addition to meeting the most important condition of them all: that this takes place during a valid war when there is no ceasefire):

1 The target is a valid military target.
2 The attack is as a last resort [min ḍarūra] (such as when the civilians have been warned to leave the place and after a period of siege has elapsed):

وجوبُ الإنذار قبل البَدْء بالقَتْل لأنه لا يجوز أن يقتَلَ إلاَّ مَن يُقاتل

3 There are no Muslim civilians or prisoners.
4 The decision to attack the target is based on a considered judgement on the part of the executive or military leader that by making the attack, there is a good chance that the war or battle will be won.

(Furthermore, this position is subject to khilāf among our jurists with regard to whether the military target can be a Jewish or Christian [Ahl al-Kitāb] or other non-Muslim one, since the sole primary text that is invoked to allow this exception concerns an incident restricted to the same 'mushrikīn' as in the Verse of Sūra al-Tawba in Question II above.)

Intentionally to neglect any of these strict conditions is analogous to not fulfilling the conditions [shurūṭ] for a prayer [Ṣalāt] with the outcome that [the action] becomes invalid [bāṭil] and ineffective [fasād]. This is why the means of an act ['amal] must be correct and valid according to the rule of Law in order for its outcome to be sound and accepted, as expressed succinctly in the following aphorism of Imām Ibn 'Aṭā Allāh (may Allāh sanctify his soul!):

مَن أشْرَقَتْ بدايتُه أشرقت نهايتُه

[He who makes good his beginning will make good his ending.]

In our Law, the ends can never justify the means except when the means are in themselves permissible, or mubāḥ (and not ḥarām), as is made clear in the following famous legal principle:

وَسِيْلَةُ الطَّاعَة طاعةٌ ووسيلةُ المعصية معصيةٌ

[The means to a reward is itself a reward and the means to a sin is itself a sin.]

Hence, with even a simple act such as opening a window, which on its own is only mubāḥ or ḥalāl, that is, neither worthy of reward nor sinful, when a son does it with the intention of enhancing his mother's comfort on a hot summer's day before she asks for it to be opened, the originally non-consequential act itself becomes *mandūb* [recommended] and the son is rewarded in his *'amal*-account for the Next World and incurs the pleasure of Allāh.

WaLlāhu a'lam wa-aḥkām biṣ-ṣawāb! [God knows and judges best what is right!]

Question V

If it is said: 'In a classic manual of Islamic Sacred Law, I read that "it is offensive to conduct a military expedition [*ghazw*] against hostile non-Muslims without the caliph's permission (though if there is no caliph, no permission is required)". Does this not mean that though it is *makrūh* for anyone else to call for or initiate such a *jihād*, it is nevertheless permissible?'

We say:

لا غَزْوَةَ إلا في الجهاد

[There can be no battle except during a war!]

Secondary legal texts, like primary proof-texts (a single Verse of the Qur'ān from among the relatively few *Āyāt al-Aḥkām* or a Ḥadīth from among the limited number of *Aḥadīth al-Aḥkām*), must be read and understood in context. The conclusion that it is permissible – however repugnant – for anyone other than those in authority to declare or initiate a war is evidently wrong, since it violates the principal rule of engagement discussed in *Faṣl* II above.

The context is that of endangering one's life [*taghrīr bil-nafs*] when there is already a valid war with no ceasefire, as seen in the above example from the *Iḥyā'* passage, and is therefore not that of executive concerns such as declaring a war and the like. This is also obvious from the terminology used: a *ghazw* [a military act, assault, foray or raid; the minimum limit in a modern example is an attack by a squad or a platoon (*katība*)] can take place only when there is a state of *jihād* [war], not otherwise.

FĀ'IDA

Imām Ibn Ḥajar (may Allāh be pleased with him!) lists the organizational structure of an army as follows: a *ba'th* [unit] and several such together, a *katība* [platoon], which is a part of a *sariyya* [company; made up of 50–100 soldiers], which is in turn a part of a *mansar* [regiment; up to 800 soldiers], which is a part of a *jaysh* [division; up to 4,000 soldiers], which is a part of a *jaḥfal* [army corps; exceeding 4,000 soldiers] making up the *jaysh 'aẓīm* [army].[14]

In our School, it is offensive but not completely prohibited for a soldier to defy or, in other words, to take an initiative against the wishes of his direct superiors, whether his unit is strong or otherwise. In the modern context, this may include cases when soldier(s) disagree with a particular decision or strategy adopted by their superior officers, whether during a battle or otherwise.

The accompanying classic commentary to the text quoted will help clarify this:

> [Original Text:] It is offensive to conduct an assault [whether the unit is strong (*man'a*) or otherwise; and some have defined a strong force as 10 men] without the permission of the authority ([Commentary:] or his subordinate, because the assault depends on the needs [of the battle and the like] and the authority is better informed about them. It is not prohibited [to act without his permission] (if there is no grave endangering of one's life even when that is permissible in war.)[15]

Question VI

If it is said: 'What is the meaning of the rule in *fiqh* that I always hear, that *jihād* is a *fard kifāya* [communal obligation] but when the *Dār al-Islām* is invaded or occupied it is a *fard 'ayn* [personal obligation]? How do we apply this in the context of a modern Muslim state such as Egypt?'

We say: It is *fard kifāya* for the eligible Muslim subjects of the state in the sense that joining the army is voluntary when the state declares war with a non-Muslim state (non-Muslim subjects are evidently not religiously obligated but can still serve). It becomes a *fard 'ayn* for any able-bodied Muslim when there is conscription or a nationwide draft if the state is invaded by a hostile non-Muslim force, but only until that hostile force is repelled or the Muslim authority calls for a ceasefire. As for those not in the military, they have the option to defend themselves if attacked, even if they have to resort to throwing stones and using sticks:

بأيّ شيءٍ أطاقوه ولو بحجارةٍ أو عصا

FURŪ'

When it is not possible to prepare for war [and rally the army for war (*ijtimā' li-ḥarb*) and a surprise attack by a hostile force completely defeats the army of the state and the entire state is occupied] and someone [at home, for example] is faced with the choice of whether to surrender or to fight [such as when the hostile force comes knocking at the door], then he may fight. Or he may surrender, provided that he knows [with certainty] that if he resists [arrest] he will not be killed and that [his] wife will be safe from being raped [*fāḥisha*] if she is captured. If not [that is to say, he knows he will be killed even if he surrenders and his wife raped when captured], then [as a last resort] fighting [*jihād*] becomes personally obligatory for him.[16]

Reflect upon this legal ruling of our Religion and the emphasis placed upon preserving human life and upon the wisdom of resorting to violence only when it is *absolutely necessary* and in its proper place; and witness the conjunction between the *maqāṣid* and the *wasā'il* and the meaning of the conditions when fighting actually becomes a *farḍ 'ayn* for an individual!

Question VII

If it is said today: 'In the [Shāfi'ī] *madhhab*, what are the different classifications of lands in the world? For example, *Dār al-Islām, Dār al-Kufr* and so forth, and what have the classical *ulamā* said their attributes are?'

We say: In accordance with empirical fact [*tajriba*], Muslim scholars have classified the territories in this world into *Dār al-Islām* [synonyms: *Bilād al-Islām* or *Dawla Islāmiyya*; a Muslim state or territory or land or country, etc.] and *Dār al-Kufr* [a non-Muslim state, territory, etc.].

The definition of a Muslim state is: 'any place in which a resident Muslim [authority] is capable of defending itself against hostile forces [*ḥarbiyyūn*] for a period of time, where its decisions have the force of law at that time and thereafter, is a Muslim state'.[17] A non-Muslim who resides in a Muslim state is, in our terminology: *kāfir dhimmī* or *al-kāfir bi-dhimmati l-muslim* [a non-Muslim in the care of a Muslim state].

By definition, an area is a Muslim state as long as Muslims continue to live there and the political and executive authority is Muslim. (Think about this, for the Muslim lands are many, varied, wide and extensive; and how poor is the insight of those who have tried to limit the definition of what a Muslim state must be, and thus, whether or not they realized what they were doing, have attempted to reduce the extent of the Muslim world!)

As for a non-Muslim state, it is the absence of a Muslim state.

As for *Dār al-Ḥarb* (sometimes called *Arḍ al-'Adw*), it is a non-Muslim state which is in a state of war with a Muslim state. Therefore, a hostile non-Muslim soldier from there is known in our books as: *kāfir ḥarbī*.

FURŪ'

Even if a *kāfir ḥarbī* resides in or enters a Muslim country that is in a state of war with his home country, provided of course he does so with the permission of the Muslim authority (such as entering with a valid visa and the like), the sanctity of his life is protected by our Law, just like that of the Muslim and non-Muslim subjects of the state.[18] In this case, his legal status becomes a *kāfir ḥarbī bi-dhimmati l-imām* [a hostile non-Muslim under the protection of the Muslim authority], and for all intents and purposes he becomes exactly like the non-Muslim subjects of the state. In this way, the apparent distinction between a *dhimmī* and a *ḥarbī* non-Muslim is academic and a distinction in name only.

The implication of this rule for pious, God-fearing and Law-abiding Muslims is not only that to attack non-Muslims is illegal and an act of disobedience [*ma'ṣiya*], but also that the steps taken by the Muslim authority and its enforcers, such as in Malaysia or Indonesia today, to protect the places of non-Muslims, including churches or temples, from the threat of attacks and bombings, are included under the *bāb* of *amr bi-l-ma'rūf wa nahy 'ani l-munkar* [the duty to intervene when another is acting wrongly; in the modern context: enforcing the Law], even if should it cost the life of the Muslim enforcers [*muḥtasib*] whose task it is to protect the non-Muslims.

Question VIII

If it is said: 'In what category of land are those who live in the European Union, and what is the *ḥukm* of those who are here? Should they theoretically leave?'

We say: It is clear that the countries in the Union are non-Muslim states, with the possible future exceptions of Turkey or Bosnia, for example, should they become a part of the Union. The status of the Muslims who reside and are born in non-Muslim states is the converse of the above non-Muslim status in a Muslim state: *muslim bi-dhimmati l-kāfir* [a Muslim in the care of a non-Muslim state] and from our own Muslim and religious perspective, whether we like it or not, there are similarities in their guest status which should not be forgotten.

There is precedent for this status in our Law. The answer to your question is this: they should as a practical matter remain in these countries and if possible learn to cure the schizophrenic cultural condition in which they may find themselves – whether this be the sense of a torn identity in their souls or their dissociation from the general society. If they cannot do so, but find instead that their surroundings are incompatible with the life they feel they must lead, then it is recommended for them to leave and reside in a Muslim state. This status is made clear in the *fatwā* of the *Muḥaqqiq*, Imām al-Kurdī (may Allāh be pleased with him!):

> He (may the mercy of Allāh – Exalted is He! – be upon him!) was asked: In a territory ruled by non-Muslims, the Muslims have been left [in peace] except that they pay tax [*māl*] every year just like the *jizya*-tax in reverse, for when the Muslims pay them, their protection is ensured and the non-Muslims do not oppose them [i.e., do not interfere with them]. Thereupon Islam is practiced openly and our Law is established [meaning that they have the freedom to practice their religious duty in the open and in effect become practising Muslims in that non-Muslim society]. If the Muslims do not pay them, the non-Muslims could massacre them by killing or pillage. Is it permissible to pay them the tax [and thereby become residents]? If you say it is permissible, what is the ruling about the non-Muslims mentioned above when they are at war [with a Muslim state]: would it or would it not be permissible to oppose them and if possible, take their money? Please give us your opinion!

The answer:

> Insofar as it is possible for Muslims to practice their religion openly according to their rights [in that country], and they are not afraid of any threat [*fitna*] to their

religion if they pay tax to the non-Muslims, it is permissible for them to reside there. It is also permissible to pay the tax as a requirement of it [residence]; indeed, it is obligatory [*wājib*] to pay them the tax for fear of their causing harm to Muslims. The ruling about the non-Muslims at war is that, because they protect the Muslims [in their territory], it would not be permissible for the Muslims to murder them or steal from them.[19]

The *ḍābiṭ* for this *mas'ala* is:

وَإِنْ قَدَرَ على إظهار الدين ولم يَخَفِ الفتنة في دينه ونفسه وماله لم تَجِبْ عليه الهجرةُ

[If someone is able to practise his religion openly and is not afraid of threat to his religion, life and property, then emigration is not obligatory for him.]

FURŪʿ

Our Shāfiʿī jurists have given detailed consideration to the case of Muslims residing in a non-Muslim state, and they have divided the legal rulings about their emigration from it to a Muslim state into four sorts (assuming that an individual is able to emigrate and has the means to do so):

1 *Ḥarām*: it is prohibited for them to leave when they are able to defend their territory from a hostile non-Muslim force or withdraw from it (as in the case of a border state, buffer area or disputed territory) and do not need to ask for help from a Muslim state. The reason is that their place of residence is already, technically [*ḥukman*], a 'Muslim state' even though not in name [*ṣūratan*], since they are able to practise their religion openly even though the political or executive authority is not Muslim; and if they emigrated it would cease to be so. This falls under the *fiqhī* classification of *Dār Kāfir Ṣūratan Lā Ḥukman*, which is equivalent to *Dār Islām Ḥukman Lā Ṣūratan*.

2 *Makrūh*: it is offensive for them to leave their place of residence when it is possible for them to practise their religion openly and they are happy to do so.

3 *Mandūb*: leaving becomes recommendable only when it is possible for them to practise their religion openly but they find themselves unhappy to do so.

4 *Wājib*: it becomes obligatory to leave when it is the only remaining option, that is, when practising their religion openly is not possible. A legal precedent is the position in the aftermath of the *Reconquista* in Spain (conditions that no longer prevail in Spain today) when the Five Pillars of the Faith were actively proscribed, so that, for example, Muslim homes were required to keep their doors open after sunset during the fasting month of Ramaḍān in order that the Spanish authorities could check that the communal act of breaking the fast was not taking place.

Question IX

If it is said: 'Would you say that in the modern age with all the considerations surrounding sovereignty and inter-connectedness, these classical labels do not apply any longer, or do we have sufficient resources in the School to continue using these same labels?'

We say: As Imām al-Ghazālī used to say:

إذا عُرِفَ المعنى فلا مُشَاحَّةَ في الأسامي

[Once the real meaning is understood, there is no need to quibble over names.]

Labels can never be relied upon; it is the meaning behind them that must be properly understood. Once they are unpacked, they immediately become relevant for all times; just as with the following loaded terms: *jihād, mujāhid* and *shahīd*. For Muslims who fail to notice the relevance of our own inherited medieval terms with the modern world, the result may be that they will live in a schizophrenic cultural reality and will be unable to identify with the surrounding society and will not be at peace [*sukūn*] with the rest of creation. Just as the *sabab al-wujūd* of this article is a Muslim's misunderstanding of his own medieval terminology from a long and rich legacy, the *fitna* in the world today has been the result of those who mis-understand our Law.

Pay heed to the words of Mawlānā Rūmī (may Allāh sanctify his secrets!):

Go beyond names and look at the qualities, so that they may show you the way to the essence.

The disagreement of people takes place because of names. Peace occurs when they go to the real meaning.

Every war and every conflict between human beings has happened because of some disagreement about names.

It is such an unnecessary foolishness, because just beyond the arguing there is a long table of companionship, set and waiting for us to sit down.

End of the *masā'il* section.

Tatimma

It is truly sad that despite our sophisticated and elaborate set of rules of engage-ment and in spite of the strict codes of warfare and the chivalrous disciplines that our soldiers are expected to observe, which have all been thoroughly elaborated and codified by the orthodox jurists of the *Umma* from among the generations of the *Salaf*, there are today in our midst those who are not ashamed to depart from these sacred conventions in favour of opinions espoused by persons who have received no training in the Sacred Law at all and certainly none sufficient to be considered a *qāḍī* or a *faqīh* – the rightful heirs and sources from whom they should be receiv-ing practical guidance in the first place. Instead they rely on engineers or scientists and on those who are not among its *ahl*, yet speak in the name of our Law. With these 'reformist' preachers and *dā'ī*s comes a departure from the traditional ideas about the rules of *siyar/jihād/qitāl*, i.e., warfare. Do they not realize that by following them they will be ignoring the limitations and restrictions cherished and protected by our pious forefathers and that they will be turning their backs on the *Jamā'a* and *Ijmā'* and that they will be engaging in an act for which there is no accepted legal precedent within orthodoxy in our entire history? Have they forgotten that part of the original *maqṣad* of warfare/*jihād* was to limit warfare itself and that warfare for Muslims is never total war, so that women, children and innocent bystanders are not to be killed and property not to be needlessly destroyed?

To put it plainly, there is simply no legal precedent in the history of Sunni Islam for the tactic of attacking civilians and overtly non-military targets. Yet the awful reality today is that a minority of Sunni Muslims, whether in Iraq or Beslan or elsewhere, have perpetrated such acts in the name of *jihād* and on behalf of the *Umma*. Perhaps the first such mission to break this long and admirable precedent was the Hamas bombing on a public bus in Jerusalem in 1994 – not that long ago. (Reflect on this!)

Immediately after the incident, the almost unanimous response of the orthodox Shāfi'ī jurists from the Far East and the Hadramawt was not only to make clear that the minimum legal position from our Sacred Law is untenable for persons who carry out such acts, but also to warn the *Umma* that by going down that path we would be compromising the optimum way of *Iḥsān* and that we would thereby be running a real risk of losing the moral and religious high ground. Those who still defend this tactic, blindly invoking a nebulous *uṣūlī* principle justified from *ḍarūra* while ignoring the *far'ī* strictures, must look long and hard at what they are doing and ask the question: was it *absolutely necessary*, and if so, why was this not done before 1994, and especially during the earlier wars, most of all during the disasters of 1948 and 1967?

How could such a tactic have been condoned by one of our Rightly Guided Caliphs and a heroic fighter such as 'Alī (may Allāh ennoble his face!), who, when in the Battle of the Trench with his notorious non-Muslim opponent, who was seconds away from being killed by him, and who spat on his noble face, immediately left him alone. When asked his reasons for withdrawing when Allāh clearly gave him power over his enemy, he answered: 'I was fighting for the sake of God, and when he spat in my face I feared that if I killed him it would have been out of revenge and spite!' Far from being an act of cowardice, this characterizes Muslim chivalry: fighting but not doing so out of anger.

In actual fact, the only precedent for this tactic from Muslim history is the terrorism carried out by the 'Assassins' of the Nizārī Ismā'īlīs. The most famous victim of one of their suicide missions was the wise minister and the Defender of the Faith – who might otherwise have survived to confront the *fitna* of the

Crusades: Niẓām al-Mulk, the Jamāl al-Shuhadā' (may Allāh encompass him with His mercy!), assassinated on Thursday, the 10th of the holy month of Ramaḍān 485, or 14 October 1092.

Ironically, in the case of Palestine, the precedent was set not by Muslims but by early Zionist terrorist gangs such as the Irgun, who, for example, infamously bombed the King David Hotel in Jerusalem on 22 July 1946. So ask yourself as an upright and God-fearing believer, whose every organ will be interrogated: do you really want to follow the footsteps and the models of those Zionists and the heterodox Ismaʻīlīs, instead of the path taken by our Beloved (may Allāh's blessings and peace be upon him!), who for almost half of the (twenty-three) years of his mission endured Meccan persecution, humiliation and insults? Is anger your only strength? If so, remember the Prophetic advice that it is from the Devil. And is ḍarūra your only excuse for following these false prophets into their condemned lizard-holes? Do you think that any of our famous mujāhids from history, such as ʻAlī, Ṣalāḥ al-Dīn, and Muḥammad al-Fātiḥ (may Allāh be well pleased with them all!) will ever condone the Al-Muhajiroun article you quoted and these acts today in Baghdad, Jerusalem, Cairo, Bali, Casablanca, Beslan, Madrid, London and New York, some of them committed on days when it is traditionally forbidden by our Law to fight: Dhū l-Qaʻda and al-Ḥijja, Muḥarram and Rajab? Every person of fiṭra will see that this is nothing other than a sunna of perversion.

This is what happens to the Banū Ādam when the wahm is abandoned by ʻaql, when one of the maqāṣid justifies any wasīla, when the realities of furūʻ are indiscriminately overruled by generalities of uṣūl, and most tragically, as illustrated from the eternal blunder of Iblīs, when Divine tawakkul is replaced by basic nafs.

Yes, we are one Umma such that when one part of the macro-body is attacked somewhere, the other parts inevitably feel the pain. At the same time, our own history has shown that we have also been a wise and sensible rather than a reactive and impulsive Umma. That is the secret of our success, and that is where our strengths will always lie as has been promised by Divine Writ: in ṣabr and in tawakkul. It is already common knowledge that when Jerusalem fell to the Crusading forces on the 15 July 1099 and was occupied by them, and despite its civilians having been raped, killed, tortured and plundered and the Umma at the time humiliated and insulted – acts far worse than what can be imagined in today's occupation – it took more than a hundred years of patience and legitimate struggle under the Eye of the Almighty before He allowed Ṣalāḥ al-Dīn to liberate Jerusalem. We should have been taught from childhood by our fathers and mothers about the need to prioritize and about how to reconcile the spheres of our global concerns with those of our local responsibilities – since we will definitely not escape the questioning after death about the latter – so that by this insight we may hope that our response will not be disproportionate nor inappropriate. This is the true meaning [ḥaqīqa] of the true advice [*naṣīḥa*] of our Beloved Prophet (may Allāh's blessings and peace be upon him!): to leave aside what does not concern one [*tark ma lā ya'nīh*] when one's time and energy could be better spent in improving the lot of the Muslims today or benefiting others in this world.

Yes, we will naturally feel the pain when any of our brothers and sisters die unjustly anywhere especially when their deaths have been caused directly by non-Muslims, but it *must* be the more painful for us when they die in Iraq, for example, when their deaths are caused directly by the self-destroying/martyrdom/suicide missions carried out by one of our own. On *tafakkur*, the second pain should make us realize that missions of this sort, when the means and the legal particulars are all wrong – by scripture and reason – are not only a scourge for our non-Muslim neighbours but a plague and great *fitna* for this mercy-bound *Umma*, and desire *inṣāf* so that out of *maslaḥa* and the general good, it can be stopped.

To this end, we could sum up a point of law tersely in the following maxim:

$$\text{لاَ ٰ يَجْعَلُ الظُّلْمَانِ الثَّانِيَ حَقًّا}$$

[Two wrongs do not make a right.]

If the first pain becomes one of the mitigating factors and ends up being used as a justification by our misguided young to retaliate in a manner that our Sacred Law definitely and without doubt outlaws (which makes the *Al-Muhajiroun* article the more appalling, as its author will have passed the special age of forty), then the latter pain should by its graver significance generate a greater and more meaningful response. With this intention, we may hope that we shall regain our former high ground and reputation and rediscover our honour and chivalrous qualities and be no less brave.

I end with the first ever Verse revealed in the Qur'ān which bestowed the military option only upon those in a position of authority:

$$\text{وَقَاتِلُوا فِي سَبِيلِ اللهِ الَّذِينَ يُقَاتِلُونَكُمْ وَلاَ تَعْتَدُوا إِنَّ اللهَ لاَ ٰ يُحِبُّ الْمُعْتَدِينَ}$$

[And fight for the sake of God those who fight you: but do not commit excesses, for God does not love those who exceed (i.e., the Law).][20]

Even then, peace is preferred over war:

$$\text{وَإِنْ جَنَحُوا لِلسَّلْمِ فَاجْنَحْ لَهَا وَتَوَكَّلْ عَلَى اللهِ}$$

[Now if they incline toward peace, then incline to it, and place your trust in God.][21]

Even if you think that the Muslim authority in question has decided wrongly and you disagree with its decision not to make war with the non-Muslim state upon which you wish war to be declared, then take heed of the following Divine command:

يَا أَيُّهَا الَّذِينَ ءَامَنُوا أَطِيعُوا اللهَ وأَطِيعُوا الرَّسُولَ وَأُوْلِى الأَمْرِ مِنْكُمْ

[O believers, obey God, and obey the Messenger, and those with authority among you!][22]

If you still wish to insist that your authority should declare war with the non-Muslim state upon which you wish war to be declared, then the most you may do in this capacity is to lobby your authority. However, if your anger is so unrestrained and brings out the worst in you to the point that your disagreement with your Muslim authority leads you to declare war on those you want your authority to declare war on, and you end up resorting to violence, then know with certainty that you have violated our own religious Laws. For then you will have taken the *Sharīʿa* into your own hands. If indeed you reach the point of committing a violent act, then know that by our own Law you would be automatically classified as a rebel [*ahl al-baghy*] whom the authority has the right to punish, even if the authority is perceived to be or is indeed corrupt [*fāsiq*]. (The definition of rebels is: 'Muslims who have disagreed [not by heart or by tongue but by hand] with the authority even if it is unjust [*jāʾir*] and they are correct [*ʿadilūn*]'.)[23]

That is why, my brethren, when the military option is not a legal one for the individuals concerned, you must not lose hope in Allāh; and let us be reminded of the words of our Beloved (may Allāh's blessings and peace be upon him!):

أَفْضَلُ الْجِهَادِ كَلِمَةُ حَقٍّ عِنْدَ سُلْطَانٍ جَائِرٍ

[The best *jihād* is a true (i.e., brave) word in the face of a tyrannical ruler.][24]

For it is possible still, and especially today, to fight injustice or *ẓulm* or *ṭāghūt* in this *dunyā* through your tongue and your words and through the pen and the courts, which still amounts in the Prophetic idiom to *jihād*, even if not through war. As in the reminder [*tadhkira*] of the great scholar, Imām al-Zarkashī: war is only a means to an end and as long as some other way is open to us, that other way should be the course taken by Muslims.

Ma shāʾ Allāh, how true indeed are the Beloved's words, inspiring the latter-day *mujāhid* or activist to be no less brave in his or her campaign for a just cause in an oppressive country (or one needing reform) than the former *mujāhid* or patriot who fought bravely for his country in a just war:

فَاتَّقِ اللهَ ورَاجِعْ مُفَاتَشَةَ نَفْسِكَ وإصْلاحَ فَسَادِها وهو حَسْبُنا ونِعم الوَكيلُ ولا حَوْلَ ولا قُوَّةَ إلا باللهِ العَلِيّ العَظِيم

وصلواتُه على سيِّدِنا محمدٍ وآلِه وسلَّمَ ورضي اللهُ تبارك وتعالى عن سادَاتِنا أصحابِ رسولِ اللهِ أجمعين وعنَّا معهم

وفِيهم ويجْعَلَنا من حِزْبِهم برحمتِك يا أرحمَ الرَّاحمين آمين

[Fear God, and go back to controlling your self and to curing your wickedness! For indeed, He is enough for us: what an excellent guardian! There is no help or power except through God, the High and Mighty! May His blessings and peace be upon our master, Muḥammad, and his Family! And may He be pleased with our leaders, the Companions of the Messenger of God, one and all! And may we be together with them and in their company, and may He make us among their Troop. By Your Mercy, O Most Merciful of those who show mercy, Amen!]

May this be of benefit.

With heartfelt wishes for *salām* and *ṭayyiba*
from Oxford to Brunei,
Muhammad Afifi al-Akiti
16th Jumādā' II 1426
23 July 2005

III Select bibliography – Shaykh Muhammad Afifi al-Akiti

Bā'alawī, 'Abd al-Raḥmān. *Bughyat al-Mustarshidīn fī Talkhīṣ Fatāwā ba'ḍ al-Muta'akhkhirīn*. Bulaq, AH 1309.

al-Bakrī. *Ḥāshiyat I'ānat al-Ṭālibīn*. 4 vols. Bulaq, AH 1300.

al-Ghazālī. *Iḥyā' 'Ulūm al-Dīn*. Edited by Badawī Aḥmad Ṭabānah. 4 vols. Cairo: Dār Iḥyā' al-Kutub al-'Arabiyya, 1957.

Ibn 'Arabī, Qāḍī. *Aḥkām al-Qur'ān*. Edited by 'Alī Muḥammad al-Bajawī. 4 vols. Cairo: Dār Iḥyā' al-Kutub al-'Arabiyya, 1957–58.

Ibn Barakāt. *Fayḍ al-Ilāh al-Mālik fī Ḥall Alfāẓ 'Umdat al-Sālik wa-'Uddat al-Nāsik*. Edited by Muṣṭafā Muḥammad 'Imāra. 2 vols. Singapore: al-Ḥaramayn, AH 1371.

Ibn Ḥajar al-Haytamī. *Tuḥfat al-Muḥtāj bi-Sharḥ al-Minhāj al-Nawawī* in *Ḥawāshī al-Shirwānī wa-Ibn Qāsim 'alā Tuḥfat al-Muḥtāj*. Edited by Muḥammad 'Abd al-'Azīz al-Khālidī. 13 vols. Beirut: Dār al-Kutub al-'Ilmiyya, 1996.

al-Jaṣṣāṣ. *Aḥkām al-Qur'ān*. 3 vols. Istanbul: Dār al-Khilāfa al-'Āliya, AH 1335–38.

al-Kurdī. *Fatāwā al-Kurdī al-Madanī*. In *Qurrat al-'Ayn bi-Fatāwā 'Ulamā' al-Ḥaramayn*. Edited by Muḥammad 'Alī ibn Ḥusayn al-Mālikī. Bogor: Maktabat 'Arafāt, n.d.

al-Nawawī. *al-Majmū' Sharḥ al-Muhadhdhab*. Edited by Maḥmūd Maṭrajī. 22 vols. Beirut: Dār al-Fikr, 1996.

al-Nawawī al-Jāwī. *Marāḥ Labīd Tafsīr al-Nawawī: al-Tafsīr al-Munīr li-Ma'ālim al-Tanzīl al-Mufassir 'an Wujūh Maḥāsin al-Ta'wīl al-Musammā Marāḥ Labīd li-Kashf Ma'nā Qur'ān Majīd*. 2 vols. Bulaq, AH 1305.

IV Glossary of Arabic terms – Shaykh Gibril F. Haddad

Aḥādīth al-Aḥkām   ḥadīthic proof-texts for legal rulings
ahl   [1] people; [2] experts or qualified adherents or practitioners
'aql   intellect, reason
'amal   deed, action
aṣl   see *uṣūl*
Āyāt al-Aḥkām   Qur'ānic proof-texts for legal rulings
bāb   chapter or legal subject
Banū Ādam   human beings
ḍābiṭ   see *ḍawābiṭ*
dā'ī   summoner or preacher
Dajjāl   lit., 'imposter'; the Anti-Christ
ḍarūra   necessity
ḍawābiṭ   pl. of *ḍābiṭ*, standard or principal rule
Doctor Angelicus   The Angelic Scholar, a title given to Thomas Aquinas, the great
theologian of the Western Church, who is compared here to al-Ghazālī
dunyā   this world, this life
fā'ida   benefit
faqīh   see *fiqh*
farḍ 'ayn   personal obligation
farḍ kifāya   communal obligation
far'ī   adj. from *far'*, see *furū'*
faṣl   see *fuṣūl*
fatwā   legal opinion, legal response
fiqh   Islamic jurisprudence, the expertise of the *faqīh*; adj. *fiqhī* = legal
fitna   strife, temptation, seduction, delusion, chaos, trial and tribulation
fiṭra   sane mind and soul, primordial disposition
fuqahā'   pl. of *faqīh* (q.v.)
furū'   pl. of *far'* = [1] branches (of the Law), secondary legal texts; [2] corollar-
ies, corollary legal principles
fuṣūl   pl. of *faṣl* = sections or legal particulars
Ḥadīth   a saying of the Prophet Muḥammad, upon whom blessings and peace
ḥalāl   lawful, permitted
ḥaqīqa   truth, reality; true meaning; substance
ḥarām   categorically prohibited, unlawful
ḥāṣil   legal outcome
ḥukm [*shar'ī*]   legal status, legal ruling
Iblīs   Satan
Iḥsān   Excellence, the pinnacle of religious practice
Ijmā'   Consensus

ijtihād   independent judgement, personal decision

inṣāf   fairness, setting things right

Jāhilī   lit., 'ignorant'; a pre-Islamic or pagan Arab

Jamā'a   the Orthodox Community

Jamāl al-Shuhadā'   The Beauty of Martyrs, the title of the murdered vizier Niẓām al-Mulk

jihād   moral or military struggle by the *mujāhid*

jizya   poll tax imposed on non-Muslims in pre-modern times by Muslim governments

Kabīra   Major Sin

khilāf   (juridical) disagreement

khilāfiyya   fem. adjective from *khilāf* = having to do with (juridical) disagreement

kuffār   pl. of *kāfir*, non-Muslim

madhhab   school of Law

makrūh   detestable, abhorrent, abominable, disliked, legally offensive

mandūb   recommended, praiseworthy

maqāṣid   pl. of *maqṣad*, objective or ends

maqṣad   see *maqāṣid*

masā'il   pl. of *mas'ala*, question or legal discussion or case

masā'il mufaṣṣala   detailed questions and answers

mas'ala   see *masā'il*

maṣlaḥa   welfare, public/general good

mubāḥ   indifferently permissible

mufassir   exegete

muftī   one who formulates *fatwā*s or formal legal responses

Muḥaqqiq   The Careful Examiner, a title given to Imām al-Kurdī, one of the last great jurist of the Shāfi'ī School

mujāhid   one who does *jihād* (q.v.)

mukallaf   legally-responsible Muslim

mushāraka   mutual or reciprocal matter

nafs   ego, self

nasīḥa   faithful, sincere advice

qaḍāyā   pl. of *qaḍiyya*, issue or legal context

qāḍī   judge in an Islamic court of law

qā'ida   see *qawā'id*

qātil nafsah   self-killer, suicide

qawā'id   pl. of *qā'ida*, maxim or legal principle

qawl   saying or legal position

qitāl   killing, warfare, battle

sabab al-wujūd   raison d'être

ṣabr   patient endurance and fortitude

Ṣaḥābī   Companion of the Prophet Muḥammad, upon whom blessings and peace
ṣaḥīḥ   authentic, sound
Salaf   Pious Predecessors, early authorities
salām   peace
shahīd, pl. *shuhadā'*   self-sacrificing believer who dies for the sake of God alone, 'martyr'
shakk   doubtful knowledge, something undecided (50% certain)
shar'ī   adj. legitimate in the eyes of the *Sharī'a* (Islamic Law), lawful, legal
siyar   military expeditions
sunna   way, path
sūra   a chapter of the Qur'ān
ṣūra   example, illustration; a legal case in point
Tābi'ī   Successor of the Companions
tafakkur   reflection
tafṣīl   detailed legal discussion
taghrīr bil-nafs   risking one's life
tahluka   self-destruction
ṭāghūt   designating despotic, impious and ultimately Satanic forces, i.e., everything that leads astray and turns away from God
tatimma   conclusion
tawakkul   reliance upon God
ṭayyiba   goodness
thawābit   pl. of *thābit*, axiom
'ulamā'   Muslim scholars trained in Islamic theology and law
Umma   the Muslim Community at large
ustādh   teacher
uṣūl   pl. of *aṣl*, foundational principle; adj. *uṣūlī*
wahm   imaginative faculty or emotions; whimsy, merely imagining something to be possible (25% certain)
wasā'il   pl. of *wasīla*, means
wasīla   see *wasā'il*
yaqīn   certain knowledge, knowing something to be true (100% certain)
zann   probable knowledge, believing or thinking something is probable (75% certain)
ẓulm   injustice oppression, persecution

Notes

1 Editor's note: the *Fatwa*, which is widely available on the Internet, was first published separately as a booklet (Birmingham: Aqsa Press, 2005; Hellenthal, Germany:
   Warda Publications, 2005); subsequently, a second edition appeared together with

contributions by other Muslim scholars in *The State We Are In: Identity, Terror and the Law of Jihad* (Bristol: Amal Press, 2006). The *Fatwa* is reproduced here with further stylistic corrections made by the editor in collaboration with the authors.

2 Editor's note: this expression translates the Arabic expression *al-umma al-marḥūma*.

3 Editor's note: for some context on Al-Muhajiroun, see www.guardian.co.uk/world/ 2007/may/06/terrorism.jamiedoward. For the full text of the Al-Muhajiroun article, see http://mac.abc.se/~onesr/ez/isl/0-sbm/Deviant.Opinion.html.

4 Al-Nawawī, *Majmūʿ*, 21:57.

5 Qurʾān 2:195.

6 Qurʾān 2:195.

7 Al-Ghazālī, *Iḥyāʾ*, 2:315–16.

8 Related by Aḥmad, al-Bukhārī, Muslim, al-Tirmidhī, Ibn Mājah, al-Ṭabarānī, and al-Bayhaqī, with variants.

9 Qurʾān 9:5.

10 Editor's note: The Treaty of Ḥudaybiyya (called after a plain outside Mecca) is the peace treaty that was concluded between the Muslims and the pagan Meccan Confederates in 628CE. Under its terms, the Muslims agreed to give up the pilgrimage that they had intended to make at that moment. The treaty, intended to remain in force for ten years, lasted only two years, when the Meccans breached and repudiated it. This precipitated the Muslims' march on Mecca by which they captured the city without a battle, an event traditionally known as the Victory of Mecca.

11 Al-Nawawī al-Jāwī, *Tafsīr*, 1:331.

12 Qāḍī Ibn ʿArabī, *Aḥkām al-Qurʾān*, 2:889.

13 Al-Jaṣṣāṣ, *Aḥkām al-Qurʾān*, 3:81.

14 Ibn Ḥajar, *Tuḥfat*, 12:4.

15 Ibn Barakāt, *Fayḍ*, 2:309.

16 Al-Bakrī, *Iʿānat*, 4:197.

17 Baʿalawī, *Bughyat*, 254.

18 Al-Kurdī, *Fatāwā*, 211–12.

19 Al-Kurdī, *Fatāwā*, 208.

20 Qurʾān 2:190.

21 Qurʾān 8:61.

22 Qurʾān 4:59.

23 Al-Nawawī, *Majmūʿ*, 20:337.

24 From a Ḥadīth of Abū Saʿīd al-Khudrī (may Allāh be well pleased with him!) among others, which is related by Ibn al-Jaʿd, Aḥmad, Ibn Ḥumayd, Ibn Mājah, Abū Dāwūd, al-Tirmidhī, al-Nasāʾī, Abū Yaʿlā, Abū Bakr al-Rūyānī, al-Ṭabarānī, al-Ḥākim, and al-Bayhaqī, with variants.

Index

Note: 'n' after a page reference indicates the number of a footnote on that page